Becoming Modern

Individual Change in Six Developing Countries

*Written under the auspices of the Center for International Affairs,
Harvard University*

BECOMING MODERN

Individual Change in Six Developing Countries

Alex Inkeles and David Horton Smith

Harvard University Press   Cambridge, Massachusetts

© Copyright 1974 by the President and Fellows of Harvard College
All rights reserved
Second printing 1976
Library of Congress Catalog Card Number 73-92534
ISBN 0-674-06375-9 (cloth)
ISBN 0-674-06376-7 (paper)
Printed in the United States of America

to
DANIEL LERNER
and
KARL DEUTSCH
who first rode upon the tiger

Acknowledgments

Although two of us did most of the analysis on which this book is based, the conception and execution of the project as a whole is not accurately accounted for unless one adds the names of Howard Schuman and Edward Ryan. Together with the authors, these men developed the basic theoretical orientation of the entire venture and translated the underlying ideas into the practical form of a research design and a detailed questionnaire. Dr. Schuman established and directed the field staff which did the interviewing in East Pakistan (now Bangladesh); Dr. Ryan played a parallel role in Nigeria, and each supervised the coding of the materials collected by his national field team. To our profound regret, work and careers took both to new posts while we were still at an early stage in the analysis of the data. Nevertheless, their influence continued to be firmly interwoven in the fabric of the project as it was later developed.

We are also in great debt to the other directors of the national field teams who joined the project when it was further along, yet who came in time to make important contributions to its conception, design, and execution. These included: in Chile, Juan Cesar Garcia, ably assisted by Carlotta Rios and Anna Maria Pinto; in Israel, Uzi Peled; in Argentina, Perla Gibaja; and in India, Amar K. Singh. In addition, Olatunde Oloko served as associate director in Nigeria, while Amadullah Mia and Nuril Islam gave special assistance to Dr. Schuman in East Pakistan. Without the dedication these people manifested, the determination they displayed in the face of endless distractions and obstacles, and the intelligence and perceptiveness they brought to bear on every situation, the project could not have hoped to succeed even remotely as well as it did.

In this context we should also note that our ability to identify these talented young researchers and to secure their services depended, in a number of instances, on the cooperation and support given by local academic leaders such as Peter Heintz in Chile, Gino Germani in Argentina, A. F. A. Husain in East Pakistan, and K. O. Dike in Nigeria. These distinguished scholars also gave freely of their advice and criticism, and we are pleased to express our appreciation for their generosity.

In view of the scope and scale of our research we could neither process our data nor extract its full meaning without the aid of a substantial number of research assistants. Harriet Wasserstrum was an important early incumbent of the role in which she displayed great energy, gratifying promptness, an uncanny memory, and a creative imagination. Erika Fox rendered numerous and diverse services, among others playing a key role in the development of OM-500, the scale most often used in this book. After the project moved to Stanford early in 1971 Larry Meyer was our chief assistant. Although hired as a computer programmer, a part he played with consummate skill, he quickly transcended the limits of that role. The impact of his incisive comments and thoughtful criticism was felt in every section of our manuscript. Indeed, to the senior author, to whom fell the responsibility for writing the final draft, Meyer became more a colleague than an assistant.

Our full-time research assistants were supplemented by a considerable number of graduate students employed on a part-time basis. For us, their service added much needed extra hands, and the stimulus of fresh perspectives coupled with youthful energy. Three of the students found in the project materials the basis for a doctoral dissertation: Gunther Boroschek on political attitudes and values in Argentina and Chile, Rowan Ireland on the consequences of a factory's modernity, and John Williamson on attitudes about birth control. In addition, two of the longest and most productive of our associations with graduate students were those with Reeve Vanneman and Martin Whyte, who wrote excellent memoranda on numerous topics. Bonnie Erikson served as a resident statistical consultant, and the effect of her wise counsel and stern admonishments is especially evident in the chapters on the construction and content of the modernity (OM) scales. We also benefitted from the work of Sumru Aksoy on urbanism, Peter Evans on occupational patterns, Gilda Mara on ruralism, Lorne Tepperman on work experience, and Miron Zuckerman on life satisfactions. Contributions were also made by David Eaglesfield, David Lopez, Rachel Javetz, Phyllis Kazen, Howard Ramseur, Nancy Silverman, Ellen Simons, Richard Suzman, and Nancy Williamson. In addition, we enjoyed the services of several scholars well beyond student status, in particular Anna Maria Pinto, who analyzed our data on the family, and Metta Spencer who worked on a number of topics.

A project so large as ours inevitably becomes a collective enterprise, some kind of team operation, in which the administrative officer comes to play a critical role. We were extremely fortunate in having the services of three exceptionally capable incumbents in that office. From the inception of the project through the completion of the fieldwork, Sharlee Segal exercised firm, competent, and energetic control over our financial and administrative affairs. Martha Puff displayed equally sterling qualities in managing our office after the project moved to Stanford in 1971. For the greater part of the life of the project, however, our affairs were in the hands of Elizabeth Dunn. She dealt with large budgets, mountains of paper, swarms of student assistants, and a goodly number of sensitive computer programmers and senior analysts with grace and quiet efficiency. Her contribution was indispensable to the project, and the director owes her a special and personal debt of gratitude.

A study based on long interviews in six developing countries which generated tens of thousands of "open-ended" comments, presented a data-processing job of formidable proportions. That the data was transferred to IBM cards and computer tapes with great accuracy we owe to Brian Sinclair, who later also played a key role in implementing our special program for regression analysis; Marta Fisch, who also subsequently served a term as our computer programmer; and Leslie Howard, who had earlier assisted Dr. Singh in collecting the data in India. Lynn Joiner and Sonia Cairoli also did yeoman service in this cause.

The task of getting all the recorded facts out of the computer in some appropriately transformed but meaningful fashion fell to a series of efficient and imaginative programmers. In addition to those already noted we should mention Marijo Miller Walsh, who did most of the trying and massive runs in the first stages of our work in analysis of the data, and Wendy Jackson who ably carried the burden in the middle phase of our work. Burt Baldwin was responsible for a long and complex series of regression analyses, and Peter Lemieux devised our basic program for matching men by computer. Two of our undergraduate assistants, Gary Welch and John Duffy also made numerous contributions to the job of data processing over a long interval.

As we progressed in our writing, each chapter benefitted enormously from the gentle admonishments and wise counsel offered by Marina Finklestein, late editor of the Center for International Affairs. For typing and proofreading the manuscript through what must, at times, have seemed endless revisions, we owe thanks to Elizabeth Burke, Erika Fox, Corey Patterson, and Martha Puff. Amnon Igra helped with the tables, and Dean Nielsen with the footnotes, and both assisted in other ways as well. A critical reading of the penultimate draft was undertaken by Elizabeth Dunn, S. N. Eisenstadt, Bonnie Erickson, Joseph Kahl, Larry Meyer and

Howard Schuman, who made many incisive comments and numerous excellent suggestions. We admit to having accepted only a select number of these, so that any remaining faults are to be laid exclusively at our door. In the last stages of editing, proofreading and seeing the manuscript through production we benefited from the help of Karen Miller and Richard Suzman.

We have been mainly singling out individuals for appreciation. People, not institutions, do research. Yet we could not have carried out our work except for our good fortune in finding a succession of institutional sponsors with the courage to underwrite the sort of high-risk venture our project was defined as being. For their generous support we are grateful to the Rockefeller Foundation, the Cultural Affairs Division of the Department of State, the National Science Foundation, The Ford Foundation, the National Institutes of Mental Health, and the Spencer Foundation. In addition, the University of Southern California and Boston College contributed substantial amounts of free computer time.

The Center for International Affairs at Harvard University constituted a setting in every way congenial to scholarly research, with numerous colleagues who provided just the right mixture of involved criticism and independence-fostering detachment. In this association, however, the key figure was Robert Bowie, Director of the Center. His continuous interest in and unwavering support for our work over many years was critical in enabling us to carry it to a successful conclusion. Finally, when the senior author and the project headquarters moved to Stanford University, we received considerable support from Arthur Coladarci, Dean of the School of Education.

In the field, we could not have managed without the generous cooperation of institutions in our host countries. They introduced us to the local community and gave us acceptable standing there, provided us with precious space, helped us to locate interviewers, and in several cases released members of their staffs for service with our project. We are particularly grateful to the College of Social Welfare of the Dacca University, the Nigerian Institute of Social and Economic Research at the University of Ibadan, the UNESCO-sponsored Latin American School of Social Sciences at Santiago, Chile, the DiTella Institute in Buenos Aires, the Israel Institute of Applied Social Research in Jerusalem, and the Department of Psychology of the Ranchi University in India. There were many others we cannot mention for lack of space, but which we do remember. Therefore, we take this opportunity, impersonal as it necessarily is, to give our warmest thanks to those organizations and people who helped us in so many ways.

We wish also to thank all the people and institutions who have kindly permitted us to make use of material from the project previously published by the authors and subsequently adapted for use in this volume. These include:

The American Sociological Association, Washington, D.C., as publishers for David H. Smith and Alex Inkeles, "The OM Scale: A Comparative Socio-Psychological Measure of Individual Modernity," *Sociometry* 29, no. 4, December 1966.

K. Ishwaran, as editor, and E. J. Brill, Leiden, Netherlands, as publisher, for Alex Inkeles, "The Fate of Personal Adjustment in the Process of Modernization" and "The School as a Context for Modernization," *International Journal of Comparative Sociology* 11, no. 2, June 1970 and 14, nos. 3–4, 1974, respectively.

A. R. Desai, as editor, and Thacker & Co., Ltd., Bombay, India, as publisher, for Alex Inkeles, "Fieldwork Problems in Comparative Research on Modernization," in *Essays on Modernization of Under-developed Societies*, vol. 2, 1971.

Nancy Hammond, as editor, and Social Science Research Bureau, Michigan State University, East Lansing, Michigan, as publisher, for Alex Inkeles, "A Model of the Modern Man: Theoretical and Methodological Issues," in *Social Science and the New Societies: Problems in Cross-Cultural Research and Theory Building*, 1973.

Cole S. Brembeck and Timothy J. Thompson, as editors, and D. C. Heath and Company, Lexington, Massachusetts, as publisher, for Alex Inkeles, "The Role of Occupational Experience," in *New Strategies for Educational Development*, 1973.

Contents

Part IV.   Summary and Conclusion

I

The Fundamentals

1
Introduction

Every era confronts its distinctive social and political dramas. In the mid-twentieth century, center stage has frequently been dominated by the struggle of the so-called "third world," first for liberation from the colonial powers and then for development and for entry into the modern world. The sixties were to be the "decade of development." Yet many of the emerging nations developed very little, if at all, and some slid backward. To this outcome, general political instability and specific tribal, religious, and ethnic conflict made their contributions.

However, there was more to the explanation. Experience underlined what some observers had already pointed out: diplomatic recognition and membership in the United Nations do not create a nation-state. Many of the new states were actually only hollow shells, lacking the institutional structures which make a nation a viable and effective socio-political and economic enterprise. Economic and technical dependence on the colonial power had to be replaced by indigenous activities, institutions of government had to be adapted or newly created, school systems had to be revamped and extended, and all this, plus a myriad of other tasks, had to be accomplished with relatively meager resources. No wonder then that progress in nation building has not been more spectacular.

It required time to realize that nation building and institution building are only empty exercises unless the attitudes and capacities of the people keep pace with other forms of development. That such articulation is not simply, or perhaps not even primarily, a function of independence is clear from much of recent history. Mounting evidence suggests that it is impossible for a state to move into the twentieth century if its people continue to live in an earlier era. A modern *nation* needs participating citizens, men and women who take an active interest in public affairs and who exercise their rights and perform their duties as members of a community larger than that of the kinship network and the immediate geographical locality. Modern *institutions* need individuals who can keep to fixed schedules, observe abstract rules, make judgments on the basis of objective evidence, and follow authorities legitimated not by traditional or religious sanctions but by technical competence. The complex production tasks of the *industrial order,* which are the basis of modern social systems, also make their demands. Workers must be able to accept both an elaborate division of labor and the need to coordinate their activities with a large number of others in the work force. Rewards based on technical competence and objective standards of performance, strict hierarchies of authority responsive to the imperatives of machine production, and the separation of product and producer, all are part of this milieu, and require particular personal properties of those who are to master its requirements.

In addition, modern political and economic institutions alike make certain general demands on the people who work within them. They require a greater acceptance of personal mobility, occupational and geographic; a greater readiness to adapt to changes in one's mode of working and living, indeed a propensity to be an innovator; more tolerance of impersonality, of impartiality, and of differences which may characterize the diverse backgrounds of fellow employees in complex organizations. Neither type of institution has much tolerance for fatalism or passivity, but rather favors persistent effort and confident optimism.

These and related qualities are not readily forthcoming from people rooted in traditional village agriculture, locked into near-feudal landholding patterns, dominated by self-serving elites desperate to preserve their power, dependent on inadequate and antiquated public institutions, and cut off from the benefits of modern science and technology as well as the stimulation of modern mass communication. However, alongside the struggle for national liberation and development, there has been, and continues to be, a struggle for personal liberation.

Some of the men and women tied by the binding obligations of powerful extended kinship systems have sought to assert their rights as individuals. Some have tried to win more freedom of choice in residence, occupation, political affiliation, religious denomination, marriage partner, friend, and enemy. They have sought to replace a closed world, in which their lives tread the narrowest of circles, with a more open system offering more alternatives and less predestination. From a desperate clinging to fixed ways of doing things, some have moved toward readiness for change. In place of fear of strangers and hostility to those very different from themselves, some have acquired more trust and more tolerance of human diversity. From rigidity and closed-mindedness, they have moved toward flexibility and cognitive openness. They now seek to break out of passivity, fatalism, and the subordination of self to an immutable and inscrutable higher order, in order to become more active and effective, and to take charge of their individual lives and of their collective destiny.

This process, however, occurs slowly, and, unfortunately, it usually affects only a few. Naturally, every national population is large enough to include some individuals who have quite spontaneously developed the qualities which make for quick adaptation to the requirements of the modern world. Some ethnic and religious groups also seem more likely to generate individuals of this type. Swiss Protestants, East European Jews, Parsis in India, and the Ibo in Nigeria all seem to qualify. Most men and women must, however, acquire their modernity on a more individual basis. *It seemed to us there was no more relevant and challenging task for social psychology than to explain the process whereby people move from being traditional to becoming modern personalities.*

We started, then, with the conviction that men are not born modern, but are made so by their life experience. We thought we knew how the process works, and we set out to test our theory. To accomplish our objective we had to make clear what we meant by a modern man. We derived our conception of the modern man in part from the forms of conduct we saw as likely to be inculcated by work in the factory, which we took to be the epitome of the institutional pattern of modern civilization, and in part from our estimate of the qualities more generally required of incumbents of the numerous roles — such as student, citizen, audience, producer, consumer, and family member — essential to the functioning of a large contemporary urban-industrial society. The details of our conception of the modern man are spelled out below. In the course of this book we hope to discover how far this conception reflects reality, and to show how much it can help us understand the process of individual modernization.

Our next task was to convert our conception of the modern man into a tool useful for research. This we tried to do by creating a long and fairly complex interview schedule based on questions and answers each of which could be scored to indicate whether a respondent was more inclined to the modern or to the traditional pole. Using a separate subset of questions to reflect each topic, we explored all of the themes we had built into our own conception of the modern man as well as themes which other theorists had identified as relevant to judging individual modernity. One of the major challenges facing us was to discover whether these discrete elements held together in a more or less coherent syndrome which one could sensibly speak of as designating a "modern man," or whether they would prove to be a mere congeries of discrete and unrelated traits, each of which characterized some modern men and not others. Answering this challenge involved us in a complex methodological excursion into the construction of an attitude-value-behavior scale.

In fact, it proved possible to develop a composite scale to measure individual modernity in general, one which had considerable face validity, met quite rigorous standards of test reliability, and could be effectively applied cross-culturally. The effort to develop such a scale was no mere exercise. For example, a few subthemes which *we* had assumed to be part of the syndrome of individual modernity, and some which had been nominated by *others,* failed to make a case for themselves in our empirical test. The scale also provided an essential condition for the main objective of our study — to explain what makes men modern. It enabled us to distribute men validly and reliably along a dimension of individual modernity. It then became our task to explain why particular individuals fell at one or the other end of the continuum.

In the design of our sample we brought our theory and our test instrument into contact with empirical reality. Our theory states that men become modern through the particular life experiences they undergo. More specifically, it emphasizes the contribution of man's work experience to making him modern. We believed that employment in complex, rationalized, technocratic, and even bureaucratic organizations has particular capabilities to change men so that they move from the more traditional to the more modern pole in their attitudes, values, and behavior. Among such institutions, we gave prime emphasis to the factory as a school in modernity. We also thought that urban living and contact with the mass media would have comparable effects. While emphasizing such modes of experience as more characteristic of the modern world, we did not neglect to study education, which earlier research had shown to be a powerful predictor of individual modernity. We also measured other personal attributes such as age, religion, ethnic membership, and rural origin.

These and several dozen other variables which our theory, or other theories, identified as plausible explanations for individual modernity had to be taken into account in the design of our research. Interviewers trained by our project staff questioned almost 6,000 men from six developing countries: Argentina, Chile, India, Israel, Nigeria, and East Pakistan, now Bangladesh. Our goal was to reach 1,000 in each country, the sample to include peasants, industrial workers, and persons in more traditional pursuits in town, all selected to represent ethnic, religious, regional, residential, and other important social classifications. The material thus collected forms the main basis of our study.

In addition to the analysis, however, we have also presented a fairly full account of the fieldwork required to collect the data. The experience of launching and conducting this comparative research seemed important enough in itself to warrant its description in some detail. Indeed, we hope that some of the ground rules we adopted might serve as models for others. These considerations aside, however, our six countries presented conditions for the conduct of opinion research sufficiently special to make it essential that we deal in some detail with the issues raised by the "underdeveloped" status of our field-work sites.

In conducting the main part of the analysis, we sought to establish how far variation in individual modernity could be explained, and to determine the degree to which each of the different elements accompanying the modernization process makes a truly independent contribution toward making men modern. By using a composite measure summarizing each individual's exposure to some ten different modernizing institutions, we found it possible to sort out our samples with great precision. Of the men fully exposed to the institutions which our theory designated as modernizing, some 76 percent scored as modern, whereas among those least under the influence of such institutions only about 2 percent achieved modern scores on our scales. The multiple correlation between our small set of basic explanatory variables and individual modernity scores went as high as .79.

If the standard for judging our scale of modernization is the proficiency attained by other social scientists in explaining comparable social and sociopsychological phenomena, then we may claim to have come at least as far in measuring and predicting individual modernity as our profession has come in explaining any other major syndrome such as intergenerational mobility, ethnic prejudice, or political authoritarianism.[1] Even if the standard of judgment is absolute, that is, requires us to explain 100 percent of the variance in modernity scores, we can claim to have made very substantial progress. In our best performance we explain some 62 percent of the variance in individual modernity. Admittedly this leaves considerable work to be done both in improving the reliability of our modernity scales and in identifying and measuring the relevant explanatory variables. But we are well on the way.

In sorting out the influence of the separate components among the institutions which, together, provide the modernizing experience, we found some widespread expectations confirmed, while others turned out to have surprisingly little empirical support. Education, for example, proved to be a very powerful influence, whereas exposure to an urban environment seemed, at least in the developing countries, to contribute very little to making men modern. Some variables which were new contenders for theoretical importance, such as our measures of factory experience, made good their claim to being significant factors, while others, such as our measures of the relative modernity of the factory, failed to do so. A good deal of the analysis in this book is devoted to assessing and clarifying the role of such variables in explaining or predicting individual modernity. We worked with them singly and in combinations, using various techniques including matched groups, partial correlations, and multiple regression. Since some of the measures were complexly interrelated, and the causal sequence sometimes far from obvious, we added the methods of analysis of variance and path analysis. All this done, we offer a summary of what we accomplished, set down the conclusions we reached, and try to draw out some of the larger implications which our effort may have both for social science and for public policy as together they confront the problems of developing nations.

This outline of our book provides the formal agenda for the intellectual exchange with our readers which will guide us through the presentation that follows. But specialists in the study of small groups will remind us that every conference has two agendas — one, the formal or nominal business of the meeting, the second an informal, unspoken, "hidden" agenda, in which the group deals with the sentiments, feelings, anxieties, grievances, and distinctive personal propensities of its members. Something analogous may be said about books. Every book has its formal agenda, the list of topics comprising the table of contents, and its hidden agenda, which expresses some of the special animus which moves the author to write just this work in this particular way.

Our book is no exception. Its formal agenda is easy to state, and has been fully outlined above. Yet there is more to the story. In writing this book we meant also to challenge certain conceptions built into the conventional wisdom of contemporary social science, and to stimulate fresh thinking on some subjects prematurely closed to further discussion. Five such issues constituted our hidden agenda.

First, we wanted to refocus studies of national development, putting the *individual,* in particular the "common man" rather than the elite, more nearly in the center of attention.

Research on national development in the so-called "emergent" countries has been dominated by economics. Increasing the gross national product per capita has overshadowed all other concerns, among both the leaders who determine national priorities and the specialists they employ. One need not question the importance of economics to make the point that there is more to national development than a high GNP per capita. Some of the new nations have become aware of the critical importance of institution building as a concomitant of, indeed as a prerequisite for, sustained national development. Indeed, some would argue that this is what development is really all about.

Although it is an advance to give more attention to institution building, this emphasis, like the economic, neglects the individual. We have very little scientific knowledge as to how far the qualities of a nation's people are important in fostering development. Our concern in this study is to bring people back in. We feel that an essential element in the development process is the individual, and that a nation is not modern unless its people are modern. In any event, we doubt that its economy can be highly productive, or its political and administrative institutions very effective, unless the people who work in the economy and staff the institutions have attained some degree of modernity. To prove this point decisively is going to take a great deal of research. Our effort is only a beginning.

The economists who developed the leading theories which purport to explain the process of national development have often justified their failure to bring the individual into their formulas by pointing to the lack of suitable means for measuring the "quality" of national populations. We entertain serious hopes that scales of individual modernity such as we have devised will not only eliminate that excuse but will also encourage more systematic attention to this element of the modernization process. In the first few years of its availability our test has already been used in dozens of research projects, some academic and some designed to measure the effectiveness of programs of planned social change at the local community level.[2] There is every reason to assume these scales could now be used effectively with national samples.[3]

Our second motive was to challenge those psychologists who assume that everything important in the development of the personality has happened by the age of six, and certainly by the age of sixteen.

We owe to Freud many extraordinary insights into the nature of the human psyche and its development. But along with his great heritage, he left us a great burden: the dominance of the idea that the fundamentals of character are laid down in early childhood, and that they then persist relatively unchanged throughout life. This view has come to be accepted more or less as a dogma, not only by Freudians, but by most psychologists of personality. The assumption may be accurate with reference to some aspects of character, such as ego strength or the preference for one or another type of defense mechanism, but there is much more to the personality than such so-called "basic structures."

The sociologist is particularly interested in the social aspects of the personality, in attitudes, values, self-conceptions, modes of striving, patterns of moral functioning, ways of relating to authority and subordinates. While we cannot speak authoritatively about mechanisms of defense or the structure of the ego, we are quite convinced that other elements of the personality can and do change after childhood and, indeed, after adolescence. We affirm not only a broader but also a more dynamic conception of the human personality. In our view, change in the adult personality, even in relatively fundamental values and modes of psychic functioning, is not merely possible, it is a regular occurrence. We reject the essentially fatalistic view of men and women as locked for life into the personality they had developed by the time they reached adolescence.

We believe that at any stage of life, and particularly in the early and middle years of adulthood, people may experience quite substantial personal change, some deep enough to qualify for the designation of a personality "transformation." In saying this we do not have in mind the retrogressive tendencies and even breakdowns which are familiar enough in clinical practice. Rather we assume the possibility of continuing personal growth, of movement from a sense of inadequacy to a feeling of personal efficacy, from rigidity to flexibility, from narrowness to cognitive openness, from suspicion to trust, from ignorance to knowledge.

Of course, we are not asserting that such changes take place, as a matter of course, in all, or even in most, individuals. On the contrary, we agree with most other observers that such changes are the exception under most life circumstances. People who enter a stable adult situation may be expected to manifest stability in their basic personal traits. But, equally, people whose social situation changes rapidly or profoundly may be expected to reflect that fact by undergoing significant change even in quite basic attributes of at least their more "social" personality. Such changes require, of course, the right circumstances, stimulus, and social support.

The third motive in the design and conduct of this research, therefore, was to clarify theoretically and to test empirically some ideas we had about the precise aspects of social structure which produce certain specific responses in individuals. In particular, we hoped to show that when individuals respond to social milieus having a distinctive character, they are most likely to incorporate the salient features typical of the mode of functioning of the institutions in which they are intimately involved. In taking this position we meant to challenge the widespread assumption that when men come in contact with the industrial order, the most common response is a reaction against it, producing a personal style opposed to the dominant emphases of that order.[4]

In our time it has become a cliché to fault Karl Marx's economics. Many of his economic theories were indeed wrong. Many of his predictions, among them that the industrialized working class would become increasingly impoverished, have not come to pass. However, in the process of proving Marx's economics wrong we have almost completely neglected his psychology. Marx the social psychologist stands up better than Marx the economist. Marx enunciated the principle that man's relation to the means of production determines his consciousness. Marx said: "The mode of production in material life determines the general character of the social, political, and spiritual processes of life. It is not the consciousness of men that determines their existence, but, on the contrary, their social existence that determines their consciousness." In this particular statement he was referring to men mainly as owners or employees, and by consciousness he meant mainly class consciousness — that is, a sense of one's economic group interest expressed politically. In other parts of his work, however, Marx clearly took a broader view of consciousness, using the term to stand for basic social values, attitudes, needs, and dispositions, much as a contemporary psychologist might speak of the social personality. And he traced this consciousness not only to differences in ownership, but to other aspects of man's relation to the mode of production.

Marx turned from historical analysis to masterminding revolution, and much of Marxist scholarship turned from creative research to sterile exegesis. Marx's seminal insight into the ways in which man's social milieu shapes his consciousness has not been followed by systematic research. Its truth as a social-science generalization has not been tested adequately; neither have scholars indicated under precisely what *conditions* exactly which *dimensions* of the individual's total personality are most likely to change and in which *direction*. If we are to understand the human meaning of the new types of social environment we build in our urban industrial societies, we must conduct more systematic studies of the ways in which the institutional and organizational milieus we create shape the responses of the people who work in them.

Different social milieus are not alike in quality. Some have a strong character and some a weak. Institutions with a strong character should have greater power to mold people and to move them in new directions.[5] Moreover, we can identify precisely those features of different milieus which have the power to inculcate particular personality tendencies in those who live in them. Specifically, we thought we knew what it is about a factory which would make men feel more efficacious, and what elements of a teacher's conduct of her classroom would strengthen her pupils' readiness for innovation. To our knowledge these ideas had not been put to the test in anything like the degree to which we probed them in our research in developing countries. The proof of many of the points we wished to make could probably be definitively established only by setting up a series of controlled experiments. Nevertheless, the entrance of workers from traditional backgrounds into the industry of developing countries presented a natural situation sufficiently like that required for the experiment to persuade us that we could use it to test the theory of how social milieus shape personal dispositions.[6]

The fourth motive influencing the design of the research was to prove that "strong" institutions would bring about the same changes in individuals regardless of the fact that those institutions had been introduced into diverse societies and were staffed by people with distinctive cultural traits. This objective was critical in leading us to work not in one or two, but rather in six different developing countries. By selecting these to represent a wide variety of cultural patterns and nation-states, we sought to provide a basis for statements which would be really *general* in their application. In this we were perhaps expressing no more than the aspiration of any scientist. As sociologists, however, we were also combatting the sense of despair our profession frequently feels because our statements must so often be hedged about with so many reservations as to make sociology less a basic science and more a clinical discipline limited to diagnostics.

But even if sociologists are distressed because they cannot point to many principles of fairly general applicability, they tend to believe that such generalization is possible. Our challenge was directed more toward the many anthropologists who tend so strongly to emphasize the uniqueness of each culture. Such anthropologists find it extremely difficult to believe one could possibly make any statement about adaptation to industrial employment which would apply equally to Yoruba in Nigeria, Hindus and tribal Christians in Northeastern India, Bengali Muslims in East Pakistan, Yemenite Jews in Israel, Catholic descendants of Italians in Argentina, and a mixed population of Spanish and Indian origin in Chile.

Without denying the uniqueness of each culture, we wish to affirm the common human nature of the people who make up each of these diverse societies. These separate cultures may give the individual personalities in each a distinctive content, but we believe those cultures do not alter the basic principles which govern the structuring of personality in all men. We believe certain panhuman patterns of response persist in the face of variability in culture content. These transcultural similarities in the psychic properties of individuals provide the basis for a common response to common stimuli. On these grounds we concluded that men from very different cultures might nevertheless respond in basically the same way to certain of the relatively standard institutions and interpersonal patterns introduced by economic development and sociopolitical modernization. The skepticism of our anthropological critics notwithstanding, we believed valid cross-cultural generalization was possible.

The fifth program on our hidden agenda was stimulated by our doubt as to the validity of the widespread assumption that modernization can be attained only at great cost to psychic well-being.

Anthropologists are normally reluctant to generalize about the response of different cultures to their encounter with alien societies. There is, however, one outcome of such contact about which a great many anthropologists do agree. They anticipate that the introduction of urban-industrial institutions and patterns will lead, in most indigenous cultures, to massive social disorganization and to greatly intensified personal psychic stress. Anthropologists were led to this conclusion by observing the rather massive impact of powerful and populous colonial nations on isolated, small, and relatively powerless peoples such as the American Indians or the South Sea islanders. The conclusion drawn from that experience tended, however, to be generalized to people in developing countries undergoing the first stages of industrialization. J. S. Slotkin spoke for most anthropologists when he said: "No matter how compatible industrialism may seem to be, since industrialism is usually a fundamental innovation, it and its ramifications tend to produce cultural disorganization. Therefore, one is confronted by two alternative social programs: is forced rapid industrialization worth the severe cultural disorganization it usually entails, and its attendant social and personal maladjustment? Or is it more important to maintain cultural organization, conserving social and personal adjustment, even though it means slow voluntary adjustment?"[7]

We do not accept this conclusion. While not denying that in some cases small and isolated tribal peoples had been overwhelmed and virtually destroyed by contact with modern civilization, we felt the effect would be quite different for the population in the developing countries. We assumed that in such countries the size of the population and the fact that it was organized in a nation-state would play a critical role in preserving the individual's sense of personal and cultural integrity. We also noted that many of the people in developing countries had a high culture of their own, in which they could take pride and which provided firm guidance to orient individuals in their life course. Much of the change they experienced would not, we thought, seem an alien force imposed from without, but rather something much needed and accepted voluntarily on the initiative of one's own leaders.

We were also disinclined to accept the common assumption that more direct contact with the typical institutions of the modern world — the public school, the city, the factory, and the mass media — was necessarily likely to induce psychic stress and nervous tension or other forms of personal disorientation. We felt this expectation rested on one or both of two questionable assumptions: first, the belief that the village in traditional societies provides a highly secure, steady, calm, and supportive environment, so that a move to city living and industrial employment would necessarily entail a psychically less healthy atmosphere; and second, the idea that the pattern of a life in a modern setting would be inherently noxious to men coming out of a traditional setting. A more realistic view of the actual conditions of village life as experienced by most poor peasant farmers in traditional agricultural countries should lead us to predict that life in the cities, whatever its disadvantages, would be no worse, and might be better, for preserving one's psychic integrity. And we could see in urban-industrial living not only potential for strain and harassment, but also possibilities for experiences which could be broadening, be ego enhancing, and give security. To provide an empirical test for our challenge to the conventional wisdom about personal adjustment and modernization, we included in our interview some psychological tests, in particular the Psychosomatic Symptoms Test.[8]

The design of our study shapes the main outline of our presentation. The hidden agenda will, however, determine the special emphasis at numerous points. Our hope is that through both we may contribute to understanding the process of individual change, to clarifying some basic issues of social science, and to formulating more effective public policy to speed up the development of the new nations. The issues are not only complex; they are important and arouse strong responses. As we talked to various audiences about our research we found that at every point fundamental questions about our assumptions and procedures were constantly being raised: people questioned whether our conception of the modern man is not just the Western man or the capitalist man in disguise; whether the factory itself is not an essentially Western importation embodying Western values; whether, in that case, it would not attract mainly the people who are already "Western" in spirit; whether there is any reason to prefer the factory as a school for modernity over any other large-scale bureaucratic organization, including the army; whether including the tendency to "participation" as an attribute of the modern man requires that a society be democratic to be modern.

These are certainly basic questions. Before the book is finished we hope to answer these and many more. Alas, we cannot answer them all at once. Indeed, we cannot always undertake to answer them when they first come up, at least not fully. To do so would often interfere with telling the main story of our research. We do not mean to avoid these and related issues. On the contrary, we welcome the opportunity to discuss them. We must, however, beg indulgence to get to them at what seems to us the appropriate place and time. We offer a solemn pledge, however, not to forget them; those we do not get to along the way we mean to turn to in our conclusions.

2

Toward a Definition of The Modern Man

The term "modern" has many denotations and carries a heavy weight of connotations. It is applied not only to men, but to nations, to political systems, to economies, to cities, to institutions such as schools and hospitals, to housing, to clothes, and to manners. Taken literally, the word refers to anything which has more or less recently replaced something which in the past was the accepted way of doing things. In that sense, the first sailing vessels to replace the galleys propelled by oars were modern, as was the clipper ship before steam, and steam before atomic power. Approached in this way, the modern becomes a catalogue of things rather than a concept.

Numerous scholars have sought to give the idea more distinctive and coherent form. One line of thought places the society at the center of attention. The defining features of a modern nation are then taken to include mass education, urbanization, industrialization, bureaucratization, and rapid communication and transportation. Some of these manifestations, such as cities, go back in man's history to points long antedating anything we would ordinarily call modern, while others, such as industrialization, are decidedly more recent developments. In any event, the more or less simultaneous manifestation of these forms of social organization *as a set* certainly was not observed in any nation before the nineteenth century, and became really widespread in the world only in the twentieth.

The modern might, then, be conceived of as a form of civilization characteristic of our current historical epoch, much as feudalism or the classical empires of antiquity were characteristic of earlier historical eras. Just as feudalism was not present in all the world in the eleventh to the fifteenth centuries, so modernity is not today found everywhere on the globe. And just as feudalism did, so modernity varies in accord with local conditions, the history of a given culture, and the period when it was introduced. Within these limits, however, there exists a syndrome of characteristics, readily recognized at both the national and the institutional level, which marks the modern.

Robert Ward listed ten characteristics defining *economic* modernization, including intense application of scientific technology and inanimate sources of energy, high specialization of labor and interdependence of impersonal markets, large-scale financing and concentration of economic decision making, and rising levels of material well-being.[1] Samuel Huntington offered a more compact set of three processes which define *political* modernization: the replacement of a large number of traditional, religious, familial, and ethnic political authorities by a single, secular, national political authority; the emergence of new political functions — legal, military, administrative, and scientific — which must be managed by new administrative hierarchies chosen on the basis of achievement rather than ascription; and increased participation in politics by social groups throughout the society, along with the development of new institutions such as political parties and interest groups to organize this participation.[2]

Whereas this first line of analysis in the study of modernization gives emphasis to patterns of social organization, there is a second line which emphasizes the cultural and ideational. Whereas the first approach, as represented by Ward and Huntington, more stresses ways of *organizing* and *doing,* the second assigns primacy to ways of *thinking* and *feeling.* The first approach is concerned more with the *institution,* the other with the individual. The first is more narrowly sociological and political, the second more sociological and psychological.

The sociopsychological approach to modernization treats it mainly as a process of change in ways of perceiving, expressing, and valuing. The modern is defined as a mode of individual functioning, a set of dispositions to act in certain ways. It is, in other words, an "ethos" in the sense in which Max Weber spoke of "the spirit of capitalism."[3] As Robert Bellah expressed it, the modern should be seen not "as a form of political or economic system, but as a spiritual phenomenon or a kind of mentality."[4] As such it is much less tied to a particular time and place than is a definition of modernity in terms of institutional arrangements. If modernity is defined as a state of mind, the same condition might have existed in Elizabethan England, in Periclean Greece, or in Tokugawa Japan.

Of the two main foci in the study of modernization, the institution has received far more attention. Indeed, it would be a conservative estimate to say that major studies of economic and political modernization at the institutional level outnumber those at the individual level some twenty to one. This fact played a critical role in our decision to devote our energies to the study of the individual in the modernization process.

However, to do a book about the forces that make men modern, and the processes whereby those forces operate, we had first to determine who is a modern man. By what signs should we know him?

From the start we operated with the assumption that no single quality could adequately define the modern man. We believed that individual modernity could be, and generally would be, manifested in a variety of forms and contexts. In other words, we thought of it as a syndrome, or complex, of qualities rather than as a single trait. An outstanding feature of our approach to defining the modern man was, therefore, the development of a long list of themes each of which we felt might reasonably be reflected in the attitudes, values, and behavior of the modern man. Each theme was assigned a pair of code letters, such as EF for efficacy, and each question carried such code letters before its number to indicate the dimension it was assumed to measure. Eventually we nominated twenty-four dimensions of individual modernity for consideration as part of the syndrome. These constitute the main themes we eventually built into our measures of the modern man.[5]

Although each theme was expected to make its case on its own merits, we did not come upon them as completely independent, unrelated entities. Rather, they were selected more or less as sets, each representing a different perspective or organizing principle. As it turned out, the distinctions we initially made among these sets did not consistently shape the subsequent analysis presented in this book. We have preserved them in this chapter, however, for several reasons.

For one thing, some of the distinctions *do* figure in the later analysis. For another, the distinctions provide a convenient basis for simplifying the presentation of our long array of themes. Most important, however, is the fact that these perspectives played a substantial role in alerting us to the themes we *did* measure. Obviously, even twenty-four themes cannot exhaust the list of dimensions with which we *might* have dealt. We are often asked what led us to study one or another theme, or why we left out some aspect of individual modernity which our interlocutor assumes to be important. A full explanation would require separate discussion of each such theme. But a fairly accurate general answer would be that the theme was or was not suggested to us by one of the three perspectives which guided our selection of themes. These were the *analytic,* the *topical,* and the *behavioral* perspectives.

The Analytic Perspective

With the exception of Japan, and Russia if you wish to include it with the East, all the major nations we can consider modernized are part of the European tradition. This makes it extremely difficult to disentangle those elements of the social and cultural system which are distinctive to, and necessary for, the maintenance of a modern society from those which are really "traditional" for these European societies but have, in a sense, been "dragged along" into the contemporary era together with the more modern institutions. For example, everyone has noted how the Japanese, and indeed the elites in most of the underdeveloped world, adopted the Western businessman's suit and his shoes, even though in fact these are in no way necessary for running a modern society. In formulating our conception of individual modernity we wished to avoid blindly imposing European standards of value upon the citizens of developing countries. To do so would have been not only arrogant, but also totally inappropriate for a cross-cultural study done simultaneously in Asia, Africa, and South America. Yet it did not seem to be possible, or even meaningful, to think of a "value-free" measure of individual modernity.

Our solution to the problem was to derive our list of modern *personal* qualities from the presumed requirements of daily living in a modern and complex *society,* and, in particular, from the demands made on a worker or staff member in a modern industrial establishment.

Since industrialism first arose and received its widest diffusion in the countries loosely classified as capitalist, there was in this some risk that our modern man might be cast too much in the image of "capitalist" man. We felt we could reasonably well guard against this tendency, however, because the senior author of this study had spent some twenty-five years in research on the social structure and the people of the Soviet Union.[6] By drawing on this experience he was able to identify modern personal qualities of more general significance, that is, those which were equally important to effective functioning of both capitalist and socialist societies.

Even Soviet society, however, would seem to many to be too much part of Europe to satisfy the objective of developing an image of the modern man transcending more parochial cultural limits. We decided, therefore, to peg our list of modern qualities more specifically to the particular requirements of running a factory.

We will encounter little argument, we trust, when we propose that the factory is one of the distinctive institutions of modern society. Industrialization is a very large part of the modernization process; indeed, many would claim it to be the *essential* element. Industrialization, in turn, rests on the factory — the large-scale productive enterprise, bringing together large numbers of men in one work place, systematically ordering their relation one to the other according to rational considerations expressed in formal rules, relying on concentrations of inanimate power and the innovative application of technology, and guided by a hierarchy of authority largely resting on technical skill and administrative competence.

The factory as an institution has no nationality: it is not English or French, or Dutch, or, for that matter, European. It played as great a role in the development of the Soviet Union as it had done earlier in the United States, was as important in the emergence of Japan as it had been in the rise of Great Britain. The factory does not inherently violate the important taboos of any religious group, major or minor. No general proscriptions against entering or working in such a place are posed by the Islamic, Hindu, or Buddhist religions, and representatives of all these persuasions have found it easy to take up work in factories. *We proposed, then, to classify as modern those personal qualities which are likely to be inculcated by participation in large-scale modern productive enterprises such as the factory, and, perhaps more critical, which may be required of the workers and the staff if the factory is to operate efficiently and effectively.*

There are, of course, many ways of looking at the factory as an institution. We do not claim that our list of qualities and requirements of factory life is exhaustive or even definitive. In fact, we narrowed the range of the themes we would consider by focusing particularly on those features of factory organization which we assumed would be notable to and would most influence a naïve worker fresh from the countryside. This was justified by our special interest in the factory as a learning setting, as a school, if you will, in new ways of arranging things, of thinking, and of feeling which contrast markedly with the traditional village. In any event, we assumed that each of the themes we selected was a salient feature of the factory, and one likely to be influential in shaping men's response to their environment.

As we present the individual themes it will, we trust, be apparent how each reflects qualities which would make one a more effective citizen of a modern complex society. Unfortunately, the connection between factory work and our analytic themes may not immediately be equally apparent. In order to get on with the presentation of our model, however, we prefer to put off until Chapter 11 a detailed explanation of how we derived these themes from an examination of the factory as an institution. At this point we present only a brief description of each of the personal qualities we selected to define the modern men within the framework of our analytic perspective. As we list them here they represent only our best estimate at the time we began our study. Whether they would, in truth, reflect empirical reality was an open question at the time we delineated them in the form which follows.

1. *Openness to new experience* constituted the first element in our definition. We thought traditional men would be less disposed to accept

new ideas, new ways of feeling and acting. Here, therefore, we are dealing with a psychological disposition rather than with the specific techniques or skills which a man or a group might possess because of the level of technology they had attained. Thus, a farmer who works with a wooden plow can be more modern, in our sense, than someone who already drives a tractor. In testing for openness to new experience, for example, we asked questions such as the following: "Suppose you could get along well enough where you are now, earning enough to provide food and other necessities for yourself and your family. Would you be willing to move to another place far from here where the language and other customs are different if *there* you could live twice as well as here?"

Our assumption, of course, was that a man open to new experience would more readily respond to the opportunity we described. In this case the readiness to move might, naturally, be tempered both by the economic pinch the man felt and by how much he cared about improving his standard of living. No question, however, is entirely unambiguous or unidimensional, and some of the most interesting problems in analysis come from disentangling the diverse influences which come to bear on an individual's answer to any one question. The readiness for new experience may express itself in a variety of forms and contexts — in willingness to adopt a new drug or sanitation method, to use a new seed or a different fertilizer, to get to know new and different kinds of people, or to turn to an unfamiliar source of news. Individuals and groups may, of course, show more readiness for the new in one area of life than another. But we can also conceive of the readiness to do things in a new way as a fairly pervasive characteristic which makes itself felt across a variety of situations. And we judged those with this readiness to be more modern.

2. *The readiness for social change* is intimately related to, but goes beyond, the openness to new experience. The latter asks something for oneself, the former allows it to others as well. By readiness for change we referred especially to the acceptance of changes in social organizations such as greater political participation by wider segments of the population, increased social and physical mobility, fuller opportunities for women, freer relations between superior and subordinate and between young and old. We defined the modern man as one who could more readily acknowledge the process of social transformation taking place around him in developing countries, and who could more freely accept the changed opportunities which others, previously more restricted, might now be enjoying. He is, in a sense, less rigid, less anxious about allowing others to do things in a new way, in sum, less rooted in tradition.

3. The realm of *the growth of opinion* represents the next in our complex of themes. This area may itself be divided into a number of sub-

themes or scale areas. We defined a man as more modern if he had a *disposition to form or hold opinions* on a large number of the issues arising not only in his immediate environment, but also outside of it. Daniel Lerner has shown that in the Middle East individuals within any country, and, in fact, the populations of different countries, vary greatly in their ability or readiness to imagine themselves in the position of prime minister or comparable government leader, and thus to offer advice as to what should be done to resolve the problems facing the country.[7] The more educated the individual and the more advanced the country, Lerner found, the greater is the readiness to offer opinions in response to this challenge. The more traditional man, we assumed, would take an interest in fewer things, mainly those which touched him immediately and intimately, and even when he held opinions on more distant matters, he would be more circumspect in expressing them.

We assessed the individual's readiness to hold opinions on a wide range of subjects and issues through a series of different measures. For example, we noted the number of times he responded to our questions by saying, "I don't know," or "I never thought about that," and the number of themes he introduced in reply to questions about the most serious problems facing his nation, his local community, and his family.

We also judged a man to be more modern if his orientation to the opinion realm was more flexible. We meant by this that he showed *awareness of the diversity of attitude and opinion around him,* and did not close himself off in the belief that everyone thinks alike. In our conception, a modern man is able to acknowledge differences of opinion; he has no need rigidly to deny differences out of fear that they will upset his own view of the world. He is also less likely to evaluate opinion in a strictly autocratic or hierarchical way. He does not automatically accept the ideas of those above him in the power hierarchy or automatically reject the opinions of those below him. In other words, *he puts a positive value on variations in opinion.* We tested these values by asking people whether it is proper to think differently from the village headman or other traditional leader, and, at the other end, by inquiring whether the opinions of a man's wife or young son merited serious consideration when important public issues were being discussed.

4. Intimately related to our study of opinion, but conceived as a separate dimension, were our measures of *information.* For us, being modern meant not merely having opinions, but being more energetic in acquiring facts and information on which to base them. If a man is asked whether he has an interest in world politics, it is terribly easy to say yes. It is quite another matter for him actually to know where Moscow and Washington are, and to identify them as national capitals.

5. *Time* is another theme our measures dealt with at some length.

We felt the more modern man would be oriented to the present or the future rather than to the past. We assumed he would more readily accept fixed schedules as something appropriate, or possibly even desirable. We also considered it more modern to be punctual.

The relation of time orientation to measures of modernity is complex. It presents an opportunity to point out that the classification of men as modern or traditional according to our measures often would not accord with the assignment they would receive in common practice. For example, we believe the Mayan Indians had a sharper sense of time than their Spanish rulers, and they preserve it to this day. The qualities we define as modern can, in fact, be manifested by a group which seems relatively unmodern when judged by the level of technology or amount of power it possesses. Our conception of the modern rests on properties of the person, qualities of a sort which could emerge in any time or place. What is crucial is the coherence of a set of related properties. The fact that these qualities may be widely diffused in industrially advanced nations does not mean that they cannot appear in nonindustrial cultures.

6. *Efficacy,* the sixth theme, weighed heavily in our conception of the modern man. In our view, the modern individual believes that man can learn how to exert considerable control over his environment. He thus advances his own goals, rather than being dominated by the forces created by more powerful men or by nature itself. We felt, for example, that a man who was efficacious would more likely respond positively to the question, "Do you believe that some day men will fully understand what causes such things as floods, droughts, and epidemics?" We believed that the more efficacious man, even though in fact he had never seen a dam, would say, "Yes, I think that some day man will do that."

The sense of efficacy is, of course, not limited to feelings concerning man's potential mastery over nature. It includes, as well, the sense that one can effectively do something if officials are proposing what one considers to be a bad law, and the belief that care will help prevent accidents, that human nature can be changed, that men can arrange their affairs so that even nations can live in peace. As we saw it, then, the modern man's sense of efficacy would express his confidence in his ability, alone and in concert with other men, to organize his life so as to master the challenges it presents at the personal, the interpersonal, the communal, the national, and even the international levels.

7. *Planning* is a theme closely related to efficacy and time, which we initially allowed to stand in its own right. We rated as more modern the man oriented toward long-term planning, both in public affairs and in his private personal life. We asked such questions as: "What does the country need most: hard work by the people, the help of God, or a good plan on the part of the government?" And in the more personal

realm we put the question: "Some say that a boy should be taught to handle things as they come up without bothering much about thinking ahead. Others say that a boy must be taught to plan and arrange things in advance. What do you think?"

8. *Calculability* or trust: By our definition the modern man should have more confidence that his world is calculable, and that people and institutions around him can be relied upon to meet their obligations. We assumed that the modern man would be more prepared to trust a stranger than would the traditional man. He would not agree that everything is determined either by fate or by the whims and the inborn character of men. In other words, he believes in a reasonably lawful world under human control. This was, therefore, a theme we also expected to find closely related to the sense of efficacy.

9. The *valuing of technical skill,* and the acceptance of it as a valid basis for distributing rewards, was an additional quality we expected to find in the modern man. Of course every culture values some skills, and among these are skills which clearly merit the designation "technical," for example, hunting and farming. What we especially had in mind, therefore, was a shift in preference from skills which were more valued in the traditional village setting to those which are more required in the industrial world. Thus, we asked whether a wise farmer or an agronomist could give better advice on how to combat a plant disease, and whether one should particularly encourage a boy's interest in "machines and how they work." In this context, we were also interested in the sense of *distributive justice,* by which we meant the belief that rewards should be distributed according to rule rather than whim, and that the structure of rewards should, insofar as possible, be in accord with skill and output. However, in our effort to measure feelings about distributive justice we were rather less successful than we were in tapping the valuation of technical skill.

10. *Aspirations, educational and occupational:* Each culture has a traditional wisdom, and it is assumed to be most widely diffused among and most strongly believed by the peasantry and others who make up "the common folk." In more traditional societies such formal schooling as exists is frequently used mainly for purposes of religious education, and is devoted to inculcating and preserving traditional values. The secular schools which we take so much for granted in the more developed nations are genuine innovations in some of the underdeveloped countries. The subjects they teach and the values they disseminate often compete with, may indeed challenge and contradict, the traditional wisdom. We defined the more modern man as having interest in and placing higher value on formal education and schooling in skills such as reading, writing, and arithmetic. The traditional man might see modern

learning and science as an intrusion into a sacred realm which should be left a mystery or approached only through religion. By contrast, we expected the modern man to feel that science and technology benefit mankind by providing solutions to pressing human problems. Moreover, we assumed the modern man would prefer to see his son leave the occupations sanctioned by tradition and take up one of the modern occupations more intimately associated with these newer ways of doing things.

We measured attitudes in this realm by inquiring how much schooling a man should try to get for his son if costs were no obstacle, by asking whether schools should emphasize morality and religion or the practical skills, and by soliciting the father's preference for his son's future occupation.

11. Awareness of, and respect for, the *dignity* of others is a quality many people feel has been lost in the modern world. In making a judgment as to whether this quality was, in fact, more deeply instilled and more widely distributed in traditional societies, a great deal would clearly depend on *which* traditional society one used as a standard of comparison. Many intellectuals are firmly convinced that *all* men enjoyed greater personal dignity, even if they consumed fewer goods, when they lived in the preindustrial, preurban age. We were not persuaded of the truth of this dictum. Indeed, in our study we adopted the rather radical position that the factory may be a training ground which inculcates a greater sense of awareness of the dignity of subordinates and restraint in one's dealings with them. We felt that the manager-worker relation respects that dignity more than is common in the relation of the owner, boss, chief, or patron to the peasant in most traditional villages. Indeed, we expected the modern man to be more protective of the dignity of weaker and subordinate persons, not only in the work settings but in other relations, such as those with women and children. Thus we asked, "Which of the following is more correct regarding a boy's dignity: Is it less important than a man's; as important; or more important?"

12. *Understanding production* was the last of the regular themes suggested by the analytic perspective. Its questions were designed mainly to assess how far a man grasped the logic underlying decision making at the basic level of production in industry.

Two additional themes derived from the analytic perspective were *particularism* and *optimism*. However, some of the field directors were unable to build them into their questionnaires. Consequently, these themes were not, as such, included in the basic set of twenty-four later built into our general measure of modernity, although some individual questions were used in some countries.[8] *Particularism* measured the extent to which men believed in universalistic rules applied equally to all, rather than feeling it more appropriate that one should favor friends and relatives and in other ways rely mainly on personal influence. We saw this theme as closely related to that on distributive justice. *Optimism* dealt with feelings about fate and the inevitability of things. We considered this theme to be closely related to our measures of efficacy. We would classify a man as more traditional if he was more particularistic and more fatalistic.

The Topical Perspective

Effective as it was in leading us to some themes, the analytic perspective did not particularly call to our attention many other matters which had been emphasized over the years in discussions of individual modernity.[9] Our staff, and numerous other scholars, had generated a large number of propositions about the ways in which modernization is presumably linked to attitudes toward religion, the family, social stratification, and a host of other topics. Many of these propositions enjoyed wide acceptance; others ran counter to popular impression. What struck us most was that almost all had actually been the object of very little systematic research. We therefore felt an obligation to include in our study as many questions as possible bearing on these hypotheses. These sets of questions represented our topical themes.

Whereas our analytic model represented a single coherent theoretical *viewpoint,* the topical themes derived from a more heterogeneous collection of propositions touching on a variety of nominally discrete *subjects.* Nevertheless, the psychological thrust of the specific items we introduced under these topical headings was often similar to that characteristic of the questions and themes grouped under the analytic rubric. The distinction between the two perspectives should, therefore, not be seen as hard and fast. Neither should one think about them as "our" model and "their" model. We were deeply convinced of the relevance for individual modernity of most of the elements built into the themes representing the topical perspective.

1. *Kinship and family.* With the possible exception of religion, no institution of society is more often depicted as either an obstacle to or a victim of modernization than is the extended kinship structure. Wilbert Moore summed up prevailing opinion when he said: "In general, the traditional kinship structure provides a barrier to industrial development, since it encourages reliance of the individual upon its security rather than upon his own devices."[10] The image of these family ties as a *victim* of the modernization process is well presented in M. B. Deshmukh's report on the migrant communities in Delhi, where he observed, "The absence of social belonging, the pressure of poverty, and the evil effects of the urban environment made . . . the family bonds, regarded to be so sacred in the villages . . . of absolutely no importance" in the migrant colonies.[11]

After reviewing the question we concluded that there was certainly some truth to the frequent assertion that increasing urbanism and industrialism tended to diminish the vigor of extended kinship relations. We had little reason to doubt that when urbanism increased the physical distance between kin, and industrial employment decreased their economic dependence, the strength of kinship ties as manifested in common residence, frequent visiting, and mutual help in work would decline. A series of our questions inquiring about residence, visiting patterns, mutual help, and the like was designed to test whether these assumptions were true.

While ready to follow popular assumptions up to a point, we also came to the rather radical conclusion that in some ways industrial employment might actually *strengthen* family ties. We felt that many of the common assertions about the family and modernization were much too sweeping and general, that they confused the extended with the immediate family, and that they failed to discriminate between degrees and types of kinship relatedness. It could well be, for example, that, while the experience of modernization weakens *extended* family ties, it strengthens those to a man's family of *procreation* and leads him to cling less to his mother and cleave more to his wife. While a man may give less attention to his more extended kinship ties after moving to the city, the increased stability and improved well-being that characterize his life as an industrial worker may lead him to accept more fully some of his kinship obligations than would his less secure and more impoverished brothers still earning their living as peasants in the village. We tested these relations with a set of questions on kinship obligations, such as: "Suppose a young man works in a factory. He has barely managed to save a very small amount of money. Now his relative [selected appropriately for each country, such as a distant cousin] comes to him and tells him he needs money badly since he has no work at all. How much obligation do you think the factory worker has to share his savings with this relative?"

2. *Women's rights.* Intimately related to the changing pattern of family relations, yet distinct, is the question of the status of women in society. Most of the traditional societies and communities of the world are, if not strictly patriarchal, at least vigorously male dominated. The extreme example, perhaps, is found in the Islamic and Hebrew religions, in which a man each day says a prayer of thanks to God for not having made him a woman. We predicted that the liberating influence of the forces making for modernization would act on men's attitudes, and incline them to accord to women status and rights more nearly equal to those enjoyed by men. We tested the men's orientation through questions on a woman's right to work and to equal pay, to hold public office, and to freely choose her marriage partner.

3. *Birth control, or restriction of family size.* Few points about the contemporary world have been better documented than the fact that in

many underdeveloped countries population is increasing so rapidly as to equal and sometimes exceed the rate of increase in the supply of food and other necessities. Despite an annual rate of growth of some 3 percent or more per year in gross national product, many of these countries are either standing still or even falling constantly behind in the standard of welfare they provide for the population and in the general development of their economy. One obvious approach is to reduce the number of children born to the average family. Although birth control depends in great measure on scientific technology and on particular practices guided by that technology, even the most spectacular advances in science, such as new contraceptive pills, cannot have the desired effect except as they may be supported by the motive to use them and by patterns of interpersonal relations that make that motivation effective. To assess attitudes in this area, therefore, we inquired into our respondents' ideas of the ideal number of children and into their readiness to limit that number under various conditions.

4. *Religion* ranks with the extended family as the institution most often identified both as an obstacle to economic development and as a victim of the same process. The classic case of resistance is that of the Asian religions, and many studies going back to Max Weber's have noted that religion may be a major obstacle to modernization because it is often the bulwark of tradition and a repository of beliefs and values incompatible with modern science, technology, and the idea of progress.

Many students of the subject argue rather vigorously that the individual's adherence both to the fundamental doctrine of his traditional religion and to the religious ritual and practice it requires of him will inevitably be undermined by urban living, industrial experience, and scientific education. Thus, speaking about West Africa, Dr. Geoffrey Parrinder noted: "It is sometimes said that Africans are 'incurably religious.' Whatever this may mean, it is true that African society has traditionally been permeated with religion. But the ancient religious beliefs cannot stand the strain of modern urban and industrial life. The higher religions themselves have been attacked by what someone has called 'the acids of modernity.' "[12]

Systematic evidence for this proposition is, however, much less ample than one might imagine. We thought it appropriate, therefore, to attempt to ascertain the facts by asking a series of questions designed to measure religiosity and secularism, and we inquired into such matters as the role of God in causing and curing sickness and accidents, and whether a holy man or a great industrialist contributes more to the welfare of his people. We also took note of the regularity with which our subjects prayed or otherwise fulfilled the formal ritualistic prescriptions and proscriptions of their religion.

We were prepared to find that the influences which are assumed to make for attitudinal modernity in general would also lead to greater secularism, and that increased education, urbanism, and industrial experience would also lead to more faith in science and related remedies, and to less reliance on religion. Yet we also made the less conventional assumption that the fulfillment of religious obligations in practice, especially in ritual, might actually increase as peasants left the village and became workers in urban industry. As in the case of the fulfillment of kinship obligations, we reasoned that the poor and harassed peasant would often lack the funds to pay for special religious services, and would have neither time nor energy to undertake many of his ritual obligations, especially as the lack of local facilities might increase the trouble to which he would have to go in order to do so. We concluded, therefore, that in the city, with religious facilities often more numerous and easily accessible, and income steadier and more substantial, the industrial worker might well find it less of a burden to meet the formal requirements of religious observance.

5. *Aging and the aged.* The special role of the aged is intimately linked to the strength of the family and the vigor of religion. The respect, even veneration, shown for the aged in traditional society is often noted as one of its most distinctive marks, as well as being considered as one of its outstanding virtues. It is widely believed that one of the most common, indeed an almost inevitable, tendency of modernization is to erode respect for the aged, and to foster a youth culture in which old age is viewed not as a venerable state to which one looks forward, but rather as a dreadful condition to be approached with reluctance, even horror.

On this issue, as on the family and religion, we were not inclined automatically to follow the dominant opinion. It did seem clear that the structural changes accompanying modernization might undercut reverence for the aged. In an era of technological revolutions, for example, it would be hard for the village elder relying on his long personal experience alone to preserve his authority indefinitely in competition with the agricultural expert relying on the latest scientific advances. Also, as young people came to earn their own living in factories and shops without dependence on their father's land or animals, it seemed inevitable that the father's authority over them should be lessened. The mass media and other models of new and competing styles of life would, in turn, make it difficult for the elders authoritatively to enforce the old norms and ways of doing things.

Yet we also felt that many analysts had perhaps exaggerated the corrosive effects of industrialism on the treatment of the aged. There is nothing in urban living per se which *requires* a person to show disrespect for the aged, and nothing in industrial experience which explicitly *teaches* a man to abandon the aged. In the villages, too, many an old man and woman has been abandoned by children too poor to support them. We reasoned that steadier wages and generally more stable conditions of life for the gainfully employed industrial worker could well enable him better to fulfill his filial and other family obligations. And he might well be just as respectful of the aged as his more traditional counterparts still farming in the villages.

6. *Politics.* Political modernization has been cited by many scholars as an indispensable condition for the modernization of economy and society.[13] The terms "participant" and "mobilized" often are used to characterize the citizen of a modern polity. There is an expectation that he will take an active interest not only in those matters which touch his immediate life, but also in the larger issues facing his community. His allegiance is supposed to extend beyond his family and friends to the state, the nation, and its leaders. He is expected to join political parties, to support candidates, and to vote in elections. Comparable expectations about mobilization and participation are placed on the citizens of developing communist countries run by a single party, such as China and Cuba, as are placed on those in more "mixed" systems, such as India or Chile.

Our study was not designed to answer the question whether or not a society could modernize its economy while still managing with a traditional political system. Nor is our study appropriate for testing how far modern political institutions can operate effectively without "participant" and "mobilized" citizens. But we could discover the degree to which men who were otherwise modern would also be modern in their orientation to politics. The design of our study also gave us an unusual opportunity to identify the social forces generating the qualities which sociological studies had identified as necessary or desirable in the citizens of a modern political system.

We therefore added a large number of questions, in some countries as many as fifty, permitting us to assess the political attitudes and behavior of our subjects. These included questions concerning political participation, attitudes toward politicians and the political process, evaluations of the effectiveness of the government, and levels of political knowledge and information.

7. *Communications media, mass and nonmass.* Just as wearing a watch is often the first dramatic sign of a man's commitment to the modern world, so acquiring a radio may be the thing that really incorporates him into that world. In his study of modernization in the Middle East, Daniel Lerner treated the individual's relation to the mass media as one of the key elements in his scheme for classifying people as traditional, transitional, or modern. Indeed, Lerner held that "no modern society functions efficiently without a developed system of mass communication." The model of modernization, he claimed, "exhibits certain compo-

nents and sequences whose relevance is global. Everywhere, literacy has tended to increase media exposure; increasing media exposure has 'gone with' wider economic participation (per capita income) and political participation (voting) . . . That same basic model reappears in virtually all modernizing societies on all continents of the world."[14]

Since other students of modernization, among them Ithiel Pool and Karl W. Deutsch, had also placed heavy emphasis on mass communication as one of the key elements in the modernization process, we felt obliged to deal with it in the topical model.[15] Our working assumption was that a modern man would more often expose himself to the media of mass communication, to newspaper, radio, movies, and, where available, television. We considered it much more problematic that he would simultaneously shun the more traditional sources of information and advice, such as village elders, traditional political leaders, or religious functionaries. The results of research on communications behavior have suggested that those who very actively establish contact with sources of information tend to be outstanding in the frequency of their contact with *all* sources, modern and traditional. We were quite strongly convinced, however, that when it came to *evaluating* the different sources of information, the more modern men would have greater confidence in the newer mass media, whereas the less modern would rely more on the more traditional sources. Indeed, we expected the most traditional to look on the "newfangled" mass media, such as the movies, as possibly dangerous and harmful to morals, especially those of the young.

In evaluating the role of the information media we had to decide whether to consider use of the media more as an indicator or more as an independent cause of individual modernity. We resolved the issue by a compromise. Measures of exposure to the mass media — for example those indicating how often a man listened to radio broadcasts or read the newspapers — were defined as independent variables, part of the set of presumed "causes" of individual modernity. On the other hand, we treated attitudes and values about the communication process — such as considering the movies to be inherently dangerous to public morality — as more relevant in measuring the dependent variable of individual modernity.

8. *Consumerism.* His role as a consumer struck us as one of the most problematic aspects of the life of a citizen in a developing country. On the one hand, we hear repeatedly that economic development is impossible unless the great bulk of the population enters the money economy and begins to demand and buy modern items of mass consumption. Otherwise, the argument runs, the market will be too small to support profitable national industries, the circulation of money too weak to satisfy the requirements of a modern monetary system, the base of the tax system too narrow, and so on. On the other hand, we often hear of runaway infla-

tion in developing countries, a process presumably created by an un-controlled demand for consumer goods which far outstrips capacity to produce. Outlays then exceed income by excessive amounts. And insofar as these excessive outlays are for consumption rather than for invest-ment for future production, deficit financing and mounting inflation will follow each other in a vicious circle. Economic stability will be under-mined, further investment hindered, and economic stagnation or even retrogression must follow.

Economists can perhaps resolve the apparent contradiction between these two models of development. For our part, we found ourselves re-luctant to decide whether it should be considered modern to believe in saving, or to feel that newly acquired income should be spent on beds, sewing machines, radios, bicycles, and other mass-produced goods. In the end we came down on the side of spending. We predicted that the less modern man would be guided by his tradition and encouraged by his condition to consider frugality a virtue and feel that chasing after goods was a frivolous and perhaps slightly immoral preoccupation. By contrast, we expected the stimulus of the city and work in industry to make men more aware of the kinds of goods available and to persuade them that there was a plenitude of goods in the world for all to have. We also anticipated that the urban worker's firmer financial position, plus, perhaps, easier access to credit, would stimulate him to affirm a con-sumption ethic. Through various questions we solicited information as to the goods a man owned and would like to own, and sought his views on frugality as against spending.

9. *Social stratification.* Traditional societies are generally defined as having closed class systems, in the extreme case possessed of the rigid-ity of a caste structure. In the commonly accepted theoretical model of the traditional society, mobility is at a minimum, with men born into the positions in which they will die, and sons succeeding their fathers genera-tion after generation. Status and prestige are assigned mainly on the basis of long-established hereditary family connections. Authority is feared and respected, often held in awe, and treated with elaborate shows of submission and deference. This model, which we know does not al-ways accord with empirical reality, is often counterposed to the modes of an open, modern society in which all of these features of stratification are supposed to be quite different.

Along with the changes in social structure accompanying moderniza-tion, we expected attitudes and values about stratification to shift signif-icantly in the modern system. We anticipated that modern men would assign prestige more on the basis of education and technical skill than on grounds of traditional status, and that they would believe mobility to be possible for oneself and especially for one's children. Because the move to industrial labor or white-collar work is perceived by most who experience it as an improvement of their social standing, we expected the more modern men to feel more a part of society, citizens on an equal footing with others in the national society.

10. *Work commitment* presented an issue closely related to considerations of stratification. Many observers of the industrialization process in the newly developing countries concluded that in such places it is difficult to develop a stable industrial labor force. These observers reported that men often came to work in industry only when pressed by economic circumstance, and as soon as they had accumulated some cash returned to their villages or to other traditional pursuits. As a result, the investment in training these men was lost, and production proceeded haltingly for lack of a regular labor supply.

Since this issue was clearly of some importance, we decided to test whether men who were attitudinally more modern also had a firmer commitment to industrial labor, preferring it to agricultural employment and considering themselves as having taken on a new social identity as industrial workers.

This completes the list of special topics we undertook to study as a supplement to the analytic perspective. As we noted earlier, our initial approach was to treat these topics as an unrelated assemblage of individual themes. For each we made a different assessment of its relation to modernization. Nevertheless, examination of the full array leads one to the supposition that at least some subsets of these themes could reflect a common underlying dimension of modernity. Men more independent of the extended family might well also be more interested in practicing birth control, more accepting of scientific rather than religious explanations of natural events, and more ready to participate in the newly emerging citizenship roles. Moreover, closer inspection of the themes developed from a topical perspective made it apparent that they were not necessarily tightly sealed off from those suggested by the analytic perspective. There could be much in common between themes initially introduced under different auspices. For example, readiness to adopt new methods of birth control suggests both openness to new experience and a sense of personal efficacy, and the granting of rights to women might well be related to readiness to respect the dignity of individuals who are less powerful or prestigious than oneself.

The Behavioral Perspective

Sociology is often charged with being too abstract, too divorced from social reality. Even when he leaves his study to go into the field, the sociologist almost invariably puts an instrument, usually a questionnaire, between himself and direct observation of social action. Insofar as the sociologist wishes to study large numbers of individuals he does not have many alternatives. And many people are too quick to dismiss as unimportant those changes in men which are limited to attitudes. We are not persuaded of the justice of the point. What men do is much influenced by the climate of opinion in which they find themselves. If a man, especially a young man, hears all around him an opinion which is conducive to more modern behavior, he is more likely to act in accord with his own impulses in that direction even if the elders are expressing only *opinion* and are not themselves personally acting in a more modern way.

But we also realized that a questionnaire need not restrict itself to questions concerning *attitudes*. The questionnaire may also be used to elicit information concerning the *behavior* of the man who answers it. We were acutely aware of the possibility that many of our subjects might espouse, might even have sincerely adopted, modern attitudes and opinions, while still continuing to act in their traditional way in the course of their daily human relations. We wished, therefore, to obtain as much information as we could about the actual behavior of our subjects. The materials we gathered for that purpose we called "behavioral measures," and taken together they represent the third perspective on individual modernity which guided our selection of themes to measure.[16] Since later in this book we devote a chapter to the behavioral measures, we need review them here only briefly.

The "self-reported" behavioral measures were those on which the subject rated himself by stating that he did or did not do certain things. For example, he was asked to indicate whether he had voted, to report how many times a week he attended religious services, read a newspaper, or listened to a radio, and whether and how often he talked with his wife about politics, his job, and raising the children. Such self-reported behavior is, of course, subject to many distortions. A man may not remember accurately, or he may remember very well but give one or another answer according to the impression he wishes to create. The same risks are run in inquiring into opinions, however. We could not, therefore, allow the possibility of distortion to rule out altogether the use of self-reported behavior as evidence of individual modernity.

Nevertheless, we were sufficiently impressed by the potential limitations of the self-report to supplement it with such *objectively* ascertained measures as we could reasonably mobilize. Some of these were built into our interview procedure, which permitted us to rate all of our subjects. For example, to test a man's claim that he read the newspaper or listened to the radio every day, we asked everyone to name several newspapers and in some countries radio programs as well. We also tested them on the extent of their knowledge of political leaders who figured prominently in the news. We must acknowledge that a man might really listen to the radio and yet not be able to tell you the names of any programs, but quite apart from judging his truthfulness, we learn something important about him when we make this discovery.

Finally, along with objective measures based on testing the subject himself, we collected additional information by drawing on factory records and the judgment of factory foremen. However, these supplemental measures were not used systematically in the analysis reported in this book.

An Overview

Taken together, the three perspectives served as a convenient organizing principle within which to encompass the considerable diversity of the various areas which we explored in our research. Indeed, this seems an appropriate point to draw together the different elements touched on in the preceding pages. Therefore, we present in Table 2–1 a complete list of the major elements in our questionnaire, each identified by its code letters and grouped under the perspective which had led us to it.

Useful as the three perspectives were in organizing our thinking, they did introduce some artificial, or at least arbitrary, divisions not neces-

Table 2–1.   Main themes and areas of the questionnaire by key letter and perspective.

			General			
		(SAM)	Sampling criteria			
		(BD)	Background data			

Analytic perspective		Topical perspective		Behavioral perspective	
AS	Aspirations[a]	AC	Active public	AC	Political activity
CA	Calculability		participation[b]	AR	Arithmetic test
CH	Change orientation	AG	Aging and the aged	CO	Consumption behavior
DI	Dignity	CI	Citizenship[b]	GO	Verbal fluency
EF	Efficacy	CO	Consumption attitudes	IN	Information test
GO	Growth of opinion	FS	Family size	MM	Media information test
IN	Information	ID	Identification with nation[b]	OT	Opposites word test[c]
NE	New experience	KO	Kinship obligations	PT	Psychosomatic test[c]
OP	Optimism	MM	Mass media	RE	Religious activity
PA	Particularism	RE	Religious attitudes	ST	Sentence completion test[c]
PL	Planning	SC	Social class stratification	WR	Family behavior
TI	Time	WC	Work commitment		
TS	Technical skill and	WR	Women's rights		Interviewers' ratings[c]
	distributive justice				Supervisors' ratings[c]
UN	Understanding				Factory records[c]

[a] Includes both occupational and educational aspirations.

[b] In the discussion of the topical model in the text, these three themes are treated together under the heading "Politics."

[c] These themes were not included in the themes used in developing the overall modernity scale. For a detailed analysis of the Psychosomatic Symptoms Test, see Chapter 18.

sarily found in nature. With regard to information and mass communication, for example, the three-perspective approach induced us to treat general attitudes related to that theme as part of the analytic model, views about the media as an element in the topical model, and the frequency with which a man could identify public figures and capital cities as a measure in the behavioral model. Obviously one could sensibly ignore these distinctions, and treat all these questions as different aspects of a more general study of mass media and opinion in developing countries.

These arbitrary distinctions within a single realm had their analogue in our approach to all the dimensions taken together. Although each perspective was initially justified in its own terms as theoretically distinct, we recognized that most of the separate themes listed in Table 2–1 could reasonably be conceived of as manifestations of a more general, unified, underlying dimension of modernity encompassing elements suggested by all three of the perspectives. In other words, we perceived that a man strong in the qualities of the analytic model, such as efficacy and readiness for new experience, might also be interested in politics, be inclined to grant women more rights, and so on through various themes suggested by the topical perspective. This same man might also, on our behavioral measures, prove to be well informed about the content of the mass media. Clearly, then, our materials permitted us to develop a fourth perspective on modernity, one much more general, in that it included elements suggested by the analytic, topical, and behavioral perspectives. We designated this summary by the letters OM, standing for a measure of *Overall Modernity*. However, we should keep in mind that this general measure of modernity was initially only a theoretical construct. Until we empirically tested the facts, it remained an assumption, a hypothesis only, that elements we were led to by the three perspectives would indeed combine to yield a relatively unified measure of individual modernity.

3

The Research Design and
Sample Structure

One of our prime interests was to discover the effect of factory work as a modernizing influence on men whose life experience was formerly limited to agricultural and related pursuits in a traditional village. One plan we considered was to search for newly established factories being set down in the countryside and recruiting their workers from the surrounding villages. Such factories would have provided a kind of natural experiment which well suited our scientific objectives. We could have moved into the villages and studied the people before they entered industry, returning some years later to examine them again. If between the time of the first test and the time of the second the men who had meanwhile worked in factories had become more modern, we could conclude that it was the factory experience which had made them so. This conclusion could be all the more firmly held, of course, if we found that other men, who had continued to work at their more traditional pursuits, did not become more modern between the first and second tests.

On reflection, we realized that this simple natural experiment, appealing as it might be, did not provide a practical basis for our research design. To count on finding newly established factories, especially in the countryside, seemed very risky. It would also have meant limiting ourselves to the unusual rather than the average factory, since most plants are established in or near cities. In addition, the requirement that we return to the original site years later presented us with a logistical problem of substantial magnitude. On a small scale we did finally do interviews with the same men revisited after a four-year interval, as described in Chapter 11.

For our main effort, however, we decided not to attempt a truly longitudinal study, but rather to undertake its nearest equivalent.

The Four Basic Groups

In a strictly longitudinal study we would have examined the same individuals at two different points in time. In our approximation of that design we interviewed everyone more or less simultaneously, but selected the individuals to represent points on a continuum of experience through time. Instead of comparing the same man before he entered the factory and after he had been there a certain length of time, we compared two men who were presumably alike in all other characteristics except for the fact that one had more factory experience than the other. The same approach served to distinguish men on other variables in which we were particularly interested.[1]

Thus, we established the main poles of our comparison: at one end of the scale we were to have cultivators still living in their traditional villages and working at making a living in agriculture; at the other pole we were to have men from those very same villages who had moved to the city and spent three or more years in industrial work while their country cousins over the same period of time continued work on the farms. Hence the comparison between the cultivator (Group 1 in Fig. 3–1) and the industrial worker of long standing (Group 4), constituted the most basic of the elements of our research design. It is indicated by the line C-1 in Fig. 3–1. Since these two groups were to be alike in all other major respects — sex, age, education, religion, ethnicity, and the like — we assumed that any difference in their average "individual modernity" scores could be attributed to the influence of factory work and other experiences associated with it.

A very powerful challenge might be raised as to the validity of this conclusion. It is the challenge posed by possible selection effects. The same challenge must be faced by all studies which purport to test longitudinal influence by our proposed method of equivalence. And it is a test to which most such studies fail to provide a satisfactory answer.

The challenge is posed as follows: How can we be sure any observed differences result not from the experience of factory work, but because farmers are differentially recruited for industrial labor on the basis of their already-existing psychological traits? We defined individual modernity as including such qualities as openness to new experience, orientation to future time perspectives, emphasis on planning, a sense of personal efficacy, and the like. Clearly these are the very same personal qualities which might lead a man to leave his traditional village and seek his fortune as an industrial worker in the new life of the burgeoning industrial

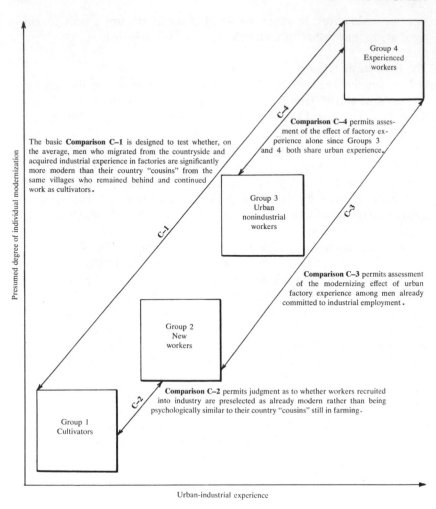

The basic **Comparison C–1** is designed to test whether, on the average, men who migrated from the countryside and acquired industrial experience in factories are significantly more modern than their country "cousins" from the same villages who remained behind and continued work as cultivators.

Comparison C–4 permits assessment of the effect of factory experience alone since Groups 3 and 4 both share urban experience.

Comparison C–3 permits assessment of the modernizing effect of urban factory experience among men already committed to industrial employment.

Comparison C–2 permits judgment as to whether workers recruited into industry are preselected as already modern rather than being psychologically similar to their country "cousins" still in farming.

Group 4
Experienced
workers

Group 3
Urban
nonindustrial
workers

Group 2
New
workers

Group 1
Cultivators

Presumed degree of individual modernization

Urban-industrial experience

Figure 3–1. Simplified analysis model.

cities. Insofar as migration from the countryside was highly selective of individuals possessing psychological attributes such as those defining modernity, that fact alone might account for any observed difference in the average modernity scores of workers as compared to their "cousins" still in the villages. There would then be no basis for arguing that the factory is a training ground for teaching men to be modern. To meet this challenge we developed two lines of defense which determined our sampling procedures in fundamental ways.

First, we decided to test the truth of the widespread assumption that psychological factors determine whether a man leaves farming to enter industry. For this purpose we needed a sample of recent migrants just entering factory employment. If these new workers were not more modern than their counterparts still in the countryside, differential recruitment on psychological grounds could hardly be the explanation for any observed difference between cultivators and experienced workers. The second line of defense accepted the possibility that newly recruited workers might indeed be more modern than those who remained on the farm. Even if that were true, however, the factory might still be a very effective training ground, modernizing its selected recruits far beyond the point they had reached earlier. Whether this occurred could be checked by comparing new workers with more experienced workers.

Both lines of defense pointed up the importance of obtaining a sample of new workers, Group 2 in Fig. 3–1, and highlighted the crucial importance of comparing them with the cultivators, on the one hand, and the experienced workers, on the other. These comparisons are indicated in Fig. 3–1 by lines C-2 and C-3, respectively. For these comparisons to be really meaningful, furthermore, we had to set fairly strict requirements limiting the sampling of new workers to those with less than three months of factory experience, and requiring that they be roughly of the same age, religion, ethnic group, and educational level as the cultivators and experienced workers with whom they were to be compared in their respective national samples.

Looking now at the fuller picture (Fig. 3–1) it will be seen that we had in effect created the steps of a ladder, representing the equivalent of a longitudinal design. Underlying this design is a simple model to explain the process of individual modernization. It assumes — and the project operated on this assumption — that men leave the village and enter industry not mainly because they are already psychologically modern men, but rather because objective factors in the countryside, especially economic necessity, force them out. Hence, we placed the new workers only slightly higher on the modernity scale than the cultivators. In this model the influence of factory work as a modernizing influence is assumed to be substantial, and to have a continuing additive effect year by year. Experienced workers are therefore placed quite a bit higher on the modernity axis. There are, of course, many other ways in which this arrangement might have been conceived, each representing a model of the development process. At various later points in this book some of these alternative models will be presented and tested against the facts. For present purposes, however, the simpler model should serve to convey the imperatives which guided our definition of the sampling criteria.

Many of our readers have no doubt noticed a considerable weakness in our argument which, in our eagerness to get on with the job of explaining the main line of our investigation, we have up to now failed to acknowledge. The skeleton in the closet is called urbanism, and we can no longer deny the insistent rattling coming from that quarter.

Since most factories are located in or near cities, it was clearly most practical to study workers in such plants. But insofar as men coming from the countryside to work in factories were also thereby becoming urban residents, and experiencing the presumed modernizing influence of the city, how could we be certain it was not the city rather than the factory which was acting as the school for modernity? One solution, of course, was to go back to the idea of studying factories in the countryside whose workers still lived in their traditional villages. Indeed, each field director was instructed to locate and study all such factories he could conveniently reach. In India, moreover, we focused our study in large part on this one issue. Nevertheless, in most countries there were very few factories in the countryside, and we were obliged to reckon with the fact that our industrial workers would, in most cases, also be urban residents.

To disentangle the influence of factory work from the accompanying urban experience, we established another sample group: the urban, but nonindustrial, workers whom we refer to as the UNIs. These men were to be in all other respects like the workers and cultivators, except that they experienced life in the city without the presumed benefit of working in factories or, indeed, in any comparable large-scale organization. They were, instead, to be drawn from such occupational groups as street vendors, kiosk operators, pedicab drivers, and the help in small restaurants and food shops. If the industrial workers proved much more modern than the cultivators, but the urban nonindustrials did not, we might conclude that factory work and not the experience of the city alone was the prime factor in inducing individual change toward more modern attitudes. Again, numerous other patterns might emerge, and they are reviewed, along with the evidence, in the chapters on urbanism as a modernizing factor.[2] For present purposes, however, it is necessary only to call attention to the status of the UNIs as a standard sampling category, referred to as Group 3 in Fig. 3–1, and to the line C-4 as defining the most important comparison in which that group was to be involved.

Elaboration of the Sample

To have studied only these four basic groups — cultivators, new industrial workers, experienced industrial workers, and urban nonindustrial workers — in a number of developing countries should perhaps have been a sufficient challenge, but various considerations urged us on to a more complicated design. For one thing, if we had restricted ourself to the four main groups, we would necessarily have left several very important questions unanswered. Indeed, we knew that if some of them remained unanswered, serious challenges might be raised to any conclusion we could draw from our sample design. In addition, we recognized that in some of the countries in which we hoped to work, a comparable study might not be mounted for many years to come. It seemed imperative to take this opportunity to collect as much data as we could on as many issues as we could manage. Though we were, of course, motivated by our intellectual and scientific interests to give more weight to some issues than to others, the pressures enumerated above led to the further elaboration of the simple straight-line model of modernization pictured in Fig. 3–1.

With regard to the issue of urbanism, for example, we did not limit ourselves to the UNIs, but also established one other sampling requirement which was included in the instructions to our field directors, even though it did not require the creation of a separate sample group. To provide a broad base from which they could draw their sample of factories, the field directors were free to work not only in the main industrial city, but in secondary and tertiary cities as well. Indeed, they were urged to select factories from at least three cities, including the main industrial center and two lesser, presumably smaller and more provincial places. Insofar as these cities could be ranked on a scale of cosmopolitanism, we expected to have an additional means to assess the impact of urban experience independently of factory work. This test could be effected by comparing men who were alike in amount and kind of industrial experience but who lived in cities varying in cosmopolitanism. If the urban setting alone made a contribution independent of factory experience, those working in factories in the more cosmopolitan centers should, with the same degree of factory experience, nevertheless be more modern.

Urbanism also entered into our sampling criteria in a rather different way, as defining not the adult but the childhood experience of our respondents. We introduced this dimension to test the popular idea that the quality of individual modernity is essentially an attribute of personality very likely laid down in the early years of life. If so, those raised in the presumably more modern setting provided by the city as against the traditional village should be more modern adults. Since our most general concern was to understand what makes men modern, we clearly could not afford to ignore this possible source of influence. In addition, it provided a severe test of our assumption that the factory is such an effective school for modernization. If it turned out, as we believed it would, that men raised in the city would, on the average, enter adulthood more modern than those raised in the country, then the factory might have very little new to teach them. They would, in a sense, have reached a certain plateau. If, on the other hand, the factory were as good a school of modernity as we believed it to be, then even these relatively modern men of urban origin could become still more modern under the influence of the factory.

To obtain the necessary groups we established as a sampling criterion

Figure 3–2. Sampling design.

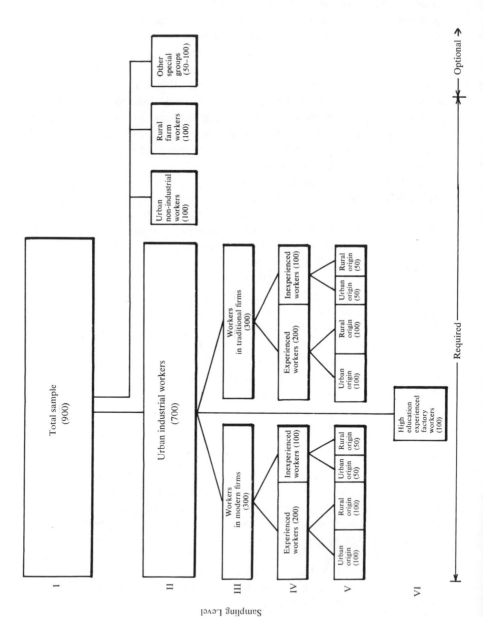

that, wherever appropriate, each national sample be selected so that half the men were of rural and half of urban origin. This clearly was not applicable to those still farming, but it did enter into the selection of the urban nonindustrials and the two levels of workers, new and experienced. In Fig. 3–2 the urban/rural origin groups are placed on level V.

Just as we elaborated our definition of urbanism, so we developed more complex definitions of factory experience. We assigned major theoretical importance to the distinction between "modern" and "traditional" factories. If the factory is a training ground in individual modernization, the more modern it is, the greater should be the impact of work in it. Furthermore, we had reason to believe that in some of the countries we studied many of the factories would be poorly organized and would approach human-relations problems in a very traditional way. We assumed such characteristics would be important influences in determining how effective any given factory would be as a school for modernity. In addition, we had to face the practical fact, from a sampling point of view, that in some countries the relatively modern factories, in which we were most interested, might be so small a minority that without special controls our sample of presumably modern "factories" would end up being mainly a set of very traditional work organizations. We therefore required our field directors to represent equally the more modern and more traditional factories, wherever possible matching one from the modern side with a traditional plant of the same size producing a similar product. This sampling criterion accounts for level III in Fig. 3–2. Factories were also sampled on the basis of size and the type of product they manufactured.[3]

The last of the sampling groups which each field director was obligated to include was composed of the especially highly educated workers. Our general sampling procedure called for keeping the average education of the several sample groups as uniform as possible. This, however, did not allow us to assess what education well above the average might do for modernity. To permit that assessment, we added the special group of industrial workers more highly educated than those normally entering our samples. (They are shown on level VI in Fig. 3–2.) So long as these well-educated workers were in all other respects like the less well-educated worker groups, a comparison of the two sets would tell us the independent contribution of higher than average education in making men modern.

Optional Samples

This completed the set of sample groups which each field director was required to find insofar as was feasible in his given field conditions. We were rather uncompromising in insisting that these groups be included in each country. Moreover, within each national sample the several groups had to be chosen so as to be basically alike in age, sex, education, and "culture," meaning by the last religion and ethnicity. These standard sample groups could, however, be supplemented by the individual field director, resources of time and staff permitting. He was free to gather additional samples having special relevance for our general design or having particular significance for understanding the modernization process in the country in which he was working.

Among the optional samples we recommended the field directors try for were groups of students at the high-school or university level. Such a sample was, in fact, collected in four of our six countries. In several cases, however, the student group proved to be rather different in basic characteristics other than education. We therefore decided to exclude the student groups from the analysis in this book.

A set of men who had entered industry but subsequently had left it, either to return to agricultural labor or to enter the ranks of the urban nonindustrials, defined another optional sample of obvious importance. Just as the greater modernity of men in the factory might come about through the recruitment of men more modern to start with, so could greater modernity come about through the factory's differential *retention* of the more modern and *expulsion* of the less modern men. If such a process operated, then in time those remaining would be much more modern, not because they had learned to be so in the plant, but only because the less modern men had been weeded out. Unfortunately, such exindustrial workers proved extremely difficult to find, and no field director succeeded in filling that optional sample cell. This scarcity, plus other considerations to be discussed later, led us to conclude that the possible screening of the industrial labor force to weed out traditional men could not alone account for any greater modernity we might find among experienced factory workers.

A third optional sample group involved the dimension of religion and ethnicity. In predominantly Moslem East Pakistan, for example, we sought out a special small sample of Hindu workers.

These provisions for collecting optional groups completed the formal sampling instructions. In Table 3–1 we have reprinted the original instructions exactly as they were set down at a meeting of the field directors at Calcutta in August 1963.[4] In addition, Fig. 3–2 presents the basic sampling design chart fundamentally as it was originally developed at the same time.

Various forces acted in different ways to prevent us from achieving the ideal sample design in all countries, with respect to both numbers and composition as described in Fig. 3–2. First, in some countries the special characteristics of the population seemed to preclude filling some of the cells except at great effort and expense. Thus, men of urban origin were so scarce in East Pakistan, and men of rural origin so infrequent among the Oriental Jews of Israel, that no differentiation by origin was attempted in the sampling in either country.[5] Second, the limited resources of money, personnel,

Table 3–1. Initial sampling provisions for variates.[a]

Variate	Criterion
1. Sex	Select only males
2. Age	Select only men between the ages of 20 and 30 (or between 18 and 32, if it proves necessary in order to get enough cases to fit our other sampling requirements). Attempt to maintain approximate equality of age on the average among the major matched sampling groups
3. Education	Attempt to maintain approximate equality (within 1 school year) of years of schooling on the average among the major matched sampling groups, within but not across countries
4. Culture	Attempt to maintain approximate homogeneity of culture for all of the major matched sampling groups. The field director in consultation with the project director, will decide what constitutes a "cultural area" or "cultural group" for a given country. We have in mind here, basically, such things as language, religion, and perhaps various elements of "ethnicity"
5. Residence and type of work	Select urban industrial workers, rural farm workers or cultivators, and a group of urban nonindustrial workers (such as small tradesmen, porters, taxi drivers, etc.)
6. Amount of industrial experience	Among urban industrial workers, select experienced and inexperienced workers. Experienced workers we define as men whose total experience in industrial firms is between 5 and 10 years (or, if necessary to get enough cases, between 3 and 15 years). Inexperienced workers we define as men whose total experience in industrial firms is 3 months or less, preferably less
7. Rural vs. urban origin	Among urban industrial workers, select half from urban and half from rural origins, insofar as possible. Urban origin is defined as not having a farmer-cultivator for a father, and living mainly in an urban area for the first 15 years of life. Rural origin is defined as having a farmer-cultivator father and living mainly in a rural area for the first 15 years of life.
8. Modernity of firm	Select industrial firms so as more or less to balance traditional vs. modern firms
9. Type of firm	Attempt to diversify industrial firms with respect to type, selecting firms of all major types according to the product dealt with (food, metals, chemicals, etc.)
10. Size of firm	Attempt to diversify industrial firms with respect to size, selecting firms of all sizes of labor forces from 50 and upward

a For a discussion of criteria for sampling, see note 4.

and time available to some of the field directors obliged them to stop short of the goal in filling certain sample cells as required by our compact. Third, the opportunities for learning something distinctive in a given country sometimes made it more compelling to concentrate our sampling energies on dimensions other than those emphasized in the basic design. This was most clearly the case in India, where the general design was greatly altered to permit us to concentrate on the impact of "industrialization without urbanization" in isolated company towns. Nevertheless, the ideal design was fundamentally achieved in at least the great majority of the core sampling dimensions in all six countries. Table 3–2 presents the basic statistics on the actual composition of the sample in each of the countries, utilizing the sampling categories identified in Fig. 3–2.

Comparative Analysis

The planned comparisons between the various groups in Fig. 3–2, and the service those comparisons were expected to perform, were basically the same as those already dealt with in the discussion of Fig. 3–1. This simple pattern of cell comparisons was not, however, to be the main mode of analysis we undertook. To follow this simple pattern exclusively, it would have been necessary that our sampling procedures function perfectly to insure that in each of the cells all other things were indeed equal to those in the comparable cells. Alas, it was not possible to maintain this standard in the actual field conditions we encountered.

For example, in several countries it proved impossible, despite our best efforts, to maintain exactly the same average level of education in the sets of farm workers as against industrial workers. The latter almost invariably had a higher average education. The scarcity of individuals who fitted our stringent sampling criteria forced the field directors to seek their cases over a range wider than that originally planned on such variables as factory experience, education, and age. In addition, it proved very difficult to keep the factors of ethnicity, religion, and district of origin constant when recruiting special groups such as new workers or urban nonindustrials.

We anticipated that these inequalities could eventually be adjusted by the process of matching, which would insure that the groups in any two cells would, on the average, be alike in all important respects but the one under investigation.[6] But we also decided, early on, to make a virtue of necessity, and to capitalize on the natural range of variation on most of the criteria we used in sampling. Narrow as the range might be, it permitted us to do more refined analysis of a number of variables about whose modernizing influence our study would otherwise have had little or nothing to say. Moreover, we could thus hope not only to judge whether our main measures, such as factory experience, were important as modernizing

Table 3–2. Sample composition.

Sample	Urban industrial workers[a]								Urban nonindustrial workers (UNIs)	Cultivators	High-education experienced factory workers[b]	Total
	Modern firms				Traditional firms							
	Experienced		Inexperienced		Experienced		Inexperienced					
	Urban	Rural	Urban	Rural	Urban	Rural	Urban	Rural				
Desired, Sample Design I	100	100	50	50	100	100	50	50	100	100	100	900
Achieved, Sample Size												
Argentina	178	120	57	37	105	78	13	4	56	98[c]	69	817[d]
Chile	149	124	79	71	133	80	22	30	106	109[c]	28	931
East Pakistan	0	282	0	52	0	255	0	62	112	177	0	1001[e]
India	0	122	0	200	0	0	0	0	250[f]	350	378	1300
Israel	150	0	27	0	94	0	57	0	92	103	115	739[g]
Nigeria	96	69	33	17	129	67	33	25	101	100	51	721

[a] Factory workers were defined as "experienced" in each country if they had at least the specified number of months of total factory experience: Argentina, 13; Chile, 12; East Pakistan, 36; India, 36; Israel, 18; Nigeria, 18. They were defined as "inexperienced" in each country if their total experience (months) was Argentina, 0–12; Chile, 0–12; East Pakistan, 0–7; India, 0–6; Israel, 0–6; Nigeria, 0–6.
[b] Factory workers were considered to be in the "high education" category in each country if they had at least 10 years of formal education in Argentina, Chile, East Pakistan, India, and Nigeria, and at least 9 years in Israel.
[c] The majority, 69, of the Argentinian cultivators were employed by large estates, but 29 were self-employed small-holders; similar proportions apply for Chile.
[d] Includes one worker whose urban rural origin was not known.
[e] Includes 58 cultivators working in the Comilla cooperative. Except in Chapter 13, only the 177 non-Comilla, noncooperative cultivators are used in the standard analysis. The total also includes three factory workers whose modern traditional factory rating was unknown.
[f] The 250 urban nonindustrial workers in India included 102 workers in public and private institutions and 148 independent workers.
[g] Includes 90 factory workers whose modern-traditional factory rating was unknown, and 11 the amount of whose factory experience was unknown.

influences, but to specify precisely what *weight* each carried relative to the other. We could thus move to multivariate regression and path analysis, and to analysis of variance. To that end we needed to treat our sampling criteria not solely as the basis for defining distinctive groups, but rather as more or less continuous variables.

Furthermore, our sampling criteria were not the only variables in which we had an interest. They were only those whose natural variation we felt we could not trust to chance. There were many others we measured in our questionnaire, but did not control in selecting cases to enter the sample. We thus trusted to chance that on these dimensions the natural variation in the populations studied would be sufficient to support later analysis. This was true, for example, of "objective" background factors such as father's occupation and education, and more "subjective" ones such as the recall of treatment by teacher and parent.

The individual characteristics which served originally as sampling criteria, plus the additional independent variables which we measured by our questionnaire, came to as many as fifty. Some, like factory experience, stood alone pure and simple. Others were part of a set, essentially variants of a basic underlying dimension. For example, our measure of economic status was separately expressed in three forms: cash income, number of consumer goods owned, and quality of housing. Table 3–3 lists the main independent variables we measured and used in varying degrees in different stages of the analysis.

To sum up, we note three attributes of our approach to sampling for this study:

First, we did not seek representative samples, but rather highly purposive quota samples, with individuals and groups selected because of their relevance to testing our theory about the relative impact of the key modernizing variables on individual modernity.

Second, within those limits of our experimental design, we did use conventional randomization procedures to ensure that we did not bias the selection of either research settings or individuals.

Third, we stressed the comparability of the sample *structure* from country to country. Again this militated against representativeness, and, in particular, meant that our results could not be generalized to the total population of the country from which the cases were drawn. But we were mainly interested in generalizing not about national populations but about processes, in particular the processes of modernization, as they operated in select occupational groups. Each country study therefore replicated the next. We have, in effect, made six independent studies of the same set of hypotheses. Any finding which holds across all, or even most, of the countries in that set must be considered to have a great deal of cross-cultural validity.

Table 3–3. Independent variables.

A. Personal and family characteristics
Age
Religion
Ethnicity
Marital status
Number of children
Parents' socioeconomic status
Father's education
Perceived modernity of home experience

B. Origin
Rural-urban origin
Geographical place of origin

C. Residence
Years of urban experience since age 15
Urbanism of present residence
City of present residence

D. Socioeconomic level
Gross Income: FW and UNI
Economic level: cultivator
Housing quality
Consumer goods possessed
Social status (self-rated)

E. Education
Years of formal education
Years of total education
Perceived modernity of school experience

F. Intelligence and skill
Literacy level
Opposites test score
Overall capacity measure
Skill level (coder-rated)
Skill level (self-rated)

G. Occupational characteristics
Occupational type
Total months factory experience
Months experience in present factory
Months experience in prior factory
Number of factories worked in
Work commitment scale
Work modernity valuation scale

H. Factory characteristics
Urbanism of work location
City of present factory
Size of present factory
Year present factory founded
Product of present factory
Number of benefits of present factory
  (worker estimate)
Overall modernity of present factory
  (project-rated)
Modernity of prior factory (worker-rated)
Perceived modernity of total factory
  experience

I. Information-media exposure
Personal-media exposure
Newspaper exposure
Radio exposure
Movie exposure
Television exposure
Mass-media exposure scale

J. Work-behavior scales
Interviewer summary rating
Supervisor summary rating
Leadership scale
Work-stability scale
Workmanship scale

4

The Conduct of The Fieldwork

Our research was carried on in six so-called "underdeveloped" nations. In most of them research such as ours was rare, and in some almost unknown. In each of them, we set up our own field organization, selected and trained our own, largely local, staffs, and conducted an exceptionally detailed interview dealing with fundamental issues and lasting up to 4 hours.[1] The conditions under which we worked were in some ways quite unusual, and this influenced both our mode of operation and what we could learn by it. Some aspects of that experience would be of interest primarily to specialists themselves planning comparative research, and we can pass over those because we have elsewhere published a full account of our field experiences.[2] But other aspects of our fieldwork raise issues concerning which most readers of this book will want to satisfy themselves, since they bear heavily on the validity and reliability of the information on which our analysis rests.

Selecting the Countries

The first issue is raised by the selection of the countries in which we conducted our study. Of course, the countries selected had to meet conditions which related to our scientific purpose. But people want assurance, in addition, that the character of the particular sites we chose was not such as to bias the outcome of our analysis.

Dealing with this issue requires that we briefly restate our objectives. Ours was not the ordinary public-opinion poll in which one seeks to predict from a small sample the views of a larger population. Rather, our concern was to discover the ways in which people in a very particular set of circumstances were influenced to change in specific directions as a result of being subject to certain special influences. In other words, our design had some of the character of a natural experiment. Nations were of interest to us, therefore, not because they were representative of all other nations, but rather because they were home to groups of people who met the requirements of our experimental design.

There was, moreover, no scientific basis for setting an upper limit on the number of countries to be studied. Of course, it was clear that we should work in more than only one country. Otherwise, we could not be sure that our findings had not been determined by some accidental concatenation of circumstances in a single country. Yet the limits of our resources constrained us to restrict our effort to only a few countries. We settled, then, on the goal of not less than three nor more than six countries.

The choice of specific countries was in good part shaped by our research design, which greatly reduced the number of appropriate sites. Only those nations could qualify which had already experienced substantial industrialization, and in which there were sufficient current industrial activity and growth to insure some flow of labor from the countryside to the city-based factory. This immediately ruled out large parts of Africa, Asia, and, indeed, South America.

A second indispensable requirement was that any country we worked in should have a reasonably open society, with at least moderate political stability. Interesting as it might otherwise be, a society in political turmoil could not be expected to welcome a team of interviewers attempting protracted interviews on delicate social and political issues. On the other hand, we knew that political stability would afford us no advantage if it was the end product of political repression. If people were afraid to speak the truth and describe their experiences as they really felt them, our whole procedure would have been meaningless.

The third requirement was that the general level of institutional modernization, and particularly the level of development in the nation's universities, be high enough to offer some promise of local support of our work. As outsiders we needed the guidance and assistance of local men who could supplement our research skills with their intimate knowledge of their country and its culture. For such collaboration to be effective, we had to find local scholars who had had sufficient experience in social research to communicate effectively with us, and to provide at least part of our staff needs. Also, to permit us to sample the factory workers intelligently we had to be assured that the governments concerned had already collected basic census data on industrial plants, labor-force statistics, and the like. Thus, the range of eligible nations narrowed still further.

Finally, we were fairly well agreed that we should include representatives of the three great continental areas other than Europe and North America, since these incorporated the overwhelming majority of the world's developing nations.

Within these objective limits the final selection of the countries was determined by a combination of factors including the personal preference of the staff, the potential cooperation of the local institutions and scholars, the availability of funds to cover expenses to be paid in local currency, the necessary absence of any objection to our work on the part of local governments, and the special interest of one or another setting for developing some basic aspect of our project. The details of the final selection are not essential to our account here, and in any event have been given elsewhere.[3] Suffice it to say, then, that through a complex interaction of the considerations just mentioned, we decided on East Pakistan, Nigeria, and Chile as the first three countries in our study. As the work progressed, we added India, Argentina, and Israel. Of these, only the choice of Israel seems to require special mention.

Israel's entry into our study *was* due to special circumstances. Just as India was meant to be paired with East Pakistan, and Argentina with Chile, so we had hoped to have Ghana for contrast with Nigeria.[4] But at the time we began our fieldwork it seemed unlikely that the political dictatorship then running that country would permit our type of study to be done there. The scientific contacts we had in Israel, and the promise of funding for our work there, led us to consider it as an alternative.[5] In themselves, these inducements would not have been sufficient, since at that point we felt our staff to be overextended. But Israel had other attractions.

Israel qualified as one of the young "emerging" nations, and it was decidedly a "developing" country even if not necessarily an "underdeveloped" one. Nevertheless, it seemed very much an extension of Europe, despite its location in the Middle East. Since we lacked a European or North American standard of comparison, we concluded we might capitalize on this very quality. We thought we could thus test whether our underlying ideas applied equally well to an essentially European population, even if it was so only by origin. Still, we remained uncomfortable about including a country in which the presumed level of modernization of the population might be so different from that in the other five settings.

As it turned out, our reservations proved beside the point. We quickly discovered that there were very few Jews of European origin in the social strata we wished to sample, namely, that of young men of relatively low education working on the production line in industry. Those who could meet our sampling requirement proved to be overwhelmingly from the countries of the Middle East, Asia, and Africa. Although they were Jews by religion, their culture was not that of Europe. They could reasonably be considered the equivalent of the groups entering our sample in the other countries since they had had relatively little formal education and had come originally from settings not yet part of the modern world. Indeed, the presence of these "Oriental Jews" in our sample permitted us to study the modernization process as it impinged upon a people with a markedly traditional culture who had suddenly moved into a quite modern and predominantly European national setting.

The major characteristics of the countries we studied are set out in Table 4–1. As a standard of comparison we included comparable information on the United Kingdom and Greece, selected to stand, respectively, as examples of the more highly developed and the less developed European countries. Before we examine some of the relevant statistics in Table 4–1, however, we must again call attention to the fact that ours were not representative national samples. Therefore, the conditions which prevailed for each of these nations as a whole did not necessarily apply in the particular regions from which we drew our samples, nor to the specific groups we reached with our interviews. The data in Table 4–1 are, perforce, national in scope, whereas in half our cases we were obliged to restrict our investigation to one region of the country. In Pakistan we worked only in the eastern wing of what was then a two-part country, in Nigeria only in the western region, and in India only in the province of Bihar. Nevertheless, national statistics can serve to convey an impression of the general setting in which our samples lived, and to highlight certain important contrasts in the conditions to which they were exposed, in the period just before we conducted our interviews.

For our purpose, the most important indicators were those reflecting the level of industrial development. Whereas in England, Japan, and even Italy, the proportion of gross national product originating in industry came to 30 percent or more, in our countries it ranged from a low of 3 percent in Nigeria to a high of 23 percent in Israel. The proportion of the labor force in industry, and other measures (shown in Table 4–1), indicate that, at best, our sextet of countries was only moderately industrialized. They were well suited to the purposes of our study, because in them we could examine the impact of industrial work in a setting in which it had not become the predominant mode of economic activity, but was, rather, a new and relatively alien infusion into a more traditional agricultural, crafts, or trading economy. This even held for Israel, despite its relatively high standing on many of the economic indicators.

Beyond this common characteristic, however, the six nations displayed very marked diversity. On almost every measure, be it one relating to education, health, mass communication, or wealth, our countries covered an exceedingly wide range. Our group included representatives of the poorest in the world, and others which, on indices of modernization and develop-

Table 4–1. Selected indicators of economic development.[a]

Indicator	Argentina	Chile	East Pakistan	India	Israel	Nigeria	Greece	U.K.
1. Gross national product per capita (1957 $US)[b]	490	379	70	73	726	78	340	1,189
2. Economic growth (annual per capita increase, 1950–60)[b]	−0.4	1.3	0.3	1.0	5.8	1.2	5.3	2.3
3. Industrial employment (percent of working-age population, 1960) [b, c]	18	17	7	8	18	—	12	35
4. Wage and salary earners (percent of working-age population, 1955)[b]	43	43	22	19	38	3	21	61
5. Manufacturing (percent of gross domestic product, 1960)[c]	22	20	13	17	23	3	—	35
6. Percent of labor force in agriculture (1955)[b]	25	30	65	71	15	59	48	5
7. Population increase (annual rate, percent, 1958–61)[b]	1.7	2.4	2.1	2.2	3.0	1.9	0.9	0.7
8. Crude birth rate per 1000 population (average, 1955–59)[b, c]	24	36	20	39	28	50	19	16
9. Number of inhabitants per physician (1960)[b, c]	670	1,600	11,000	5,800	400	27,000	790	960
10. Infant mortality per 1000 live births (average, 1955–59)[b, c]	60	118	—	146	36	78	41	24
11. Percent illiterate in population 15 years and over (1950)[c]	14	20	81	81	6	89	26	1
12. Primary and secondary school pupils (percent of population aged 5–19, 1960)[b]	57	58	20	29	69	25	53	80
13. Number of radio receivers per 1000 population (1960)[b, c]	175	130	3	5	194	4	94	289
14. Daily newspaper circulation per 1000 population (1960)[b]	155	134	7	11	210	8	125	506
15. Domestic mail per capita (1960)[c]	65	13	6	8	56	3	23	191
16. Percent of urban population in cities of 20,000+ (1955)[b]	48	46	8	12	61	11	38	67
17. Urban-population growth (annual rate, percent, in cities of 20,000+ (1950–60)[b]	—	.47	.28	.18	.39	—	.61	.10

[a] All figures given should be regarded as only approximate. This applies particularly to the years indicated. They were selected to represent the period just prior to our field work, but for particular measures the original sources often were forced to rely on different years according to availability for any given country. Different census periods, different conventions for arriving at national statistics, and differential accuracy in national record keeping and reporting all affect the precision with which these figures represent the true values for the measures cited. These considerations are too refined for our purposes, but interested readers should consult the original sources, given in notes b and c.

[b] Bruce M. Russett, Howard R. Alker, Karl W. Deutsch, and Harold D. Lasswell, *World Handbook of Political and Social Indicators* (New Haven, Conn.: Yale University Press, 1964).

[c] *United Nations Statistical Yearbook, 1964* (16th issue; New York: United Nations, 1965).

ment, equaled or exceeded the less advanced countries of Europe, such as Greece.

Of course we were not assuming that our six countries constituted a strictly representative sample of the world's developing nations. We sought only to reflect the wide range of conditions found there. Such variety was important to establish the generality of our theory. If we could show factory experience to have a modernizing influence despite the cultural and, as we now see, the economic diversity of the nations studied, it would indeed have proved itself a truly autonomous force.

This same diversity, however, held open to us the prospect of testing different and competing predictions as well. For example, some people anticipated that the factory would have its modernizing effect mainly in the least-developed countries, because there the sharp contrast between the factory and the rest of life would produce "the shock of learning." Others predicted the opposite; that is, they argued that in a really traditional society, the other forces would be so powerful that the factory experience in itself would not be able to make men modern. By selecting our countries so that they covered a good part of the range found in developing countries, we placed ourselves in a position to test these competing predictions.

Gaining Unbiased Access to the Community

Since we were not specialists in the culture of any of the countries in which we conducted our fieldwork, there was a very real possibility that our own particular national origin, combined with the nature of our local sponsorship and staff, might have biased our information either by closing off certain channels or by pushing us more or less exclusively into others. The issue is not artificial, and it was an object of concern to us. We consider that the best answer to this challenge is to point to the effectiveness with which we met the formal sampling requirements described earlier and firmly set before we went into the field.

The factories to enter our sample were selected from official lists on the basis of size and product. Special bias could have resulted only if we had been selectively admitted to some plants, let us say those owned by companies based in the U.S., while being systematically excluded from others. But, as we note below, we had a nearly perfect record in gaining entry to the plants which were objectively selected as appropriate for our sample.[6] Similarly, we selected the men to be interviewed within each factory on the basis of objective characteristics such as age and birth place. And again, as will be shown below, an extremely small proportion of the men thus selected either refused to be interviewed or broke off after starting.

The critical feature of our fieldwork was that it was not conducted solely by a team from Harvard University, but rather was in every instance the result of a collaborative effort involving a local institution and its staff. Indeed, only two Americans from Harvard lived in Chile, one each in Nigeria and Pakistan, and none at all in the other countries. In all cases, therefore, the fieldwork was virtually a completely local undertaking proceeding under the supervision of a national of the country who served as a codirector of our project. Moreover, the local field director had a strong personal interest in seeing to it that the data collected were of the highest quality because in time he would himself be using them to prepare a separate analysis specifically focused on the situation in his country.[7]

Our connection with well-established local institutions, our sponsors in them, and our national codirectors were essential elements in establishing both our place in the community and the legitimacy of our enterprise. Our work could be accurately described to people as a cooperative venture between Harvard and the local university or research institute. This facilitated our securing cooperation from the widest circle of relevant organizations and individuals.

Valuable as our advance work in public relations may have been in guaranteeing our general freedom to work in the community, the critical contacts were those with the factory managers. Since we hoped to do most of the interviewing in the factory, and if possible during working hours, their cooperation was essential. The selection of factories to be included in the sample was determined by their objective characteristics, but the pattern of contact with the managers depended on the field director's sense of what was appropriate in the given country.[8]

Once the manager was reached, we explained our research in much the same language we had used for more public presentations. We stressed that we could offer him no immediate concrete benefit, only the possibility that what we learned might be useful to management in guiding its labor relations in the long term. In the short run, we were asking him simply to support an international cooperative venture which we believed had significance for developing countries and which might contribute to the advancement of knowledge and to the development of the country.

In plants in which there were trade unions, we felt we could not approach the workers without approval of the union any more than we could enter the factory grounds without the permission of the factory manager. Our methods for approaching trade-union leaders were similar to those for managers and seemed about as successful. We had the impression many of the union leaders hoped that our listing of the workers' grievances during the course of our interview, and our general inquiry into the factory as a *social* environment, might stimulate policies more favorable to the workers.

In one way or another all the field directors echoed Dr. Schuman's sentiment when he wrote about his experience in East Pakistan: "Cooperation from factory officials was generally excellent — much better than I had anticipated. This was due to the right mixture of support from the government and local and foreign university sponsorship combined, and other factors in our general procedure."

In addition to these specific measures we adopted and followed a set of general guidelines. To protect the reputation of our sponsoring institution, to assure the friendly reception of future social-research projects and to honor our obligations to those who gave us their confidence, the field staffs agreed to observe the following principles: full and frank disclosure of the nature of our work, including our sources of support; absolute respect for the confidential nature of all information we collected, whether from managers, cultivators, or workers, with particular emphasis on the absolute anonymity of all interviews; strict neutrality and noninterference with regard to issues of policy which might be agitating the people of the factories and farms in the country in which we were working, combined with a willingness to offer freely such technical competence as we might have to all those entitled to call upon it, whether from the management or the labor side; and scrupulous observance of local law and custom, to be maintained even if nationals, or segments of the foreign colony, might be quite casually flouting them.

Insuring the Integrity of the Interview

All opinion surveys, no less in developed countries than elsewhere, are vulnerable to the risk that interviewers may seriously bias the outcome by their method of conducting the interview, and, in the extreme case, by doing incomplete interviews, or even by turning in a totally fabricated record.

We felt that we were in a quite good position so far as the integrity of our interviewers was concerned, because in most cases they formed part of a relatively permanent team in regular and fairly intimate contact with the local field director. Nevertheless, we asked each field director to set up control procedures appropriate to the local situation.

Perhaps the most elaborate and stringent were those established by Dr. Singh in India. In evaluating these measures, as described below by Dr. Singh, it should be kept in mind that these rules were not the solution adopted by a suspicious foreigner blundering around in an alien culture. They represented the considered judgment of a native of the country who knew his own culture and students, and whom we can certify from long experience to be a man of firm but gentle disposition. Dr. Singh wrote in his field report as follows:

The problem of ensuring honest fieldwork is an extremely important, though delicate issue. The interview was a difficult one, since the actual time taken was about four hours. In such situations one is likely to get what may be described as the "tea-shop bias," that is, the filling in of the questionnaires in a tea shop. I had devised several checks to minimize the possibility of such hazards. First, I was careful in selecting the interviewers. I had even preferred some academically less brilliant interviewers to those who could not face the strains of the interviews without impatience and grudge. Secondly, every interviewer was required to give sureties from two responsible persons that he would refund all the money spent on him if it was found that he had dishonestly filled in the questionnaires. Thirdly, we had obtained some information from independent sources. This was factual information regarding the interviewee's age, father's occupation, salary, overtime, name of the native village, etc. The interviewers did not know about these things. As soon as the questionnaires were returned we checked this information. Fourth, we used a quick check with a large number of respondents to find out if the interview was really done, where it was done, who did it, how long it lasted, etc. And finally, we tried to give as many facilities to the interviewers as possible, such as housing accommodations in places distant from Ranchi when fieldwork required travel.

The measures adopted elsewhere were generally not so extensive nor so rigorous as those taken by Dr. Singh, but serious attention was given to the issue everywhere.[9] All the field directors agreed with Dr. Singh that the best assurance of strict integrity was careful selection of interviewers and intimacy of association with them in the course of the work. We believe this to be demonstrated by the close correspondence between our interviewers' statements and the results of our regular spot checks on their performance.

We cannot claim that we achieved a perfect record in all places at all times. However, we do feel we maintained a standard of integrity for our interviews which was at least the equivalent of that in any study done in the most advanced countries.[10]

Insuring the Cross-National Comparability of our Questions

Although we considered the research done in each country an independent and self-contained test of our hypothesis, it clearly was important that we should be testing fundamentally the same values and attitudes in all six field settings. Inevitably, we cast our thoughts in the forms provided by our own culture, and our questions were originally written out in English. This raised formidable problems of translation as we moved from culture to culture and language to language. The question inevitably arises: how could we be sure that we were still talking to people about the same things as we moved across the set of six countries? We feel the ultimate test of our success lies in the evidence, presented in later chapters, that the structure or pattern of answers we obtained to our battery of questions was remarkably alike from one country to another. Nevertheless, an understanding of the procedures we used in developing and translating our questionnaire may allay some of the anxiety so often aroused by this issue.

In preparing our questionnaire we naturally relied heavily on the field experience of others who had gone before us.[11] However, we also undertook extensive field testing of our own. When the three field directors left Cambridge in the first months of 1963, they did not carry with them a fixed questionnaire. Instead, we had prepared a set of memoranda outlining the main themes which defined, in theoretical terms, the concept of individual modernity and the related topics we hoped to study. For many of these we had also prepared a well-elaborated set of coded questions, some of which we had already pretested.[12] For others, however, we had not yet formulated questions, but rather had general guidelines for conducting exploratory open-ended interviews which we hoped would suggest appropriate questions. And for a few themes we had no more than sets of general specifications, which could be given substance as interview material only on the basis of some field experience. We anticipated that we could broaden our thinking, sharpen our design, and improve our questions by elaborating them in the settings in which they would eventually be applied.

In addition, we expected to learn a great deal of special relevance from our local collaborators. Indeed, in the end we spent almost six months pretesting the questionnaire before we settled on the final form.

We were attempting to measure subtle and elusive psychosocial properties of the person and his mental functioning, tapping such dimensions as his sense of efficacy, his openness to new experience, and his time orientation. Yet the people to whom we would talk were mainly very unsophisticated men, possessed of little or no formal education, who worked at highly concrete manual tasks. We therefore faced a decided challenge: to develop questions which would be simple enough to be comprehensible and meaningful to the men we would interview, and yet subtle enough to permit us to score the answers on the more abstract dimensions of our conceptual scheme. Our difficulty was greatly increased by the necessity of using questions simultaneously meaningful in six different societies and in as many or more additional cultural subgroups.

We sought to resolve the problem by restricting our questions to situations and relations which, we reasoned, should be meaningful to almost anyone, anywhere. So we asked: Does a boy learn more of the truth from old people or from books? Would you prefer your son to have a job running a machine at 150 rupees a month or to be a clerk in an office at only 100 rupees? Can you usually count on the others working with you to do their share of the work? Can a man be really good even though he does not believe in religion? If a boy is poor but ambitious and hard working, can he still expect to get ahead in life? Even these questions assumed familiarity with such things as machines and offices. And there was no shortage of ambiguities concerning matters such as the referrent of "religion" or the different meanings people can read into the idea of "getting ahead in life."

We took a series of related measures to deal with these problems. For the several national teams locally in charge of the study, we prepared a version of our questionnaire which was not limited to the wording of the questions to be put to the interviewee, but which also contained "field director's notes" fully explaining those questions which we felt might be so cryptic or colloquial in English as to leave doubt as to our intentions. Beyond that, we relied on protracted discussion with the local staffs, in which we explained each of our main concepts in detail to make clear its relation to our general objective. This explanation was followed by a discussion of each question, in which we expounded the role it was expected to play in measuring some more general attitude, and explained the particular choice of ideas, situations, and even words used.[13] We considered this common understanding of our underlying ideas and their concrete embodiment in questions to be the best insurance against a process of "drift." Such a drift might, in the end, have left us with only minimally comparable questionnaires in the several countries.

We know that despite our intense desire not to blur critical cultural distinctions in the process of describing standard situations, we decidedly missed in some cases. Nevertheless, we are satisfied that conceptual misunderstandings, at least of a more serious variety, were not numerous. Almost all of our concepts were eventually fairly well rendered in the thought system of each of the several cultures involved, even though there were times when this could be done only by awkward or wordy constructions and circumlocutions. Insofar as there were less serious misunderstandings which escaped our attention, we believe them to have been neither so numerous nor so consistent as to give the interview a basically deviant style in any country.

However good our mutual understanding of the questions, their comparability might still have been greatly reduced in the process of translation. No doubt the best insurance against the "drift" resulting from translation would have been to find a single field director who was entirely fluent in all the languages we used. Barring that unlikely event, we could hope for field directors who at least knew both English and the local language.

In those cases in which the field director was not fluent in both languages, and to a lesser degree elsewhere, we attempted to control the quality of the translation by having various third parties retranslate the questionnaire back into English. This device, now widely utilized in cross-national research, proved highly effective. It served not only to locate simple mistranslations and to identify concepts which could not be accurately rendered in the local language, but also to expose instances in which the local staff had clearly not understood the original concept in English or had incorrectly interpreted the purpose behind a question.

The retranslation back into English repeatedly proved its value by exposing a substantial number of outright errors which had crept into the translation. For example, question CH-3, on the acceptance of new methods in agriculture, describes two boys working in the fields who "pause" in their work and then "discuss" the methods of raising rice or corn. The boys came out of the Hebrew translation "neglecting" their work and "arguing" about the new techniques. This was not the same thing at all, and we put the translator back to work. We believe virtually all of such simple mistranslations were caught and effectively corrected. They would not even have been identified, in any event not until it was too late, except for our use of the retranslation technique.

Even when the translators did not make mistakes, they could create real problems for the interview. Since we were everywhere dealing mainly with people of very low education, and often with men living in very isolated conditions, our questions had to be couched in the simplest possible language. But translators are generally educated men. They find it hard to render something in the common speech, even if it is so rendered in the original. Moreover, it is easier to maintain reasonable equivalence from one language to another if one sticks to somewhat more standard educated speech.

Even if it upset the local staff's sense of propriety, we insisted that they find and use the words of the common people, no matter how bizarre, ungrammatical, or even vulgar they sounded to our translators. Consequently, our questionnaire everywhere underwent a second process of translation in the effort to render it into the common speech. This was often difficult, because the local language experts seemed almost invariably too sanguine in their assumptions about the working vocabulary of the poor people. Fortunately, some of our interviewers came from the same class background as our interviewees, and were therefore able to render great service in this program of simplification. Dr. Singh's field report describes the process thus:

> The problem of translation was even greater in India because of the heterogenous nature of our sample, which included tribal and nontribal persons from villages and cities. We tried to make the language as simple as we could so that the uneducated farmers could understand it. We used a very low-level Hindi which is spoken by

both tribal and nontribal persons, and sacrificed the sense of grammar for the sake of proper communication. We used words which, strictly speaking, are not grammatically correct from the academic point of view, but nonetheless are used in day-to-day conversation. The correct Hindi word for "religion" is "dharma." People of low education speak it as "dharam." We preferred the word which people use. For "husband" the correct word is "pati," but the people from lower strata, particularly tribals, used the word "adami" for it, which literally means "any man." We used both, keeping "adami" in brackets to be used in tribal cases.

The Conduct of the Interview

Our questionnaire was very long, and dealt with a wide range of complex issues. It contained up to 438 questions, depending on the country, and required 4 hours to complete in those instances where the field director decided to use a substantial number of optional questions.[14] The majority of our interviewees were not accustomed to long verbal exchanges. The issues raised by our questions sometimes had never been presented explicitly to them before. Even in the case of problems they had previously encountered, no one had ever before asked them to *express* their opinion. The whole idea of an interview was something new in many of the countries. In any event, most of the men in our samples had never heard of the idea, let alone met anyone who had had the experience. We had to be sure, therefore, that the way in which we helped to define the situation and the manner in which we conducted the interview did not induce men to bias their answers in some misleading fashion. After a man was selected for our sample, we explained the general scientific purpose of the interview, speaking sometimes first through the personnel or trade-union officer, but always adding a statement of our own in face-to-face contact at the start of the interview. The absolute integrity of the interview was explained to him, to allay fears that what was said would be known by anyone else in a way that could directly identify it with the interviewee personally.

We made every effort to insure that the interview was conducted in what at least approached complete privacy. Usually we had a private room in each factory. In those instances where interviews had to be conducted in the open at the bench, we took pains to see that no one was loitering about or looking on, at least not within earshot. When these conditions could not be satisfied at the plant, we brought the man back to our project headquarters. Inevitably, these nearly ideal conditions prevailed less often in the interviews with the urban nonindustrial workers and the cultivators. Nevertheless, more than 90 percent of the interviews in all countries were judged by the interviewers to have been conducted either in "absolute privacy" or under conditions in which, though there might have been some onlookers, they did not interfere. Less than 1 percent were conducted under conditions such that onlookers were "a serious problem," and those mostly in the countryside or with urban nonindustrials.

The critical factor in the success of the interview, however, was its intrinsic interest and the way in which it was conducted. The simple natural problems of everyday life with which our questions dealt successfully engaged the attention of almost everyone. Although some claimed that "so much thinking" was hard work for them, our interviewees generally enjoyed the opportunity to have so many votes to cast on such basic questions of life. We sought to ease their task by offering nicely balanced alternatives from which a man might choose, thus freeing him of the necessity of formulating the matter entirely for himself. At the same time we gladly accepted any comments and emendations, which were carefully written down by the interviewer. This impressed the interviewee with the seriousness of the enterprise and the importance of his answers. It also provided us with a large body of qualitative material we could use to interpret the precoded answers.

Our interviewers were instructed and trained not to impose any point of view, not to lead the interviewee, nor in any way to seem to judge him either for the content of his answers, the language he used, the ideas he expressed, or the ease or difficulty with which he handled the questions. Of course there were inevitably some cases in which the individual, the situation, or the culture, one or all, produced tensions and even conflict.[15] Nevertheless, we believe that in the overwhelming majority of cases, the interview turned into a pleasant personal exchange satisfying to both interviewer and interviewee. Despite our fears, fatigue was generally not an issue. The interviewers got much more tired than the interviewees. Professora Gibaja spoke for all the field directors when she said:

> Despite previous fears and expectations, we [in Argentina] got a high degree of cooperation and sincerity from the respondents, who, in general established very good relations with the interviewers, and could, with good will, overcome the difficulties that no doubt many of them encountered in the experience of being interviewed. Doing the interview during working hours had its positive side. The worker was free from his work for 3 or 4 hours; almost always he was taken into a comfortable place where he could smoke or have coffee; and above all he experienced a new situation. Most of the interviewers were young students with a positive attitude toward the respondent; they wished not only to obtain answers, but probably to live out a personal experience in an environment completely different from their own. This attitude of the interviewers tended to decrease the anxiety which being interviewed produced in certain workers, and their personal approach eased the strain and made the interview a pleasant experience.

These personal impressions are strongly supported by some of the statistics we collected. Interviewers overwhelmingly rated the interviewees as "generally" or "very" cooperative, the range going from 85 percent in India to 98 percent in East Pakistan. There is little reason to believe these estimates inflated. We neither criticized interviewers for having uncooperative subjects, nor praised them for having cooperative ones. If the interviewer wanted to protect himself against complaints he would have been much better advised to shift the blame onto the interviewee by saying the latter was "uncooperative." Moreover, these positive images of cooperation by the interviewee were evidently *not* influenced by some "halo effect" which bathed the whole exchange in a glow of indiscriminate good will. Our interviewers could clearly take a critical view of the interviewee. For example, 65 percent of the interviewees in Pakistan were rated by their interviewer as being "very cooperative," but only 4 percent as being "very flexible," and only 18 percent as being "very intelligent."

The statements and actions of the interviewees support the judgment of the interviewers concerning the cooperation. In Nigeria, for example, only three interviews were broken off, out of a total of 723 which were begun. Of the three, two men later agreed to continue, and did complete the interview. The record was about the same in all the other countries except Israel, in which the number broken off was above 50. The majority of these were relocated, however, and the interview completed, admittedly in some cases only when the local rabbi interceded to plead our cause. Many of those who dropped out were not yet completely at home with Hebrew and therefore complained that the interview was such hard work "it broke your head."

We had no power over anyone except for that which derived from a personal appeal. We in no way restrained anyone. We had nothing to offer as reward other than the interview itself. We began a total of about 5,600 interviews with workers and farmers in the six countries. Of these, the number who broke off the interview *and* failed to continue later was less than 30. Thus, some 99½ percent found either us or the interview attractive enough to stay with it for up to 4 hours. This is, we believe, an exceptional record. We are, of course, proud of it, and hope that our experience will persuade others that detailed life-history interviews by the survey method are feasible even in developing countries. But more important, in this context, are the implications of the low proportion of disrupted interviews for the interpretation of our results. That fact insured that whatever differences we might find between and within groups could not be an artifact of selection or screening within the interviewing process itself. Our procedure clearly did not squeeze out men of lesser modernity, nor lock in those of higher modernity.

Response Bias and Comprehension of our Questionnaire

It required good will to sit through a 4 hour interview. We evidently generated enough of that. Yet that good will could have been our undoing had it motivated men to say just anything which came into their heads in order to be able to offer *something* in answer to our questions, whether understood or not. This raises the issue of "response bias," a potentially serious problem in all attitude studies, and one likely to be critical in research in foreign cultures.

The tendency toward genial agreement with whatever the interviewer may ask is a form of response bias known as "acquiescence set." It can produce seriously misleading, indeed even totally spurious, results, especially in samples such as ours. There is another type of response bias which is almost as powerful as the agreeing tendency, known as the "social desirability set." This set is assumed to represent a certain general psychosocial disposition, but one also thought to be more common among the less well educated. When questioned, a person with this set tends to select the answer he believes will make the best impression on others, regardless of what he himself actually believes.

To avoid difficulties with these types of response set we adopted a firm rule at the outset of our study not to make regular use of the agree-disagree format, or, indeed, of any other invariant pattern for wording questions and answers. Some few of our questions requested an answer in terms of agree-disagree, or "yes-no." Some others presented a small scale from "very important" to "not important," or the like. In content, however, the questions were highly varied, and we took pains to insure that the direction of the modern and traditional answer was not always the same. Equally important, we cast the great majority of our questions in such form that the individual was always presented several alternatives on an issue. These were couched in such terms as to make them all have the quality of being commonly socially acceptable. For example, in inquiring into job choices we asked: "Which of these two jobs would you prefer your son to take: A machinist's job at 400 per month *or* a white-collar desk job at 300 per month?" And in testing the sense of efficacy we put the balanced alternatives as follows: "Some say that accidents are due mainly to bad luck. Others say accidents can be prevented by care. What do you say?"

In addition to varying our question style and format, and offering balanced alternatives, we sought to offset the effects of response set by the organization of our questionnaire. If one asks a string of questions on the same theme, the chances are an intelligent interviewee will perceive one's purpose, and may then slant his answers so that he will appear in what he assumes is the best light from the interviewer's point of view. This can be especially germane if one is trying to find out whether men are responsible or careless, superstitious or scientific, kind or cruel, and, of course, modern or traditional.

We felt that the form and content of our questions did a good job of concealing our purpose and that they kept hints as to the "right" answer to a minimum. Nevertheless, we also arranged our questionnaire so that it did not call too much attention to the analytic variables which were our chief scientific concern. The interview was, therefore, not organized in sections dealing with our main themes such as efficacy, dignity, time, or openness to new experience. Instead, it was arranged and described to the interviewee under broad topical headings, such as family life, work experience, community life, friendship, and so on. The questions relating to our analytic themes were then scattered, as appropriate, throughout these more topically organized sections of the interview. It would have taken a very perceptive and alert person indeed to discern that we were really more interested in analytic variables, like dignity, than in the topics like "family life." More important, there was nothing in the arrangement of the question to give the least suggestion that one answer was in any way preferable to any other. These qualities should be apparent from an examination of the core questions reproduced in Appendix A.

By these means we believe we reduced to an absolute minimum the danger that any pattern which might emerge from our data could be the result of response set. Indeed, we may have carried our efforts too far. To some degree everyone thinks in sets and categories. It helps a man to clarify his position on an issue when he must deal with a variety of questions on the same topic all at one time. By varying the pattern of our questions as much as we did, and by so scattering those on a given theme throughout the interview, we probably inadvertently and unnecessarily lowered the correlation between questions related to each other, and lowered the resultant reliability of our attitude scales. This was especially likely to happen in our case because less well-educated people have a difficult time expressing their ideas as consistently as they may feel or believe them, unless they are helped out by a good deal of structure brought into the discussion from outside.

Given the level of education of our samples and the limited worldly sophistication of the milieus in which they grew up and now lived, it might be argued that the risk of response set of the sort just discussed was less serious than the possibility that our respondents failed really to understand us, and we them. The efforts we made to render our concepts in simple terms, to control distortion in the translation, and to couch our questions in the common language, all reflect our concern to evoke personally meaningful responses.

How well we succeeded, in the end, in communicating effectively with our interviewees, and they with us, may be judged from a set of measures we devised to check on our performance. At the end of each interview, the interviewer rated his subject's comprehension and understanding of the questionnaire. The proportion whose understanding was rated as only "very poor," that is, as in the lowest category, ranged from less than 1 percent in Nigeria to a maximum of 9 percent in Argentina and India.

A check on the accuracy of the interviewers' own impressions may be derived from the distribution of our R or repetition scores. To the left of each question there were three blank boxes, one to be checked by the interviewer every time it proved necessary to repeat a question for the interviewee. After three repetitions the interviewer was supposed to pass on to the next question, and the person was scored DK/NA (Doesn't Know/No Answer.) There was, as one might expect, great individual variation in the number of times questions had to be repeated. One poor soul in Chile, and another in Argentina, each racked up 577 repetitions, an average of more than one per question.[16] However, the median number of repetitions *per interview* was quite modest, ranging from 6 in Argentina to 30 in East Pakistan. Taking into account the base for the number of questions to which the R score was applied in the different countries, that works out in the case of East Pakistan as one repetition every nine questions, and in Argentina, one for every 73 questions.

To our knowledge, this technique of scoring repetitions was never tried before, so we have no comparative basis for judging performance. Considering the typically limited education of our respondents, however, we interpret the results as indicating that our interviewees understood us quite well. Moreover, in the typical study these results would have been classified as "Doesn't Know" or "No Answer," and that would have been the end of it. A little patience on our interviewer's part often indicated that these people really did have something to say.

The data on the repetition score are supported by the frequency of DK/NA (Doesn't Know/No Answer) responses. We have the information for only three countries, and only as applying to the approximately 166 questions in the "core" questionnaire. In those cases, the average number of DK/NA responses per subject was: Chile, 0.4; Israel, 4.2; Nigeria, 1.6. The number of DK/NA responses, of course, reflects not only the understanding of the questionnaire by the respondent, but the diligence of the interviewer in pursuing an answer. Nevertheless, the fact that failure to answer was limited to about two questions per hundred for the average respondent was decidedly encouraging. Indeed, it is a standard of performance rarely attained in regular national surveys in even the most highly developed countries.[17]

All our efforts to repeat questions and keep down the number of DK/NA responses may be challenged by saying that our technique may have encouraged people to say anything which came into their heads, whether they understood the question or not. We have powerful evidence that this was not the case. In East Pakistan we undertook a special test of the understanding of our questionnaire. The technique, which we call the "random probe," involved following the interviewee's choice of one of our fixed alternatives with some further query such as: "And why do you say that?"[18] The answers were scored on a scale from 1, for complete understanding, to 5, indicating serious misunderstanding. The score of 5 was assigned even when the respondent's explanation of his reply was quite clear in itself, but was not in accord with the choice he had made among the fixed alternative answers to the question. In short, the scoring was very stringent.

The random probe was applied only to ten questions during the course of any one interview. It might, therefore, be unreliable as a way of rating the level of understanding of any one person. However, each separate attitude question in the questionnaire was probed by this procedure during the course of 50 different interviews. In our view, this provided quite a reliable basis for judging how well any particular question was understood. Moreover, the probing technique was used in each of 1,000 interviews in East Pakistan, with ten probes per interview. Therefore, there were altogether 10,000 different probes, which provided a very stable basis indeed for judging the comprehension of our questionnaire as a whole.

Using the scale from 1 to 5, the median score for the entire set of questions was 1.4, essentially a B+ performance. Of the 200 questions to which the technique was applied, 87 percent were rated as having been understood "well" or "very well." This was not only cheering news about our success in writing intelligible questions; it also indicated un-mistakably that in all but a few cases our interviewees not only under-stood *what we were asking,* but understood and could explain and justify *what they were answering.*

Checking this general impression on an individual basis, we found almost 90 percent of the interviewees were scored as having understood our questions at the B level or better. Only 22 out of 1,000 men had a mean score of 3 or worse. These were the C and D men, who failed in substantial degree to understand the questions. When we consider that almost 40 percent of the East Pakistan sample had not been to school at all, and only 12 percent had completed six or more years, the level of understanding of our questionnaire which they manifested was highly reassuring, not only with regard to East Pakistan, but, by extension, with regard to the other countries where, after all, the average level of education of our respondents was much higher.

Communications and Drift

Each field director was expected to bring in a study strictly comparable to the others, yet one which was realistically adapted to the local conditions. If each man had dealt with every issue according to his own lights, the drift away from a common design could have gone so far that the individual-country studies could no longer serve their scientific purpose of each being a more or less exact replication of the other. On the other hand, to insist on rigid adherence to a set of fixed criteria faced the field director with the prospect of squandering his resources in what could seem to him obviously futile searches for scarce information. Or it might oblige him to collect clearly misleading or inappropriate information.

With work going on in six countries spread over three continents, there were inevitably many failures of communication. Quite apart from outright misunderstandings, moreover, the field directors were simply forced to make many decisions without any consultation, merely because of the pressure of local circumstances, limited resources, and dwindling time. All this contributed to the drift which pulled each national project away from the standard of strict comparability with the others, and thus away from the fulfillment of its mission in the overall design. There are, therefore, some points in the analysis at which we lose one or two countries from our six-country set. On the whole, however, we feel this drift was kept to a reasonable minimum. The study design, and the array of the questions and their form, were sufficiently close in all the countries to permit using each national study as a more or less exact replication of the others. When the data from all six countries were assembled in Cambridge we could tell that the integrity of our master plan had been well preserved. Our basic procedures, and the efforts of the field directors, had insured us the opportunity to attempt a truly transnational analysis of individual modernization with data in whose relevance and reliability we could quite firmly trust.

II

Measuring Individual Modernity

5
Two Case Studies

We have so far discussed individual modernity only as a rather abstract concept. It would not have been productive to give more detail until it could be seen in the context of our research plan and method. Now the time has come to present the traditional and the modern in more concrete terms. To do so we will offer below sketches of two men selected because they well represent the modern and traditional man as we conceive him. Neither is the most extreme example we could find; indeed, quite a few in our samples were further out toward the modern or the traditional pole, as the case may be. But we wanted our examples to be rather alike in certain objective characteristics, which narrowed the range of variation. However, the contrast between the men we selected is sharp enough to make quite clear what we mean by a modern and a traditional man. We should note in this connection that whenever quotation marks are used in the profiles which follow, they indicate the man's own words as volunteered by him as a supplement to his answer.[1] The words used as fixed alternatives in our questionnaire are presented without quotation marks.

Our traditional man is Ahmadullah, a Pakistani farmer living in a village quite far from any urban center. He was 28 years old, and had never been to school. When our interviewer pointed out to him that a man may do all sorts of work, Ahmadullah nevertheless said he was highly satisfied to be a farmer. "If I work hard," he told us, "I can get crops by the grace of the Almighty, and can live with my wife, children, and parents. We can eat crops we grow ourselves, and keep ourselves alive." Ahmadullah was not searching for new experience; indeed, he considered the great advantage of agriculture to be that farmers "stay in their own home, while the factory workers must go away from home."

Our modern man is Nuril. He was 27 years old and an industrial worker. He had had one year of schooling. Employed for the last 10 years at the Plant X of the P. Metal Industries in East Pakistan, he worked as a moulder, pouring brass from the furnaces. His work involved regular contact with machines. Nuril said that he was only moderately satisfied to find himself in this type of work. Nevertheless, he preferred industrial to agricultural labor. He appreciated the regularity with which he was paid in that line of work, and the fact that the wage permitted him to "live well" and even to "send money home at the end of the month." But the purely financial advantages were only part of the story. Nuril said there are other advantages, most notably the chance for new experience because "we can meet different people in town."

Common Backgrounds and Contrasting Perspectives

Ahmadullah and Nuril had roughly comparable backgrounds. The districts they came from were different, but both were typical East Pakistani regions devoted to rice cultivation by small-scale farmers. Both men grew up in relatively isolated villages. Nuril's was the more so, being 30 miles from the district center at Comilla, while Ahmadullah's village was 16 miles from the subdivision headquarters in Mymensingh District. Each was raised by a farmer wholly engaged in cultivation, who had had no education. In Nuril's case, however, it was his uncle who raised him, his father being away, working as a sweeper on the railway. Nuril's father had been to school, evidently for about a year, but given his circumstances this does not seem likely to have given the boy much of a head start toward modernity. During their first 15 years of life, neither Ahmadullah nor Nuril had any experiences in an urban environment. Since Nuril migrated at 18, however, he had had something like 10 years of life in the city of Dacca before the interview took place.

Being Bengali, Muslim, and uneducated, the two men understandably shared certain cultural and social values. For example, they both showed considerable anxiety about communal tensions, and expressed vigorous hostility toward India and the Hindus. Thus Ahmadullah said that the biggest problem facing Pakistan was "the four million Muslims in India who were being tortured by the Hindu ruler there." Asked his view of the Hindus in turn, Nuril said "they are killing Muslims in India and are driving away the Muslims from India."

Both Ahmadullah and Nuril rejected the idea that a man who had no religion at all could be a truly good man. Even for a family which already had several sons as well as daughters, they preferred the next to be a male child. And they explained this choice in the same terms. Thus Ahmadullah said, "If a son is born he will be able to earn money and help his parents when he grows up." Nuril echoed these sentiments in saying, "We are poor, and he will be able to support me by earning money." Both men also argued that, compared to the dignity of a man, it was much less important to worry about assaults on the dignity of a mere boy.

On these few points the two agreed. But there were, in fact, surprisingly few such points. Despite the similarity of their background and education, Ahmadullah and Nuril came across to us as markedly different in the quality of their minds, the extent of their knowledge of the world, their feelings about themselves, and their relations to others both more and less powerful and advantaged than they were.

Informed Contact With Outside World

The contrast between the two was perhaps most striking in their knowledge of the world and things in it. Although he had had only a single year in school, Nuril had taught himself to read, and passed our literacy test quite well. Ahmadullah said he almost never saw a newspaper; Nuril claimed to see one several times a week, and gave credibility to his claim by naming three papers. He also claimed to get information several times a week from the radio, his local government (the so-called union-council), and religious leaders. Ahmadullah reported that he never got news from any of these sources. Furthermore, not having had much contact with the movies, he indicated he had no idea whether their effect on morality was good or bad. By contrast, Nuril was firmly convinced that they were a good influence. Understandably, Ahmadullah could not correctly identify any of the array of political figures or places with which we presented him, whereas Nuril knew eight of the eleven, missing only on Jinnah, Moscow, and a local politician.

Nuril not only knew about this world — he evidently felt himself much more a part of it. When Ahmadullah was asked what he considered himself first and foremost when presenting himself to outsiders, he responded by naming his village, whereas Nuril chose the much broader identification of being "a Bengali." If he got conflicting advice about a public issue, Nuril would rather follow a national leader, while Ahmadullah would follow a local chief. Asked what kind of news interested him most, Nuril wanted to hear about events in all of Pakistan, whereas Ahmadullah preferred word about religious festivals.

The Sense of Personal Efficacy

Nuril communicated a strong sense of personal efficacy. He felt that the outcome of things depended very much on himself, and that others bore responsibility for their individual actions. Ahmadullah was relatively passive, even fatalistic, and very much dependent on outside forces, above all on the intervention of God. Confronted by the incomplete sentence stub, "When the farmers work in the field then . . . ," Ahmadullah responded, "Then in the name of God they wait to get the crops." Nuril was not for waiting; he responded by saying, "Then they work hard." Asked why he would not attempt to switch from farming to other work, Ahmadullah replied, "I am a very ignorant man. I can only do cultivation work." Presented with the situation in which he got a new and better plow, he responded rather doggedly that in that case he would continue merely to "plow the land." When told, in the comparable sentence-completion test for workers, that a new machine had replaced the old, Nuril completed the sentence by "feeling pleasure to do the work."

Nuril's optimism came through in his belief that within 30 years everyone in East Pakistan would own a radio and a camera; Ahmadullah was firm in believing they would not. Told of a boy who was killed by a car while crossing the road, Ahmadullah assumed this had happened because the boy "was ill-fated and it is God's wish," whereas Nuril concluded that if the boy had been more cautious "he might not have met this accident." Ahmadullah thought a solution to the problems of his local community depended mainly on God's help, but Nuril assigned prime importance to hard work by the people. Asked to choose for himself among jobs ranging from those with many responsibilities to those with none, Nuril preferred a job with many whereas his compatriot wanted one with only a few responsibilities. Although Nuril joined Ahmadullah in rejecting the use of a pill as a way of preventing conception, he did not simply leave it at that. He went on to explain his decision in a way which again showed his propensity to accept personal responsibility, saying: "One should not stop the power of conceiving by taking tablets. One can stop issue by self-restraint."

Neither man had joined any civic or public organizations, and neither could recall ever having actually written or spoken to a public official. Ahmadullah went further to say that he had never thought about any public issue sufficiently to really want to do something about it, whereas Nuril claimed he had, and added proudly: "We have built a road in our village." The contrast between the two men was heightened by their statements as to what they would do if a law they considered unjust was under discussion in their local government council. Nuril said he would ask the chairman of the council not to enact the law, whereas Ahmadullah replied, "I can't do anything. I am just an ordinary man."

Openness to New Experience
Ahmadullah not only lived in a closed and unchanging world, he seemed to prefer it that way. Offered the choice of living anywhere he might prefer, he nevertheless named his own village. Nuril also wanted to

stay where he was, which was in Dacca. But he declared that if he could make twice as much money by moving 1,000 miles to West Pakistan he would move; Ahmadullah would not. Nuril was stimulated by the thought of meeting new people, and affirmed confidently: "I can meet them and I can know them." Ahmadullah was less certain and more cautious. Ahmadullah thought it wrong for a couple to attempt to limit the number of children they would have, whatever the form of birth control they might adopt; he would not vote for a woman to hold high public office; he maintained that the husband should speak for the entire family; and he argued that it was best to stick to old tried and true methods of raising rice rather than to experiment with new seeds and methods of cultivation. Nuril disagreed with him on each of these issues. Moreover, he approved having scientists explore what made a baby turn out a boy or girl, or how a seed turned into a tree, whereas Ahmadullah did not think poking around in such matters was a good thing.

Readiness For Change

Ahmadullah had the impression that the freedom of women to do things was not changing, and when asked how he felt about the situation he replied, "I don't feel anything personally." By contrast Nuril said he thought the situation of women was changing rapidly, and approved, saying: "It is good; education is good." Indeed, for a Muslim and a generally devout man, he showed himself ready to go quite far in accepting new freedom for women. Although he acknowledged being *a little* worried about illicit relations developing where men and women worked together, he allowed that there were circumstances under which a young woman should be permitted to work away from home, explaining himself by saying, "If there is nobody to look after her, she should be given the chance to stand on her own." In these same matters Ahmadullah was worried *a lot* about illicit relations, and would under no circumstances permit a girl to work outside the home.

Education and Occupational Aspirations

It may be observed that in the developing countries faith in education is surprisingly widely diffused among all segments of the population. Ahmadullah was no less vigorous than Nuril in urging education for a bright boy who came from a background like his own, saying he would like his son to go "as far as would be possible." He was, however, vague as to just how far that might be, whereas Nuril was much more precise in specifying "matriculation," meaning to about ten years of schooling, as the goal. The two men differed a good deal, furthermore, in their ideas about what should go in the school, what its effects and uses were, and what the long-term objectives of a young scholar should be.

Asked what is the goal of education for a young man, Ahmadullah responded with some charm that "it adds knowledge and makes gentle." Nuril took a much more utilitarian view, declaring that with education "one can keep his accounts; one can read and write letters; one can be a salesman in a shop." Considering these practical views, we are not surprised that he thought it most important for the school to concentrate on teaching a useful trade, like machine repair, whereas Ahmadullah thought it more appropriate to study the Koran and other religious matters. The result was that neither gave prime emphasis to the third alternative which the question presented, the mastery of reading and writing. Should a young man succeed in getting a lot of education, however, Ahmadullah proposed that he go into the more traditional "public service," whereas Nuril would prefer that he follow the more modern profession of engineering.

Nuril was ambitious not only for his son, but for himself. While Ahmadullah said he would be content to continue for the rest of his life as a cultivator of the land, Nuril said he would prefer, if he could, to shift to some other kind of work, and spoke of having his own metal-working shop. He also had rather definite ideas about what he might do with his good fortune should he succeed in advancing himself. In addition to a radio and a camera, of which we had shown him pictures, he volunteered the information that he would like some day to own a wrist watch, a torch light, an electric fan, and even a motor car! Ahmadullah said he did not wish to own either the radio or the camera, no doubt a sensible decision given his village location. There was, however, one additional purchase he cared to make, two bigahs of land, totaling two-thirds of an acre.

Relation to Traditional Authority

At the end of their meeting the interviewer of Ahmadullah was moved to note about him that "he always used to speak things in the name of God." This did not necessarily mean that he was more strict in the observance of his religion. Nuril claimed he prayed alone at least once every day, and that he participated in a religious congregation at least once every week. Evidently Ahmadullah did neither. His constant references to God more reflected his sense of submission to this and all other forms of established authority around him. This quality of submission and self-rejection was so marked that his interviewer was prompted to note that Ahmadullah very often punctuated the interview by declaring, "I am but a foolish man; what can I say?"

Ahmadullah admired the holy man, who was very devout, more than the factory manager, whom Nuril praised because "he has given jobs to many." When it came to assigning relative weights to diverse opinions,

Ahmadullah said the village headman's views should count for more, whereas Nuril wanted the opinion of the common people to carry equal weight. Faced by the incomplete sentence stub, "Most bosses . . . ," Ahmadullah became flustered and could not think what to say, but Nuril responded readily that most bosses "do not work hard." Ahmadullah also had trouble dealing with the question of how much attention the country's leaders were paying to the opinions of ordinary people like himself. He was finally recorded as "don't know." Nuril did not have any trouble making up his mind; he said straight out that the government was paying no attention at all to common people like himself! In case he were to receive conflicting advice on a public issue simultaneously coming from a religious leader and a government leader, Ahmadullah would follow the religious leader and Nuril the government man. Faced with a similar conflict of loyalty as between the head of his family and the head of his village council, Ahmadullah would follow the family head; Nuril the council head.

Nevertheless, almost no one is perfectly consistent in his attitudes, and Nuril's liberation from the influence of parental authority was far from complete. If he had to choose between a job he liked and another he didn't like but which his parents preferred, then he, like Ahmadullah, would follow his parents' preference, explaining that "as one's parents brought one up, so one should act according to their opinion." Ahmadullah provided his own show of independence by joining Nuril in urging that a girl should pick her own husband. In case the parents objected to the choice, however, Ahmadullah would give in and counsel her to follow the parents' preference. Not so Nuril; he would advise the girl to follow her own feelings "because if they are married, they will not be happy if the girl does not like the person she married." A modern view indeed.

The contrast between the two men was especially evident in their response to questions about one's relation to the aged, often taken to be a key element of traditional cultures. Asked what were one's obligations to the old, both made clear their acceptance of a major responsibility. Ahmadullah said succinctly, "One's obligation is to support them, to obey them." Nuril waxed warm on the subject, and elaborated his answer as follows: "One should attend the old and take care of them. One should give them all their needs. One should get medical care if they are ill." It is notable, however, that he said nothing about obedience.

Our impression that Nuril felt more independent of the authority of elders was confirmed by his reply to other relevant questions. He claimed, for example, that one could get more of the truth from books and schooling than one could from merely listening to the old. Ahmadullah took the opposite point of view. Asked whether he would follow the advice of a "party of the old" or a "party of the young," Ahmadullah opted for the old, Nuril for the young. He went on to explain: "The old know about the old days. Young people understand more than the old about the present time." This then was his declaration of independence.

The standard social-science model of traditionalism in authority relations specifies a duality in asserting that the man who is most blindly submissive to traditional authority is himself more likely to be domineering and punitive with his subordinates. Ahmadullah seemed to fit the model. If he had a foolish wife who squandered the family's last bit of money on some bauble, he would beat her. Nuril was prepared only to give a sharp warning, much further down toward the "soft" end of the scale of punishments we proposed. Ahmadullah's response to a hypothetical subordinate who made a stupid mistake which caused the waste of much material was more severe than Nuril's. And when asked what his government should do with the prisoners they took in an unprovoked invasion, he said, "They should all be brought into jail," whereas Nuril was willing to stop at having his country "treat them strictly, so they become disciplined."

What the Sketches Told Us

In the course of our research, we conducted almost 6,000 interviews. From these thousands we selected two men who seemed to convey the contrast between what we mean by a modern and a traditional man. Obviously, since each stands for hundreds of others, these cases are being asked to carry too much weight.

The two men happened to be Pakistani. The pair could just as well have been from any of the five other countries. Indeed, we did develop profiles for roughly comparable pairs from the other countries. Nevertheless, East Pakistan seemed our best choice because it is so unambiguously an underdeveloped country and a new nation. In addition, the use of the "random-probe" technique in Pakistan gave the interviewee more opportunity to put things in his own way, and we were eager to have these men speak in their own words as far as possible.

Ahmadullah and Nuril happened to be a farmer and an industrial worker, respectively, but we might have paired a farmer and an urban nonindustrial worker, or even two industrial workers. Each occupation and each national group would offer its own special contrasts, but in each setting we could find a more modern and a more traditional man. As for this particular pair, moreover, it was not hard to find them. The profiles of both men represent common types, who appear again and again in our interviews, even if not always in such pure and seemingly distilled form. Nevertheless, they were not chosen at random. They were selected because we wanted to illustrate certain points. Having been so selected they cannot be taken as proving anything. That comes later, and is the job of a larger number of cases speaking in statistical terms. But these profiles did tell us three important things.

First, the profiles gave us confidence that the concepts we had developed to describe and study the relative modernity of individuals were indeed serviceable. This was a real issue because many of the qualities we treated as important attributes of the modern man were not described for us in any of the standard vocabularies of personality psychology. Our concepts were, in many cases, developed especially for this study of the individual in the modernization process.

The path leading down to contemporary psychology is strewn with the wreckage of concepts which proved to be only fancies of the scientific imagination. Empirical investigations have repeatedly failed to support the inference that certain hypothesized psychological dispositions could be accurately discerned in nature, that is, could be commonly found in real men. The sketches of Ahmadullah and Nuril, however, testified to the reality and serviceability of our concepts. After reading Ahmadullah's profile one can no longer seriously doubt that the concept of "personal efficacy" identifies a discernible personal disposition which, in his case, came out quite clearly and coherently in his attitude toward work, birth control, accidents, nature, government, public officials, and almost every other topic we touched on. Similarly, others of our concepts passed some rough test of serviceability in these sketches. They seemed to us to identify relatively distinctive personal attributes clearly discernible across a variety of the situations to which our questions elicited a response.

We recognize, of course, that the evidence of the sketches is limited. Our feeling that we could reliably characterize Ahmadullah and Nuril in a more or less "clinical" way as to level of information, sense of efficacy, openness to new experience, independence of authority, aspirations for advancement, and the like did not in itself prove that we had delineated concepts and devised measures for them which met the standards of good sociopsychological research. To do so required further technical exercises, demonstrations, and proofs of a more statistical nature. When such procedures are attempted later in this book it will be apparent that characterizing large numbers of individuals on these same dimensions is often more difficult or ambiguous than it seemed to be in these two cases. We also found that some of our concepts were not nearly so serviceable as were those of efficacy and openness to new experience. Indeed, our sketches of Ahmadullah and Nuril quickly raised some doubt as to whether or not we could successfully test value orientations concerning calculability, planning, or the aged, and whether such measures, if developed, would really serve effectively to distinguish one man from another.

The second thing our two sketches told us was that it is apparently sound to assume that different measures of individual modernity may cohere in a simple syndrome, permitting one to speak of men in fairly global terms as more "modern" or more "traditional." Nuril was not only better informed than Ahmadullah; he was also markedly more efficacious, open to new experience, ready for change, ambitious and aspiring, more active in politics, independent of his parents and other traditional authorities, more in favor of birth control, more in contact with the mass media, and so on over a number of other dimensions.

Our theory had predicted that some such pattern would emerge. After the fact it seems quite reasonable that it did, as illustrated in these two cases. But it did not *have* to be that way. It might well have turned out that Nuril was very open to new experience but was not very efficacious, and that he had high aspirations, but very little independence of traditional authority. If the sketch of Nuril's attitudes and values had revealed such a pattern, it would have been difficult to describe him as unambiguously "modern" and Ahmadullah as unmistakably "traditional," which is what we feel it is reasonable to call them. Instead, at every step, we would have had to specify in what particular respect Nuril seemed modern, and in what particular respect Ahmadullah seemed traditional. And if one wished to give a summary statement about each man, it could not have been done in simple global terms, but would have required the presentation of a fairly complex and detailed multifaceted profile.

Of course, by themselves, our two cases could not establish how frequently the general syndrome would prevail, and how far, if at all, the more complex differentiated profile would emerge as the only valid way to describe individual modernity. Again there were standard procedures and statistical tests which could help to resolve these issues, and we will later present the relevant findings. For now, however, we limit ourselves to the implications we drew from our two profiles.

The sketches gave us confidence that it would make sense to give each individual a single score expressing his overall modernity. We could see that such a summary measure would not be making a hash which disguised the distinctive character of the ingredients of individual modernity. And it certainly would be very useful in distinguishing in a simple way between sets of individuals who were not so sharply and obviously contrasting as were Ahmadullah and Nuril on almost every relevant subdimension of individual modernity.

The sketches also gave us confidence in our assumption that individual modernity was not exclusively a reflection of superior education. Of course one cannot build a social-science generalization on a single case, nor even a dozen. We knew that to prove this point would require an elaborate statistical demonstration with hundreds of cases. But the sketches showed us what was possible.

Nuril had had only one year in school. Yet it could hardly have been this one-year advantage over Ahmadullah, who had not attended at all, which accounted for Nuril's being so strikingly more knowledgeable and so markedly more modern in every attitude and personal disposition. Nuril may have been born brighter than Ahmadullah, but it does not seem reasonable to assume he was born more modern. His modern attitudes and disposition were surely something he had acquired along the way. But where, and how? Both men were raised by uneducated farmers and grew up in isolated villages. For this pair, therefore, we cannot assume that differences in their origin and early social milieus were responsible for their contrasting personal qualities.

When we look to Nuril's later life, however, we find he had experienced the impact not only of migration, but also of 10 years of city life, factory employment, and exposure to the modern media of mass communication. Which of these, if any, and in what proportions and combinations, account for the fact that he seems so modern? Our theory identified factory experience as potentially very important. Nuril had worked 10 years in a factory, but was different from Ahmadullah in many other ways as well. From the single case we cannot hope to disentangle that knot of experiences. Moreover, this single case should not be interpreted as telling us that education is unimportant; we will see plentiful evidence that it is very important indeed. Our single case did, however, give us assurance that a man *can* become very modern in spirit without the benefit of education. At the same time it drove us to examine large numbers of cases with detailed and refined measurement to determine what other forces may have been at work and in what ways. And to do that we had to abandon the more clinical case method and develop systematic measures which lend themselves to statistical manipulation. The construction of such measures is the central focus of the rest of Part II which follows.

6
Constructing the OM Scale:
An Overall Measure of Modernity

One of the central theoretical and practical concerns of our project was to establish whether individual modernity was a general syndrome rather than a mere congeries of discrete elements. Many scholars argue that individual modernization does not come about in a highly consistent way. They hold that most men change profoundly in some dimensions while remaining extremely traditional in other respects. We readily acknowledged that such mixed patterns were not merely possible, but quite common. Nevertheless, we believed that in most individuals personal modernity was, in fact, a quite general *syndrome* such that having one modern characteristic, say a strong sense of personal efficacy, would quite regularly be associated with manifesting other modern characteristics, such as favoring birth control, joining voluntary organizations, and taking an interest in world affairs.

In addition to our interest in the theoretical aspects of the problem, there were practical reasons for pressing the "syndrome" issue. To establish that there was a general syndrome of modernity promised to simplify greatly the task of analyzing and presenting our results. Otherwise, we faced the prospect of separately exploring the relation of each of as many as thirty different themes to the whole array of our independent variables. Although many of these topics were clearly important enough to be looked at separately, in their own right as it were, we were impressed by the great economy of time and space which would result, if we could establish a good summary measure of individual modernity.[1]

Having decided to develop the OM Scale as an overall measure of modernity, we had to determine how to go about doing so. The problem was not purely technical. The quality of the index or scale that one creates, by whatever method, depends a great deal on what one puts into it.

Since the analysis in the remainder of this book rests almost exclusively on the OM scales, we assume the prudent reader will want to know a good deal about how they were put together. He is, otherwise, buying the proverbial "pig in a poke." Moreover, in the process of constructing the several forms of the OM scale described below we clarified a number of *substantive* issues, thus giving this review of scale construction more than purely methodological interest.

The Basic Components

Before proceeding to construct an overall measure of modernity, we had to screen the questions we had asked in order to decide which we thought were really relevant, given the kind of measure we wanted. The first and rather obvious step was to eliminate all the background questions. It would, of course, have been possible to create a measure of the modern man that combined information on his social characteristics, such as age and occupation, with material on his attitudes and values. The main purpose of our research, however, was to show how far and in what ways modern attitudes and values could be *explained* by differences in social characteristics such as education and urban residence. We considered attitudes, values, and behavior as our "dependent" variables, distinct from the social background and experience measures which we intended to use as "independent" variables. A measure of the modern man which from the outset combined his socioeconomic status with his attitudes would have precluded studying the systematic interrelation of these two distinctive sets of personal attributes.

Because of our special interest in behavior, we next segregated the questions which clearly dealt with self-reported behavior, such as those requesting an individual to tell whether he had voted in the last election or talked about politics with his wife. There were 12 such questions.[2] To them we aggregated 35 "items" which tested behavior "objectively," these being mostly tests of information, such as identifying Nehru or giving the names of newspapers.[3] We did not segregate these behavioral items because we felt such questions should play no role in determining who was considered modern. Rather, we did it because of our theoretical interest in the distinctive behavioral model of the modern man. Since we planned to test how far men modern in attitude also *acted* in a more modern way, we needed to construct at least one version of our overall modernity measure based solely on attitudes and values, excluding the behavioral and informational items.

There remained a pool of questions which were not on backgrounds, did not report behavior or objective "test" information, and had been asked in at least four of the six countries, which we considered the minimum standard of comparability. In the remaining pool, however, there were numerous questions we had added to our questionnaire not because we had strong theoretical reason to assume they would be part of a modernity syndrome, but rather because we, or often someone else, considered it intrinsically interesting to explore a certain subject using our type of sample. Before beginning our analysis, therefore, we decided to have the available field directors and senior staff rate all the questions which had been used in our questionnaire. The raters were told they could ignore the distinction between the analytic and the topical discussed in Chapter 2. Rather, they were to assess each question on its own merits, judging whether or not it unambiguously tapped some aspect of individual modernity as they understood the project to have defined it. We then placed in the "prime" or "core" category only those questions which met the strict test of being selected by five of the six raters. Seventy-nine of our questions so qualified, and are identified as such in Appendix A, as composing OM-1.

At the time the field directors rated the questions, we had plans to develop a separate scale of political modernity, based mainly on the items which tested how far a man was an active or "participant" citizen.[4] Therefore, the raters were asked to exclude from consideration any questions which tapped that dimension. We later ascertained, however, that there was good agreement on some 17 questions related to active citizenship which the staff felt could properly be aggregated to the core set of 79 they had approved earlier.

Of the questions which remained, some dealt with issues which at least some of our field directors or research associates did indeed consider relevant to the definition of a modern man. Others had been identified as relevant by at least one leading student of modernity working elsewhere. We did not feel we could dismiss those questions out of hand. Therefore, the director and assistant director of the project undertook to screen all the remaining questions to ascertain which should qualify, even if only in a "secondary" way, as part of the total pool of questions we would use to define the modernity syndrome. Twenty-three additional questions were thus selected as relevant.[5]

Putting these categories together, the maximum pool of items we had available to consider in constructing an overall measure of modernity was then 166: 79 were core or prime questions on attitudes, values, and opinions; 23 were secondary questions of the same type; 17 tested a man's readiness to be an active, participant citizen; and 47 dealt with behavior either as self-reported or as elicited by the project through its "objective" tests of information and verbal fluency. All had been selected on purely theoretical grounds without reference to, or even knowledge of, how they related empirically to one another or to the independent variables.

Having determined which *questions* were relevant for measuring individual modernity, we had to decide next which *answers* we would classify as modern and which traditional. We had conceived of the alternative answers to each question as constituting a continuum running from the traditional to the modern. Which end of the continuum was considered modern and which traditional was determined theoretically. Since there were usually three, four, and even five alternative answers to each question, however, we still had to face the decision as to what should be the precise "cutting point" on the continuum of answers which would determine whether a man fell on the traditional or the modern side for that particular question. Our guiding principle was to select that point in the distribution of answers to any question which came closest to putting half of the country sample on the modern side and half on the traditional side. *This procedure was done separately for each question in each country.* We thereby insured the maximum variation of modernity scores within each country, although we did so at the price of reducing the strict comparability of any absolute OM score from one country to another.[6]

Constructing the OM Scales

Once we had decided which end of the response continuum was modern and which traditional, and then found the appropriate median "cutting points," computing the modernity score for each individual was simple. Answers on the traditional side of the median were scored 1, on the modern side of the median 2. The "ones" and "twos" received by each individual were summed and then averaged by dividing that sum by the number of questions he had answered. The fact that some people failed to answer a number of questions was therefore no problem. The overall score became a "best estimate" based on the questions answered. In our computer printout everyone received a score between 1.00 and 2.00. This was the equivalent of having everyone's score expressed on a scale from 0 to 100, the form in which we have reported the results in this book.[7]

This method had the virtue of great simplicity, both for arriving at the individual's score and for expressing it in a readily comprehensible manner. The resulting scale may be thought of almost as a kind of aptitude test, with scores expressed in the familiar range from 0 for those who miss on everything to 100 for a perfect score. We felt these advantages greatly offset some of the disadvantages which this, like any other method, must have.[8]

By applying the method just described to the pool of 166 items that we considered appropriate measures of individual modernity, we constructed a number of different forms of the OM scale. These various forms were designed to meet certain methodological challenges we could anticipate, or to facilitate some special type of analysis we planned to undertake. However, the content of all the forms was broadly similar.

Moreover, a man's score on each form of the OM scale summed his responses and expressed his modernity in a single number ranging from 0 to 100. It was quite simple, consequently, to assess the agreement of one form with another. As the results which are reported in Table 6–1 and Table 6–3 make abundantly clear, each form tended to assign any given man much the same standing as modern or traditional.

Since different subsets of the items were used in the several forms of OM, this basic agreement of the resultant scores gave us further confidence that there was a general syndrome of modernity which our questions consistently tapped. Moreover, the consistency of a man's score from one version of the OM scale to another also permitted us to simplify our presentation of results in this book by basing it mainly on that single version of the scale which best satisfied our theoretical and technical requirements. However, other versions of the scale were used at various stages in our analysis and results based on them are included in this book. In addition, the version we use most often was built up from earlier models, so that understanding it requires some acquaintance with those earlier forms. Furthermore, seeing how the several forms of the scale were conceived and constructed gives some insight into the role which particular types of subject matter played in defining the modernity syndrome. These considerations argue the desirability of presenting, even if quite briefly, an account of our procedure in constructing the OM scale in five different ways.

OM-1: The Core Attitude Scale Derived From Theory

The first summary modernity scale we constructed, bearing the appropriate title OM-1, was designed to give us a measure of modernity which was purely attitudinal and excluded questions on the respondent's political role. We did not build it that way because our theory of the modern man required us to exclude from consideration either a man's behavior or his orientation to political participation. On the contrary, in our view, the definition of a modern man *should* include those elements of his social role. However, we had considerable interest in discovering how far a man who had modern attitudes also behaved in a more modern way. We also intended eventually to explore the orientation to political issues of men who were judged modern by other criteria.[9] To test either of those relations in an unambiguous way we had to construct a version of the OM scale limited entirely to attitude and value questions and excluding questions touching on political participation.

Apart from these considerations, however, OM-1 had special status as a test of the soundness of our theory about what constituted individual modernity. In its construction we used exclusively those 79 attitudinal questions which our staff had rated as unambiguously part of the syn-

Table 6–1. Selected characteristics of the OM scales.

Characteristic	OM scale	Argentina	Chile	East Pakistan	India	Israel	Nigeria
Number of items	1	78	79	77	78	78	79
in the scale	2	118	119	114	117	118	116
	3	163	164	162	164	167	157
	500	100	100	100	100	100	100
	519[a]	80	85	87	93	87	78
Mean score	1	54	56	57	60	59	59
	2	53	54	53	58	57	56
	3	53	53	51	54	57	55
	500	55	57	52	61	58	56
	519	55	58	51	59	58	58
Median score	1	54	56	56	62	59	58
	2	54	54	53	59	58	56
	3	53	53	51	55	58	55
	500	56	57	52	63	58	56
	519	56	58	51	61	59	58
Standard deviation	1	9.0	8.7	8.5	13.5	9.3	8.5
of scale	2	7.6	7.3	7.5	10.7	8.0	6.9
	3	8.3	8.1	8.2	11.3	8.4	7.6
	500	11.4	11.2	10.7	13.9	10.6	10.5
	519	12.4	11.7	11.5	13.7	11.1	11.7
Range of scores	1	22–82	28–90	32–86	6–91	19–79	27–82
observed	2	28–74	28–79	27–84	31–81	25–75	29–76
	3	26–76	25–78	28–80	20–77	16–77	32–79
	500	23–81	22–87	24–86	9–90	14–88	29–86
	519	22–84	21–90	20–84	9–89	8–91	28–88
Average item-to-scale	1	.19	.19	.19	.30	.20	.19
correlation	2	.16	.16	.17	.24	.17	.15
(unadjusted)	3	.18	.18	.18	.24	.18	.16
	500	.24	.24	.22	.30	.22	.23
	519[b]	.47	.44	.42	.53	.43	.43
Average item-to-scale	1	.13	.12	.12	.25	.14	.12
correlation	2	.11	.09	.12	.20	.12	.11
(adjusted for	3	.18	.14	.15	.22	.15	.13
autocorrelation)	500	.20	.20	.18	.27	.18	.19
	519[b]	.35	.33	.30	.43	.31	.31
Reliability:	1	.76	.74	.74	.88	.77	.74
Spearman-Brown	2	.77	.75	.77	.87	.78	.73
formula	3	.84	.84	.85	.91	.85	.81
	500	.86	.86	.84	.91	.84	.85
	519	.84	.82	.80	.88	.81	.82
Kuder-Richardson	1	.68	.67	.64	.86	.55	.63
formula	2	.71	.65	.72	.85	.71	.66
	3	.72	.82	.83	.91	.83	.79
	500	.85	.83	.80	.90	.82	.82
	519	.80	.78	.73	.85	.75	.76

[a]These items were combined into 19 subscales to compute a man's OM-519 score.
[b]For OM-519 the figures given are not item-to-scale correlations, but are rather subscale-to-scale correlations.

drome of individual modernity. Of course, our official definition of modernity also included behavior and political orientations not measured by OM-1. Nevertheless, we acknowledged that if the attitudes measured by these 79 core questions proved not to cohere at least reasonably well, then our theory about modernity as a complex syndrome would be seriously challenged.

The outcome of constructing OM-1 strongly indicated that we were very much on the right track. OM-1 demonstrated unambiguously that the questions we had been using as indicators of modernity were clearly related to some common theme or dimension which, on the face of it, could reasonably be called a syndrome of individual modernity.

If we had just been guessing blindly, half the questions would have been correlated with the scale in a positive direction, and half in a negative direction. The actual results, presented in Table 6–2, were quite different. The number of questions with negative correlations to the overall OM-1 scale score was limited to the range from 3 to 13 percent, depending on the country. Moreover, instances of such negative correlations which were statistically significant (at .05 or above) were limited to the range from 0 to 7 percent.[10]

By chance alone an average of less than one item in each country would have been positively correlated with the scale score at about the .01 level of significance. Even following our strict standard, which corrected for autocorrelation effects, we found no less than 48 of the 79 items in each country correlated with the scale at the .01 level or better representing, with variation by country, between 61 and 90 percent of all items in the scale. In other words, the overwhelming majority of all the questions we had identified on theoretical grounds as appropriate to measuring attitudinal modernity did in fact make a consequential and statistically significant contribution to the measurement of that quality in the individuals in our six countries.

These results testified to the effectiveness of our theory in correctly identifying the modern and the traditional responses. Moreover, we here had strong evidence that men in developing countries were highly consistent in the way in which they "came down" on one or the other end of a set of attitude and value measures selected by theory to represent a continuum from the modern to the traditional. In other words, we had obtained a clear indication that the diverse attitudes and values which had been measured in our questionnaire did hold together as a set, defining a general syndrome of individual modernity.

Perhaps the simplest way to summarize the coherence of a set of items such as those used to construct OM-1 is to use a measure of scale reliability. By the Spearman-Brown (S-B) formula the reliability indices for OM-1, presented in Table 6–1, ranged from a low of .74 in Nigeria, Chile, and East Pakistan to a high of .88 in India. The more stringent Kuder-Richardson (K-R) formula yielded somewhat lower figures.[11] Overall, these reliabilities would be rated quite satisfactory by the standards usually applied to tests of individual attitudes and values.[12]

Indeed, we felt the scale reliabilities earned by OM-1 were sufficiently high to warrant stating that there clearly is a general syndrome of individual modernity, even when modernity is judged by attitudes and values alone. Yet there was no compelling reason to limit ourselves to this one measure. OM-1 was constructed as it was partly in order to provide a special measure for later analysis, and partly as a pure test of our theory. We could therefore lift some of the restrictions in search of a measure of individual modernity with still higher reliabilities, subject, of course, to the

Table 6–2. Percent of adjusted item-to-scale correlations statistically significant, for selected OM scales.[a]

Correlations which are—	OM scale	Argentina	Chile	East Pakistan	India	Israel	Nigeria
Positive and	1	65	65	69	90	65	61
significant	2	61	56	63	81	56	55
at .01 level	3	64	68	70	80	70	59
	500	89	96	92	94	86	83
Positive and	1	70	73	71	94	76	67
significant	2	69	67	68	85	67	63
at .05 level	3	69	73	73	86	77	65
	500	96	98	95	96	96	88
All positive	1	87	94	90	97	97	89
(significant	2	88	87	89	90	93	86
or not)	3	83	85	88	91	93	82
	500	98	100	99	100	100	100
Negative and	1	4	0	0	1	0	1
significant	2	2	3	2	6	1	3
at .01 level	3	4	3	2	3	2	4
	500	0	0	0	0	0	0
Negative and	1	6	0	1	1	0	1
significant	2	6	3	3	6	2	4
at .05 level	3	9	3	4	4	2	5
	500	0	0	0	0	0	0
All negative	1	13	6	10	3	3	11
(significant	2	12	13	11	10	7	14
or not)	3	17	15	12	9	7	18
	500	2	0	1	0	0	0

a The numbers of item-to-scale correlations upon which these percentages are based are given in Table 6–1.

condition that this search should not require us to depart substantially from our theoretically derived conception of the modern man.

OM-2: An Expanded Attitude Scale

OM-2 took into account all the items from OM-1, plus some 40 others.[13] These 40 items, which may be identified in Appendix A, qualified because we relaxed two of the constraints applied in the construction of OM-1. First, certain items tapping our respondents' orientation toward politics and their role as citizens were allowed to enter the new scale. There were 17 such questions. Second, we included a large set of questions, some 23 in number, which had earlier been excluded because there was no consensus in the project staff in favor of including those items in the definition of a modern man, even though the questions had been identified by other researchers as appropriate measures for this purpose. Unless such questions were allowed to enter the competition by being included in the pool used to make up an OM scale, one could not resolve the issue as to whether or not they really were useful indicators of a man's standing on the modern-traditional dimension.

Many of the items whose relevance for measuring the modernity syndrome we had questioned on theoretical grounds did indeed fail to demonstrate empirically that they should have been considered part of the syndrome in the first place. We can express this in terms of a success rate, "success" being defined as the proportion of items having corrected item-to-scale correlations significant at the .01 level or better in the expected direction. As noted earlier, the 79 items in OM-1 had a success rate ranging from 61 to 90 percent, depending on the country. The success rate of the 40 items added to make OM-2 was in the much lower range of 38 to 64 percent. This was, of course, still a quite respectable performance. By chance alone the success rate would have been about 0.5 percent. Although this outcome was a compliment to our original theory for being sharply honed, it also indicated that we might have been too strict, or too parochial, in our original definition of the modern-man syndrome. Many of the items about which our staff had not reached consensus nevertheless showed themselves to be statistically part of the modernity syndrome. And as a result of including those questions we had, in OM-2, a broader and more catholic conception of the modern man. By purely technical standards, however, adding the 40 additional items to the 79 in OM-1 improved the quality of the original scale very little, if at all. We felt there remained enough room for improvement to require us to go still further in our search for a maximally reliable scale.

OM-3: The Maximum Scale

OM-3 was constructed by adding to the items in OM-2 all those in which the individual reported his behavior rather than merely his attitudes and values, plus those which *objectively* tested his behavior as manifested in giving the correct answer to various tests of information, as in response to the questions: "Where is Moscow?" and "Please give us the names of some newspapers." Approximately 47 such additional units were included in the pool, making the score on OM-3 an average of 166 responses. As with OM-1 and 2, the OM-3 score for each individual was based on the average for all the questions he answered expressed on a scale from 0 to 100.

How well he kept informed had seemed to us certain to be an important indicator of the modern man. The improvement in the quality of the OM scale which resulted from adding the behavioral and information items to the OM-2 set gave a strong empirical confirmation to our expectation. Relative to OM-2 the reliability index earned by OM-3 jumped markedly in all six countries, as may be seen in Table 6–1. The K-R indices now ranged from a low of .72 in Argentina to a high of .91 in India, with a median of .83.[14] Such reliabilities are decidedly on the high side, equal to the performance set by the better standard scales commonly used in sociopsychological research in the most developed countries.[15]

These reliabilities marked OM-3 as a scale of excellent quality. The results, described in Tables 6–1 and 6–2, provided strong evidence for the argument that the large pool of items we considered as relevant to defining a syndrome of individual modernity did indeed cohere to a marked degree. Taken together they constituted quite a stable measuring instrument. In using it we could have considerable assurance that a man identified by the scale as modern at one time would be so defined at another time, and that two men who were truly alike in their attitudes and behavior would earn similar scores on the OM-3 scale.[16] Moreover, the quality of the scale, particularly reflected in the high reliability indices, gave us some assurance that if individual modernity were truly related to our independent measures such as education and factory experience, this scale would permit us to see that relation clearly.[17] In brief, we were quite ready to use OM-3 as our main measure of individual modernity in the analysis of the causes and social correlates of individual modernity. Indeed, a substantial part of the work of our project reported in this book and elsewhere was initially done using OM-3.

Challenges to OM-3

Despite our general satisfaction with OM-3, we had to acknowledge that certain substantial theoretical and methodological challenges could be directed at it. In our view, those challenges did not significantly impugn the integrity of the scale or the appropriateness of our using it. Nevertheless we saw no point in allowing such reservations as had been raised to cast any doubt on the reasonableness of the conclusions we were reaching, and we therefore decided to develop a scale free of the acknowledged defects of OM-3.

One of the blemishes of OM-3 would be considered by many to be more or less cosmetic, but some specialists in scale construction viewed the matter more seriously. As we pointed out in discussing OM-1, we felt we had been exceptionally successful in selecting questions in advance which later proved to be related to the larger syndrome of individual modernity. Nevertheless, a substantial number of questions which were counted in computing each person's score were not making any meaningful contribution to the accurate measurement of his relative modernity. On the average about one in four of the items weighed in computing OM-3 scores was not positively correlated with the overall scale at the .05 confidence level or better. Among these items, moreover, there were some, happily few, which actually had significant *negative* correlations with the overall score. In those cases the scoring system gave a man credit toward being modern even when he chose what we had discovered empirically to be the more typically traditional answer. Although this might have been fatal on a short scale, its effect was modest in one as long as OM-3. For that reason the defect could be held to be a minor issue. Nevertheless, it was clear that some benefit could be obtained from "cleaning up" OM-3 by eliminating the items which made no statistically significant contribution or which, through our error of judgment, were scored opposite to the way they evidently should have been.

A more serious challenge to OM-3 could be raised on the grounds that it lacked balance, and might indeed be untrue to our original theoretically defined conception of the modern man. Our system of using key letters to identify the different sets of questions yielded 24 themes, ranging from AC, for "active citizenship," to WR, for "women's rights."[18] It must now be acknowledged that as we developed the questions for our study we evidently had been very casual about the *number* of questions we formulated to test each theme. Some themes, such as efficacy and aspirations, were represented by at least 13 questions, whereas others, such as work commitment and aging, were represented by only 2 each. Most overrepresented were the questions on geography, politics, and consumer goods, along with the measures of verbal fluency such as those based on a count of the number of words or themes given in an answer. Such questions alone numbered 23, and because of the multiple coding of some, they contributed 35 units to the OM-3 score.

This outcome had not been a product of a conscious policy. Very likely we prepared only two questions to test the fear of aging because we were not much convinced that it was actually very relevant to the modernity syndrome. In other cases, the theme did not readily lend itself to formulating questions. Yet the project staff certainly did not consciously decide that in our definition of the modern man measures of information should carry twice the weight of questions dealing with efficacy, which in turn, should carry twice the weight of questions about citizenship and birth control.[19] There seemed good reason, therefore, to construct a summary measure of individual modernity which, compared to OM-3, would be both "clean" and "balanced."

OM-500 and 519: "Clean" and "Well-Balanced" Scales

To clean OM-3 of dross we set the rule that no item should be considered eligible for this new scale unless it could be shown to be making a statistically significant contribution to the scale score.[20] To insure that the new OM scale was balanced, we set the rule that each theme — such as efficacy, information, women's rights — should be represented by not more than five questions. We sought to represent as many themes as possible from our original theoretically derived set, subject to the rule limiting us to questions making a statistically significant contribution. To meet this requirement we needed a larger set of questions to draw on. We enlarged the pool of available items by recoding some questions we had bypassed earlier because they had presented difficult coding problems. Moreover, since some themes, as defined by the original alphabetical key, were represented by only a few questions, we regrouped and combined some of the "small" themes into new themes now containing more items. In this regrouping, however, we preserved as fully as possible the basic structure of our original conception of the modern man as defined by the 24 themes previously described in Chapter 2.

The new clean and balanced scales were constructed in two different ways. They bore numbers beginning with 5 to indicate that they were part of our fifth series of OM scales, the fourth series having been constructed for special purposes not relevant here. OM-500 was based on 100 questions. Nineteen subthemes were represented, wherever possible by five items each, but in any event, not less than three. The remainder necessary to reach 100 units were selected from items in the miscellaneous category.[21] Each item was counted in the usual way as modern or traditional, to yield a score from 0 to 100.

OM-519 was not based as usual on the items, but rather on subscales. There were 19 of these, one for each theme, hence the scale's designation as OM-519. Each man's modernity was measured separately on each theme, and then the 19 theme scores were averaged to yield the man's overall modernity rating.[22] But here again the system yielded a score from 0 to 100.[23] This procedure, used to score 519, ensured the best balance, since by it we weighed each theme in strictly equal fashion, regardless of the number of questions by which the theme happened to be represented.

Despite these differences, however, OM-500 and OM-519 were virtually identical scales, as shown by their intercorrelations in Table 6–3.[24]

Both OM-500 and OM-519 yielded very high reliabilities, even using the Kuder-Richardson test. OM-500 came in with a range from .90 in India to .80 in Pakistan, and the excellent median over all six countries of .83. Because it was based on fewer units, OM-519 earned lower reliabilities, but the levels it attained also indicated that it was a scale of excellent quality.

Thus, these new scales had nearly all the virtues of OM-3 without any of its presumed defects.[25] Their high reliability made them an eminently suitable basis for exploring the relation of individual modernity to those life experiences which our theory identified as its probable causes. Unlike

Table 6–3. Intercorrelations of selected OM scales.

Country	Scale	OM-1	OM-2	OM-3	OM-500	OM-519
Argentina	OM-1	1.00				
	OM-2	.92	1.00			
	OM-3	.87	.91	1.00		
	OM-500	.82	.83	.90	1.00	
	OM-519	.82	.82	.90	.98	1.00
Chile	OM-1	1.00				
	OM-2	.93	1.00			
	OM-3	.85	.89	1.00		
	OM-500	.80	.80	.90	1.00	
	OM-519	.78	.78	.89	.98	1.00
East Pakistan	OM-1	1.00				
	OM-2	.94	1.00			
	OM-3	.84	.89	1.00		
	OM-500	.84	.89	.93	1.00	
	OM-519	.83	.85	.90	.98	1.00
India	OM-1	1.00				
	OM-2	.97	1.00			
	OM-3	.94	.95	1.00		
	OM-500	.95	.94	.95	1.00	
	OM-519	.94	.94	.95	.99	1.00
Israel	OM-1	1.00				
	OM-2	.94	1.00			
	OM-3	.85	.91	1.00		
	OM-500	.83	.86	.91	1.00	
	OM-519	.81	.83	.90	.98	1.00
Nigeria	OM-1	1.00				
	OM-2	.93	1.00			
	OM-3	.82	.85	1.00		
	OM-500	.78	.78	.90	1.00	
	OM-519	.75	.73	.87	.97	1.00

OM-3, however, these newer scales were under no suspicion of giving undue weight to tests of information or any other single element in the array of themes our theory had identified as potentially relevant. We resolved, therefore, to use one of the fifth OM series whenever possible in our analysis in this book. The mantle fell on OM-500, mainly because one could so easily interpret the meaning of any difference between two scores on that test. Each point higher or lower on OM-500 always simply meant one more question, out of one hundred, answered in either the modern or the traditional direction. In all tables and charts in this book, therefore, references to OM are to be understood to mean OM-500, unless otherwise indicated.

Despite the improvement in scale quality represented by OM-500 and 519, the results obtained with them actually gave us very little reason to fault the OM-3 scale we had created earlier and which we had used in so much of our preliminary analysis. The intercorrelations of OM-3 with the new 500 scale were above .90 in all six countries. This meant that the OM-3 scales were actually extremely well qualified to stand as substitutes for the new scales. In addition, we should note that even with our rigorous cleaning operation, the K-R reliability ratings earned by OM-500 were greater than those earned by OM-3 in only three of six countries, as indicated in Table 6–1.[26] Any analysis done with OM-3, therefore, could be used with the confidence that the method of constructing the scale did not make it substantially less representative of our initial idea of the modern man than the more "balanced" scales OM-500 and OM-519.

OM-500 and OM-519 complete the set of scales which figure significantly in this book. Some other forms of the OM scale which we constructed have been mentioned in footnotes. One version of the scale we cannot relegate solely to a footnote, however, is the so called "short form," OM-12. This form was a distillate of the larger scales, containing a mere fourteen representative questions. They were, however, the items which we found most effective in measuring modernity in all six countries. Since OM-12 is so brief, it can be scored in the field in a matter of minutes. Its effectiveness in identifying modern men accurately, easily, and economically induced some fifty researchers, of whom we have knowledge, to incorporate it in studies launched between 1966, when the scale was first described in *Sociometry*, and 1972. Others whose first contact with OM will be through this book will likely wish to use it, and so we have described it separately in Appendix B. However, OM-12 was not used in this book, since the longer forms of the scale described above more accurately reflected our conception of the modern man and also had higher reliabilities.[27]

Summary

To sum up, we succeeded in constructing a set of scales which measure individual modernity *in general*. They permitted us conveniently to express each man's score on a scale from 0 to 100. These scales took into account a man's attitudes, values, and behavior over the whole range of issues, topics, and themes identified by our theory, and by those of others, as being relevant to the definition of a modern man. We recognized that the distinctiveness of a man's reaction to each separate aspect of his life experience might be blurred by this procedure, which blended the discrete elements of response into a common denominator of "individual modernity." Nevertheless, we found unambiguous statistical evidence that this operation was not artificial, forced, or capricious. If it had been, we would not have obtained the high scale reliabilities we did.[28] Those reliabilities meant that for our best measures, such as OM-3 and OM-500, our scales had between 80 and 90 percent variance in common with the "true" modernity score, could we but measure it without error.

Because of the way in which we constructed our questions and organized our questionnaire, the high reliabilities we obtained simply could not, even in small part, be attributed to some spurious factor such as response set.[29] Considering the theoretical analysis which lay behind the selection of our themes, and the face validity of the questions used, the outcome of our efforts in constructing the OM scale very strongly indicated that there is a general factor or syndrome of individual modernity which influences, or is reflected in, the individual's response to the particular issues with which he is confronted in many different realms of life and in many diverse social relations.

In declaring that we have established the existence of a common element, or underlying theme, in the responses to our questionnaire, we are not asserting that individual modernity is unidimensional. To say there is *a* common theme is not to say there is *only one* theme. The very method of constructing our OM scale, drawing as it did on questions from so many different themes, itself highlighted the multidimensional nature of individual modernity. That fact will be further evident when, in the next chapter, we analyze in detail the *content* of the OM scales we created.

7

The Content of OM:
The Concept of Individual Modernity
Reexamined in the Light of
Empirical Evidence

Our success in constructing the OM scale as a measure of overall modernity put us in a position to ask two further questions: First, in the light of the empirical evidence now available, were we obliged to revise substantially our original *theoretical* formulation of the modern man? And second, to what extent is the modern man basically the same in each of our six countries? Again, as in Chapter 6, we wish to emphasize that we do not undertake to answer these questions exclusively, or even primarily, to satisfy methodological critics. We consider the results to be substantive and to have bearing on important theoretical issues.

Our theory defined individual modernity as a complex or syndrome of personal qualities. We identified a large number of themes, aspects, attributes, and forms in which a man could demonstrate his modernity. Each main theme was identified by a pair of code letters, such as WR for "women's rights," and each question was tagged with one of these pairs of code letters plus a number. The complete list of these main themes was presented in Table 2–1. Although the themes were there organized into three groups or "models," we should recall that in the actual construction of the OM scales we overrode those distinctions and allowed each theme to compete independently on its merits for a place in the overall modernity syndrome.

The items which entered into the construction of OM-1 represented twenty of those themes, and four more were represented by the larger set of items in OM-3. We should now ascertain whether any of the themes which theory had identified as attributes of the modern man failed to sustain that claim when the structure of the syndrome was tested empirically.

On What Should Be Excluded from Our Definition of the Modern Man

To answer this question we had to decide what was to be the standard for concluding that a theme had "failed" to prove itself part of the modernity syndrome. Establishing that standard proved complex, but we hope that it can be made relatively unambiguous.

In any given country, any one question's contribution to the general scale defining individual modernity could be readily judged by the size of the item's correlation with that larger scale. A fairly stringent rule of thumb would require that in any given country an item should yield an "adjusted" correlation to the scale statistically significant at the .01 level, using a two-tailed test, in order to qualify as having made a contribution to the individual scale score in any given country.[1] Any item producing such a correlation might confidently be considered to deal with material significantly related to the larger syndrome of individual modernity.

In both absolute and relative terms a substantial number of questions included in OM-3 failed to produce an adjusted and positive correlation with the overall scale at the .01 level of statistical significance. The number of such failures ranged from a low of 33 items in India to 64 in Nigeria. Across all six countries 31 percent of the observed item-to-scale correlations in OM-3 were not statistically significant at the .01 level. The number was large enough that if those "failures" were all concentrated in one or a few themes, that concentration could easily have disqualified those themes as part of the OM syndrome.

In order not to be arbitrary we had to have some objective standard for judging that a theme had, by empirical performance, failed to sustain its initial theoretical claim to a role in defining the larger syndrome. We could not accept the argument that a theme was related to the modernity syndrome merely because *some* items representing the theme could be individually shown to pass a statistical test of relevance. Rather, we had to insist that the *proportion* of such significant relations tested for each theme be, in some specified degree, in excess of what would be expected by chance alone. Technically, any theme which had substantially more than 1 percent of its questions showing item-to-scale correlations at the .01 level had thereby established that its relation to the modernity syndrome could not be dismissed as a statistical accident. But it was not obvious *how much* better than chance a theme ought to do in order to stay in the running as part of the OM syndrome. With too lax a standard it might prove impossible to disqualify any theme; and with too strict a standard we ran the risk of excluding themes which really could make a claim, even if a modest one, that they were relevant to measuring individual modernity. We decided that for our initial screening any theme which did not show 10 percent or more of its correlations to be at the .01 level would be considered as having failed to validate its claim to being part of the OM syndrome. Our standard was more strict than that set by the most commonly used statistical criterion, but not so severe as to rule out of consideration themes which made only a modest contribution to men's OM scores.[2]

Our statistical standard was met by all of the themes entered into the competition, whether by the project's theory or by the theory of others. As Table 7–1 shows, following the 10-percent rule we could not, even for a single theme, say that we had been able to cast serious doubt on its status as empirically part of the syndrome which defines a modern man. Indeed, all the themes did very much better than was required by the rule. None of the 24 themes in OM-3 had fewer than 38 percent of its positive and adjusted item-to-scale correlations significant at the .01 level. The probability that this proportion would have been obtained by chance, even in

Table 7–1. Percent of adjusted item-to-scale correlations for six countries positive and statistically significant: by subtheme.

		OM-1		OM-3	
		Level of significance		Level of significance	
Theme		.05	.01	.05	.01
AC	Active public participation	a	a	97	97
AG	Aging and the aged	83	50	58	50
AS	Aspirations[b]	81	76	85	80
CA	Calculability	67	61	47	40
CH	Change orientation	75	75	58	47
CI	Citizenship	92	92	93	93
CO	Consumption	72	72	77	73
DI	Dignity	56	43	50	38
EF	Efficacy	92	89	80	76
FS	Family size restrictions	100	94	80	71
GO	Growth of opinion	50	37	76	70
ID	Identification with nation	70	70	69	53
IN	Information	a	a	100	100
KO	Kinship obligations	56	50	47	47
MM	Mass media	71	63	79	79
NE	New experience	93	93	88	88
PL	Planning	73	67	65	56
RE	Religion	87	83	83	81
SC	Social class stratification	83	83	62	58
TI	Time	60	48	58	50
TS	Technical skill[c]	56	50	66	44
UN	Understanding production	a	a	80	60
WC	Work commitment	a	a	91	91
WR	Women's rights	66	64	56	52

a These themes were excluded from consideration in the construction of OM-1.
b Includes occupational and educational aspirations.
c Includes distributive justice.

the case of themes represented by only two questions, was less than .00001. In the case of the themes with more questions the probability was even more remote.[3] Obviously this outcome strongly supported the view that individual modernity is a very general syndrome incorporating a wide variety of elements. Moreover, the more or less equal and proportional representation of themes reflecting both the analytic and the topical perspective confirmed the correctness of the decision to override such distinctions in constructing the OM scale.

We could, then, feel confident that all the themes which we had considered relevant, as evidenced by their inclusion in the scale, had a significant relation to OM. To say this was not to assert, of course, that all the themes were equally strongly related to the syndrome. And it by no means argued that all the separate *questions* we asked served us equally well. So far we had merely rejected a null hypothesis, one which asserted that there were themes in our set which were unrelated to the general modernity syndrome. Such null hypotheses are often simple and extreme; after we have rejected one we are still left with a wide range of alternatives to explore.

The perfect record achieved on this first test might lead some readers to wonder whether there is *any* characteristic of men which, by our procedure, would *not* have been proved statistically a part of the modernity syndrome. Fortunately, it is quite readily apparent that we were not working with an unfalsifiable proposition. After all, the six countries together provided 300 item-to-OM-3 correlations *not* positive and significant at the .01 level. As we noted above, any concentration of those could easily have invalidated a number of themes, even the relatively larger ones. Our modal theme had six questions which, with six countries involved, yielded a total of 36 item-to-scale correlations per theme. If 33 of those had failed to qualify, then according to the 10-percent rule the theme would have been knocked out. A theme with fewer questions, say 3, could have been disqualified by using up only 17 of our pool of "bad" correlations. Obviously, with any degree of concentration, we had enough ammunition easily to disqualify perhaps 6 to 8 themes. We did not succeed in knocking out any. This came about because those questions which yielded poor item-to-scale correlations were scattered over numerous themes, rather than being systematically concentrated in one or a few of them. This suggested that the observed failures reflected measurement error aggravated by the problem of working in six different cultures, rather than following from the presence of irrelevant themes in the set we had selected as bearing on the definition of the modern man.[4]

Two Challenges To Our Conclusion

However, we foresaw certain challenges to the adequacy of our procedure for screening the relevance of themes to OM, and sought to meet them. For one thing, some might question our having applied our "10-percent rule" to the pooled results for six countries. We recognized that our doing so might have permitted a theme to qualify merely because in one country *all* the items were closely tied to OM even if the same theme was consistently unrelated to the measure of modernity in other countries. If that had happened, it would hardly be reasonable to speak of the theme in question as being, in any *general* sense, part of the OM syndrome.

Inspection of our master chart of item-to-scale correlations by country made it seem highly unlikely that any standard theme was managing to stay in the competition merely because it "worked" in only one country or even two. Nevertheless, we undertook a systematic check of those themes about which there could be some doubt because less than 50 percent of their items in OM-3 had met our criterion. There were five such themes — calculability, change orientation, dignity, kinship obligations, and technical skill valuation. It was notable that the weakest of these themes had 38 percent of its item-to-scale correlations significant at the .01 level or better, which in itself was no mean feat. But that was not the issue any longer; it was whether the qualifying correlations had been contributed by only one or two countries.

To check the point we set the following rule: if, for any theme, any two countries accounted for two-thirds of the qualifying items, then the theme would be considered lacking in *general* relevance to the modernity syndrome.[5] When we applied this rule, all five of the basic themes which had been challenged passed the test. None showed more than 50 percent of its significant correlations to be contributed by only two countries, whereas for a theme to be disqualified by our rule two countries had to account for 66 percent of the significant correlations.[6] We had again failed to exclude from the definition of the modern man any of the 24 main themes which entered into the construction of OM-3.

There was yet another challenge to what now seemed an inevitable conclusion. Some of our *main* themes were so broadly defined that a theme as a whole could pass muster even though some of the *subthemes* it encompassed would not survive if put to the test while standing entirely on their own. Simply to poke around in search of subsets of items which performed badly, however, could have become a very arbitrary, even a capricious, procedure. To avoid this pitfall we worked out a definition of the subthemes on theoretical grounds before resuming the empirical test of performance. The larger themes were, where relevant, broken up into smaller subthemes, and some items originally in different themes were now combined if they seemed clearly to define a relevant subtheme. The original set of 24 themes thus divided yielded 35 subthemes, each of which could now be subjected to the same test of relatedness to the OM syndrome which we had applied to the original set of 24 main themes.[7]

A New Standard of Performance

Since we were rescoring the subthemes we also reviewed the standard of performance we had been using. Our first approach, embodied in the 10-percent rule, treated each theme as if it were on trial for its life, and therefore insisted on the standard "innocent unless proved guilty." Only if it could be shown beyond a reasonable doubt that a theme was *un*related to the OM scale would we have excluded it from the syndrome defining individual modernity. Some of our critics thought that standard to be too lax. They argued that we should view the matter more as one evaluates an application for membership in a club. Instead of requiring that the statistics show why a theme should be excluded, they argued that each theme should make a good case for *inclusion*. In response, we decided on two new and much more strict statistical procedures for screening the 35 subthemes.[8]

One of those methods cast doubt on the relevance of three subthemes. The other challenged the same three and added two more (see Table 7–2). From these challenges one could conclude, at least according to our strict standard, that in comparison with more traditional men, modern men:

are not markedly more trusting;[9]

are not particularly less likely to accept their obligation for support of a relative;[10]

do not much more often harbor illusions that the mere possession and consumption of goods in themselves brings goodness or contentment;[11]

are not decidedly more likely to perceive difference of opinion between their views and those of others around them;[12]

are not substantially less likely to be severe with people who fail to perform their duties well and responsibly.[13]

Some of our readers may be surprised by these results, others confirmed in a suspicion that they had entertained all along. We rested quite comfortable with the outcome because more than half of all the questions implicated in this set, and at least two-thirds of those used in each of three of the subthemes, had been rated by our project staff as not particularly relevant for judging individual modernity.

Most important to us, however, was the fact that 30 of the 35 *sub*themes we had considered worthy of consideration had passed a rigorous test proving that they were indeed unmistakably part of the OM syndrome. In the face of that record, we were not distressed by the rejection of five subthemes, for three of which we had made no brief anyhow. This outcome demonstrated that our measure of modernity was a reasonably well-delineated phenomenon. It did not indiscriminately include everything and anything.

Summary of the First Stage

To sum up, we could not unambiguously deny any of our major themes the right to claim some role as part of the larger syndrome defining the modern man. When working with subthemes, however, and applying a stricter standard, we did cast some doubt on the right of 5 of 35 to be treated as part of the modernity syndrome.

We interpreted the results we obtained as strongly confirming the correctness of our original hypotheses as to the characteristics of the modern man. But the main point here is not to judge how right our theory was. Of the 24 main themes, or the 35 subthemes, many, indeed as many as half, could have failed to win a place in the larger syndrome without invalidating the idea that there is a general quality we may appropriately call individual modernity. *The main thrust of our findings was that individual modernity is clearly a very broad, multifaceted phenomenon.* Modernity is not something which exists so encapsulated in the person that it manifests itself only in special tests on a few very specific topics. It seems rather to be a general quality reflected in attitudes, values, and behavior in many and diverse realms of social action.

On Whether There Is a Single Key Element in the Delineation of the Modern Man

While each of the 24 main themes had sustained its claim to be part of the OM syndrome, it did not follow that they were all *equally* important in delineating the modern man. Some key themes might have been "doing all the work," while the rest got a more or less free ride. For example, the number of questions we used in OM-3 to test information and verbal fluency was substantial, and our experience with them showed them to have a consistently outstanding record in yielding high item-to-scale correlations. It therefore seemed essential to satisfy ourselves that it was not the set of information items alone which really determined a man's modernity rating. Indeed, we realized that if that proved to be the case we should be obliged to recast fundamentally our original theoretically derived conception of the modern man.

The issue could, in good part, be resolved by comparing OM-2 and OM-3. As noted earlier, we had constructed OM-2 like OM-3 but without any tests of information or behavior. OM-2 had a median reliability across the six countries of .77 by the Spearman-Brown formula. Although that was down from the median reliability of .85 earned by OM-3, it was still quite respectable. Moreover, OM-2 was shorter, and this had a deleterious effect on its reliability. When we compensated for this factor of length by means of the Spearman-Brown prophecy formula, we found the reliability of an OM-2 scale as long as OM-3 would have had a median reliability of .82 for the six countries, that is, much closer to the median reliability actually earned by OM-3.[14]

We concluded, therefore, that the information items, no matter how numerous and strong in their relations to the modernity syndrome, were

Table 7–2.   Item-to-scale correlations (adjusted) for OM-3 positive and significant for six countries: by subtheme.

Subtheme	Number of items in subtheme	Number of items-to-scale correlations generated by subtheme[a]	Percentage significant at—	
			.05 level	.01 level
AC Political activism	3	17	100	100
AG Role of aged	2	12	58	50
AS(1) Educational aspirations	4	23	83	78
AS(2) Occupational aspirations	4	24	88	83
CA(1) Calculability of people's dependability	3	18	61	44
CA(2) Calculability of people's honesty	3	18	33	28
CH Change perception and valuation	7	41	61	54
CI Citizens political reference groups	3	17	94	94
CO(1) Consumption aspirations	3	18	78	67
CO(2) Consumer values	2	12	42	33
DI Dignity valuation	7	42	50	38
EF(1) General efficacy	7	42	69	67
EF(2) Efficacy and opportunity in life changes	8	48	71	58
EF(3) Efficacy of science and medicine	3	18	100	100
FS(1) Family size—attitudes	2	12	75	58
FS(2) Family size—birth control	3	18	83	83
GO(1) Growth of opinion awareness	2	12	50	33
GO(2) Growth of opinion valuation	3	18	50	50
ID Political identification	3	15	67	53
KO(1) Extended kinship obligations	5	29	38	38
KO(2) Kinship obligation to parental authority	2	12	100	100
MM Mass-media valuation	4	24	83	71
NE(1) Openness to new experience—places	2	12	67	67
NE(2) Openness to new experience—people	4	21	100	100
PA Particularism-universalism	2	12	58	58
PL Planning valuation	6	34	65	56
RE(1) Religious causality	3	18	78	72
RE(2) Religious-secular orientation	3	18	78	72

Table 7–2.   (Cont.)

Subtheme	Number of items in subtheme	Number of items-to-scale correlations generated by subtheme[a]	Percentage significant at—	
			.05 level	.01 level
SC Social class attitudes	3	18	78	78
TI Time (punctuality) valuation	4	24	58	50
TS Technical skill valuation	3	18	67	44
WR(1) Women's rights—general	5	30	57	53
WR(2) Women's rights—work and school	2	12	50	50
Information measures	20[b]	117	95	92
Behavior measures	8	44	77	77

[a] In most cases this is the number of items in a subtheme multiplied by six (the number of countries). In some cases the number of correlations will be less than this product since not all items were used in each country.
[b] Indicates the number of items coded, not the number of questions asked. Several different versions of a question are sometimes recorded.

very far from being the "indispensable ingredient" in defining individual modernity. Furthermore, since the set of information items was the largest single block with an outstanding record of item-to-scale correlations, as indicated in Table 7–1, there was reason to assume that no other single theme, such as efficacy, could hope to qualify as the irreplaceable element in the measurement of individual modernity. Of course the information and efficacy themes are an important part of the larger syndrome, and they added to the reliability of our general measure. But the exploration just completed did not lend much credence to the idea that the larger syndrome is so much determined by one or two characteristics as to make the others of peripheral importance.

Additional evidence was provided by a factor analysis of OM-519. That scale, it will be recalled, was constructed by averaging the scores on 19 different themal subscales.[15] As may be seen in Table 7–3, all 19 themes generally had consequential loadings, that is, loadings of .30 or above, in all six countries.[16] Moreover, the loadings all fell within the same relatively narrow range.[17] The results of the factor analysis could, therefore, have been interpreted as telling us that the themes were all more or less equally important, except for the unmistakable fact that the information subscale had loadings quite a bit higher than any other. Was it, after all, the key element in defining individual modernity?

Table 7–3. Factor loadings of 19 themes in OM-519 on the first factor emerging from a principal-components factor analysis.

Theme	Argentina	Chile	East Pakistan	India	Israel	Nigeria
Active citizenship	.35	.54	.47	.40	.49	.43
Change valuation	.51	.48	.42	.53	.27	.37
Dignity valuation	.47	.40	.23	.56	.41	.49
Economic aspiration	.35	.37	.39	.31	.21	.27
Education valuation	.43	.49	.29	.59	.42	.43
Efficacy	.52	.45	.54	.72	.50	.44
Family size	.32	.29	.40	.53	.50	.28
Information	.77	.73	.62	.76	.57	.72
Minority opinion valuation	.50	.39	.41	.45	.49	.48
Modern family	.52	.37	.33	.53	.40	.48
Modern religion	.47	.45	.41	.61	.47	.40
New experience valuation	.53	.46	.47	.60	.52	.48
Nonparochial allegiance	.55	.47	.56	.70	.47	.45
Planning valuation	.54	.47	.33	.31	.42	.50
Responsibility valuation	.46	.48	.41	.44	.42	.41
Technical skill valuation	.45	.46	.58	.68	.42	.43
Urban-industrial preference	.32	.32	.37	.31	.35[a]	.45
Verbal fluency	.38	.49	.43	.27	.33	.37
Women's rights	.39	.35	.33	.57	.46	.31
Latent root	4.30	3.91	3.54	5.49	3.60	3.71
Percent of total variance	22.6	20.6	18.6	28.9	18.9	19.5

[a] In Israel, Particularism valuation is substituted for Urban-industrial preference.

If certain themes were really indispensable, then it followed that without including them in the factored set we should be unable to regenerate a modernity factor at all like the one already created when those special themes had been included. In several countries we experimented by simply leaving out of the factor analysis either the measures of information and verbal fluency or the measure of efficacy, and in the extreme case we left out all three. Some price was certainly paid for omitting these, our best subscales. Despite such drastic measures, however, the remaining subscales yielded virtually the identical factor structure as before, still unmistakably identifiable as the modern man we had delineated by other methods.[18]

Thus, our experience in factor analyzing OM-519 gave further evidence that the OM scale is a rather general measure to which each of a large number of diverse elements contributes moderately, without any subset of those elements dominating, let alone independently determining, the basic character of the whole. *Individual modernity is, then, truly a syndrome, a complex and diffuse personal quality manifest in attitudes, values, and behavior in numerous and diverse realms of social action. No one element is indispensable. No single attribute of the person, not even how well informed he is, can stand alone as the indicator representing the whole syndrome.*[19] Rather, each of a large number of different themes makes some contribution to defining the modern man. The omission of some elements, even the more central ones, can be compensated for by other elements which, in a sense, step in to take their place. From knowing any one characteristic relevant to a man's modernity one can predict any other characteristic at a level which may be statistically significant but will also be highly imprecise. By contrast, if we know a large number of the elements measured by our OM scale we can make a sound general characterization of the man as modern or traditional.

The definitive syndrome of individual modernity, now empirically established, included keeping informed about the world and taking an active role as a citizen; valuing education and technical skill; aspiring to advance oneself economically; stressing individual responsibility and seeing the virtues of planning, including family planning; approving social change and being open to new experience, including the experience of urban living and industrial employment; manifesting a sense of personal efficacy; freedom from absolute submission to received authority in family, tribe, and sect, and the development of newer nonparochial loyalties; and the concomitant granting of more autonomy and rights to those of lesser status and power, such as minority groups and women. Taken together this set of qualities empirically delineates the modern man.

On the Universality of the Content of OM

Creating the OM scales and establishing that in all six countries they met a fairly stringent statistical test of coherence put us in a position to ask a further question of some importance: How far is the man defined as modern in one country like the man defined as modern in the next?

At one level of analysis we have already answered this question: the two men would definitely be much alike. We can say this because in each country the pool of items used, the scoring procedures, and the method of constructing the overall modernity score were more or less identical. Given all these constraints, the fact that a statistically satisfactory general scale emerged everywhere was itself strong evidence that the content and internal structure of the OM syndrome was basically the same in all six countries. One must be particularly struck in this connection that the standard pool of items produced average item-to-scale correlations and scale reliabilities varying only within an exceptionally narrow range across the set of six countries. The facts may be reviewed in Table 6–1.

There are, however, certain peculiar properties of scales and scale construction which might reasonably lead a cautious man to want more detailed evidence before accepting our assertion that the OM syndrome is "basically the same" in all six countries. Given a large enough number of items and a diverse group of test populations, such as we had, we could, theoretically, have come out not with one scale truly common to all, but rather with a set of scales, even one for each country, each with a distinctive character although each in turn had reasonably high reliability. This would have come about if in each national sample different items strongly cohered as a subset, while yet having moderate but consistent relations to whatever the larger set had in common. We were obliged, therefore, to ascertain how far the questions which were important in giving OM its character in each country were alike or different as we moved from one country to the next.[20]

The Best 50 Items in All Countries

To judge the standing of different questions as "central" or "peripheral" to the OM syndrome, we listed them in rank order according to the size of each item's correlations with the overall scale score, repeating the process separately for several different forms of the OM scale. By this means the "best 50" questions were identified for each country. The next step was to compare the different "best 50" lists for all six countries to ascertain the degree of overlap. The results, presented in Table 7–4, indicate that what was central in defining individual modernity in one country tended to be central in defining it in another.

We judged an item to be highly comparable cross-nationally if it was in the top set in as many as four of the six countries. Any item which met that standard clearly should be considered as a key element in the definition of individual modernity. Applying that standard to OM-3 produced striking results. Of the 154 items used in all countries, 30 appeared among the top 50 in four or more countries.[21] But we knew that OM-3 was subject to the challenge that it contained 35 "items" measuring information and verbal fluency which generally performed quite well. If only information tests were commonly on top in defining OM, we could hardly claim that the entire OM *syndrome* was cross-national. We therefore reran the experiment using OM-2, thus excluding the information-testing items from the competition. The number of items in the top 50 in four of six countries actually rose to 38. The probability of obtaining that number by chance alone is the infinitesimal one of approximately 10^{-23}.[22]

Table 7–4. Cross-country overlap among items in OM-3 with the highest item-to-scale correlations.

Identification labels[a] of items appearing in top 50 in—			
all 6 countries	5 of 6 countries	4 of 6 countries	3 of 6 countries
AC- 6	CO- 1[c]	AS- 1	AC- 1[b]
CO- 7[c]	CO- 2[c]	AS- 5	AC- 2[b]
EF- 3	EF-11–12	AS- 7	AS- 6[c]
EF- 8	GO- 1[c]	CH- 3	CI- 7
EF-14	GO- 2[c]	CI- 2[c]	EF- 2
IN- 1	IN- 2x	CI- 2	ID- 1
IN- 2	IN- 7	FS- 3	IN- 4x
IN- 3		FS- 4	IN- 7x
IN- 4		MM- 6	KO- 2
IN- 5		MM-10–12	NE- 2
IN- 6		NE- 5	NE- 3
MM- 8[c]			PL- 4
			RE-11
			RE-14
			WC- 2
			WR-11
Totals 12	7	11	16
Cumulative totals 12	19	30	46

a These identification labels can be used to examine the content of each item in Appendix A.
b Item coded for self-reported behavior.
c Item coded for demonstrated verbal fluency.

Clearly we had tapped a highly regular phenomenon. We could, therefore, go beyond our earlier statement that the large pool of modernity-relevant items defines a broad syndrome of attitudes, values, and behavior. The several national measures of OM not only had the larger set of items in common; they also had in common a basic subset which was central in defining the larger syndrome. Within the larger pool, those items which played the key role in defining the modern man in *one* country tended to be very much the same questions which were central in defining the modern man in the *next* country. To convey some sense of what emerged as central in defining the modernity syndrome, Table 7–4 lists the items according to the number of countries in which they figured as part of the top 50.

Twelve items achieved the impressive record of appearing in the top 50 in *all six countries*.[23] Eight of those were tests of information and verbal fluency. Knowledge of geographical places and political figures, and of the names of books, newspapers, and consumption items, clearly was invariably an important characteristic of the modern man in all six samples. But the information test was far from being the only theme represented among the questions which worked best in defining modernity. Three of the 12 items central in all six countries were explicitly measures of the sense of *personal efficacy,* and a fourth clearly reflected the same tendency. More or less invariably, the man with a high score on the OM-3 scale tended to believe that one's position in life depends more on one's efforts than on fate (EF-3), that a job with many responsibilities (and hence opportunities for exercising personal control) is preferable to a job with no responsibilities (EF-8), and that scientific research delving into the nature of things is beneficial (EF-14). Further, he had many times in the past become so concerned with some public issue that he really wanted to do something about it (AC-6).

The 7 items in the top 50 in *five out of six countries* confirmed the impression gained from those on top in all countries. Most of the additional items were measures of information and verbal fluency, the latter tested by two questions which measured the number of problems the respondent saw facing his town and his country. The man with a higher OM-scale score tended to report a larger number and variety of problems in response to both questions. Again, however, a question tapping the sense of personal efficacy entered the set. The man with a high OM-scale score was more likely to state that what his country needs most is more hard work on the part of the people or good government planning, rather than good luck or God's help.

Moving on to those questions in the top 50 in four of six countries, we found the information and verbal-fluency questions giving way to others, and the content of the modernity syndrome broadened notably. Only one more verbal-fluency test was added, while the other 10 new items seemed largely to reflect "instrumental activism" and "cognitive openness." As delineated by these items, the man who scores high on the OM-3 scale: has high educational aspirations for his son, and high occupational aspirations for himself and his son; feels that discussing new ways of doing things is good; accepts the idea of birth control, and would have his wife use a contraceptive treatment; would do something to block an unjust law being considered in the local legislature; thinks he could understand the thinking of a foreigner very different from himself; places his trust in the mass media rather than in personal media for world news, and prefers national or international news rather than sports, religious, or hometown news.

These items, briefly described, cover a wide range of situations, from very personal practices in the home to public actions to be taken in regard to legislation. Collapsing all the information-testing items into one category, whether labeled "IN" or not, we still have nine different alphabetically defined themes represented up to this point: Information, Active

Citizenship, Aspirations, Efficacy, Change, Citizenship, Family Size, New Experience, and Mass Media. Taken together they reflected the breadth of the overall modernity syndrome, and its potential relevance to all phases of life.

At the same time, it was not too difficult to see a common thread running through these items. Nearly all of them helped to portray a man actively engaging his environment in an attempt to master it, intellectually or physically, or both, and constantly striving to influence, change, or mold it to his design. The man who scores high on the OM scale tends to be active in thinking, discussing, doing, interacting. He is knowledgeable, and yet he is open to new ideas and ways of doing things. He is also seeking to increase and utilize this knowledge to control his destiny. It is in this sense that the modern man, as defined by a high score on our OM scale, may be called an "instrumental activist." By contrast, the traditional man, as defined by a low score on the OM scale, tends not only to be less knowledgeable and less verbally fluent, but also to have a more closed mind and to be more passive in his relation to the world and his immediate environment.

This impression of the modern man could be further checked by examining the 16 additional items which appeared in the top 50 in at least *three out of six countries* as presented in Table 7–4. Again a few dealt with information and verbal fluency, but the rest gave a varied and more complete view of the modern man. Individuals with high OM scores tended to have higher job aspirations, to believe that prevention of accidents is more a matter of carefulness than luck, to hold that medicine is more effective than prayer in curing a sick person, to favor making one's own job choice and mate choice rather than automatically following parental wishes, to belong to more organizations, to prefer planning affairs in advance, to like meeting new people and getting to know a stranger better. All of these elements fit rather well with the picture of the modern man as a knowledgeable instrumental activist who is open to the broader world and to new experiences.

Correlatively, the modern man is more likely to take the advice of his government than the advice of his church or some equivalent organization, and is more likely to identify himself with his nation rather than with his ethnic group, religion, or village. Lastly, the modern man is more likely to state that charity should be given to the poor because of generosity rather than because of fear of God. These items helped to emphasize that psychosocial modernity is not merely knowledge and verbal fluency, nor is it limited even to instrumental activism and cognitive openness. To the nine areas represented earlier we had added questions representing an additional six themes, for a total of fifteen. The additions were: Identification, Kinship Obligations, Planning, Religion, Work Commitment, and Women's Rights. The addition of these themes further emphasized how far modernity is a broad syndrome of characteristics in which efficacy and information play a leading role, but in which numerous other elements are strongly represented as well.

The Factor-Analytic View of the Universality of OM Content

How far the content of OM is basically the same in all six countries could also be assessed by factor analysis. As noted above, factor analysis yields so-called "loadings" which express how much a single component in a set of measures has in common with the set as a whole. So long as we included the same components in the analysis for each country, we were in a position to assess whether the pattern of factor loadings yielded by the various themes was similar or markedly different in the several countries.

We need only look back to Table 7–3, which presented the results of a factor analysis of OM-519, to see the marked similarity of the "internal structure" of the scale in all six countries. This similarity of structure was revealed in the first instance by the fact that without exception the factor loadings were positive, and fell overwhelmingly in the narrow range from $+.25$ to $+.55$. This outcome was particularly striking because factor loadings so often vary greatly over their theoretical range from $+1.00$ through 0 to -1.00. Secondly, it is notable that the themes which had high or low loadings in one country tended to have similar standing in the others. For example, the subscale testing information had the highest loading in all countries. At the other pole, the measure of preference for urban industrial living was fairly consistently very low in rank, as was the measure of economic aspirations. These findings supported the conclusion that the general structure of individual modernity is basically alike in all six countries.

The Issue of Coherence Reexamined

The factor analysis we performed on the fifth series of OM scales permitted us to take a new approach to the problems of the coherence of the overall modernity scale, a problem which was a central issue in the preceding chapter. We there took the position that an underlying theme unites the elements of the syndrome of individual modernity, at least sufficiently to justify measuring that quality by reference to a single summary score. To make that statement was, in effect, to assert, in the language of factor analysis, that the various elements we built into the OM syndrome define a "common factor."

We considered the scale based on subthemes, namely 519, as the most appropriate for our purpose.[24] We then applied three standards for judging whether or not our data revealed the existence of a "common factor" underlying OM-519. Just as the criteria for acceptable scale reliabilities are not absolute, but rather are determined by convention, so are the standards used in judging the outcome of factor analysis. The standards we chose were selected on the basis of the experience of psychological testers, insofar as we judged that experience to be relevant to the instruments and procedures of our project. Since the standards were quite technical we have relegated their full discussion to a footnote for the specialist.[25] It must suffice here to point out that none of the 19 subthemes formed an exclusive separate factor, but rather that *all* tied nicely into the same main factor, which was not only of good size but relatively distinctive in its quality. In nontechnical language, we established that there was indeed a common factor one could quite reasonably take as delineating a general syndrome of individual modernity.[26] Moreover, we found that the common factor was virtually identical to what had already been constructed as the OM scale.[27]

The factor analysis thus provided significant additional justification for our decision to combine the different subthemes into one global summary measure characterizing each individual's *overall modernity*. The statistical tests we applied showed that this was not an arbitrary or unreasonable procedure which blindly counted unrelated things and summed them up as an artificial "x number of somethings." Although each of the different aspects of modernity we measured has its distinctive meaning, all the subthemes clearly share a common property which justifies their being combined in a summary measure expressing that commonality.[28]

Practical and Theoretical Implications

Our finding that the central element in OM is basically the same in all six countries has substantial implications, practical and theoretical.

At the theoretical level it suggests that certain personality syndromes are truly cross-national or transcultural. The nature of the human personality, its inner "rules" of organization, is very likely basically the same everywhere. The elements or components of personality do not, and we think in substantial degree cannot, vary randomly or even relatively freely with reference to one another. Rather, there seems to be a system of inner, or what might be called structural, constraints in the organization of the human personality. These structural constraints create a strong probability that an individual, whatever his culture, who has or acquires certain personality traits will be more likely also to have or acquire others which naturally "go with" one or another basic personality syndrome. This conclusion seems to us to follow from our evidence that the modern-man syndrome includes the same elements and has the same basic structure in our six different societies.

Our findings also indicate to us that when men from very different cultures are subject to basically the same set of situational pressures they are likely to undergo personality changes moving them, *in common*, toward certain specific new modes of psychic functioning. This part of our theory we will establish more fully in the analysis later in this book. We should note here, however, that it is this presumed propensity of men to change in certain regular ways under the influence of standardized social environments which formed the basis for our prediction that in all six countries, however diverse their cultures, men exposed to factory work and to other presumably modernizing milieus would become more modern individuals. Furthermore, this same propensity to change provided the basis for our assumption that in time the very content of personality will everywhere become more alike as the people in what are now very different cultures come more and more to experience similar life conditions.

At a more practical level, our finding that the core content of OM was basically the same in the different countries promised greatly to simplify our tasks of analysis and exposition in the rest of this book. If the core of the modernity syndrome had been markedly different in each country, we could not talk of "modernity" in general but would have been obliged to affix a national tag to the term modern whenever we used it. Moreover, whenever we sought to relate our measure of individual modernity to the independent variables, we would, in effect, have been relating those variables to something different in each country. If, then, the diverse modernity measures had responded differently to the standard independent variables in each country, we would have been unable to tell whether that was so because the modernity measures were different or because their relation to the independent variables had a truly special character in each country. Perhaps we would successfully have mastered this challenge, but only through an enormously complex analysis country by country. Even after having developed a measure of individual modernity which had basically the same content and structure in each country, we could not be sure that it would relate to the independent variables in the same way in all our six countries. If we had had to work with a measure of individual modernity having a different content in each country, there would have been only a very small probability of reaching any generalizations valid cross-nationally.

Summary

To sum up what we have done and discovered in these chapters on the construction and content of the OM scale we note the following:

1.   It proved possible reliably to characterize each individual more or less globally as relatively more modern or traditional by using the general or summary measure we called OM, an index based on answers to the whole range of attitude, value, information, and behavior questions used in our study.

2. That we constructed this summary measure should not be interpreted as meaning that we consider individual modernity to be unidimensional. On the contrary, our theoretical orientation strongly emphasizes that it is a multidimensional phenomenon. The statistical evidence available to us supported that theoretically derived assumption. No one of the several different aspects of modernity taken alone is even remotely adequate as a substitute for the set as a whole. In putting the themes together in a summary measure, all we assume is that the larger set has enough in common that an index combining them all more than adequately meets the technical standards set by psychologists who specialize in the measurement of general individual characteristics. We acknowledge that this combined index may not do full justice to the distinctiveness of each subtheme, but we are obliged to postpone such more detailed study of the separate themes for later analysis.[29]

3. The chief *theoretical* implication of the combined index is that it establishes the existence of a general quality of the personality which may reasonably be called individual modernity. The chief *practical* justification for using OM as a general index is that it greatly simplifies what would otherwise have been an inordinately, perhaps impossibly, complex task of analysis and presentation.

4. Several versions of the OM scale were constructed with different combinations of questions from our larger pool. That all had adequate reliability increased our confidence in the reasonableness of our procedure. One of these, a short form of the scale containing only 14 items, has great practical significance since it permits one to score men for modernity under field conditions in a matter of minutes. In general, however, the longer scales had higher reliability and were, therefore, most suitable for assessing the role of the different social factors we believed to be associated with individual modernity. The availability of these different versions of the OM scale promised to facilitate certain special types of analysis we will undertake later.

5. There were some personal attributes which the theory of our project staff, or others, had identified as presumably part of the syndrome of individual modernity but which nevertheless failed to legitimate their claim in our empirical investigation. They proved, at least by the standards we adopted, not to be part of the complex of qualities displayed by men who earned high scores on the general index of individual modernity. For example, modern men evidently are not outstanding in trust (as of merchants or relatives); they are not markedly less inclined to fulfill their obligations to kin than are the more traditional men in our study; and they are not decidedly more inclined to believe that endless striving for money and goods is desirable or brings happiness.

6. Despite these departures from the predictions of at least certain

experts, the modern type of man, as he emerged from the statistical testing of our empirical investigation, fit extremely well the "ideal-typical"
conception originally suggested by our theory. We identified some 24
major themes, ranging from "active citizenship" through to "women's
rights," each of which serves to differentiate significantly the more
modern man from the more traditional.

7.   Although certain characteristics — such as being well informed
and efficacious — were somewhat more central in defining who is a modern
man, no single theme so predominated as to be indispensable. Individual
modernity emerged as a truly general syndrome which manifested itself
in a wide variety of attitudes, values, and behavior in different realms of
interpersonal and social action.

8.   To a striking degree, what defines a man as modern in one country also defines him as such in other countries. By diverse tests we ascertained that the content and structure of the set of attitudes, values, and
behaviors which constitute the syndrome of individual modernity is basically the same in all six countries. This led to the conclusion that there is
not only a *potential* but, at least in one sense, an *actual* psychic unity in
mankind. Each culture gives its average man a profile of attitudes and
values different from that of men from other cultures. But in each society
there are selected types of men whose psychological propensities are
markedly like those of men from quite different cultures. Men who are
modern in one country would be recognized as modern men in other
countries. *The modern man is a cross-national, transcultural type who
can be identified by our scales whatever the distinctive attitudes with which
his culture may otherwise have endowed him.*

Having established these points, in particular having developed the OM
scale as a summary measure of individual modernity, we were in a position
to explore the forces which make men modern.

8

The Social Correlates of
Individual Modernity

However elegant its structure, a scale is pointless if it does not "work." In the first instance, it should effectively discriminate among individuals. We have already seen that the OM scale did that, and did so reliably. Within the limits of a maximum range from 0 to 100, the men in our sample earned scores all the way from a low of 6 to a high of 91 points.[1] Any scale which can do that is performing quite well in distinguishing one individual from another. Nevertheless, this accomplishment was not sufficient to support the claim that the OM scale met its objective.

Establishing the Validity of the OM Scale

To prove its worth a scale not only must distinguish one individual from another, but must do so *accurately*. The usual method for establishing the validity of a scale is to apply it to people whose characteristics are already known by some other independent criterion, which is why this approach is called the "criterion method of scale validation." If we were devising a test of psychic adjustment, for example, we might compare the scores of patients in a mental hospital with those of individuals whom psychiatrists had rated as well adjusted. If the scale was any good we would expect it correctly to identify the criterion group of hospital patients. Even the method of validation by a criterion group of "known" quality is full of vicissitudes, as the example just given will surely suggest. Our problem, however, was even more serious. There simply is no generally accepted external criterion by which we can certify a man to be modern.

Indeed, one objective of our project was precisely to establish who were the modern men.

Our theory of modernization offered a way out, but it also put us on the horns of a dilemma. The theory held that certain institutions and experiences have the capacity to change men in ways which make them more modern. We assumed that the more such experiences a man had been exposed to, the greater would be the degree of his individual modernity as expressed in his attitudes, values, and behavior. Therefore, if the OM scale was valid it should have assigned higher scores to men who had been much exposed to modernizing institutions and experiences. In other words, our theory indicated that we should take certain objective social characteristics as defining the external criteria by which to test the OM scale. Accordingly, those who were better educated, who worked in industry rather than agriculture, who lived in the city rather than the countryside, and who made above-average use of the mass media should have scored as more modern.

Although this sounded very plausible, we had good reason to hesitate before committing ourselves to this method for testing the validity of the OM scale. The proposed approach suffered from the defect that it assumed the correctness of the very theory we were attempting to test. We therefore faced the prospect of being confronted by a dilemma should we discover that individuals more exposed to modernizing experiences *failed* to score higher on the OM scale. We had to recognize that if such were the outcome we would be faced with two alternative explanations without being able to choose between them. One alternative would be to argue that the fault was in the OM scale. In other words, one might maintain that the institutions cited did actually change men in ways which made them more modern, but that the OM scale failed to reflect those changes. Adopting that explanation would imply that our theory of change had been correct, but the OM scale was invalid. The second alternative would be to assume that the OM scale was quite good at telling which men were truly modern, but that the institutions cited did not contribute to making them so. Adopting that interpretation would lead to the conclusion that the scale was valid, but that our theory about the causes of individual change had been incorrect.

Although we were distressed by the prospect of great ambiguity should the OM scores *fail* to be positively associated with modernizing experiences, we saw no alternative for establishing the validity of the scale. And we took comfort in the realization that should the OM scores indicate greater modernity among those more exposed to modernizing experiences, we would be a double winner. That result, we felt, would establish simultaneously that the OM scale was valid as judged by an external criterion *and* that increased exposure to modernizing institutions brought about greater individual modernity. Thus, our causal theory would be proved correct, and the scale established as valid, simultaneously.

An Index of Exposure to Modern Institutions

More readily to measure exposure to modernizing experiences we devised a simple summary index based on ten main independent variables, such as education and years of factory experience. With regard to each of these presumably modernizing experiences, those with little or no exposure were given a score of 1, those with intermediate contact a score of 2, 3, or 4. These "points" were summed across the ten variables, so that a man could have a summary score from 10 to 40. On the basis of these summary scores we divided the sample frequency into deciles, ranging from those having had least to those having had most contact with institutions and experiences presumed to have the capacity to modernize (Fig. 8–1).[2]

The incumbents of the lowest decile were, typically, farmers with little education, men without urban or factory experience, having a low standard of living, without much contact with the mass media, coming from traditional schools, and from homes in which the father had had little or no education. In the highest decile, the typical individual was a man who had all or almost all the presumed advantages; he had been relatively well educated, had a skilled and well-paying job in industry, came in very regular contact with the mass media, and so on. The rest of the sample was spread out between these extremes in one or another decile. In the middle ranges, men with the same score on the scale might have earned it on the basis of a different array of modernizing experiences. In other words, for this exploration we arbitrarily treated all modernizing experiences as equal in importance and, in a sense, as interchangeable.

Having thus arranged the men according to the degree of their contact with modernizing settings, we were in a position to ascertain what proportion of those in each decile scored "high" on OM.[3] The results were unambiguous and striking. The more men were exposed to what we defined as modernizing influences, the more likely they were to score high on our test of individual modernity. This pattern was found with marked regularity within each country, and with strict consistency across the six countries, as is evident in Fig. 8–1. Typically, only about 2 percent of those in the lowest decile on the experience index scored high on OM, whereas more than 76 percent of those in the top decile earned the designation of modern men. At the other end of the scale, as many as 97 percent of the men with the least contact with modernizing institutions were scored low on OM, whereas as few as 1 percent of those with multiple advantages were rated as traditional men. Summing up this experience in the form of a correlation coefficient, we found the median correlation between OM-

Figure 8–1. Percent modern by increasing levels of modernizing influences.(a)

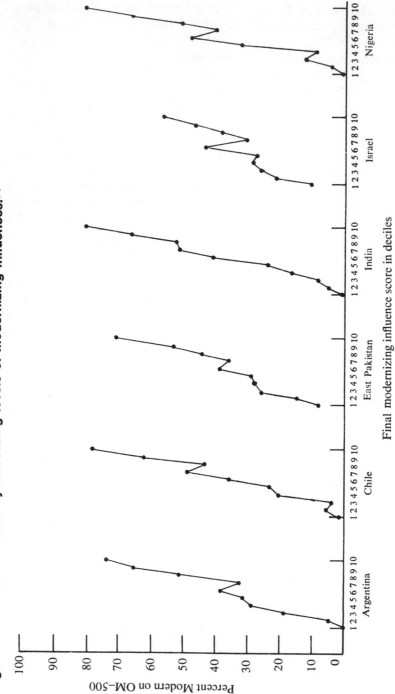

(a) Modern indicates a score in the top one-third of the frequency distribution on OM-500 in each country.

500 and the modern experience scale to be, for all subjects, a robust .63, significant well above the .001 level.[4] Although there was some variation from one country to the next, the same basic pattern was manifest in all, as reflected in the close bunching and the persistent sharp upward thrust of the graph lines for all six countries in Fig. 8–1. In all six countries there was strong evidence that the OM scale effectively identified as modern the men we had expected to be so on the basis of their objective social characteristics.[5]

Men who had experienced none of the modernizing forces fell almost entirely into the category of those low on OM. Among the men who had enjoyed as many as ten forms of modernizing experience, very few, never more than 8 percent, displayed the attitudes and values we defined as traditional. This is as good a performance as one can expect of any current psychosocial test, even those used mainly in the developed nations.[6] It is even more impressive if we take into account that we were working within a narrow range of social differentiation. The OM scale's capacity to discriminate would have been considered highly satisfactory even if we had been working with a much wider range of educational and occupational experience, such as one would obtain in a more heterogeneous representative national sample. The fact that the OM scale worked so well within the limits of a relatively homogeneous sample, representing only a modest part of the actual range of educational and occupational experience, marked the scale as a highly sensitive instrument.

The effect of modernizing experiences on the individual may also be expressed directly by giving actual OM scores. In general, each step up the ladder on the exposure scale found the group located there to have a higher average OM score than that on the rung below. In the median case, those in the lowest decile had an OM score of 44, those in the highest decile, 65. In this median case, each step up the ladder of exposure meant a gain of approximately 2⅓ points on the OM scale. In the extreme case, that of India, the mean OM score increased from 42 to 75, a gain of 3⅔ points per step.

A glance back at the results previously presented makes it evident that the gap separating those with none and those with as many as ten modernizing experiences seems less dramatic when it is expressed in terms of mean OM scores than it is when expressed in terms of the percentage "high" on modernity. This should be kept in mind in approaching results to be presented later in this book. When we say one group has an average OM score 3 points higher than another group, that may not sound like very much, especially on a scale which is thought to run from 0 to 100. To think exclusively in those terms can be misleading. Even taking into account all the modernizing experiences we measured, the greatest gap between the groups (as against the individuals) most and least exposed to modernization was 33 points on the OM scale, and in the median case it was only some 21 points. If, then, at a later stage in our analysis, we should say, as we will, that getting an additional year of education moves a group as much as 2 points up on the OM scale, that statement should be understood as indicating that it moved them not 2 percent but rather closer to 10 percent of the distance it effectively could have moved them. In other words, when we take into account the actual calibration of our scale, a 2-point gain is certainly worth noting and a 3-point gain is substantial, especially if these gains occurred under conditions in which other variables were simultaneously controlled.

Objectives for Further Analysis

Having established that the OM scale met the test of validity by an external criterion, we had the necessary precondition for pressing ahead with our investigation. We knew that having many modernizing experiences went with being modern in attitude, value, and behavior. Yet, while acknowledging that the outcome could, theoretically, have been different, we never seriously believed that it would. The main concern of our project was to go beyond this global finding to more refined analysis. Although the summary index of exposure to modernizing experiences served a useful purpose, it also covered up distinctions in which we had a particular interest. When using the index we had no way of knowing which of the numerous measures built into it were strongly associated with individual modernity and which weakly, or not at all. In constructing the experience index we arbitrarily treated all the modernizing settings as if they were of equal importance. In fact, some may have contributed substantially to the individual OM scores, but others may have helped little or none at all.

Indeed, the simple (zero-order) correlations of the ten variables built into our experience index suggested, in Table 8–1, that the contribution of the different modernizing experiences was probably far from equal. Education and mass media were strongly and consistently correlated with individual OM scores, whereas the rated modernity of a man's home and school milieu related inconsistently, and generally weakly, with OM. These facts pointed to a series of analysis tasks which still lay ahead of us.

First, we wanted to be sure that the observed association between any given life experience and individual modernity was truly independent, and not merely an artifact of the association between the variable measured and some other variable having the true power to influence the individual. Second, we had to clarify the causal connection between various presumably modernizing institutions, on the one hand, and individual modernity, on the other. Third, we wanted to know the relation to individual modernity of variables not included in the set of ten used to construct our index of exposure to modernizing experiences.

Table 8–1. Correlations of ten independent variables with OM-500[a]

Variable	Argentina	Chile	East Pakistan	India	Israel	Nigeria
1. Formal education	.60***	.51***	.41***	.71***	.44***	.52***
2. Months factory experience	.24***	.36***	.26***	.11**	.26***	.29***
3. Objective skill	.34***	.25***	.24***	.33***	.23***	.23***
4. Mass-media exposure	.43***	.46***	.36***	.55***	.42***	.43***
5. Number of factory benefits	.09*	.13***	.10**	.25***	.17***	.28***
6. Years of urban experience since age 15	.35***	.37***	.20***	−.02	—	.22**
7. Urbanism of residence	.45***	—	.11**	.25***	−.01	.36***
8. Modernity of home-school setting	.11**	.22***	.01	.26***	.01	.02
9. Father's education	.33***	.33***	.21***	.42***	.02	.17***
10. Consumer goods possessed	.44***	.35***	.35***	.38***	.17***	.42***
N for variables 1, 4, 7, 8, 9, 10	817	929	943	1198	739	721
N for variables 2, 3, 5	663	715	654	700	544	520
N for variable 6	239	305	654	700	—	184

[a] Asterisks denote significance as follows: *, at .05 level; **, at .01 level; ***, at .001 level or better.

These three additional tasks of analysis did not exhaust but rather merely illustrated the job yet to be done in coming to understand the forces which make men modern. Before launching that analysis, however, it is necessary that we explain the procedures on which it will be based.

The Nature of our Method

In Part III of our book we present a set of chapters, each focused on a single major independent variable such as education, occupational experience, mass-media exposure, or home and school modernity. Each variable so studied has been identified in some popular theory as defining a social context which should, in its own right, produce more modern men. However, there is often a complex pattern of association linking these variables. We have noted, for example, that the location of most factories in cities and towns meant that for every year he was in the factory, the average worker also gained a year of urban experience. Men who grew up in rural areas generally got less schooling than those who were raised in cities; workers usually have more education than farmers; some ethnic groups are more inclined to go into handicraft work than others, and so on. These social patterns result in a complex array of statistically significant intercorrelations among the various background variables. Table 8–2 reports the facts, limited to Argentina to economize space. However, much the same picture was presented by the data for the other five countries.

Given these patterns, any measure of exposure to a particular institution could have a spuriously high correlation with individual modernity. Both for scientific understanding of the process of individual change and as a basis for sound public policy, we had to try to disentangle these influences to discover which forces are truly independent causes of individual modernity, and which only *seem* to be so because of their accidental association with the true causes. We were faced with a series of linkages such as that of city life with factory experience, of parental background with a man's own education, of an ethnic group's cultural heritage with the particular occupation that heritage led a man to take up. We wanted to know — indeed, for purposes of soundly establishing public policy we must know — whether an independent contribution to individual modernization is made by one or the other member of these pairs of presumed causes, or, as the case may be, by both.

In most of our samples, the qualities we preferred to study in relatively pure form were in fact thoroughly mixed up with the other characteristics of the men interviewed. A major task of our analysis program, therefore, was to find methods which would permit us to disentangle the diverse influences which had acted on each group of men.

The technique most commonly applied by sociologists toward that end is a multiple cross-tabulation in which one or more variables considered extraneous by the researcher are "controlled" while the analyst examines the relation between the two variables which are the real object of interest to him. Although this procedure has served for many years as an aid to sociological analysis, its inadequacy has been increasingly manifest.[7]

In place of the more conventional cross-tabulation we utilized several techniques to test the degree to which any form of social experience might be a truly independent influence in shaping individual modernity. One we relied on quite heavily is a special procedure we call the matching technique. By this means men were matched to be statistically indistinguishable in a large number of characteristics whose influence we wished to control, while being different on the one variable whose independent influence we wished to assess. Thus, when we wished to test the

Table 8–2. Intercorrelations of ten independent variables, for Argentina.[a,b]

Variable	1	2	3	4	5	6	7	8	9	10
1. Formal education	1.00									
2. Months factory experience	.01	1.00								
3. Objective skill	.35***	.35***	1.00							
4. Mass-media exposure	.27***	.19***	.11**	1.00						
5. Number of factory benefits	.07	.02	.08*	.05	1.00					
6. Years of urban experience since age 15	.01	.71***	.25***	.25***	.09	1.00				
7. Urbanism of residence	.34***	−.03	.07	.33***	−.03	.00	1.00			
8. Modernity of home-school setting	.11**	−.01	.00	.10**	.01	−.06	.07*	1.00		
9. Father's education	.36***	−.01	.16***	.18***	.00	.15*	.26***	.01	1.00	
10. Consumer goods possessed	.40***	.23***	.25***	.30***	.04	.36***	.32***	.10**	.26**	1.00

[a] Asterisks denote significance as follows: *, at .05 level; **, at .01 level; ***, at .001 level or better.
[b] The minimum N upon which these correlations are based is 662 except for variable 6, for which the minimum N is 220.

influence of occupation, we started with two pools of men, one all farmers, the other all factory workers. Each farmer was then matched to a worker who was like him in all the respects we considered important enough to require us to control for their influence. Typically, men were matched to be alike in education, ethnicity, religion, urban or rural origin, father's education, income, modernity of home and school background, contact with mass media, skill, age, and marital status. Since the resultant sets of men were alike in all important respects save one, in this case occupation, any difference in their modernity score could unambiguously be attributed to the influence of the match variable without fear that the outcome was a spurious effect produced by the influence of other uncontrolled factors.[8]

To find men who were reasonably closely matched was a slow and demanding procedure, although we in time discovered how to have the computer do it for us.[9] Since we knew exactly which men entered into each match set, our analysis was much less a blind procedure than are most statistical methods. We could almost see the machinery at work. The method did, however, have its drawbacks as well. For one thing, the rigorous requirements of the matching procedure often left us with a very small number of cases. Consequently, the reliability of the statistical results yielded by the matched groups was often uncertain. Differences between the groups could qualify as statistically significant only when they were quite large. Moreover, the requirements of matching sometimes led to the selection of sets of men who were rather unrepresentative of their fellow workers as a whole.

Every method of analysis has its inherent limitations. Nevertheless, to decrease the chances that the distinctive properties of the matching procedure might somehow systematically mislead us, we supplemented it whenever possible by at least one other method. That which we use quite regularly in the next set of chapters is the method of partial correlation, a method which is, especially compared to matching, a relatively conventional procedure. Like the matches, partial correlations can control simultaneously, or "hold constant," a whole series of peripheral influences while allowing the examination of two variables at the center of one's interest. Unlike the matching procedure, the partial-correlation technique takes into account information available for *all* the sample, rather than being limited to a specially selected subset. It has the disadvantage, however, that it is a relatively blind technique. It rests on a complex set of statistical assumptions and, once results are obtained, it is difficult to ascertain exactly what lay behind the outcome.

Matching and partial correlations, while logically analogous, rest on quite different procedures and statistical assumptions. We felt, therefore, that whenever the results yielded by the two methods were in agreement, we could take that as strong ground indeed for reaching certain conclusions. Insofar as the outcomes did not agree, however, we faced the prospect of substantial ambiguity in deciding which method, if either, to rely on. Happily, as we shall see, there were few instances in which we had to make a choice; the two methods agreed remarkably throughout the analysis.

With both the matching and the partial-correlation techniques, one runs the risk of what has come to be called "the partialing fallacy."[10] One can easily fall into this error by inadvertently including in the set of control variables one which is essentially a duplicate, or functional substitute, of that whose independent influence one wishes to assess. To choose a flagrant case, if one wished to assess the influence of years of schooling, but included among the variables controlled "highest grade attended," the outcome most probably would be to make schooling appear as a variable powerless to explain anything. This would, however, be a spurious result, an artifact of the particular statistical method and the way in which it was being used.

In less glaring instances of redundancy, the partialing fallacy is nevertheless easily committed. Take, for example, the complex of variables: length of factory experience, skill level, and income. Clearly these are measures of quite different things. Nevertheless, there is a strong probability that men who are in the factory longer will gain in skill and will consequently earn more. If one were testing the independent effect of factory experience on modernity, but simultaneously controlled for skill level and income, one would, to a degree, be committing the partialing fallacy.[11] Of course, certain analysts are interested precisely in disentangling the relative contribution of each of these aspects of occupational experience, and there are special methods which permit one to make some progress toward that goal. We use the methods of regression analysis and path analysis in Chapter 20 to achieve a similar end.

In the chapters immediately following, however, we are mainly concerned with assessing how far the various presumed causes of individual modernity qualify, each in turn, as truly independent factors. The method we use makes it very important that we be on guard against the partialing fallacy. We have been highly aware of the issue, and throughout the analysis have endeavored to give full details concerning the variables controlled. We also undertake to approach the data in a variety of different ways so as to minimize the dangers of being prisoner of any single method.

Contexts and Causes of Modernization

9

The School as a Context
for Modernization

In large-scale complex societies no attribute of the person predicts his attitudes, values, and behavior more consistently or more powerfully than the amount of schooling he has received. Almond and Verba echoed the experience of numerous other students of social structure when they reported in their five-nation study that "among the demographic variables usually investigated — sex, place of residence, occupation, income, age and so on — none compares with the educational variable in the extent to which it seems to determine political attitudes."[1] In the light of this experience we considered it an essential test of the soundness both of our conception of individual modernity and of OM as a scale that scores on it be significantly related to measures of education.

Schooling and OM Scores

For the total sample, the OM scale met this test and did so smartly, yielding strong or robust correlations with education in each country as follows: Argentina, .59; Chile, .51; East Pakistan, .41; India, .71; Israel, .44; and Nigeria, .52.[2] In the everyday experience of those working with attitude surveys, correlations of this size are seldom attained, and not often exceeded, even with samples covering the full range of education.[3] Ours, by comparison, included only a limited segment of that range, since most of our subjects had less than 8 years of schooling.[4]

Typically, fewer than 10 percent of the men with the least education were classified as modern, that is, had OM-500 scores in the upper third of the distribution (Table 9–1). By contrast, of the men whose education was the highest in their country sample, some 80 percent or more

Table 9-1.   Percent high on OM-500[a] for increasing amounts of education.[b]

Years of Education	Argentina	Chile	East Pakistan	India	Israel	Nigeria
0	—	—	17 (394)	2 (299)	—	—
1	—	—	32 (75)	0 (13)	—	—
2	—	4 (56)	35 (95)	9 (44)	—	—
3	2 (48)	8 (119)	43 (96)	11 (62)	20 (20)	—
4	9 (91)	22 (135)	41 (112)	16 (51)	12 (73)	9 (34)
5	8 (91)	16 (130)	50 (101)	21 (75)	23 (77)	3 (34)
6	26 (93)	42 (376)	67 (60)	27 (48)	24 (102)	9 (123)
7	41 (381)	56 (25)	59 (32)	19 (108)	10 (39)	21 (159)
8	60 (15)	72 (32)	69 (36)	28 (54)	34 (306)	43 (320)
9	84 (19)	89 (27)	—	41 (61)	42 (31)	—
10	90 (31)	100 (13)	—	55 (182)	69 (51)	90 (10)
11	88 (16)	—	—	77 (303)	85 (20)	80 (25)
12	—	—	—	—	81 (16)	—
13	100 (11)	—	—	—	—	—

a "High on OM-500" means a score in the top one-third of the frequency distribution within eac country.
b Numbers in parentheses are values of N upon which the percentages are based; a dash means tha fewer than ten men are at that level of education in our sample.

were commonly rated modern. In between, each step up the education ladder generally brought with it a fairly regular and substantial increment in the proportion of modern men.[5] Moreover, this tendency was consistently manifested in each country, regardless of the segment of the educational range it represented. It was evident both in the East Pakistan sample, in which the typical man had only 2 years of schooling, and in Argentina, where he had 7. This can be shown most clearly by expressing each individual's level of modernity and education as standard scores. When this was done, as in Fig. 9–1, the line reflecting the relation of individual modernity to increasing education had a remarkably similar slope in all six countries despite the fact that the educational range in each was quite different. Taken together, these findings indicate that education was a prime factor in determining the level of a man's modernity.

Although this first result was very encouraging, we wanted to be sure that schooling was a truly independent contributor to modernization. The amount of schooling a man has is usually intimately tied to his other social characteristics. Urban children generally have more opportunity for schooling than rural residents; wealthier parents, and those themselves well educated, are likely to keep their children in school longer; certain ethnic groups value education greatly and see that their children get more of it; men in highly skilled jobs generally have more education,

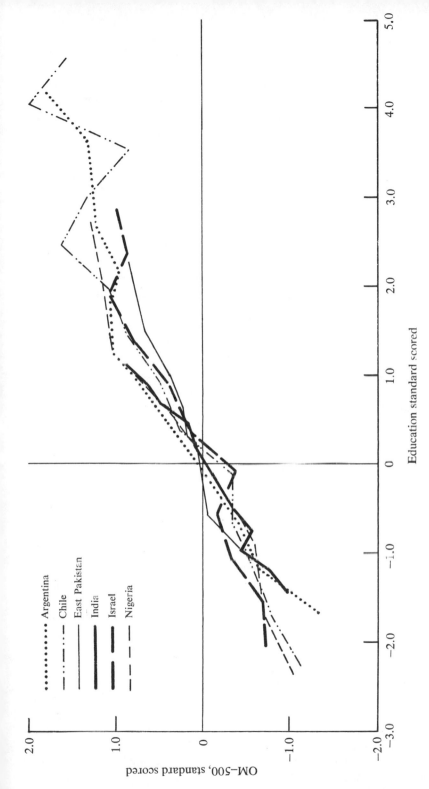

Figure 9–1. The relation of standardized scores on education and individual modernity (OM-500).

and so on. Insofar as these social attributes are also strongly correlated with education, their cumulative influence, rather than education per se, could have been the real explanation for individual modernity. To test this possibility we consulted evidence from both the matches and partial correlations.[6] In this analysis we rely mainly on the factory workers, as our largest group and the one in which we were particularly interested.[7]

We were not surprised to find that when we controlled for the influence of important variables with which education is closely linked, most notably mass media, the strength of the correlation of education and modernity was brought down. Nevertheless, as is evident in Table 9–2, the partial correlations of education and modernity were generally strong, whatever the combination of other variables controlled in the partialing process. When other early socialization factors — such as father's education, rural origin, and ethnicity — were simultaneously partialed out, education still produced the very respectable median correlation of .40 with modernity.[8] When later-life attributes — in particular factory experience, mass-media contact, living standards, urbanism of residence, and modernity of work place — were brought under statistical control, education still performed well, yielding a median correlation of .40. Indeed, even when the ten variables in our basic Set A (Appendix C) were taken into account, education still yielded a median partial correlation with modernity of .34, and all were significant at better than the .001 level.[9] These figures tell us that the originally observed high correlation between education and modernity was to some extent an artifact of the link between men's education and other social characteristics such as their occupation, origin, or mass-media exposure. The evidence lies in the fact that the controls applied in Set A reduced considerably the variance explained by the simple correlation. Yet the fact that education so well survived a quite rigorous process of partial correlation also tells us that it was, in its own right, a very powerful *direct* and independent factor in determining men's modernity.

The match (Table 9–3) confirmed the conclusion reached through partial correlation. The match created two sets of factory workers, one with "less" and the other with "more" education.[10] Each education pair, however, was selected to be statistically indistinguishable on nine other variables, such as mass-media exposure, factory experience, and religion.[11] Despite the large number of variables thus controlled, the median correlation between individual modernity and educational ranking was strong, at .38, and the figure was significant at better than the .01 level in most of the countries. Among the "less" educated men the median proportion qualifying as modern was 13 percent, whereas among the "more" educated it was 49 percent. Again we had powerful evidence of the direct and independent contribution which education makes to individual modernity.[12]

To give the most concrete form to our measure of the effectiveness of education, we computed the number of points on the OM scale a man gained for every additional year in school.[13] In effect, this treated the OM scale as if it were an achievement test of the kind commonly used to

Table 9–2. Correlations of education and OM-500 for factory workers.[a]

Correlation	Argentina	Chile	East Pakistan	India	Israel	Nigeria
Simple (zero-order)	.55	.50	.44	.68	.48	.42
Partial, controlling for—						
Mass media	.49	.45	.32	.54	.40	.35
Factory experience	.56	.51	.42	.70	.47	.38
Mass media and factory experience	.51	.46	.33	.55	.38	.32
Early socialization	.39	.38	.37	.61	.47	.41
Late socialization	.45	.44	.28	.54	.35	.26
Set A (early and late socialization)	.34	.33	.27	.52	.37	.24
N	663	715	654	700	544	520

[a] All correlations are significant at better than the .001 level.

Table 9–3. Modernity of otherwise matched groups differentiated as having more or less education.

Modernity measure	Argentina	Chile	East Pakistan	India	Israel	Nigeria
Percent modern[a] among group with—						
Less education	16%	7%	29%	5%	44%	10%
More education	32%	43%	48%	70%	72%	50%
Mean OM score of group with—						
Less education	50	53	50	53	59	54
More education	54	60	57	71	67	61
Match correlation (Match 36Mb)[b]	.24*	.35**	.31**	.74***	.42**	.40**
N[c]	19	28	21	20	25	30

[a] "Modern" indicates a score in the top one-third of the frequency distribution on OM-500, in each country.
[b] Indicates the correlation of OM score of each man with his classification on the match variable: for "less education" and 2 for "more education." Asterisks denote significance as follows: *, at .05 level; **, at .01 level; ***, at .001 level or better.
[c] Figures given are the number of pairs in the match.

assess progress in school. Indeed, the OM scale can be viewed as measuring some kind of social capacity or skill.

While simultaneously controlling for the effect of a large number of
additional variables by strict matching, we found, in Table 9–4, that
men gained 1.8 points on the OM scale for every additional year of
schooling, whereas the most rigorous regression analysis placed the gain
at 1.7.[14] Since holding constant so many other variables might have
introduced some artificial constraints, we also computed the point gains
with fewer controls. The effect was, predictably, to give more credit to
the influence of schooling. When we controlled only for factory experience
and one other key variable, the gain for each additional year of education
rose to 2.1 OM points with the matching technique and to 1.9 for the
regression analysis.[15] Clearly the two methods gave broadly similar results, increasing our confidence in the reliability of these estimates. Just
as people presumably improved their scores on arithmetic and vocabulary
tests for each year in school, just so did our men improve their overall
modernity score by approximately 2 points per year of schooling.

At the observed rate of gain in OM scores, how well was the school
doing in modernizing men? In part, the answer is that the school did
less than it might have. Across our six countries, the median gap between
the highest and lowest scorers on the OM–500 was 64 points. If we
assume that a complete education takes 16 years, and that a man with
such an education should get the highest OM score, it follows that it would
take a gain of about 4 points per year to carry a man from the lowest to
the highest standing in modernity as he moved through his schooling.

Table 9–4.   Point gains on OM-500 per additional year of schooling for factory workers.

Type of control	Argentina	Chile	East Pakistan	India	Israel	Nigeria	Median
Strict matching[a]	1.3	2.0	1.4	2.0	1.6	2.9	1.8
Regression controlling 10 variables (Set A)[b]	1.7	1.7	1.1	1.6	1.8	1.5	1.7
Match with few controls[c]	2.8	2.2	1.6	1.6	2.0	2.3	2.1
Regression controlling only factory experience and mass media	2.4	2.2	1.3	1.6	1.8	1.9	1.9

a Match 36Mb was used, as in Table 9–3.
b For variables controlled in Set A, see Appendix C.
c For variables controlled in this match see note 15.

But our results indicate that — from their schooling alone — men gained only about 2 points per year.

However, to call on the school to produce the optimum gain of some 4 OM points per year would be to ask it alone to produce an outcome which we know was in reality the result of a substantial number of other modernizing experiences working cumulatively. As we saw in Chapter 8, the men who earned the highest score on OM had not only had the highest education, but also the most factory experience, the greatest contact with the mass media, and so on through a large set of other advantages. To say that every additional year of school produced less than half as much gain in OM score as would have resulted if education were the sole explanation of modernity comes close to saying that almost half a man's OM score was determined by his education alone.[16] Taken all together, therefore, the evidence argues that the school in developing countries, for all its presumed defects, is surely one of the most powerful means of inculcating modern attitudes, values, and behavior.

The Theory of Educational Effects

If education had not played this role we would have been distressed and surprised — distressed because it would have suggested that the OM scale was a failure, and surprised because we expected education to be a good predictor of individual modernity. Indeed, when we described our work in progress to various audiences, our expectation concerning the prominent role education would play generally aroused the least resistance. Almost everyone accepted the idea that education should modernize, but virtually no one asked why it should have that effect. Yet, what everyone took for granted was not at all obvious on grounds of logic.

Had the OM scale tested people on subjects constituting part of the typical school curriculum, that fact might have provided an obvious explanation for the high correlation of education and modernity. Yet the content of OM and of the school curriculum overlapped only with regard to measures of verbal fluency and the information questions which tapped knowledge of geography, public figures, and consumer goods. Moreover, by using OM-1 we could control the possible influence of such questions, because that form of the modernity scale tested attitudes and values only. Nevertheless, OM-1 *also* showed a very strong relation to education, with a median correlation of .36, a figure significant beyond the .001 level, and one which held that level of significance under partial correlation. It was clear, therefore, that one could not account for the higher OM scores of the better-educated men on the grounds that the formal curriculum of the school *directly* prepared for high performance on our test of modernity. Even when our measure of modernity excluded any test of information or verbal fluency, the fields in which the formal curriculum specializes, education still showed as a substantial independent cause of individual modernity.

Indeed, we know of no curriculum which provides significant *formal* instruction in how to join public organizations, to be open to new experience, to value birth control, or to develop a sense of personal efficacy, to name but a few of the themes measured by the OM scale. Since the men who received more education displayed these qualities in greater degree, there must have been a good deal of learning in the school *incidental* to the curriculum and to formal instruction in academic subjects. As children in school these men not only learned geography and acquired skills in reading and arithmetic; they evidently also learned new attitudes and values, and developed new dispositions to act, whose full significance would not be manifest until they were adults.

Of course, since we tested individuals only after they reached adulthood, we cannot say for certain that the modernity to which education evidently contributed was already manifest in them at the time the better-educated men left school. We assume that in good part it was, and have been confirmed in that assumption by evidence from other studies.[17] It is, however, not necessary to insist on the point. We are equally comfortable with the assumption that in many areas schooling merely laid the ground–work which made it possible for later life experience to give concrete content to a more general disposition established in childhood. This would seem the more likely sequence for something like the readiness to accept birth-control methods, which surely was not dealt with in most schools, whether directly or indirectly.

Mechanisms of Learning

But what are the mechanisms by which the school inculcates the attitudes and values, teaches the psychosocial dispositions, and trains in the behavior we define as modern? We believe that the answer lies mainly in the distinctive nature of the school as a social organization, something which has little to do with the curriculum as such. In our view, the school is not only a place for teaching; it is, inevitably, a setting for the more general socialization of the child. The school modernizes through a number of processes other than formal instruction in academic subjects. These are: *reward and punishment, modeling, exemplification,* and *generalization.*

These learning processes are not unique to the school. They occur in other formal organizations, and also in informal settings such as the family or the play group. However, the special nature of any organization gives distinctive form and content to the socialization process which goes on within it. We may illustrate the point by considering several of the OM themes individually. Since our purpose here is not to present an exhaustive analysis, but rather merely to illustrate an approach, we shall discuss most of the modernity themes only with reference to one or at most two of the socialization processes in the school. This should *not* be taken to mean that there is *a simple one-to-one correspondence between any one theme and any one process.* On the contrary, we believe that any one feature of the school as a social system may influence the child's development with regard to several themes relevant to the definition of individual modernity. Moreover, several socialization processes may be involved in the acquisition of any one of the attitudes, values, and modes of behaving relevant to defining individual modernity.

Consider first the acquisition of a sense of efficacy, which is one of the central elements in the personal profile of the modern man. In the acquisition of this feeling, *generalization* plays a substantial role. Generalization occurs when an individual enjoys so satisfying an experience in one specific relationship or performance that he is led to believe that he can attain comparable success in other contexts. Having mastered one or more specific skills, he comes to believe in his general capacity to acquire skills; having solved some problems, he may come to have confidence in his ability to solve others.

Before coming to school, children have already enjoyed mastering certain fundamental skills, notably walking and talking, feeding oneself, and sphincter control. If school did not intervene, however, there would usually be a lull until adolescence provided them new opportunities for mastery in hunting or farming, sex, or combat. For those who attend school, this interim can be filled with important new opportunities for mastery, learning to read, to write, and to figure being the most fundamental and perhaps the most rewarding. Each of these skills opens up new opportunities for increasingly competent behavior. The child who learns to read his schoolbooks later finds himself able to read directions and instructions and to follow events in the newspaper. The boy who learns his arithmetic can later assume more complex responsibilities on the farm or in the factory. By extension and diffusion, or what we have called generalization, a heightened general sense of personal efficacy results.

What the child learns in school about planning illustrates the process of *exemplification.* By exemplification we refer to the process whereby the individual incorporates into himself not a personal model but *an impersonal rule or general practice* characteristic of the social organization or institution as such.

School starts and stops at fixed times each day. Within the school day there generally is a regular sequence for ordering activities: singing, reading, writing, drawing, all have their scheduled and usually invariant times. Teachers generally work according to a plan, a pattern they are rather rigorously taught at normal school. The pupils may have no direct knowledge of the plan, but its influence palpably pervades the course of their work through school day and school year. Thus, principles directly embedded in the daily routine of the school teach the virtue of planning ahead and the importance of maintaining a regular schedule. The principle of planning may, of course, also be inculcated more directly through *reward and punishment,* as when pupils are punished for being late, marked down for not getting their papers in on time, and held after school for infractions of the rules. Moreover, application of the principle need not be limited to the context of the school, but may later be diffused to other settings.

By *modeling* we mean the child's incorporation into his own role repertoire of the ways of behaving, feeling, and thinking which he observes in significant and powerful *persons* in his milieu. It is the imitation of a person, as against the incorporation of a rule of organization, which distinguishes modeling from exemplification. In the school the most notable model is, of course, the teacher.

Modeling may be seen at work in various ways. When a teacher listens attentively to, and takes seriously, the suggestions of the children, he serves as a model of sensitivity to the feelings of subordinates and of openness to new ideas. If he is careful to keep his personal preferences from influencing grading, and gives marks in accord with objective performance, the teacher serves as a model of "universalism" or distributive justice. For such modeling to occur it is not necessary that the individual child be directly reinforced by rewards for his behavior, as in getting praised for having new ideas or helping younger children. Modeling is presumed to work because the greater visibility and influence of the teacher lead to incorporation of the behavior he manifests, even when he is mainly interacting with persons other than the learner. It is a process more like imprinting or introjection.

Limits on Effective Learning

The modernizing outcomes sketched above are not necessarily produced in every classroom. They represent developments which can, and often do, occur, but which are by no means inevitable. Some teachers make fun of children, humiliate, and even beat them. This hardly serves as a model of respect for the dignity and feelings of subordinates and people weaker than you are. Teachers may have favorites for whom they show every preference, not only in personal matters, but also by overlooking errors on presumably objective tests in arithmetic and spelling. Such behavior will hardly inculcate faith in distributive justice. Similarly, a teacher who gives substantial evidence of being superstitious, who shows her anxiety about witches and the evil eye, cannot make a very convincing case for the relevance of science to daily life. One who is rigid, compulsive, and doctrinaire is not likely to stimulate openness to new ideas, and so on.

Just as the teacher may lack the qualities making her an appropriate model of modernity, so may the school fail to exemplify the organizational principles we identify with the modern mode. The flow of work in the classroom may be chaotic, the school day subject to constant disruption, the annual schedule erratic, and the very continuance of the school uncertain. Such a school will not effectively exemplify the virtues of planning and will provide little training in developing fixed schedules. Moreover, either the conditions of a pupil's life outside, or the nature of the school itself, may lead his school experience to be one of continuous frustration, failure, and rejection. Insofar as this pupil generalizes from his school experience, therefore, it will hardly be by way of feeling more efficacious or more open to new experience.

Conclusion

To acknowledge that there are deficient schools and teachers, even to allow that they may be extremely common in developing countries, does not fundamentally challenge our theory. Emphasizing the common shortcomings of the school and the teacher makes us aware of how much more effective schools might be, but it does not follow that the school, imperfect as it may be, is without any effect in inculcating individual modernity. Our data show unambiguously that the schools in each of our six developing countries, flawed as they undoubtedly were, clearly had a substantial effect on the pupils exposed to their influence. Their pupils did learn. Furthermore, they learned more than reading, writing, and figuring. Our tests show that they also learned values, attitudes, and ways of behaving highly relevant to their personal development and to the future of their countries. Those who had been in school longer were not only better informed and verbally more fluent. They had a different sense of time, and a stronger sense of personal and social efficacy; participated more actively in communal affairs; were more open to new ideas, new experiences, and new people; interacted differently with others, and showed more concern for subordinates and minorities. They valued science more, accepted change more readily, and were more prepared to limit the number of children they would have. In short, by virtue of having had more formal schooling, their personal character was decidedly more modern.[18]

10

Modernity and the Mass Media

The wide diffusion of the media of mass communication is one of the best indicators of advanced economic development. This fact is patently evident not only when we contrast the new nations with the older industrial countries such as the U. S. and Britain, but equally when we compare nations within the same part of the developing world, such as Asia. In 1960 Japan had a per capita income almost five times that of India. In that same year Japan could boast of distributing 396 newspapers per thousand of population, India only 11. Overall, measures of per capita income and per capita availability of the means of mass communication correlate at above .80.[1] Moreover, the "consumption" of news and the other messages disseminated by the mass media seems to rise markedly before the rise in consumption of other "goods" typically in great demand in developed countries.[2]

The fact that the more developed *countries* have more fully elaborated mass communication suggests, but does not prove, that *individuals* more exposed to such communication are likely to become more modern.[3] The media of mass communication, being mechanical instruments, are quite neutral as to the nature of the message they disseminate. They may be used to reinforce traditional sentiments as effectively as they transmit new ideas. Thus, a fundamentalist church in the "Bible belt" of America is as likely to use the airwaves to spread its message as is the local populist political party bent on economic and social reform.

Even if the media carry a high proportion of material which might be thought of as unambiguously "modernizing," audiences have a remarkable capacity to approach this material selectively. People pay attention mainly to what they want to hear and see, filtering out that part of the message they find too foreign or too likely to conflict with their inherited traditions and established beliefs. Mass communication may, therefore, be much less effective in bringing about fundamental changes in attitudes and values than many imagine. Indeed, after reviewing hundreds of studies of the presumed effect of the mass media in the more developed countries Joseph Klapper concluded: "Mass communication *ordinarily* does not serve as a necessary and sufficient cause of audience effects, but rather functions among and through a nexus of mediating factors and influences."[4]

Despite Klapper's sober conclusion, many people assume that one could easily mobilize a great volume of evidence to prove that with increasing exposure to the mass media men become increasingly modern. Surprisingly enough, the facts were not systematically documented in the classic studies of individual modernization by Lerner, Kahl, or Almond and Verba.[5] We considered it particularly important, therefore, to use our data to test the strength of the relation between mass-media contact and individual modernity.

Media Contact and OM Scores

To summarize each individual's contact with the media of mass communication we constructed a simple index giving equal weight to radio listening and newspaper reading. The result was a seven-step scale which permitted us to rank each man on a ladder from low to high exposure. At the one extreme were the men who said they *never* listened to the radio or got news from a newspaper; at the other end were those who listened to the radio and got news from the newspaper every day.[6] Since the extent of literacy and the availability of radios varied greatly from country to country, many more men were at the high end of the mass-media scale in Argentina and Israel than in India or Pakistan. But we adjusted for this inequality of opportunity by using a different standard to define "much" and "little" contact with the mass media for each country (Table 10–1).

Using the mass-media scale we found a fairly regular and strong relation between exposure to mass communications and individual modernity. With few exceptions, the basic pattern was for each increase in mass-media contact to be associated with an increase in OM score. In Argentina, for example, those who almost never listened to the radio or got news from the press showed only 4 percent scoring high on the overall measure of individual modernity, those who occasionally read a paper or tuned in produced 14 percent of modern men, whereas among those who listened to the radio and got news from a newspaper every day the proportion of modern men rose to 53 percent. Much the same pattern was manifested elsewhere. In each country the proportion of men earning high scores on the OM scale was at least six times as great for those most ex-

Table 10–1. Percent high on OM-500[a] for increasing levels of mass-media exposure.[b]

Level of exposure to mass media[c]	Argentina	Chile	East Pakistan	India	Israel	Nigeria
1			8 (62)	3 (175)		7 (15)
2	4 (27)	4 (73)	11 (94)	11 (237)	0 (28)	
3			19 (163)	34 (341)		7 (42)
4	14 (66)	12 (105)	36 (172)	47 (136)	14 (43)	3 (60)
5	21 (139)	21 (221)	46 (296)	56 (247)	22 (121)	19 (140)
6	30 (245)	39 (290)	47 (148)	69 (49)	22 (171)	32 (170)
7	53 (328)	56 (236)	54 (66)	59 (108)	47 (361)	49 (293)

a High on OM-500 means a score in the top one-third of the frequency distribution, in each country
b Numbers in parentheses are values of N upon which the percentages are based.

c The mass-media scale is a combination of responses to questions about the frequency of newspaper reading and radio listening. A score of 1 indicates a person who never reads a newspaper or listens to the radio; a score of 7 indicates a person who does both daily. In Argentina, Chile, and Israel the first three categories, and in Nigeria the first two categories, were collapsed because of the small numbers of people at the lower end of the original scale. Otherwise, the scale scores represent the same frequency of media use across all six countries.

posed as against those least exposed to the mass media, as may be seen in Table 10–1. This fact is reflected in the very definite pattern of Fig. 10–1, which, with some minor exceptions, shows a regular and sharp increase in individual modernity with every step up the scale of mass-media contact.

Since the data in Fig. 10–1 were standard-scored, we can more easily compare the six countries despite the fact that they varied so widely in the average mass-media exposure typical for the several national populations. Figure 10–1 indicates that whether a country was relatively backward or relatively advanced in the development of mass communication did not much affect the pattern of association between mass-media exposure and modernity at the individual level. In each of the six countries, almost every step up the communications ladder produced a roughly proportional increment in individual modernity. This common tendency was also reflected in the strong zero-order correlations of OM and mass-media exposure, which, for the total sample, stood at .45 in the median case.[7]

Taking into account all the evidence we have seen so far, we concluded that the mass media were in the front rank, along with the school and the factory, as inculcators of individual modernization. The conclusion was,

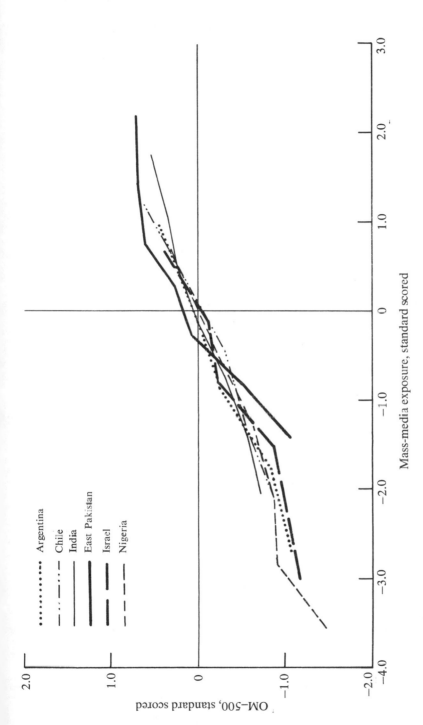

Figure 10–1. The relation of standardized scores on mass-media exposure and individual modernity (OM-500).

however, subject to challenge on the grounds that the observed zero-order correlations could have been an artifact of the association between media contact and other variables, such as education, urban residence, and occupation. Mass-media exposure was indeed appreciably correlated with other independent variables, such as education, and it could well be that the effects seemingly produced by contact with the media were really produced by these related variables.[8] To ascertain how far mass-media contact exerted a truly independent effect we had to explore its relation to individual modernity with these other variables controlled, which we could do by the matching procedure and by partial correlation. And since the industrial workers were the largest, and to us the most important, group, we elected to test those procedures with them first.

As may be seen in Table 10–2, applying controls for the influence of variables other than mass-media exposure did not oblige us to change our opinion of the latter as an important and independent factor in making men modern. The mass media evidently did not produce their effect mainly because of an incidental association between their use and the length of industrial employment. Controlling for education, a variable which is powerful and closely linked to the use of the mass media, might have been expected to call in question the independent contribution of the media. Yet media use survived this control with a median correlation of .28 which, while much reduced, was still significant at above .001 in all countries. While this reduction indicated that perhaps half of the ef-

Table 10–2. Correlations of mass-media exposure and individual modernity (OM) for factory workers.[a]

Correlation	Argentina	Chile	East Pakistan	India	Israel	Nigeria
Simple (zero-order)	.40	.38	.35	.56	.40	.39
Partial, controlling for—						
Formal education	.30	.27	.22	.29	.28	.31
Years factory experience	.38	.35	.33	.56	.36	.36
Formal education and years factory experience	.28	.25	.20	.27	.26	.29
Early socialization	.27	.23	.20	.21	.19	.30
Late socialization	.29	.31	.28	.46	.34	.32
Set A (early and late socialization)	.22	.19	.18	.19	.15	.25
N	663	715	654	700	544	520

a All correlations are significant at the .001 level.

fect of mass-media exposure stemmed from its mediation between education and modernity, there was still a substantial independent contribution left.[9] Indeed, even with nine variables in Set A simultaneously controlled, mass-media exposure everywhere defended its claim to standing as an independent determinant of OM at a very high level of statistical significance.

The soundness of this conclusion could be checked by consulting the matches. In the matching procedure we pitted men with "much" exposure against those with "little" exposure, maintaining as large a gap as we could in each country.[10] The men scored high and low, respectively, on the mass-media scale were matched to be almost exactly alike on up to thirteen other variables, ranging from education and factory experience to religion. This was done separately for cultivators and factory workers in recognition of the marked differences in opportunity for mass-media contact characterizing those groups. The resultant matches had minor flaws, but the process was basically highly successful in achieving a good match.[11] By simultaneously controlling so many variables which could be related to mass-media exposure, we ran the risk of committing the partialing fallacy. But we could also be highly confident that any differences which persisted in the face of matching were truly independent effects which did not stem from any uncontrolled correlation of the mass-media score with other powerful independent variables such as occupation or education.

Running the matched groups against OM left no doubt that the media of mass communication were a truly independent force in shaping men's modernity. As may be seen in Table 10–3, even with about a dozen other variables controlled, urban resident workers with higher scores on the mass-media index consistently had higher scores on the OM scales, the match yielding correlations highly statistically significant in all six countries. Expressing these differences in percentage terms, we found that, generally, the group more often in contact with the mass media contained twice as many modern men as did the group less frequently using the radio and newspapers. In Nigeria, for example, the proportion of modern men was 45 percent among those who frequently, as against only 19 percent among those who infrequently, used the mass media. The details are given in Table 10–3.

The Media and the Farmer

Of course, city dwellers have much greater opportunity to avail themselves of the media of mass communication than do farmers. Moreover, in the city the mass media may be assumed to interact with other sources of stimulation to produce a heightened impact. One might, therefore, expect mass-media exposure to have been more effective in modernizing

Table 10–3. Modernity of otherwise matched groups differentiated as having much or little contact with mass media.

Modernity measure	Argentina	Chile	East Pakistan	India	Israel	Nigeria
Percent modern[a] among group with—						
Much media contact	51%	41%	36%	59%	34%	45%
Little media contact	23%	26%	18%	54%	22%	19%
Mean OM score of group with—						
Much media contact	58	60	52	70	56	59
Little media contact	55	56	48	66	53	53
Match correlation (Match 25)[b]	.19**	.20*	.26***	.16*	.17*	.34***
N[c]	111	78	124	94	97	74

a "Modern" indicates a score in the top one-third of the frequency distribution on OM-500, in each country.
b Asterisks denote significance as follows: *, at .05 level; **, at .01 level; ***, at .001 level.
c Figures given are the numbers of pairs in the match.

urban workers than in influencing cultivators. On the other hand, the sharpness of the contrast between the world reflected in the mass media and that actually surrounding those dwelling in the average village of an undeveloped country could be so great as to give the media an unusually strong impact. One could well assume, therefore, that mass-media exposure should be more strongly associated with individual modernity among rural cultivators than among urban men. We were not sufficiently won over by either argument to take sides. Rather, we operated on the assumption that the media of mass communication should be an effective stimulus to individual modernity more or less equally for both cultivators and urban industrial workers.

The basic facts, presented in Table 10–4, are unfortunately not completely unambiguous. In four of the six countries, the impact of mass-media exposure among the men working the land in the villages seemed roughly equal to its effect on city workers. However, in Chile and Nigeria mass-media exposure failed to qualify as a statistically significant influence among the cultivators.

We tried to ascertain whether in those countries this outcome might be due to a real weakness in the power of mass-media exposure to modernize, or, rather, whether it resulted from some peculiarity of our rural samples there. Our efforts did not yield a definitive answer. The cultivators in Chile and Nigeria also showed less effect from schooling, as we will see in Chapter 17, which led us to suspect that our results were an artifact of the composition of the rural sample from those two coun-

Table 10–4.   Correlations of mass-media exposure and modernity (OM) among cultivators.[a]

Correlation	Argentina	Chile	East Pakistan	India	Israel	Nigeria
I. **Simple** (zero-order)	.48***	.15	.32***	.58***	.25**	.08
II. **Partial,** controlling for—						
Formal education	.39***	.15	.22*	.36***	.23*	.07
Age	.49***	.16	.32***	.58***	.26**	.08
Age, formal education, living standard	.36***	−.02	.21*	.33***	.22*	.07
Early socialization experience	.38***	.14	.18*	.32***	.22*	.07
Late socialization experience	.43***	−.00	.28***	.49***	.25**	.09
Set A (early and late socialization)	.36***	−.03	.16*	.30***	.21*	.08
III. **Control by matching** (Match 25A)	.45***	−.16	.20**	.22	.34*	.09
N's for Parts I & II	97	109	176	350	103	100
N's for Part III[b]	25	27	86	36	18	34

a Asterisks denote significance as follows: *, at .05 level; **, at .01 level; ***, at .001 level or better.
b Figures given are the numbers of pairs in the match.

tries. Such peculiarities in sample composition can have substantial effects on correlation coefficients.[12] But to insist on this conclusion could well cover up an important fact about rural patterns in those two countries which deserves further separate analysis. It seems more appropriate, therefore, to accept these two cases as exceptions to the rule that mass-media exposure is everywhere significantly related to modernity. The fact that in four of the six countries differential exposure to mass media produced so substantial an impact on the OM scores of farmers should suffice to make the case for its general importance in rural as well as urban environments.

Reservations and Affirmations

Using both partial correlations and the matches we could satisfy ourselves that the observed association between modernity and use of the mass media was not an artifact of the incidental correlation of media use with other causal variables such as education or factory experience. Unfortunately, those methods could not serve to prove that the evident link between mass-media use and modernity was not due to self-selection, that is, to the likely tendency of men already modern in spirit to express that modernity by more often making use of the newspaper and the radio. The same issue could, of course, be raised with regard to education and factory work. Since we had a distinct theoretical interest in testing the effect of factory work on modernity, however, we took special measures in designing our field work and our samples to permit us to deal with the challenge that all concentrations of modern men were due to self-selection. In the case of mass-media exposure, however, we could not measure the duration of exposure, only the degree at one point in time. And we were unable to mount a special before-and-after study.

Logically, however, there seemed every reason to accept the conclusion that contact with the mass media should progressively influence men to become more modern. In most places the mass media bring men information about many aspects of modern living; they open them up to new ideas, show them new ways of doing things, demonstrate accomplishments which can contribute to a sense of efficacy, reveal and explore diversity of opinion, stimulate and justify heightened aspirations for education and mobility, glorify science and sing the praises of technology — all of which should induce greater modernity in any individual open to influence.[13]

Of course, it is this very quality of openness to influence, associated with media use, which caused us to wonder whether the mass media are a truly independent force shaping men in the modern mold, or, alternatively, whether our results merely reflected self-selection. What brings men to the mass media may be their very propensity to respond to life as modern men. Therefore, the men who paid attention to the radio and the newspaper could indeed have been those who were more modern in spirit to begin with. Nevertheless, there seems every reason to believe that the greater modernity of those who were most often exposed to the mass media also resulted in good part from the effectiveness of the radio and newspaper as teachers of modernization.

The most appropriate model seems to us to be that of a feedback system. Men who are more modern in spirit may seek out contact with the mass media, but that contact in turn probably serves to make them more modern. Becoming modern in attitude and value, they presumably are all the more vigorous in seeking out the media of communication, thus renewing the cycle. One might, therefore, wish to discount somewhat the strength of the association our data show to prevail between individual modernity and mass-media exposure in order to allow for some influence due to self-selection. In our opinion, however, a reasonable rate of discount still leaves largely unimpaired the standing of the mass media as one of the most important of the influences which serve to make men modern.

This conclusion, moreover, had important implications for our further work. Education and mass-media use were well established in theory and fact as the most appropriate external criteria for judging the validity of any attitudinal and value measure of personal modernity. Since the OM scale was so clearly associated with both higher education and mass-media contact, the case was made for its standing as a valid measure of individual modernity. We could, therefore, use it with confidence to assess the impact of sources of influence less conventionally studied in modernization research, such as the factory, the city, and the rural cooperative, to which we turn in the chapters which follow.

11

The Factory as a School in Modernity

That the school might modernize was quite readily accepted by almost everyone. But our idea that work in factories should be a modernizing experience was met by skepticism or outright rejection from a surprisingly large number of persons to whom we initially described our project. Their reasons were by no means insubstantial.

First, and foremost, they challenged the assumption that basic changes in personality could occur with any regularity in individuals who had already reached maturity. The OM scale measures some patterns of response which lie at the core of the personality; these include the sense of personal efficacy, cognitive openness, trust, orientation to time, and modes of relating to social "inferiors" dealt with in our "dignity" theme. Modern psychology considers these attributes as basic, in the sense that they are assumed to be laid down in childhood and adolescence, and thereafter to be stable or relatively unchanging, certainly much more so than are mere opinions. Consequently, our critics were led to express the same view as Benjamin Bloom when, in his famous review of research on *Stability and Change in Human Characteristics,* he concluded: "We are pessimistic about producing major changes in a [personal] characteristic after it has reached a high level of stability."[1] Bloom had in mind mainly such attributes as intelligence or cognitive capacity, but a large segment of the community of personality psychologists takes essentially the same pessimistic view of the prospects for bringing about significant change in basic characteristics of personality after the age of 16 or 18.

The second reason our critics advanced was doubt that the factory provided a sufficiently powerful environment to bring about changes in basic value orientations and need dispositions. Some psychologists hold that there are almost no circumstances under which really basic traits of personality laid down early in childhood can be substantially altered in adulthood. Most would, however, agree with Bloom that under extreme environmental conditions, such as are prevalent in concentration camps, prisons, or "brainwashing" sessions, "one may encounter considerable deterioration in characteristics which are ordinarily quite stable."[2] This concession to the idea of adult change, however, is limited largely to instances of deterioration or retrogression; it does not apply to long-term positive transformations, that is, to growth and new development in adulthood. Those who assumed such extreme conditions to be necessary for bringing about transformations of fundamental personality characteristics in adulthood were, therefore, convinced the factory could not produce the sort of changes we anticipated.

The third line of attack was based on a challenge to our interpretation of the factory as a social organization. Our critics saw the factory in a quite different light. They argued that even if the factory *could* bring about significant personality change in adulthood, the kind of change it produced would probably make men less rather than more like the project's model of a modern man.

They pointed out, for example, that factories are hierarchically organized, and argued that therefore one should not expect them to stimulate the sort of participant citizenship required by our model of the modern man. Since technical and economic considerations must always be uppermost in making decisions in industry, they noted, there was little likelihood that the factory would train men to pay respectful attention to the opinions of subordinates and others less powerful or prestigious than they were. Our critics went on to point out that most factory workers are in a dependent and passive position. They perform routine repetitive functions, often dull and deadening, and do so mainly on the initiative of others. According to this view, workers are coerced and harried by the clock and the inexorable pace of the machine. Changes in the machinery, or in the arrangement of their work, are likely to require that they work harder, or faster, and may even threaten some of them with a layoff. Therefore, our critics claimed, factory work would encourage passivity and dependence, foster fear of and resistance to change, and stimulate a reaction against the domination of strict schedules and a preference for more spontaneously arranged work.

We felt that there were sound reasons for doubting the validity of the assumptions our critics made. The issues raised are sufficiently fundamental, we believe, to warrant turning aside briefly from the presentation of results to clarify our theoretical position.

Theoretical Foundations
Our first task was to look more closely at the assumption that the

main features of individual personality are laid down in early childhood and adolescence and persist basically unchanged into adulthood. We were at once struck by how little systematic empirical evidence there was to support that assumption. Since the idea seems to accord so well with most people's practical experience, there has been little incentive to challenge or even test this theory, which has nevertheless become almost a dogma of the psychoanalytic age.

Professor Bloom performed a great service by pulling together the research available on the stability of responses to a variety of psychological tests. These included the Kuder Personal Preference Record, which tests interests such as the mechanical and artistic; the Strong Vocational Interest Test; the Allport and Vernon Test of Values; the Thurstone Personality Scale, and others. One striking fact which emerged from Bloom's review was that virtually all of the available longitudinal studies on which so many of our conclusions about the stability of personal traits rested had been done with high school and college students. These researches, therefore, typically covered only 2 years or so of elapsed time, and in very few cases really extended very far into adulthood. Most, therefore, simply have no bearing on the question of how far basic attitudes, values, and dispositions are stable throughout adulthood. Even those few studies which covered a period of 3 or 4 years, however, indicated that a good deal of change may have taken place even in that short interval, because the correlation of test scores over that span of time was generally only about .60 on tests such as the Allport-Vernon value scale, Plant's tests of ethnocentrism, and Thurstone's personality scale.[3]

How much stability or change there will be depends, of course, on the area of personality one is testing. Apparently there have been very few, if any, truly longitudinal studies of features of personality which are strictly, or even remotely, comparable to those dealt with by the OM scale. Furthermore, how much personality change one observes in a given group will, in our opinion, depend greatly on how far the group's environment has been changing. It is noteworthy, therefore, that after reviewing the evidence with regard to the stability of adult characteristics Bloom concluded: "Much of the stability we have reported in this work is really a reflection of environmental stability. That is, the stability of a characteristic for a group of individuals may, in fact, be explained by the constancy of their environments over time."[4]

The essential feature of our modernization study, however, is its emphasis on the *change* in the social and physical environment which men experience as they shift from the more traditional settings of village, farm, and tribe to city residence, industrial employment, and national citizenship. We believed that in such circumstances the stability of personal characteristics commonly observed under conditions of social and cultural continuity must give way to a more rapid and profound rate of personal adaptation.

Finding no empirical evidence to the contrary, we proceeded, then, on the assumption that the personality can continue to develop and grow well into adulthood, and that basic change, even in fundamental characteristics such as the sense of efficacy, was more than merely *possible.* Indeed, we assumed such changes to be highly *likely,* at least when men lived under social conditions conducive to personal transformation, such as those prevailing in the sectors of developing countries experiencing the process of modernization.

We also countered our critics by affirming that basic personal change can be stimulated by life in settings less extreme or stark than prisons and concentration camps. While taking this position, we were not unaware that on completion of his intensive review of stability and change in personal characteristics Professor Bloom had stated that "a central thesis of this work is that change in many human characteristics becomes more and more difficult as the characteristics become more fully developed," with the consequence that "to produce a given amount of change . . . requires more and more powerful environments and increased amounts of effort and attention as the characteristic becomes stabilized."[5] In our view, the factory qualified as such a "powerful environment," one which should be able to impinge upon individuals with sufficiently concentrated force to bring about changes in core features of personality.

We noted, first, that contact between the individual and the factory system was not fleeting or irregular. To work in a factory means to expose oneself to its regimen for at least 8 hours a day, 5 to 6 days a week, and continuously, week in and week out, over a period of years.

Second, we believe this involvement with the factory is serious and engaging for the participants. Work is one of the most important elements in most men's lives. Moreover, in developing countries, jobs with the pay and steadiness of industrial employment are rare. That alone makes factory work particularly desirable. In addition, such employment often confers prestige. Most men in industry in these countries are, therefore, not merely sojourners casually passing time in the plant.

Third, and most important in conferring on the factory the quality of a "powerful environment," are certain features of its activity and organization. Technical constraints, the objective standard of productivity, and strict requirements of profitability all act to give the factory a firm and relatively invariant character. It does not so much adapt to men as it requires that they adapt to it.

The essential logic of machinery and mechanical processes must be rigorously observed, else the machine, or its attendant, or both, must break. It requires only a few instances in which hair, or a flowing gown, or fingers get caught in the machine, to impress the point indelibly on all who come in contact with it. This same sharpness of outline tends to be manifested in the organization of the factory. Departments, shops, even individual machines are distinctly set off and clearly demarcated. Division of labor is generally precisely and rigorously maintained. Hierarchies of authority and technical skill give a definite structure to interpersonal relations. Standards of performance tend to be objective and precise. And the system of rewards and punishments is highly relevant to all the participants, unambiguous, powerful, and by and large objectively calculated.

These characteristics of the factory which make it a "powerful environment" point to the basis for our rejection of the third challenge addressed to us by our critics, namely, that the factory's effect should make men *less* rather than more modern.

In our view, the organization of the factory and its mode of functioning embodied a series of fundamental principles to which men from a traditional background would respond favorably. We anticipated that rather than responding with confusion or reacting defensively, traditional men would be open to the lessons the factory had to teach, incorporating and adopting as their own standard the norms embedded in modern factory organization. This learning, we believed, would come about through the same processes of socialization identified by us earlier as the basis for learning modern attitudes and values in the school, namely, modeling, generalization, exemplification, and reward and punishment. These processes can be observed at work across the whole range of the main themes which defined our analytic model of the modern man, but it should suffice to illustrate the point with reference to a select few.

Efficacy. By the very nature of the forces at work in it, the factory *exemplifies* efficacy, since in it is concentrated the power to convert obdurate materials into new shapes and forms far exceeding the capacity of the unaided individual to do so. The total working of the factory affirms man's capacity, through organization and the harnessing of mechanical power, to transform nature to suit his needs. One worker we spoke to in Nigeria expressed the basic idea for us perfectly when, in reply to our questions about how his work left him feeling, he said: "Sometimes like nine feet tall with arms a yard wide. Here in the factory I alone with my machine can twist any way I want a piece of steel all the men in my home village together could not begin to bend at all."

The factory provides *models* of efficacy in the person of the engineer, the technician, and the more highly skilled workers such as tool and die makers. These men have the professional responsibility to solve problems, to develop new combinations of elements, to convert ideas and blueprints into concrete mechanical reality. In addition, the system of *reward and punishment,* in particular the bonuses, reclassification to higher skill categories, and promotion to more responsible work, should also serve to reinforce the lesson in efficacy the factory offers.

Of course, we assume that the sense of efficacy stimulated by factory experience will be *generalized,* so that the lessons learned in the factory will be extended to other life situations. In his personal affairs, and in his interventions in community life, we may expect the experienced factory worker to abandon passive fatalism and to work on the assumption that he and his community can bring about meaningful change in their lives.

Readiness for innovation and openness to systematic change. The struggle to keep costs down to competitive levels, and the constant pressure to keep up with the demands of the market, oblige factories to be outstanding among large-scale institutions in the introduction of new machinery, techniques, and administrative arrangements. We recognized that the main responsibility for effecting such changes usually lies with management, and with its associated engineering and technical personnel. We assumed, therefore, that in stimulating men toward openness to new experience and readiness to accept change, the factory would work mainly through the process of *modeling.*

Insofar as the factory as an institution is generally receptive to innovation, readily adopting new techniques for processing material, new machinery, and new personnel policies, it should also encourage openness to new experience by *exemplification.* Managerially sponsored innovation may, of course, mean harder, faster, or more dangerous work for the employee. In most reasonably modern factories, however, technical innovations are more likely to lead to safer, less strenuous, and more evenly paced work. Technical innovation may also result in higher individual productivity and elevated skill ratings. Although there is, again, no guarantee that these gains will be fed back to the workers in the form of increased earnings, in many instances the technological innovations of management do redound to the interest of the workers. Insofar as their experience was thus positive, we expected workers to *generalize* the lessons of the factory to other situations in which openness to new experience and readiness for change are called for.

By bringing together a much wider variety of men than one commonly finds in the village, the factory offers the worker an encounter not only with new ways of doing mechanical things, but with new people whose thinking and customs may be quite different from his own.[6] Since the factory is a culturally neutral ground, since it presents a firm structure which it applies more or less equally to all its members as a guide to their interaction, and since it holds up certain common standards of evaluation such as objective skill and productivity, much of the uncertainty that usually surrounds contact with strangely different people may be eliminated or at least be made more bearable in the context of the factory. A more secure basis is thereby provided for exploring new customs, and for discovering common interests and propensities, which are otherwise typically masked by the more salient dissimilarities with which people from different cultures initially confront each other. In the context of the factory the cost of exploring new ways is low, and the *rewards* may be quite gratifying. Such success in opening up relations with people who are culturally rather different from oneself may, furthermore, be *generalized* into a lessened fear of strangers and a heightened confidence in one's ability to understand foreign people and ways.

Planning and time. To attain its goal of maximizing productivity the factory must emphasize planning. The principle of planning is exemplified in the very layout of the factory, designed to permit the most rational movement of goods from their point of entry as raw material to their exit as finished product; in the flow of the work, as the product is subjected to one process after another in the technically prescribed succession; and in the coordination which insures that, despite extensive division of labor, the required tools and materials will be available at the appropriate place and at the right time.

The management of time is intimately related to planning. Industrial production requires precise scheduling in bringing together the diverse elements entering into the production process. This requirement is most evident with the assembly line, since it rigorously imposes the necessity that everyone start and stop at the same time, that each process be allocated a precise amount of time, and that each step be completed as scheduled. According to the socialization principle of *exemplification,* men working in factories should come to internalize a concern for orderly advanced planning and precise scheduling. This learning should be facilitated by the system of factory *reward and punishment* since persistent lateness brings reprimands and may lead to discharge, and bonuses are often paid for completing important jobs on or ahead of schedule.

Respect for subordinates. The predominance of rules and formal procedures in the factory should teach respect for the rights of subordinates and of other individuals of inferior standing in the hierarchy of status. Of course there are still factories run by cruel and vicious bosses, and even in the best-run plant a particular foreman or other supervisor may be able to hound and even persecute a man. By and large, however, the norm of treatment in the factory emphasizes relatively just, humane, respectful treatment of subordinates, at least compared to what goes on in many other settings in underdeveloped countries.

Factories are generally owned and operated by corporations, private or governmental. This may make them places in which authority is cold and distant, but their public character generally also insures that the extremes of personal, vengeful treatment by harsh bosses are much less manifested in them than in other types of work situations. Generally the factory is dominated by men of relatively higher education, in whom a more civilized standard of personal conduct is likely to have been inculcated than will be commonly found among absentee landowners or their overseers. Industrial managers and engineers are likely to look for their "ego tonic" outside, in the larger community, rather than seeking it vicariously through abusing the dignity of their subordinates in the plant. In addition, the trade union, generally totally absent in the countryside but quite common in urban industry, serves as an additional important source of restraint to insure that the men in the plant are treated with respect in accordance with objective rules for decent supervision.

The interdependence of men in the complex production process of the factory requires that there be a substantial flow of information *up* as well as *down* the status hierarchy. Inexperienced engineers and foremen quickly learn, often to their dismay, that their own success is heavily dependent on the cooperation and goodwill of their subordinates. The men in most immediate contact with machines and materials see and know things which are vital to the fulfillment of the factory's production goals. To be effective, therefore, supervisors cannot merely tell the men what to do; they must also pay attention to what the men tell *them* about how things are going.

In general, then, by *modeling* and *exemplification,* men working in factories should have an opportunity to learn lessons in showing consideration for subordinates, and in respecting the feelings of those weaker or of lesser status than themselves. To the extent that their views are listened to and given some weight in the decision-making process, they should also be learning to see the value of diversity of opinion as opposed to unanimity.

All of the other themes built into our analytic model of the modern man should also, in some degree, be reflected in a man's work experience in an industrial establishment. Belief in the calculability of the world and the people in it should be encouraged by the regularity of work and pay in the factory, by the fulfillment of its imperatives for close coordination in the division of labor, and by the model of responsible norm-oriented behavior usually presented by the engineering and technical personnel. A preference for universalism over particularism might well be fostered by the factory organization's embodiment of bureaucratic principles of governance through impartial rules, and its conformity to technical and normative standards. A rejection of fatalism and its replacement by optimism and active striving should be fostered by several attributes of the factory, including the steadiness and relative security of industrial work, its mastery over materials, and its evident ability to exercise some substantial control over natural forces.

Of course we are completely aware that none of the effects we anticipated is a *necessary* concomitant of industrial employment. Our description of the factory was cast in what Weber called "ideal-typical" form, in order to highlight the theoretical basis for our expectations. In doing so, we meant neither to assert that the factory was unique, nor to deny that in many, perhaps most, concrete instances it might fail to live up to its potential.

On the issue of uniqueness, we recognize not only that the factory shares many of its attributes with other large-scale organizations, but also that some of the lessons it has to teach could as well be learned on a farm. For example, it obviously takes planning, sometimes very close planning, to run a productive family farm. Nevertheless, even in those respects in which agricultural and industrial work have something in common, we expected the factory experience to be qualitatively different. And where its effect proved similar to that of farm work, we expected it to be much the more powerful influence.

The approach to timing may serve to illustrate what we mean by a qualitative difference distinguishing agricultural from industrial employment. The farmer is certainly subject to some coercive pressures of time, as in sowing and harvesting. For him, however, time runs mainly in long cycles, as by the season. Furthermore, his personal schedule on any given day can be independent of that of his neighbor. By contrast, the industrial worker feels the pressure of time more on a day-to-day and even on an hour-to-hour basis, because of the requirement that he closely coordinate his work with that of many others, or adjust his pace to that of a machine. Both farmer and worker, then, must pay attention to timing, but the industrial worker's experience is much more likely to impress on him recognition of the necessity for strict, regular, short-term scheduling.

An effect presumably produced by both agricultural and industrial work, but much more powerfully generated by the latter, may be illustrated by the sense of efficacy. One should keep in mind, of course, that we refer mainly to the situation in developing countries. There, the farmer's work is often described as expressing his harmony *with* nature, rather than his dominance *over* it. Nevertheless, the farmer who clears a field and brings in a good crop might certainly develop a sense of personal efficacy. In the traditional village, however, folklore and religion will generally encourage the farmer to believe that his success depends not on his personal effectiveness so much as on the grace of God. Moreover, what the traditional farmer can accomplish, with or without God's help, is terribly restricted by the modest power at his disposal, power usually limited to his own labor and that of one or two draft animals. By contrast, the man who moves from farm to factory links himself to a complex and powerful organization. The organization marshals for him forces which enormously expand and extend his capacity to transform objects. Once in charge of a machine, and simultaneously linked to the factory as an organization, the new worker commands not one or two horsepower, but dozens or even hundreds. We expected that under such conditions his sense of efficacy would be much more powerfully activated than if his efficacious experiences were limited to what is possible on the traditional farm.

Moreover, while acknowledging that there may be some parallels in the experience of work on the farm and in industry, we were impressed by the many ways the two milieus are distinct. The traditional farmer generally works alone, helped at most by members of his family; the work is seasonal and irregular, with long periods of enforced idleness; he produces in good part for his own consumption, and the return for his labor is generally modest, perhaps minimal; the resources he commands from the storehouse of science are extremely limited; the technology he utilizes is relatively unchanging yet ineffective against natural forces and disease; and the powerful men he deals with, such as the landowner or an overseer, are likely to show little respect for his integrity or dignity in matters vitally affecting their own special interests.

By contrast, the industrial worker is backed by the resources of a complex and powerful organization; his work is highly coordinated with that of others who have been selected on the same impersonal grounds, and whose performance is also judged by objective standards of skill and output; the work is regular and steady, and in developing countries the remuneration is likely to be well above the standard available to the average farm renter or small holder; he works under cover, protected from the elements; many of the latest advances of science, engineering, and technology are put into his hands to increase his productivity; and he operates in a frame of rules and regulations which guarantee him at least the minimum of respect for his opinions, feelings, and personal dignity.

We assumed that these differences in the two milieus, which are more or less absolute, along with others which are more matters of quality or degree, should all combine to make factory work a much more effective school of modernization. Our prediction was that those who remained on the farm, thereby experiencing maximum continuity between childhood, adolescence, and adulthood in an unchanging environment, would show very little personal change as they added years of occupational experience, whereas those who left the farm and moved into industry should manifest significant personal change with every passing year.

The Ideal Versus the Real
Many to whom we described our research plan were of the opinion that

while our model of what factories were like might apply in some exceptional cases, it was not likely to be true of the average factory, least of all those in developing countries. We were quite ready to acknowledge that factories would vary in their effectiveness as schools for modernity; indeed, it was that expectation which led us to go to considerable trouble in studying the relevance which the size, product, and relative modernity of industrial establishments might have for the process of individual modernization. Nevertheless, we were firmly convinced that even in developing countries the average factory would in sufficient degree embody the principles we enumerated above to be an effective school in modernity.

Moreover, even if it should prove to be the case that factories in developing countries left much to be desired when measured against the standard of the more developed nations, we were convinced that they would still be far ahead of the other work settings within the same countries in the degree to which they embodied the organizational principles we thought would make for individual modernity. In other words, we assumed that in developing countries the impact of the factory would depend in good part on the *contrast* between it and the other organizational milieus to which the citizens of such nations are normally exposed.

Empirical Results

It is time for an empirical test of our theory. The first step in our analysis tested the assumption that the contrast between the environment which men of rural origin had known earlier in their lives and that which they met when they moved into industrial work would produce a sharp impact intensifying the factory's effectiveness as a school in modernity.

Critics of our theory expected the ex-farmers either to be disoriented by the marked difference between the patterns they were used to and those they encountered in the plant, or to respond in a defensive way. Insofar as these newcomers to the industrial milieu were confused, they should not have learned the lessons presumably built into the factory as a social organization; insofar as they were defensive, they might have gotten the message, but should have resisted being influenced by it. In either event, if our critics were correct, the men who had moved into the factory should have been no more modern than their farmer "cousins" whom they left behind in the countryside.

To test these competing expectations we needed a match which was limited to experienced factory workers of rural origin, and which put them in competition with cultivators who were from the same district of origin as the workers and indistinguishable from them in education, ethnicity and religion, age, and the like. Match 4 (Appendix E) met these requirements, at least in five countries.[7]

The match rather strongly confirmed our hypothesis, as is amply demonstrated in Table 11–1. In all five countries which had men of rural origin, those who had moved to the factories scored as more modern than those still farming, by a very wide margin. The correlations were among the strongest we obtained with the matching procedure, ranging from a low of .34 to a high of .71 with the median at .56, all significant at better than the .001 level. The proportion of the men scored as "modern" was generally several times greater among the workers as compared to the cultivators. The median proportion of the cultivators who qualified as modern was only 2 percent, whereas 33 percent did so among the workers of rural origin.

Challenges to the Factory's Claim

Although the differences between workers and cultivators were striking, we could not claim to have provided conclusive proof that factory work modernized until we met three challenges. The observed effects might have resulted from: the *self-selection* of more modern men choosing to enter the factory; the *differential retention* of more modern men after entering; or the impact, not so much of factory experience itself, but rather its *concomitants* such as increased exposure to mass media

Table 11–1. Modernity of matched cultivators and rural-origin experienced factory workers.[a]

Modernity measure	Argentina	Chile	East Pakistan	India	Nigeria
Percent modern[b]					
Cultivators	2%	0%	16%	26%	0%
Experienced factory	11%	30%	38%	49%	33%
Mean OM score					
Cultivators	39	45	47	58	44
Experienced factory workers	50	57	53	67	59
Point gain per year of factory-urban experience	1.4	1.4	1.1	1.1	1.6
Match correlation (Match 4)[c]	.56***	.59***	.34***	.35***	.71***
Nd	63	63	176	69	21

a Israel is not included because there were no rural-origin factory workers in the Israeli sample.

b "Modern" indicates a score in the top one-third of the frequency distribution on OM-500, in each country.

c Asterisks denote significance as follows: *, at .05 level; **, at .01 level; ***, at .001 level or better.

d Figures given are the numbers of pairs in the match.

and urban living. We can deal with the first two challenges immediately, and will take up the third after turning briefly aside to describe a special set of reinterviews we undertook to resolve the issues raised here.

(a) Differential selection. We turn first to the possibility that the workers of rural origin were more modern than men still on the farm, *not* because they learned to be so while in the factory, but rather because they were self-selected, having been more modern to begin with. It is widely supposed that differences in background, which are in turn related to modernity, lead some men to enter industry more readily. We note, however, that Match 4 controlled precisely for those early socialization variables, such as education, which might have given the factory workers an advantage over the cultivators.[8] Moreover, a separate analysis we undertook of migration from the country to the city failed to indicate a large role for that phenomenon. The details of that analysis are given in Appendix D. For present purposes, therefore, we propose a much more direct answer to the self-selection argument. If our hypothesis about the factory was correct, then, whatever the basis of their initial selection, men should have increased in modernity, year by year, *after* going to work in industry.

To test the effect of factory experience, we calculated the proportion who scored modern, as men moved from the status of least to most experienced worker. By and large, as may be seen in Table 11–2, each step up the experience ladder brought with it an increase in individual modernity.[9] In four of the six countries the proportion of modern men among the most experienced workers was more than double what it was among those just entering industry. The progression was less regular for Israel and quite ambiguous in India. Typically, however, somewhere around

Table 11-2. Percent modern[a] among men with increasing amounts of factory experience.[b]

Steps up factory experience ladder,	Argentina	Chile	East Pakistan	India	Israel	Nigeria
1 (Least experienced)	22 (111)	17 (201)	26 (117)	48 (200)	20 (121)	27 (108)
2	40 (124)	34 (73)	39 (140)	58 (155)	35 (128)	30 (100)
3	36 (135)	38 (118)	35 (147)	54 (104)	41 (97)	43 (132)
4	39 (122)	43 (100)	49 (148)	48 (99)	45 (112)	51 (86)
5	46 (84)	53 (113)	56 (102)	49 (142)	35 (86)	57 (94)
6 (Most experienced)	56 (87)	53 (110)	—	—	—	—

  a "Modern" indicates a score in the top one-third of the frequency distribution on OM-500, in each country.
  b Numbers in parentheses are values of N upon which the percentages are based.
  c These steps are not comparable among countries except for step 1, which was everywhere limited to new factory workers with less than 1 year of experience. For a precise definition of each step in each country, see note 9.

25 percent of the new workers were modern, whereas some 50 percent of the most experienced fell in that classification.

This relation could be expressed simply by a correlation coefficient measuring the association between years in the factory and individual modernity. The appropriate coefficient for workers of rural origin, similar to those included above in Match 4, ranged from .11 in India to .46 in Chile, with a median of .29, significant at the .01 level for India and at the .001 level or above in the other cases.[10] This outcome seemed to us to provide conclusive evidence that the results obtained earlier with Match 4 were not merely the consequence of the differential recruitment of more modern men for factory work. *It seemed clear that men learned to be more modern, year by year, after they entered the factory.*

The point was further underscored by the correlation of years in the factory and modernity for men of urban origin. As one might expect, in at least two of the three countries in which the comparison could be made, men raised in the city evidently found the factory a less powerful school in modernity than did the men of rural origin, probably because there was less in it that was really new to them. Nevertheless, the evidence is unmistakable that men of urban origin also became more modern as they extended their stay in the factory, since for them the correlation relating OM scores to factory experience, with a median of .24, was everywhere significant at the .001 level, as indicated in Table 11–3.

Moreover, the greater modernity characteristic of men who had been in the factory longer could not be attributed merely to the fact of aging and progressive maturation. If that were the case, each year spent in agricultural pursuits should also have made the cultivators progressively more modern. That was decidedly not the case, as may be seen in the fourth line of Table 11–3. Unlike the correlation of modernity with years in the factory, that for years on the farm did not show any noticeable association between increasing work experience and modernity. The relation was as often negative as positive. More important, the correlations were very small and never statistically significant. Men did not become more modern merely as they became older and more mature regardless of where they worked. When they remained on the farm, they seemed not to change significantly one way or the other, whereas they became definitely more modern in the course of their sojourn in the factory.

(b) Differential retention. All in all, the evidence argued strongly for accepting the role of factory experience in making men modern. But an additional challenge to our conclusion could be entered. The observed effects on modernity of work in industry might actually have resulted from the factory's *preferential retention* of modern men, so that such men did not *develop* in industry, but merely *concentrated* there.

The evidence available to us indicated that it was most improbable

Table 11–3. Correlations of work experience and individual modernity (OM).[a]

Correlation	Argentina	Chile	East Pakistan	India	Israel	Nigeria
Simple (zero-order)[b]						
All factory workers	.24***	.36***	.26***	.11**	.26***	.29***
Rural-origin factory workers	.32***	.46***	.26***	.11**	—	.29***
Urban-origin factory workers	.20***	.23***	—	—	.26***	.27***
Cultivators	−.00	.05	−.01	−.02	−.03	.01
Partial, all factory workers, controlling for—						
Formal education	.28***	.37***	.26***	.25***	.24***	.20***
Mass-media exposure	.20***	.34***	.24***	.10**	.18***	.24***
Education plus mass-media exposure	.24***	.36***	.25***	.22***	.18***	.17***
Early socialization	.24***	.35***	.24***	.07*	.20***	.21***
Late socialization	.19***	.17***	.13**	.08*	.21***	.06
Set A (early and late socialization)	.14***	.13***	.14**	.08*	.17***	.05
Number						
All factory workers	663	715	654	700	544	520
Rural-origin workers	239	305	654	700	0	184
Urban-origin workers	423	410	0	0	544	336
Cultivators	97	109	176	350	103	100

[a] Asterisks denote significance as follows: *, at .05 level; **, at .01 level; ***, at .001 level.
[b] For factory workers the measure used for work experience was years of factory work; for cultivators the measure used was age.

that the greater modernity of the men who had been longer in the plant could be accounted for on the basis of preferential retention of more modern men. From the standpoint of the workers themselves, we discovered that if anyone was inclined *voluntarily* to leave the factory, it was more likely to be the especially modern man rather than his traditional counterpart. Those considering leaving were generally the more highly skilled and ambitious, who were willing to run the risk of setting up their own small business for service, repairs, or small-scale manufacture.[11] The more average man, by contrast, was apt to cling to his job in industry because such employment brought higher wages, greater security, and increased prestige. Insofar as there actually was a drain off of men, therefore, the consequence should have been that those with longer tenure in the factory would be, on the average, less and not more modern.

Turning to the role of management, we found little reason to assume they were pursuing a policy of differential retention of more modern men. Whatever screening they accomplished generally took place in the first few weeks after new men had been hired. Once management had kept a man as long as a year, they seemed inclined to keep him on indefinitely. Indeed, often the law, or trade-union regulations, obliged managers to retain men after they had been on the job a year. Overall, it was our impression that after the first year men were kept on as a group without further screening or weeding out. Yet, for policies of preferential retention to have produced the facts which we had observed, management would have been obliged constantly to cut out men at the bottom of the modernity scale. Moreover, this must needs have occurred at every level of tenure, year by year, inasmuch as the modernizing effect we had observed occurred *throughout* the range of factory experience.[12]

Finally, we observed that men released from one plant generally turned up in another; they neither left nor were pushed out of the industrial labor force entirely. This meant they had an equal chance to enter our sample, and would thus have been described in our data according to the *total span* of their industrial experience rather than in terms of how long they had been in their last factory. Consequently, even if some factory directors had made it a practice to force the less modern men out of their particular plants, that would have had little or no effect on the overall correlation of modernity and factory experience we observed for each country sample as a whole.

Taking all these considerations into account, it seemed quite clear to us that the greater modernity of men with longer industrial experience could not be accounted for by differential selection, whether self-initiated or arising from management decisions. This impression was confirmed by the relevant statistical evidence available to us.

If the men who stayed, or were kept on, year after year were predominantly the more modern, the long-term effect should have been for each "class" or "cohort" in factory seniority to be not only more modern but also markedly better educated. In fact, that had not happened. The education of men did not rise systematically or substantially with each step up the experience ladder.[13] Moreover, if the less modern men were more likely to be forced out by management, then the men who had moved from plant to plant more frequently should have been less modern. In fact, the opposite was the case. In all six countries, the fact that a man had worked in several or many factories was associated with a high rather than with a low modernity score.[14]

Additional evidence on the issue was provided by the method of partial correlation. If factories retained only the men who were more modern to begin with and if, as we know, better-educated men were more modern, then controlling for education should have erased the earlier reported simple correlation between length of factory tenure and individual modernity. Yet, partialing out the effect of education as often as not *increased* the correlation for factory experience and modernity; the median rose to .25 and all the correlations were significant at the .001 level, as may be seen in Table 11–3. The Indian case was particularly interesting, because with education controlled its correlation of factory experience and OM was comparable with the others, whereas before it had been much smaller.[15]

The situation was not much changed when we also brought under control other social characteristics on which a policy of differential retention might have rested, such as father's education, literacy, ethnicity, and religion. All these measures were combined in the index of early socialization, and when it was controlled, in Table 11–3, the correlations for factory experience with the OM score were still quite substantial, with the median partial correlation of .23, significant at .001.

We concluded, therefore, that the case was unambiguously made. Neither self-selection nor differential retention could account for the fact that the more experienced factory workers were more modern. No accidental or purposeful concentration of men of certain social characteristics, such as higher education, could be found in the ranks of the more experienced workers. There was every reason to believe that more experienced factory workers were more modern because they had become so during the course of their stay in the factory.[16]

The Worker Revisited: A Longitudinal Study

Although we were satisfied that the partial correlations and other material presented above proved that differential retention of the more modern men could not explain away the greater modernity of those who had worked longer in the factory, we discovered that some people found it hard to accept that type of evidence as definitive in settling so basic and complex an issue. The point was so vital to the theory underlying our entire study that we decided we had to provide evidence of a basically different character.

The obvious solution was to add a truly longitudinal component to our otherwise cross-sectional study, by interviewing for a second time some of our original industrial workers. If, in the intervening period of some 4–5 years, these men had substantially increased their OM scores, the argument that modernity is an unchanging attribute of men's basic personality would be decisively defeated. And there would no longer be any ground for holding that the preferential retention of more modern men accounted for the observed tendency of those with longer tenure in industry to be more modern.

We have reinterview data only for Israel and East Pakistan.[17] For this purpose we settled on a sample of 100 from each country, chosen to be, in each case, representative of the original sample of industrial workers.[18] The reinterview relied on a shortened form of the original questionnaire, processed in basically the same way as the original to give each man a series of OM scores.[19] We then compared the OM scores the men earned on the second round with those they had had on the first interview some years earlier.

The results of the reinterviews were gratifying indeed. The men in East Pakistan raised their average OM score by just under 7 points during the interval of 5 years between the first and the second interview, whereas in the shorter span of just under 4 years, the Israeli factory workers increased their average OM score by just over 4 points. The difference between the initial and the reinterview OM score was significant in both countries at well beyond the .001 level of statistical significance.[20] Expressed in terms of the points gained on the OM scale per year, the East Pakistanis had improved their score by 1.4 points per year, and the Israelis by 1.2.[21]

Up to this point our attempt to prove that men became more modern as they were increasingly exposed to modernizing institutions had rested on the assumption that our samples could be used *as if* ours was a truly longitudinal study. With the reinterviews, we proved definitely that individuals could increase their modernity in the late socialization period, because we had studied the very *same* individuals after they had been in the factory an additional period of some 4–5 years. There was no longer any *as if* element in our method. However, from the special perspective of this chapter, we were still left in doubt by the reinterview study as to whether it was the contact with the factory which produced the observed change or whether the change was brought about by the concomitant increase in exposure to other modernizing forces such as mass media, increased income, and urban experience. After all, the men we reinterviewed not only had been longer in the factory, but they also were simultaneously increasing their exposure to other "late-socialization" modernizing influences as well.

The fact that men in industry generally were simultaneously increasing their exposure to other modernizing institutions posed a challenge which could not be met by the method of following the same men over time unless one ran a complex natural experiment. Such an experiment would require that some men be sent into factories in the countryside without access to newspapers and radios, while others were sent to industry in town but were also denied mass-media contact, and so on. An experiment of that sort is obviously not feasible. With partial correlations, however, the appropriate natural experiment might be crudely approximated, since by that method we could bring under statistical control such experiences as mass-media contact while examining the relationship between factory experience and modernity.

The Challenge of Concomitant Influences

We previously noted that controlling for education, which we knew to be the most powerful of the early-socialization variables, did little to diminish, and in some cases actually enhanced, the correlation of factory experience and modernity. Sociological theory and our actual experience identified mass-media exposure as the key characteristic to be considered among the late-socialization variables. Controlling for it still left factory experience correlated with modernity at a median level of .22, significant at much better than the .001 level. Indeed, even when we controlled both education and mass media simultaneously, as in the seventh line of Table 11–3, the correlation of factory experience and OM was significant at better than the .001 level in all six countries.[22]

This seemed to us unambiguously to establish factory experience as an important independent contributor to making men modern. Nevertheless, a purist might insist that we could not stop at this point. Men who were in the factory for a longer time were also simultaneously spending more time in urban living. Moreover, the longer they were in the factory, the older they got, and, generally, the more they earned. It was possible that these factors, rather than industrial experience itself, were the real cause of the observed increase in modernity among experienced factory workers.

Of these alternative explanations, the one which had to be taken most seriously was urban experience. Urban living is theoretically quite distinct from industrial work, and as a practical matter one could set up factories in the countryside or develop cities without industry. Moreover, a strong case could be made for the assumption that city life should, in its own right, be a strong modernizing influence.

As we read the evidence, however, the influence of urban experience could not explain away our finding that men become more modern the longer they work in industry. First, we had the important information provided by the men of urban origin. Since those men had grown up in the city, urban experience very likely was no longer a new source of influence on them by the time they entered industry. Nevertheless, as we showed above, such men gained in modernity each year they were in the factory.

Second, we accepted the risk, in this case an extreme one, of committing the partialing fallacy by testing the correlation of factory experience and modernity among men of rural origin, even while adding a control for "years of urban experience after age 15" to the standard controls for education and mass media contact.[23] Surprisingly, the results firmly supported our hypothesis: factory experience continued to show a median correlation with modernity of .21, significant at .001 or better in four of the relevant countries, and at .01 in the fifth.[24]

Third, we drew on the special cases we had collected in India and East Pakistan. In both of these countries we had located sets of men who continued to live in their original villages even though they had entered industrial employment in factories built on the outskirts of town near their villages. These "village resident factory workers" had factory experience without urban experience. We compared them, first, to cultivators from the same villages, matched to be as much like the workers as possible. We could do this only in India, but in any event there men in industry were significantly more modern, indeed generally *much* more modern, than their fellow villagers who had continued in agriculture.[25] This certainly suggested that the factory could modernize without the aid of the city.

Of course, the finding just reported might be challenged on the ground that those who went into industry could have been self-selected, being more modern to begin with. The fact that the cases compared were otherwise matched to be alike in most socioeconomic characteristics weighed against that interpretation. In any event, the challenge could be met by leaving the cultivators out of the comparison and restricting our analysis to factory workers only, comparing those living in villages with those living in town. This test could be performed in India and East Pakistan.

If urban living explained the greater part of the previously observed modernity of workers, then workers with urban residence should have been much more modern than those living in villages. In neither India nor East Pakistan did it turn out that way. The factory workers who lived in the villages were as modern as the men in the same factories who lived in town.[26] The results of the matches were supported by a separate analysis relying on the partialing technique.[27] These cases, at least, gave no reason to argue that city living was a necessarily modernizing experience, and certainly gave no cause for claiming that the greater modernity of factory workers should be attributed to the influence of urban living rather than factory employment.

There remained the alternative that either aging or the extra income received by men who had worked longer in industry might account for the apparent impact of factory experience on modernity. We felt the grounds for considering these variables to be logically distinct alternatives to factory experience very much weaker than had been true for urban experience.[28] Moreover, age and income were so strongly correlated with the length of factory experience that to control for them was to maximize the danger of committing the partialing fallacy.[29] Nevertheless, to satisfy those who might insist on controlling for such influences, we did run the appropriate partial correlations.

With age controlled, the median partial correlation of factory experience and modernity was .25, easily significant at better than .001; with income controlled, the median was still .18, also significant at .001; and even adding the standard controls for education and mass media to those for age *and* income left the median partial correlation at .18, still significant at the .001 level.[30] Thus, factory experience again showed an impressive capacity to survive the partialing process, and to defend its standing as an independent factor causing individual modernity.

We thus had established that it was not merely the typical accompaniments of factory experience — such as aging, income or life in the city — which made men modern. It was something above and beyond these concomitants. What remained after they were taken into account was, of course, the day-to-day experience of interaction with the machines and the organizational arrangements which define the special character of industrial labor. Factory work, through its inherent properties, provided training in new ways of orienting oneself toward man, nature, and the social order. *The factory is an effective school in modernity.*

Conclusion

Taking all the evidence into account, we found a firm basis for asserting that industrial work had proved itself a major factor in making men modern. Men who had left the farm and spent years in industry were, as a result, much more often modern than were their "cousins" who continued in agriculture. Those who grew up in the city, and presumably had already been exposed to modes of modern living, nevertheless also found additional stimulus in the factory, so that year by year their work there led to higher OM scores. Neither differential selection or retention, nor the special nature of our samples, could account for the observed effect of the factory, a fact which became unmistakable when we reinterviewed some of the men we had first met 4 and 5 years before. Through the reinterviews we could prove that the very same individuals steadily and vigorously increased their OM scores in the intervening years of factory work. Some part of the change observed over the reinterview period had properly to be attributed to the usual accompaniments of increased factory experience, such as increased exposure to the mass media and larger incomes. But after we took that into account, it was still clear that the qualities inherent in industrial employment consistently exerted a significant influence on men's OM scores. We conclude that the factory is unmistakably a school in modernity. In its own right, the organizational experience it provides serves consistently to change men in ways which qualify them as more modern in attitude, value, and behavior.

12

Factory Modernity

We reasoned that if time spent in a factory made a man modern, the more modern the factory the greater should be the degree of individual change. In our view the factory modernized man because the factory embodies principles which teach. It followed that factories which more fully incorporated those principles in their organization and practice should have been superior schools of modernization. Indeed, we had to face the possibility that factories might not automatically teach individual modernity *unless* they had reached some minimal level of mechanization, rationality, technical proficiency, and organizational effectiveness. It could be that only factories which passed a certain threshold of modernity would have any effect at all on their workers. This possibility, furthermore, did not necessarily conflict with our established finding that there was a significant positive correlation between length of time in the factory and individual modernity. The observed outcome could have been produced by only a few of the more modern factories which were having a marked impact, while the others contributed little or nothing to the correlation.

Classification of the Factories

These considerations led us to devote substantial energies to classifying factories as modern or traditional. The field directors were requested to select the plants they sampled so that, as far as possible, half would qualify as relatively modern and half as traditional. Our sampling instructions contained an extensive guideline setting out in detail our conception of the two types of plant. The guideline developed two different dimensions of modernity. The "human-relations" dimension was to reflect the extent to which "the worker faces management as a citizen — a person possessed of rights, entitled to respectful treatment, capable of more or less equal bargaining (if only through the collective force of his union), who enters into a limited and clearly defined relation with the factory which leaves his private life outside work very largely to his own choosing." The "technical rational" dimension was to express how far "management shows much interest in the efficiency, change and continual improvement of factory organization and production." The full statement of the model ran eight pages.

Each field director was left relatively free to decide for himself how to interpret this guideline in reaching the classification of the factories. In all countries, advisory boards and technical consultants were called on in varying degrees, but the final decision was made by the field director.

His first task was to decide which establishments qualified as factories to be sampled. Everyone is, of course, free to establish his own definition of what constitutes a "factory." We had decided that to enter our sample an establishment had to engage in the production of at least semifinished materials or goods, employ at least 50 persons, make substantial use of machinery and inanimate power, and have at least three levels of authority and responsibility. In most cases the qualifications of each establishment were obvious, but there were numerous instances in which more refined discrimination became necessary. In countries in which there were few factories, the temptation to relax the criteria was substantial. In Nigeria, for example, Dr. Ryan came on a factory making bottle caps, which utilized two high-speed, thoroughly automatic machines which alone produced enough caps to supply all the breweries and soft-drink manufacturers in Nigeria. But, unfortunately, this mechanized, mass-production establishment employed only 30 workers in all its departments. It could not, therefore, qualify for our sample. If it had, it would have been rated modern.[1]

Another Nigerian establishment, one manufacturing furniture, met the division-of-labor requirement because there were a boss, a foreman, a special operator for the one power saw, and sets of workers who assembled the furniture while others put on the finish. Nevertheless, the use of machinery and power was minimal. Indeed, the method of making the furniture in this plant was basically the same as in numerous small separate craft shops employing only 5 or 6 men. Strictly speaking, this plant employed 60 men. On closer inspection, however, it developed that some 35 of them were apprentice helpers to the more experienced men. On this basis Dr. Ryan ruled that the plant did not meet our labor-force requirement, and it was excluded from the sample. Had it been accepted it would have been rated as traditional, not only for its technological backwardness, but also because of its use of the apprentices.[2]

Once an establishment was accepted as meeting our criteria as a factory, it had to be rated as modern or traditional. Fortunately, there were cases where the evidence available seemed relatively unambiguous. Consider, for example, Dr. Schuman's experience in a large East Pakistan factory employing more than 1,000 men. The director, a young man not long out of school, seemed interested in research, and gave our study his fullest cooperation. This was, however, the only thing which suggested a modern rating. The director adopted what seemed to Dr. Schuman a paternalistic and even patronizing attitude toward his workers. He showed little respect for them in Dr. Schuman's presence. For example, if the men said something which seemed foolish to their boss he made a great public joke of it, and laughed loudly and heartily for all to hear. He treated his men not so much as social inferiors, but more as a stern father might treat inefficient and naive children. Moreover, he admitted to using devious procedures in paying wages. Since the union agreement set wage levels according to skill, he arbitrarily classified many skilled men as semiskilled, and semiskilled men as unskilled, thereby insuring himself a lower wage bill. He would not attempt to bribe the trade-union leader, as he claimed other managers did, but his reason for not doing so seemed to be mainly that he might easily be found out. It was notable that this director had established a drama club for the workers, at some expense, and seemed rather pleased and proud that it was so popular. He also freely gave away the milk from the 20 cows which he, as a devout Hindu, kept fed. But this paternalistic concern for his workers did not extend to other realms. Many of his employees wore no shoes, and very few seemed to have any kind of protective clothing, even though they worked with hot molten materials which often had to be moved about in very crowded conditions. As Dr. Schuman commented: "There were no signs about safety at all. There wasn't anything that showed any concern with safety."

Virtually all of this evidence dictated a rating of "traditional" in human relations. The evidence concerning technical modernity pointed overwhelmingly in the same direction. The factory was little more than a large shed with a roof to keep off rain, with partially open sides to permit some passage of air. Some system of record keeping had been developed, but it seemed to be handled in a very informal way. The molding of the molten raw material, and other operations, were performed by very simple hand machinery. There was very little of even semiautomatic equipment. Although the operations were inherently dangerous, lighting was minimal, even on the night shift, and no fire-fighting equipment was visible. Dr. Schuman reported that at night the floor of this plant seemed like a scene from a dimly lit hell. The director, although he obviously knew a good deal in a practical way about the operation of his plant, was not technically trained in the field of its operation. That would have been less serious had he had technically trained assistants. But the plant's chief technician was an older man from another country, and one who proved to be familiar mainly with the nonmachine aspects of the plant's production. The evidence on the technical side, therefore, also pointed unmistakably in one direction. Despite its large size, this factory clearly was to be rated as traditional on both the human-relations and the technical dimensions.

This case seemed fairly clear cut. But in general the rating of factories was full of vicissitudes. Where the field director undertook the rating himself, serious questions could be raised both as to his competence to make such a difficult judgment and as to the reliability of a rating made by one person on the basis of necessarily limited knowledge. When we relied on local experts, however, we sometimes ran into a Tower of Babel. Despite our efforts to standardize the rating process, different experts tended to use quite diverse criteria in judging factories, each influenced by his professional background and personal ideology.[3] The specialist from the health department would consider only the sanitation facilities, the trade-union adviser was interested only in the management's readiness to institute grievance procedures, and the engineer took into account mainly the degree to which the firm was technically advanced. To complicate matters, each expert tended to know different factories, and even when they knew the same plant they would often not agree in their ratings.

We encouraged the field directors to acquire all relevant information they could about each factory. Indeed, in some countries the amount of detail we amassed from the industrial census, government reports, and the factory's own records was substantial, and we are planning separate reports based on that material.[4] For this book, however, we decided to rely mainly on the summary rating of the field director. Doing so had the advantage that our measuring "instrument" was the same throughout any given country, even if it was a different field director who did the rating in each country. This still seemed more consistent than relying on the quite different kinds of information accumulated about the factories from diverse sources in the several countries. Relying on the field directors also had the advantage that all the factories could be rated, whereas the other sorts of data were available for only some plants. Finally, we felt that through their deep involvement in the project the field directors were best able to grasp what the project considered really important in judging a factory. Of course, to insure that the ratings were not influenced by the result of our interviews with the workers, the modernity rating of each factory was assigned before we spoke to the workmen in it.

Checking the project's summary rating of the modernity of each factory against other standards gave us reason to believe that this relatively subjective judgment was indeed significantly related to some relevant independent measures. Two such measures were available: one, the size of factories; the other, the number of benefits, such as medical care, which each factory's workers described their plant as offering. The modernity ratings given by the field directors were consistently and substantially correlated with both of these objective measures.[5]

The fact that the larger plants were more often classified as modern made sense because such plants could more often be expected to afford advanced technology, were under greater pressure to introduce more rational organizational procedures, and were more likely to adopt more progressive personnel practices. Yet the correlation of factory size and modernity, at a median of .24***,[6] was not so high as to suggest that the measures were merely redundant, owing to an unwitting tendency of the field directors to identify bigness with modernity. Indeed, we have given above one illustration of a very small plant in Nigeria classified as modern, and an example from East Pakistan of a very large factory classified as traditional.

If the field directors had inadvertently identified bigness with modernity, that could have influenced the ratings they assigned because they knew the size of each factory at the time they classified it as modern or traditional. There was no such possibility of contamination inherent in the measure of factory benefits. The workers listing the special benefits their factory offered were completely unaware of how we had rated or might rate, their factory's modernity. Neither did the field directors know, when they made their modernity ratings, how the workers would describe the benefits offered by their employers. These judgments were, therefore, virtually absolutely independent. It is notable, therefore, that the field directors' ratings of factories on the modernity dimension and the workers' report of benefits yielded a substantial median correlation of .30***.

Of course, some will question whether the fact that a factory offers benefits — such as vacation with pay, medical services, training in new skills, and help with housing — should qualify it as more modern. In our view, this quality was definitely part of the syndrome defining the modernity of a factory. Indeed, we would more readily acknowledge as legitimate the quite different criticism that our project's rating of the modernity of factories should have had a higher median correlation with the workers' judgment of benefits received.[7] Nevertheless, we feel the substantial agreement between our rating and that of the workers gives confidence that our field directors had been consistent, and used valid criteria, in judging factories as modern or traditional.

Testing the Effect of Factory Qualities

Having clarified the nature of the factory modernity rating and finding it to possess substantial validity, we could move ahead to see what difference it made in explaining individual change.

Since all the factories in India had been rated as modern, we were left with five cases.[8] Looking first at the simple correlations (in the first line of Table 12–1), we received some encouragement in that three of the five remaining countries showed modest but statistically significant correlations between the rated modernity of the factories and the individual modernity of the men in them. But in Chile there was no evident relation, and in Israel the more modern men were actually found in the *less* modern plants at a statistically significant level.[9]

Before reaching a final conclusion, however, we had to face the probability that modern factories would systematically recruit better-educated men with higher skills and other attributes which could make them modern without any help from the factory.[10] The matching procedure permitted us to meet this challenge by comparing men who were alike in all important respects except that one group worked in modern, the other in traditional factories.[11] When these matched groups were pitted against each other, as in Table 12–1, we found, as before, that Argentina and Nigeria yielded fairly strong statistically significant correlations indicating that men working in more modern factories were themselves more modern as a result. With the stringent controls used in the matches, however, East Pakistan no longer supported our expectation, and Chile and Israel again failed to give support to our theory.

Table 12-1. Correlations of measures of factory quality and individual modernity scores (OM-500).[a]

Factory quality	Argentina	Chile	East Pakistan	India	Israel	Nigeria
All factory workers						
Modernity	.18***	−.01	.13**	—	−.11*	.11
Benefits	.09*	.13**	.10***	.25***	.17***	.28***
Size	.06	−.01	−.12**	.14***	−.11*	.06
N	663	715	654	700	544	520
Men matched on background characteristics[b]						
Modernity	.27**	−.01	−.02	—	−.06	.25**
(Match 15)	(65)	(68)	(90)		(80)	(54)
Benefits	−.01	.06	.05	.11	.29*	.12
(Match 28)	(80)	(84)	(44)	(36)	(37)	(18)
Size	−.01	−.09	−.01	.07	.07	.01
(Match 22)	(107)	(55)	(79)	(34)	(90)	(50)

[a] Asterisks denote significance as follows: *, at .05 level; **, at .01 level; ***, at .001 level or better.

[b] Figures in parentheses are the numbers of matched pairs in each country.

Being right in two of five countries hardly met our standard for establishing a generalization valid cross-nationally. Nevertheless, to obtain a correlation which could be expected by chance alone only once in a thousand tries, and to obtain that result in two of five countries, suggested that we were very likely on the right track. There seemed to be something about particular factories which intensified their impact on workers, and, if we could, we meant to find what it was.

The Role of Factory Benefits

Our modernity rating of the factories was an outsider's judgment. We wondered whether we might have done better to adopt the insider's view. If the man who worked there found his factory an agreeable and supportive milieu, then, regardless of how we judged it, he might more readily accept the lessons it had to teach. We had no direct measure of whether or not workers thought their plant modern. It would have taken too much time to have explained the concept to them. Moreover, to do so would have had the further disadvantage of alerting our respondents to the objectives of our research, and thus perhaps inadvertently influencing their answers. But our question, "Did you receive any of the following benefits from your factory?" served as a reasonable substitute.[12] The number of benefits cited by each man was counted. The rating each man gave his factory could thus be correlated with other characteristics of the plant. As previously noted, the rating of factories by this approach agreed well with the judgment of our field directors as to each factory's modernity, but not so well as to be redundant. It clearly was in many ways an independent measure and we also had reason to believe that it was a fairly reliable one, since the men from any given plant tended to agree about the number of benefits their factory offered.

The simple correlation of number of perceived benefits and individual modernity was positive and statistically significant in all six countries, and markedly so in three of them, as indicated in Table 12–1. This result led us to believe this approach to measuring factory modernity might prove more productive. But since so many other factors might have influenced the outcome, we required the check which a match could provide. In Match 28 we compared men who reported their factory as offering relatively few benefits with those who credited their plant with offering many. On the average, with some variation by country, "few" generally meant about two benefits and "many" generally meant just under five. As usual, the men were drawn so as to be otherwise alike on as many other variables as we could practically match them.[13]

Only in Israel did the match correlations, summarized in Table 12–1, yield a statistically significant difference between the set of men who rated their factories as giving many benefits and those who rated them as giving few. Of the two countries for which the matching had previously shown substantial influence to be exerted by the factory modernity rating, only one, Nigeria, again gave some indication that the benefits measure also had some meaning. With only three of the match correlations more than negligible, and only one significant, we had to conclude that defining a factory's modernity on the basis of the benefits offered by it was even less serviceable as a predictor of individual modernity than the field directors' ratings, at least when so many other variables were controlled in the matching process. We could temper the disappointment of this conclusion by noting that, in this case, the matching process may well have involved us deeply in the partialing fallacy, a situation we will attempt to correct below.[14] But up to this point there was little evidence of an *independent* contribution to individual modernity having been made by the quality of the factory when that quality was measured by ratings of the benefits offered in each factory.

The Effect of Size

Both the project directors' and the workers' ratings were basically subjective estimates, even though they had some relation to objective facts. Perhaps our inability to discover any power of discrimination in these predictors of individual modernity stemmed from this subjectivity. An objective measure would possibly have provided a more reliable standard of judgment. Of course, there is no such thing as a truly "objective" rating of a factory's modernity. We therefore fell back on our measure of the *size* of each factory as the best of the objective ratings we had.

The simple correlations of factory size and individual modernity (Table 12–1) were not too promising. In three countries there was a significant correlation, but only in the case of India did it indicate that the large factories had more modern men. In Israel and East Pakistan the small plants had more modern men. Since we knew that the size of the plant could be associated with differences in education, skill, and other personal qualities, it seemed wise to suspend judgment until we brought these factors under control through matching.

In our Match 22 on size of factory, we compared men from "small" plants with those working in "large" establishments.[15] The usual array of additional variables was then controlled to match each man from a small factory as closely as possible with his opposite number in a large one. The number of pairs we could thus obtain was everywhere sufficient and even ample. The match was of good quality.[16] The results of running these matched groups against our OM scales indicated that the mere size of a factory was of no relevance at all in determining whether the men who worked there were more or less modern. In no country, including those having given evidence to the contrary in the simple correlations, was there statistically significant evidence of an association between factory size and individual modernity once other relevant variables were controlled. Leaving statistical significance aside, we could not even point to any consistency in direction. Half the cases suggested that larger factories made for more modernity, and half favored the opposite conclusion. But since all the relations were so weak it seemed wiser to ignore direction, and to emphasize the general lack of association between individual modernity and factory size, large or small.

Alternative Explanations of the Results

Our initial experience with the various measures of factory quality was disappointing. The results did not fulfill our expectations and failed to confirm our theory. We could not too readily blame this failure on the poor quality of our measures. The men reporting on the benefits they received were not recalling events from the distant past, as from childhood, but rather were describing fairly recent experiences. Moreover, we had ourselves been able to observe at first hand what the different factories were like. We were not limited to one measure, but rather could draw on three: the project rating, the perceived-benefits report, and the size classification. How then could we account for the weak results? Several explanations seemed to merit serious consideration.

One alternative was not to apologize, but simply to accept the facts and acknowledge that our theoretical expectations had been wrong. Factories do modernize, but modern factories do not necessarily modernize more rapidly or more thoroughly. Rather than be upset by this finding we might be pleased, because it gave us one of the rare opportunities to show that not everything in social science is obvious, no matter how much it may seem so. Dozens of people to whom we had described our research plan said: "Well, it's a nice idea, but why bother? It's obvious that modern plants will more effectively modernize the men in them. That's true almost by definition, isn't it?" We were simpleminded enough to believe that the connection existed, but stubborn enough to insist on getting the evidence, even at the risk of being ridiculed for trying to prove the obvious. Lo and behold, the obvious turned out not to be true.

As the truth, even when unexpected, becomes more familiar, it also becomes more acceptable. We can argue that, after all, a factory is a factory. Because of the strict qualifications on which we insisted, all the factories in our sample used power, had machinery, involved substantial division of labor, depended upon technical competence, and transformed raw materials into finished goods by utilizing some degree of mass production supported by complex rational organization. It might then be argued that insofar as these are the basic prerequisites for making the factory a school in modernization, and since all those we studied possessed it, all should have been more or less equally effective. The qualities which make a factory modern do not change the most fundamental aspects of the organizational forms used in *all* industrial production. The qualities which make a factory modern may constitute little more than a marginal type of differentiation, and their effect, therefore, may be only very modest. And that would have been all the more the case in our research, because we had set so high a standard in defining the minimum qualifications to be met before a productive establishment could qualify as a "factory."

Moreover, we were encouraged to stick to our findings because they were in agreement with the results of a massive study of American public schools. The so-called "Coleman Report" also found that the effectiveness of schools bore very little relationship to their "quality," so long as one first controlled for the effect produced by the socioeconomic characteristics of the children in the schools studied. In the Coleman report the quality of the school was defined by measures of its physical facilities and its curriculum, which may reasonably be interpreted as analogues to our measures of a factory's rated modernity, size, and benefits provided.[17] Evidently, social scientists — ourselves included — had in the past been too quick to accept the common-sense assumption that just because one has a modern physical plant, a more "advanced" staff, and a streamlined organization, one can do a better job of training people than can institutions which put on a plainer front and go about their tasks in a more routine manner without the special qualities we associate with more "progressive" outfits.

This possibility had, indeed, been anticipated by some members of the project staff. In retrospect, we found particularly prescient certain observations which Dr. Schuman recorded in his diary in 1963, after he had completed his first factory visits. The factory which stimulated him to this comment was the very Pakistani plant described in detail at the beginning of this chapter. Despite Dr. Schuman's firm classification of that factory as very traditional according to the standards of our project, he had grave doubts as to whether it really would be a less effective school in modernity. After his visit to the plant he wrote the following comment in his diary:

> In general, what seemed paradoxical was that many of the workers here probably had to exercise more skill — although they may have been less conscious of it — than workers in a much more modern factory. And I have the feeling that this is something that I'll meet from now on: that the modern factories will not necessarily be the ones where the men actually have more contact with modern techniques. These men were having contact not with absolutely modern techniques, but with techniques that were modern as compared to what they may have practiced in their village. And they were having more intimate contact with these techniques. Moreover, since the

equipment was generally primitive, the men could probably understand what they were doing much more than, say, the men in the very modern government flour mill who were working tremendous machines, most of which they could not understand because that equipment was run by mechanisms that were covered up, not visible. In this factory basically everyone could pretty well understand the process and could feel a very intimate part of it. This makes me wonder a bit about the "traditional-modern" distinction in the way that we have been using it. Should we not get out of the frame of reference of the specialists who are basing their ratings on advances in technology relative to other factories, or in terms of safety conditions, or of amenities for the workers? In all these respects this factory may have been very backward, but from the standpoint of a man's actual contact with the industrial process, I am not sure at all that it is backward as a learning experience.

A Composite Measure of Factory Modernity

Having completed a series of empirical probes of the issue of factory modernity we were quite ready to acknowledge that the evidence did not support the assertion that the factories rated "modern" on various dimensions in fact consistently made men significantly more modern than did traditional plants. But before we definitively rejected the proposition that the quality of a factory must play some special role in how fast or how far men become modern, we felt that we had to meet some objections to the way in which we had gone about testing the effects of factory modernity.

For one thing, our matching procedure might somehow have covered up the effect which more modern factories actually have. The matches based on the project rating, on size, and on the benefits measure, gave some hints that the more modern factories did indeed more often have modern workers. The persistent difficulty was that the differences observed were too small to qualify as statistically significant. Moreover, in each match we had controlled for the effect of at least one of the other closely related variables. Factories rated modern were compared to factories rated traditional only insofar as they were equal in size, and vice versa; and the match on benefits was controlled for both factory size and rated modernity. A good case can be made for the appropriateness of such controls for certain purposes. Yet we had to recognize that if factory modernity is a *syndrome* made up more or less equally of the qualities these three matches dealt with separately, then our procedure might have artificially obscured the underlying relation. In other words, we had committed the partialing fallacy.

We had two means available to set matters to rights. First, we could rerun the matches, taking care not to control any of the other basic factory-quality measures, thus avoiding the partialing fallacy. We did this, and found the results provided no more evidence of the independent contribution of factory modernity, benefits and size, than had the earlier matches.[18]

There remained, then, the second alternative, which was to rate the factories on the basis of the combination of all three measures. This had the virtue of permitting the potential contribution of each aspect of plant modernity to accumulate along with the other effects, thus more naturally reflecting the power of that complex of qualities which together perhaps more accurately defines factory "modernity."

We thereupon constructed such a composite measure of factory quality, giving equal weights to the project rating, the measure of size, and the workers' report of benefits. This procedure gave us a match of good quality, and one with a very comfortable number of cases in each country. Alas, this composite measure of factory quality, represented by Match 59 in Table 12–2, was no more, indeed, was even less, discriminating than the original project modernity rating standing alone. Only in Argentina was there a modestly significant correlation favoring the modern factory. The correlations for India and Israel also met our minimum standard, but they were not high enough to be statistically significant with the number of cases available in the matches.

The limitations imposed by the small number of cases entering the match could be overcome by using the full sample of workers and partial

Table 12–2. Correlations of composite measure of factory modernity and individual modernity (OM).[a]

Correlation	Argentina	Chile	East Pakistan	India	Israel	Nigeria
I. **Simple** (zero-order)	.12**	.06	.05	.22***	.07	.20***
II. **Partial,** controlling for—						
Early socialization experience	.06	.03	.02	.12**	.11**	.11*
Late socialization experience	.10*	−.00	.05	.14***	.05	.15***
Set A(early and late socialization)	.06	−.01	.02	.05	.08	.10*
III. **Match correlation**[b]	.12*	−.03	−.02	.14	.10	.03
N's for Parts I & II	663	715	654	700	544	520
N's for Part III[c]	161	153	79	37	145	52

a Asterisks denote significance as follows: *, at .05 level; **, at .01 level; ***, at .001 level or better
b This match pitted men from factories rated low on the composite measure of factory modernity versus men from factories rated high.
c Figures given are the numbers of pairs in the match.

correlations to control other variables. With a composite measure of factory quality similar to that used in the matching, the full sample of factory workers yielded significant correlations with individual modernity in three of six countries, as indicated in Table 12–2. All three correlations were reduced, but remained significant when we controlled only the other late-socialization variables. This certainly indicated that factory quality is not an inconsequential matter. Our gratification with this outcome was, however, rather diminished when we applied controls for the full array of late- and early-socialization variables in Set A. Then only Nigeria continued to show a significant correlation. We were obliged to conclude, therefore, that once the main background variables were controlled, the quality of the factory, at least as measured by our composite rating, had only a very weak, even if fairly consistent, positive effect on the modernity of the working man.

Additional Measures of Factory Quality

Another possibility for explaining these meager results was that our conception of factory modernity was at fault. There are other ways of conceiving modernity than by expert rating, size, and workers' perceptions. The critical factor might, for example, have been the attitudes of the managers. After all, these are the men who determine the psychosocial climate of the factory and probably serve as the most important role models for the men who work under them. Or again, it might be that the most important determinant was the "quality" of the other men with whom our interviewees had worked. In some plants the men were, on the average, much superior in education, experience, and other qualities associated with modernity. If a man learned to be modern mainly through his associations with work mates, their character might have been more important in shaping the individual's modernization than even the ideology of management. Such an outcome, moreover, would have been predicted on the basis of the main conclusion of the Coleman report.

Still a third approach argued that the key to modernization in the factory context lies in the degree to which a given plant permits the workers an opportunity to exercise meaningful control over the course of their life at work. This theme of workers' control over the pace, the patterning, and other aspects of the work process was particularly emphasized in Blauner's study of worker satisfaction in American industry, but it had been stressed as well in Crozier's research in France, and by Sayles, March and Simon, and others.[19] These and other studies indicated that when workers can negotiate with management, have more autonomy in arranging the work process at their own discretion, and control some of the resources vital to effective management, their sense of efficacy is enhanced, and their *engagement* with their work is deepened. Such conditions should, in turn, operate to make men more open to the lessons the factory has to teach.

These theories about the qualities of factories deemed relevant to worker modernization certainly did not exhaust the list we might have compiled, but they were among the more notable. We felt that by studying the factory qualities identified by these theories we should be able to quiet any suspicion that our earlier failure to find factory modernity a consistently significant force in individual modernization was due merely to our mistakenly having limited ourselves mainly to the three measures of modernity we have used so far.[20]

To test the relevance of these additional dimensions we developed a special measure of each quality which these new theories identified as an important attribute of the factory.[21] To rate the managers' attitudes we relied on a special questionnaire we had administered to the men who ran the plants from which we drew our worker samples. These managers were asked their views as to the best policy to adopt in regard to a series of questions facing management, for example: How valuable can the workers' initiative be as a contribution to increased production? Is it vital to inform workers ahead of time as to changes in the flow of production planned by management? How much attention should one pay to the feelings of the workers?

To assess the *quality of the work force* we developed a composite measure, based on company or government statistics, which gave us the age, education, average skill level, and other characteristics of the workers in each factory. The degree of workers' control was assessed by a scale which took into account features of each factory's organization, such as the use by management of time and motion studies and formal production controls.

To assess the ability of these new variables to explain worker modernity we did not undertake new matches, but rather turned to a computer-based multiple analysis of covariance program. This program permitted us to deal with the argument that the modernization of the worker is too complex and subtle a process to depend on the presence or absence of only a single factor, but rather requires some special combination of elements to bring it about. Fortunately, the main virtue of an analysis of covariance lies precisely in that it permits one to study interaction effects. Our analysis of covariance tested the power of a very large proportion of all the possible combinations of six measures, namely: rated modernity, factory size, managers' attitudes, worker control, work-force quality, and a sixth measure of the relative "isolation" of the factory from large urban centers.

These measures were tested alone, then in pairs, and finally in a number of instances in the more likely seeming combinations of three. As in the case of the partial correlations, several other important variables were controlled at the same time.[22] We could thus test how far these combinations of factors could give new life to the theory that some special qualities of the workplace, going beyond the mere fact that it is a factory, play a substantial role in influencing how far a man will become modern.

In only four countries was there enough information to score all the factories on all the relevant dimensions. To interpret the results, presented in Table 12–3, requires a discussion more technical than we feel it permissible to introduce in our main text. In nontechnical language, however, we may say the following:

1. The extra contribution to explaining individual OM scores which came from the interaction of several factory qualities in combination was

Table 12–3. Analysis of covariance relating factory qualities to individual modernity: betas significant on OM-3.[a]

Factory quality	Argentina	Chile	Nigeria	Pakistan
Tested alone				
Factory modernity	.15***	—	—	.03***
Size	—	—	—	.08***
Workers' control	—	—	.06***	.03*
Managers' attitudes	—	—	.08***	—
Qualities of workers	—	.06*	—	.05***
Isolation	.03*	.15**	.15***	.09*
Tested in pairs				
Factory modernity by—				
Size	—	.07**	—	.13***
Workers' control	—	—	—	.15***
Managers' attitudes	—	—	.14**	—
Qualities of workers	—	—	—	.11***
Isolation	—	—	.09***	—
Size by managers' attitudes	—	.15**	—	—
Workers' control by qualities of workers	—	—	—	.06*
Managers' attitudes by qualities of workers	—	.17**	—	.15**
Tested as a set of three				
Factory modernity by size by workers' control	.07*	—	—	—
Factory modernity by workers' control by managers' attitude	.05**	.08**	.09**	—
Factory modernity by managers' attitudes by isolation	—	—	.14**	—

[a] Asterisks denote significance as follows: *, at .05 level; **, at .01 level; ***, at .001 level or better. Varying the "order of entry" of the various measures in no case altered the significance levels of the betas, although the values of the betas themselves did fluctuate somewhat. A dash (—) means "not significant" rather than indicating that the combination was not attempted.

often statistically significant. This happened sufficiently often to indicate there is something to the hypothesis that one should not study different factory qualities in isolation one at a time.

2. Even with the aid of such interaction effects, we could generally not explain a great deal of an individual's modernity by reference to the qualities of the factory he worked in, once we had taken account of the length of time the man had been in the factory and his skill level.

3. There was unfortunately no pattern in the way the combinations of factory qualities could be drawn upon to explain individual modernity. The two-element combinations of qualities were generally more powerful predictors of individual modernity than were single qualities, but alas, the three-element combinations did not explain more than the sets of two elements. Moreover, except for the combination of modernity and size, which worked in two of four countries, no pattern was important in more than one place. This was quite different from our experience with variables such as education, mass-media exposure, and factory experience, which worked everywhere in about the same way.

One can hardly build a general theory on the basis of such results. The best we can say is that certain qualities of the factory which test its modernity seemed — in some combinations, in some countries, at some times — to have a statistically significant effect on the modernization of the worker. Or to put it more positively: in every country we found some single feature of the factory, or some combination of qualities, which seemed substantially to influence the modernization of the individual beyond the effect produced by merely spending time in *any* factory, but this single factor, or combination of elements, was distinctive to each country. Moreover, once we discovered it, we found that its impact was modest.

Conclusion

We conclude, therefore, that the sheer amount of time a man spent in a factory was a much more powerful determinant of how modern he became than was any single attribute or combination of attributes of that factory. When the time spent in the plant was taken into account, the special qualities of the factory — whether it was modern or traditional, large or small, staffed by well-educated or less competent men, or run by liberal or conservative managers — seemed to add little, at least on a regular basis, to the effect of the factory as a school in modernization.

We emphasize, of course, that this is a statistical generalization expressing our experience in six countries across a large number of factories. We have found quite a bit of evidence that here and there one encounters outstanding exceptions.[23] In those cases, either enlightened management or other special features of the factory evidently played a special role in significantly speeding up the modernization of the men who worked there. To discover more precisely which plants have this outstanding ability to modernize men more rapidly and more completely, and then to search out the distinctive qualities of those unusual factories, must be the object of a special research which will go beyond what we have been able to accomplish so far.

13

The Role of Agricultural Cooperatives

In selecting the factory as our chief exemplar of a modernizing institution, we did not assume that its capacity to make men modern arose exclusively from the use of machinery and inanimate power. Although we assigned these an important role, our emphasis was more on the factory as a particular form of social organization, characterized by rational planning, ready acceptance of new technology, authority based on technical competence, coordination of the efforts of large numbers of individuals, and treatment according to impartial rules. But factories do not have a monopoly on such principles of organization and standards of performance. We were, therefore, eager to test the modernizing influence of institutional settings, other than the factory, which nevertheless shared some of its noteworthy characteristics. The rural cooperative seemed to us to qualify as such an institution.

In contrasting the factory so sharply with the typical village, we did not mean to suggest that agricultural pursuits as such made men traditional. On the contrary, we were quite convinced that under the right circumstances men living in villages and continuing to work in agriculture could be helped to become more modern at as brisk a pace as that characteristic for men in factories. We were, therefore, quick to take advantage of the opportunity to study the impact of the rural cooperatives organized by the Pakistan Academy for Rural Development. They represent our first test of the power of nonfactory and nonurban settings to bring about the modernization of adults. Israel provided us with an additional opportunity to explore the issue, since we could there study the *moshav,* a quite different form of agricultural cooperative. The social situation of the farmers in these two settings was, in certain important respects, quite different from that shaping the lives of the other cultivators in our several national samples.

Most of the cultivators we interviewed were small landholders producing mainly for subsistence, although some were partially involved in cash crops for a market. These smallholders lived in largely self-governing villages in which the overwhelming majority of the villagers were also small private farmers, each running his own family farm. This pattern prevailed exclusively in Nigeria and India, almost exclusively in East Pakistan, and for about one-third of the cultivator sample in Argentina.

All of the Chilean farmers, and two-thirds of the Argentinian, were essentially agricultural laborers on large estates working for wages in cash and in kind. Although most of these farm laborers did not own land, their service on the estates generally carried with it the right to cultivate personal plots of variable size. Their status was, therefore, technically different from that of the nominally independent farmer elsewhere.

Yet even the independent farmer in India and Pakistan often farmed a tiny plot, hired himself out to work the land of others, and was heavily in debt to rich landowners and to money lenders. All this contributed to making him not so different from the Chilean and Argentinian farmer, except that the latter worked for what was nominally a "large organization." These organizations were, however, the epitome of what we think of as traditionalism in agriculture. They were large estates, *fundos* as they are called in Chile, dominated by a *patrón* who was generally an absentee landlord living in the capital city and leaving most of the responsibility for his farm to an overseer. The absentee owner took little or no interest in technological improvements, machinery was used only minimally, modern seeds and methods of cultivation were not regularly introduced, and human relations were dominated by the classical paternalistic pattern of extreme superordination on the one hand, and extreme dependency on the other.

There were, however, two important exceptions to the conventional pattern predominant in our samples of cultivators. In East Pakistan, in the area now forming Bangladesh, we collected a special subsample of farmers who had been enrolled in the so-called "Comilla" cooperatives. And in Israel all of our farmers participated in a special form of agricultural co-op known as the moshav. As we noted in the introduction to this section, these groups permitted us to determine how far men who continue in village agriculture may nevertheless attain a high level of modernity when some of the organizational principles common in industry are brought to the countryside by the cooperative movement.

Agricultural Cooperatives in East Pakistan: The Comilla Experiment[1]

The Comilla experiment takes its name from both the town and the district of Comilla, headquarters for the Pakistan Academy of Rural Development. Just a few years before our field work began in East Pakistan in 1964, the Academy had launched in the villages surrounding Comilla town what is widely acknowledged to be one of the most impressive of contemporary ventures in organizing cooperative farming. Since we were getting part of our Pakistani sample of cultivators from that district, Dr. Schuman took the initiative and included in his interviewing a special subsample of men who lived in the villages touched by the cooperative program.

The Comilla District was one of the seventeen provinces into which the former eastern wing of Pakistan was divided. It was also the administrative center for Kotwali Thana, a smaller unit comparable to the county in the United States. In 1960, four years before our interviews took place, Comilla District and Kotwali Thana were quite typical of East Pakistan, except for the distinction of having been chosen, respectively, as the headquarters of the Academy of Rural Development and the site of an experimental program in agricultural cooperation. Over 90 percent of the people in the thana were engaged in agriculture. They worked minuscule plots, commonly only one-fourth of an acre, on which they practiced ancient methods of cultivation.[2] Even these tiny plots were generally heavily mortgaged, and almost everyone was deeply in debt to the money lenders. Less than 20 percent of the people could read. The religious orientation of the population, overwhelmingly Muslim, was profoundly conservative. It was a timeless, changeless place in which the prospects for rapid development seemed poor indeed.

It was precisely this challenge which led Dr. Akhter Hameed Khan to locate his newly founded Pakistan Academy for Rural Development in Comilla in 1959–1960. A history of failure had characterized numerous efforts to bring about rapid agricultural development in East Pakistan. Such efforts had included establishing rural branches of banks and developing cooperative societies in the villages. But Khan believed he could break the discouraging cycle of failure which had characterized previous ventures, replacing the piecemeal efforts of the past with a truly comprehensive program which would attack the problem of rural backwardness on a number of fronts at once.

Unlike earlier programs, however, this one was not to come exclusively from above. Rather, Khan's main principle was to work more closely with the people, in tune with their aspirations and the reality of their situation. This required that his institute be located not in the capital city, where schools of agriculture were so often placed in developing countries, but rather in the heart of the agricultural land and in the midst of the

cultivators toward whom his program was to be directed. Since the project was to be experimental, he also needed freedom both from the interfer-
ence of important officials and from many of the usual bureaucratic
rules and regulations. Because A. H. Khan had the friendship and the
support of Ayub Khan, then President of Pakistan, he was assured not
only resources but special powers to experiment with new methods
of local administration coordinated with the program of the Academy
for Rural Development.[3]

Under these auspices the Academy was founded in 1959, and began
actual operations in 1960. The experiment was initially limited to Kotwali
Thana, the county surrounding Comilla town, an area of 107 square miles
with a population of somewhat over 150,000, living in about 150 villages.
As experience accumulated and the success of the program became apparent, it was extended to other thanas, but at the time we came on the
scene in 1964 it was solidly established only in Kotwali Thana, and our
report is limited to the experience in that one county.[4]

Exercising the unusual powers he had been granted, A. H. Khan substantially integrated the activities of the Academy, the cooperative
movement, and the local government officials concerned with development. The Thana Council, a coordinating institution consisting of the
elected leaders of the local "union councils," met at the Academy. Local
government officials concerned with development, such as the Agricultural Officer and the Fisheries Officer, also sat with the Council. They
could thus learn at first hand the concerns of the people, and could communicate their intentions back to the villages through the Council members. The Academy also was headquarters for the Central Cooperative
Association, linking the village cooperatives which were the key element
in the entire scheme, and provided the Association with administrative
direction, technical assistance, and financial support. Finally, the Academy
was home to the training school of the thana development center. Each
day of the week a different group of village representatives came in for
training in agricultural practice, public health, family planning, and the
like, and these representatives were expected to carry the word back to the
villages.

The Co-op Program

The Pakistan Academy for Rural Development brought into the lives
of those it reached three intimately related ingredients which were
almost totally lacking before its arrival: organization, resources, and
participation.

Before the advent of the program initiated by A. H. Khan each vil-
lager in Kotwali Thana was limited to his own pathetically meager
resources, plus what little help he might get from his equally poor and

beleaguered relatives. Apart from those relatives, and such limited knowledge as his traditional culture endowed him with, he faced the world pretty much alone on his small plot of land. Thus, when the first instructors were sent out, they found that "it was very difficult to get the villagers to discuss their problems with the instructors or with one another . . . each family felt its troubles were unique."

The Development Program transformed the situation of the residents of Kotwali Thana by making it possible for them to join cooperative societies which linked their members to others in the village, to a Central Cooperative Association uniting the various village societies, and to the Academy. Through the Academy they were, in turn, linked to the world, because the Academy could draw on the resources of both the government of East Pakistan and the scientific community of the entire world.

With the cooperatives came a plethora of new information, new roles to play, and new techniques to use. The Central Association had special sections for agricultural extension, water development, provision and maintenance of tractors, and marketing. Outside the cooperative movement, the Academy organized programs for training midwives and enlisted local religious leaders in programs for running schools. Thus, the Academy Development Program linked the formerly isolated cultivator to a large number of new and effective organizational networks, each of which could serve to broaden his horizons and widen the base of social support on which he could rely.

The organizational framework fostered by the program also brought to the village cultivator a host of resources which would otherwise have been denied him. The Academy program placed special emphasis on loans to cooperative members, which enabled villagers to pay off the heavy indebtedness with which most were encumbered. For the first time in generations, many came to own their land outright and so could free themselves from the money lenders whose interest rates ran to 50 percent and more. Among the many resources which the development program made available to the farmer in Kotwali Thana, some were of a purely local nature, like land and money; some, like roads, specially dug "tube wells," and tractors, depended on funds which ordinarily only the national budget could supply; and others, such as the new, more productive, and disease-resistant strains of rice, were benefits yielded by the international scientific community. Previously, access to virtually all of these resources, but most assuredly to those stemming from the national budget and international science, would have been only a remote possibility likely never to materialize for the average cultivator on his tiny plot. Through the work of the Academy Development Program these remote possibilities became current realities in the daily lives of thousands of cultivators in Kotwali Thana.

Nevertheless, neither the organization nor the resources brought by the Academy would, in our opinion, have been sufficient in themselves to insure the success of the development program. We believe that the distinctive feature of the Academy's approach was its emphasis on participation. The Academy's leader, A. H. Khan, insisted that the people themselves "must make plans to increase their production." "Loans cannot make them richer," he said, "unless they increase their [own] income."

Those of our readers whose image of the typical village assumes it to be preeminently the natural home of mutual trust, cooperation, and aid may be surprised by so much emphasis on participation as something which had to be *brought* to the villagers by the development program. But the idyll of the village entertained by so many of the world's urban intellectuals is seldom the reality in any particular village. As one of the Academy's reports put it: "There is much factionalism in the villages, and these [requirements for cooperation] are not easy prerequisites. The first few cooperatives were a real venture in faith for their members, and the instructors spent many patient hours with each new group."[5]

The development program, therefore, was designed to encourage self-help and to provide a variety of opportunities for participation in local affairs. To stay in good standing in his co-op, and in particular to have the privilege of obtaining loans from it, each member was under strict obligation to save money on a weekly basis. No matter how poor he was, each farmer was obliged to put *something* into the cooperative funds on a regular basis. To obtain a loan, furthermore, each individual, and the cooperative as a whole, had to present a production plan. The details were worked out in general discussion at cooperative meetings. The plan had to show by name which member would borrow how much for what purpose. The loans, however, were given by the Central Association to the local co-op as a whole, rather than to the individual. The total loan was guaranteed by the cooperative community, so that all had an interest in the fulfillment of the obligation of each. In each case, therefore, the loan application was reviewed by a jury of peers who had a personal stake in having the loan put to productive use, and who could judge from intimate knowledge whether or not the venture was practical. Use of the pumps for irrigation at the deep wells also required extensive cooperation and mutual coordination of each member with the others.

Other opportunities for direct participation in local affairs were numerous. The more effective and energetic could become co-op organizers, the leaders who organized the weekly meeting in the village and represented the local co-op at the Central Cooperative Association and at the Academy. Any cultivator could also serve as a Model Farmer for his village, thus becoming a leader in the introduction of new seed, stock, and techniques. New posts as supervisors, marketing agents, and accountants were created, as well as new jobs in maintaining and operating the tractors and pumps which had been introduced. The development program also brought to the village a certain amount of instruction in literacy, birth control and family planning, health, animal husbandry, and fish culture. Some individuals were selected for more intensive training at the thana headquarters, and then brought back their knowledge to the village, giving instruction open to everyone, whether a member of the cooperative or not.

The Academy Development Program was evidently highly successful in attaining its official objectives of establishing village cooperatives and advancing agricultural modernization. Starting from zero in 1959, the number of village co-ops reached 59 by mid-1962, and rose to 122 by mid-1964. Between the fiscal year 1961–62 and fiscal 1964–65 the average member's deposit in his cooperative society doubled, going from 52 to 103 rupees. The cultivation of new varieties of rice doubled each year from 1961 on, so that by 1964 the use of these higher-yield and more resistant strains had increased from six to eight times over the 1960 level. In the geographical area of the experiment, 75 percent or more of the population had by 1964 adopted such practices as chemical fertilizing, inoculation and vaccination of the family, and saving and borrowing through the village cooperative.

Modernity and Cooperation in Comilla

Impressive as these results were, they could be challenged by some who would say the figures are mainly a testimonial to the energy and determination of the Academy staff, which came in from outside. They would ask: "How far do these figures reflect a real change in the local people themselves, one which was internalized by them and which could be expected to persist even if the Academy and its organizational apparatus and resources were no longer there to press for and reward the adoption of new ways of doing things?"

This is a reasonable question, even in the framework of the objectives which the Academy Development Program set itself. Many specialists in development argue that only "self-sustaining" growth merits designation as truly successful development. Impressive as the Comilla figures on the number of inoculations and acres planted to new rice strains might be, they could not answer the question as to how far the psychology of the people had been changed in a basic and presumably lasting way. The body of data collected by our project, however, provided precisely the information needed. Furthermore, as a basis for evaluating the success of the Comilla experiment our data had the great advantage that, unlike the economic statistics presented above, they did not come from the Academy itself, but rather from a completely independent and disinterested source.

To test the success of the Academy Development Program in changing the attitudes and values of typical Pakistani cultivators, Dr. Howard Schuman, our field director for East Pakistan, administered our standard questionnaire to 58 cultivators from 17 different villages in Kotwali Thana. The men to be interviewed in Kotwali Thana were selected on the same basis as in the villages elsewhere. In each village chosen for study, a list of all men eligible according to our sampling criteria was prepared on the basis of local records and informants. Men were considered eligible if they were between 20 and 30 years of age, known to be of rural origin, not educated beyond the eighth grade, and employed more or less exclusively as tillers of the soil. No attempt was made in sampling to use cooperative membership as a criterion for selection. As it turned out, our interviews in the experimental villages included men who were not members of the cooperatives as well as those who were, as would be expected by chance alone. This outcome was essential to permit the full range of comparisons we meant to make later.

Table 13–1 presents the men we studied in the Comilla District arranged in a special sequence of groups, selected to highlight the extent of their contact with the cooperative movement. The men in each cell were carefully matched so that they were alike in important respects, such as

Table 13–1. Match results for effect of Comilla cooperative movement on individual modernity (OM-500): Match 45 (4-way).[a]

	Work setting		
	Nonco-op village	**Co-op village**	**Factory**
		Nonco-op member	Co-op member	
Mean OM score	46	51	60	54
Percent high on OM	20	25	65	35

Match number	Correlations[b,c]
45e	⌐————.19—⌐
45f	⌐————.54***————⌐
45h	⌐———.45***⌐
45j	⌐——–.31*—⌐

a This 4-way match involves 80 men in four groups of 20 men each. The first three groups consist of cultivators resident in Comilla District; the fourth group consists of factory workers of Comilla origin.

b Asterisks denote significance as follows: *, at .05 level; **, at .01 level; ***, at .001 level or better.

c A positive correlation indicates that the group on the right is higher on OM-500.

education and age, while differing in their relation to the cooperatives.[6]

Cell 1 includes cultivators from villages in which there were no co-operatives. These were typical Bengali villages, and since all were from outside Kotwali Thana, the men living in them were not exposed in any way to the special influence of the Academy program. This group represents, therefore, the base line against which the other groups may be assessed.

Cell 2 includes cultivators from villages in which there were coopera-tives, but these men were themselves not members of the co-ops. Approxi-mately half of the families in villages with cooperatives were not members of the organization. Nevertheless, they were exposed to certain programs undertaken by the Academy which were open to everyone in the village, regardless of whether or not he was in the co-op. This applied, for exam-ple, to the literacy campaigns, to instruction in animal husbandry, and to the health and birth-control programs.

Cell 3 includes the men who were actually members of the coopera-tives. They therefore came in contact not only with all the programs applied to the cooperative village at large, but also to the numerous others available only to members. They were eligible for loans, could use the tractors, were supplied with special seed, participated in the group plan-ning sessions, held office in the co-op, played the role of instructor to other farmers, and so on.

Cell 4 includes men who were originally from the Comilla District, but had later migrated to Dacca and other cities to enter industrial work. They, therefore, had no contact with the cooperatives, but instead had had extensive experience in the presumably modernizing context of the factory.

First, comparing men from typical villages with the nonmember resi-dents of the co-op villages, we see, by comparing cells 1 and 2, that the nonmember did gain from merely living in co-op villages, but the gain was modest. Compared to men living in Comilla District villages un-touched by the cooperatives, the noncooperating residents of co-op villages had, on the average, a substantial 5-point advantage in OM score. How-ever, only 5 percent more of those living in co-op villages were rated as modern. Moreover, the match correlation, at .19, was not statistically significant. We may recognize this outcome as similar to that experienced rather frequently when development programs are limited merely to giv-ing advice, or to talking to people, instead of involving them in direct action based on personal commitment. The programs based on listening rather than doing often have some modest impact, but rarely produce a major personal change.

The results were different, indeed strikingly so, when we came to the critical comparisons involving actual members of the cooperatives. The members of the co-ops were, of course, exposed to the full impact of the movement's organizational imperatives, rather than merely to its informational campaigns. The effect showed in their performance on the OM scale.

Comparing co-op members with men from other parts of their own district of Comilla but living in nonco-op villages, produced a robust match correlation of .54 with OM, significant at the .001 level despite the small N of 20 cases. Of the co-op members some 65 percent were classified as modern men, whereas a mere 20 percent of the other Comilla villagers won that designation. This may be seen by comparing cell 1 with cell 3 in Table 13–1.

Even within the very same village, those who were co-op members proved to be much more modern than those who were not, as shown by the comparison of cells 2 and 3 in Table 13–1. Of the nonmembers in the cooperating villages, only 25 percent earned the designation of modern men, whereas 65 percent of the actual co-op members were so classified. The members were on the average all of 9 points higher in OM score than were nonmembers living in the same villages. The resultant match correlation, a strong .45, was significant at the .001 level.

Indeed, so marked was the superiority of the members that they actually substantially surpassed in modernity our sample of industrial workers with many years of factory experience. On the average, the rural co-op members had an advantage of 6 points on the OM scale over the industrial workers who had earlier migrated from farms in Comilla. Among the co-op members the percentage scored as modern was almost double the percentage of the industrial workers so classified.

Challenges to the Findings

The greater modernity manifested in the villages reached by the cooperative movement, and particularly that recorded by the actual members of the cooperatives, came through as a finding as strong and clear cut as any we obtained by the matching method. The contrast between co-op members and nonmembers among the cultivators in East Pakistan was as sharp as the difference between the highest and lowest educational groups in even those countries where the greatest gap in years of schooling separated the two sets of men constituting the match. In East Pakistan, under the controlled conditions of matching, every year in a factory was worth only about 1 point on the OM scale; every year in school produced a gain of about 1.5 points; whereas each year of exposure to the co-op movement as a nonmember netted approximately 1.7 points, and every year spent in the co-op as a member yielded a gain of 4 points or more per year.[7]

We saw this outcome as striking testimonial to the power of the cooperative movement to bring about rapid and dramatic changes in adult men still working in agriculture. Before we affirmed that conclusion, however, we had to meet certain reservations which might be raised about our findings.

To begin with, we needed assurance that the results were not an accidental artifact of our method. We checked the outcome of the matches against the data from a multivariate regression analysis. Although that method did not permit anything like the flexibility in arranging various combinations which the matches had allowed, it strongly supported the conclusion that the people in cooperative villages were indeed outstandingly modern.[8]

Second, we needed assurance that there was not something special about Comilla District, some unique regional character, which made people from that district more modern by virtue of the local cultural tradition. This was actually not a decisive issue because the analysis presented above was based on sets of men living exclusively within the Comilla District. Nevertheless, we can give assurance, based on several checks, that the average level of modernity of cultivators from Comilla was statistically indistinguishable from that manifested by men of comparable social status who lived in other districts of East Pakistan.[9]

Next, we had to deal with alternative explanations of our results. The first challenge was addressed to our finding that within Comilla District the villages having cooperatives were more modern than those without that organization.[10] Could that not have come about because only the villages with more modern men invited the co-op organizers to come in? In other words, how can we be sure those particular villages were not more modern from the outset?

In reply we note that the particular villages in which the Academy first established itself — and on which our results were based — were not selected by the Academy because they were more modern, but rather because they could readily be reached from the town of Comilla where the Academy had its headquarters. Moreover, the 17 cooperative villages we studied were purposely chosen by us from among more than 100 available because they were as far from Comilla town as possible, and hence farthest from the zone of its likely influence.

Distance from the town aside, we generally recognize a village as being spontaneously modern in spirit if it invests more in schooling. Yet the average educational level in the villages which developed co-ops was indistinguishable from that of the villages which did not.[11] Finally, we have the Academy's testimony, cited above, as to the deep resistance it met when it first introduced the cooperative idea to these villages. All this indicates there was nothing unusually modern about the typical spirit of those villages before the Academy came in to introduce the cooperatives.

There remained, though, the last challenge, resting on the assumption that only the most modern men in each village joined the co-op. If that had been the case, co-op members would have scored more modern on our tests without necessarily having learned to be more modern as a result of their participation in the cooperatives. Unfortunately, we could not, for the cooperatives, repeat either of the two procedures with which we answered a similar challenge to the idea that the factory is a school in modernity.[12] Nevertheless, there were several strong reasons to believe that the results we obtained did not follow mainly from processes of individual self-selection, but rather reflected the impact of contact with the cooperative organizations.

First, there was the fact that in villages in which the cooperative was installed, even men who did not actually join the movement were more modern than men in villages without the co-ops, whether located in Comilla or in other districts.[13] As we noted, the cooperatives directed some of their programs to everyone in the village. The fact that these programs were effective with nonmembers obviously cannot be explained on the basis of an allegation that the *nonmembers* may have been self-selected from among those already modern. The Academy's programs must have been rather powerful to influence people who had decided not to join the co-op, even after it was established in their village. There is every reason, therefore, to assume that the co-op programs would have been all the more effective with co-op members who were fully exposed to the cooperatives' efforts over longer periods of time.

In any event, if only the most modern men joined the cooperatives the social attributes typically associated with modernity should have been much more common among co-op members. Since education is the best indicator of modernity, we scanned that first. We found that just as co-op villages did not have higher average education, so *within* any village co-op members had not had more schooling than nonmembers. Indeed, the similarity in the social profile of the member and the nonmember was quite striking.[14]

Finally, to render plausible the argument that the members were already modern men and were recruited on that basis, one has to explain where all those modern men suddenly came from. We had evidence, already presented, that the average village in Comilla District to which the cooperative movement had not yet arrived was usually no more modern than the average village in other districts. Since, in the typical village of Comilla District, there was no excess supply of modern men waiting to be recruited, the greater average modernity of the villages with cooperatives should logically have resulted from experiences the men had after the arrival of the cooperatives.

Conclusion

Taken all together the evidence seems to us to point unmistakably to the conclusion that the cooperatives were a very powerful school in modernization. The co-op program made available new information, new ideas, and new technological resources. It thus helped men to a stronger sense of their competence and personal efficacy. It also provided new role models in efficacy and competence in the persons of the instructors sent to the villages. By their disinterested professional stance the representatives of the Academy encouraged a new sense of trust in others, and provided a model of respect for the dignity of people less powerful and advantaged than oneself. The rules for running the cooperative provided lessons in planning and were a training ground in the principles of distributive justice. The outcome of the Academy's efforts showed that even in the most neglected and backward of villages one can, by introducing the right kind of social organization, stimulate fully adult farmers to change in fundamental ways their attitudes, values, knowledge, and behavior, and to do so at a rapid rate. The Comilla project stands, therefore, as one of the most important demonstrations of the possibility of creative and humane social change in the annals of social experimentation and innovation.

The Moshav: Agricultural Cooperatives in Israel

On learning that we had worked in Israel and had included farmers in our sample there, almost everyone assumed that we had studied men from the well-known kibbutzim. In fact, none of our Israeli farmers were kibbutz members. Because we limited our sample in Israel to the so-called "Oriental Jews," we were obliged to take all our Israeli farmers from a different type of agricultural settlement known as the *moshav*.

Very few of the Oriental Jews found their way into the kibbutz after their migration to Israel. Actually, it is not clear whether the kibbutzim, dominated as they were by Jews from Eastern Europe, were ready to accept the Oriental Jews. In any event, the authorities assumed that these later immigrants would not make a good adjustment in such decidedly communal settlements, and so those of the Oriental immigrants who were steered into agricultural settlements at the time of their arrival in Israel were sent predominantly into the moshav.

The kibbutz is a collective settlement in which production and consumption, and indeed many other phases of life such as child socialization, are on a strictly communal basis. By contrast, the moshav — which dates back to 1921 — is not communal but is rather a cooperative development. The basic unit is a separate family household working its own small section of land. Ownership of that land, however, is not vested in the individual, but rather in the state. Within any moshav the plots of land are as equal as they could be made, allowing for inevitable natural variation. The sources of financing are public rather than private. An elaborate system of credit, supply, and marketing services is provided by a public authority. In the moshav major emphasis is given to agricultural extension services; new crops and seeds are regularly introduced on the advice of agricultural technicians; and the whole enterprise is strongly oriented toward the market. Most of the necessary services, and especially the use of machinery and the marketing of the crops of the moshav village, are undertaken according to principles of cooperation.

This brief description should suffice to indicate that the moshav is a rather special form of agricultural enterprise, at least as compared to those we studied elsewhere. Like the Comilla cooperative movement it was the object of a concerted effort from outside the community to introduce new principles of organization and new technology into agriculture within the framework of a cooperative movement.

The moshav differed from the Comilla cooperative villages, however, in that its members were not traditional farmers. Most of the original moshav members had had quite different, often urban, occupations before they were directed to the farms.[15] Since we limited our interviews to men under 33, however, very few of these older original settlers were in our sample. Those we interviewed were rather the children of the original settlers. Only a third had spent their entire childhood on the farm, but, depending on their age and the time their parents had reached Israel, almost all had spent some of their formative years there. In any event, at the time of interview all were active members of a moshav, earning their living through agriculture.

In East Pakistan we could compare farmers having different degrees of involvement in the cooperative movement. In Israel, however, all of the cultivators in our sample were members of the moshavim. This obliged us to limit our comparison in Israel to farmers, on the one hand, and those in nonfarm occupations, on the other. Of these, the industrial workers were, of course, of greatest interest. If, by its very nature, farming was a dulling occupation, the moshav members in Israel should have scored much lower in modernity than did their compatriots working in industry, just as farmers did in all the other countries. But if the experience of life in a cooperative could provide a stimulus which was the equal of urban living and industrial employment, then the moshav members should have had modernity scores indistinguishable from those of the workers.

To resolve the issue we followed our standard procedure, creating a match to compare the cultivators with industrial workers whom they were like in all important respects. The outcome in Israel was markedly different from that we had encountered everywhere else. In the other five countries the match pitting the regular cultivators against the industrial workers favored the workers overwhelmingly, with a median match correlation of .56. In the other countries the smallest contrast shown by the match of cultivators and industrial workers was found in East Pakistan, yet even there the correlation in the match was .34, significant at the .001 level, and the OM score of the workers was 7 points above that of the cultivators. In Israel, by contrast, the match correlation was only .08, below minimum standard and not statistically significant at even the .05 level; and the workers had an OM score less than 2 points higher than that of the moshav members.[16] In other words, everywhere else the city worker was much more modern than his country cousin, whereas in Israel the moshav farmers were virtually equal to the industrial workers in their modernity.

Another way of testing whether the moshav had any special effectiveness as a school in modernization was to use the urban nonindustrial workers as the standard of comparison rather than the factory workers. With the application of the usual controls for matching, the four other countries in which the comparison could be made showed the UNI's to be more modern than the farmers, and usually significantly so.[17] In the other countries the UNIs, on the average, were 14 percentiles higher in rank than the cultivators; in Israel, the situation was reversed and the cultivators stood 15 percentiles higher in the overall distribution of OM scores.

These results provided further evidence supporting the conclusion we had drawn from the Comilla experiment: cooperative organization can give farmers a stimulus toward individual modernization roughly equal to that provided by industrial employment. In both the Comilla cooperatives and the moshavim, the members jointly planned many elements of their work, especially as it involved finances, the use of machinery, and the marketing of their produce. The experience of planning and the sharing of responsibility for coordinating complex activities serves as a stimulus to individual modernization. In both cases the farmers were given access to, and encouraged in the use of, agricultural machinery. New seeds and new techniques of cultivation were regularly introduced by agricultural extension agents, who also served as personal models of development. In these and other ways, we concluded, the moshav had provided a special occupational setting whose properties were sufficiently different from those of the traditional agricultural village to make it more nearly equal to the factory as a school in modernization.

Reservations and Conclusions

Before we accepted this conclusion, however, we had to satisfy ourselves as to whether or not some other special aspect of the moshav might be accounting for the performance of its members on the OM scale.

The observed outcome could not be explained away on the basis of differential recruitment. The families sent into the moshav were generally directed there by the immigration and relocation authorities. Usually the authorities sent people into the moshav because there were empty places there at the moment a particular set of families arrived. Indeed, one of the complaints against the moshav was that so many families were there against their will, and the policy of involuntary assignment was eventually abandoned.

Another alternative explanation for the modernity of the moshav members was that of those assigned there only the more modern men had stayed on. If that had happened, the residue of men we met and studied could have been modern all along, rather than having been modernized by the experience of cooperative farming. It was equally plausible, however, that the men who had initially been more modern found farming too limiting for their talents and ambition and moved on to urban and perhaps industrial jobs, leaving behind in the moshav only those who had initially been less modern.

On another tack, we faced the possibility that if the Israeli factory had had no ability to modernize, the farmers would have been rather like the workers because neither the moshav nor the factory was a school for modernization. That explanation had to be rejected, however, because in Israel the correlation between OM scores and years of factory experience, and the point gain in OM score for each year of factory work, were as strong as in other countries.[18] The Israeli factory definitely *was* a school for modernity, and if moshav members did not lag behind it seems reasonable to conclude that that was because their cooperatives were also effective schools for modernization.

There were, however, several characteristics of the moshav farmers which made them distinctive in ways not controlled by the standard matching procedures. The moshav farmers came disproportionately from two countries, Yemen and Aden, and immigrants of that origin had the reputation of being especially energetic and enterprising. In addition, on the average the farmers in our sample had come to Israel quite a bit earlier than the workers, and at a younger age, so they had had more time to be acculturated there. Finally, we had to confront certain special facts about the geographical location of the moshav farms. The farmers we studied in Israel lived overwhelmingly in the so-called Jerusalem corridor, the stretch of land connecting Jerusalem with Tel Aviv. It is a highly urbanized region, well provided with all amenities such as electricity and piped water; radios and newspapers are readily available; and one can easily get into town by regular bus service over good roads. It was possible, therefore, that the moshav members were so close to the workers in modernity because they had so extensively shared with them the advantages of the modern urban culture.

In response to these facts we reconstructed the standard match of cultivators and factory workers for Israel, selecting the cases to meet the objections just raised. All the workers had to be from Yemen and Aden, just as the moshav men were, and the two groups were matched very closely on the length of their stay in Israel. In addition, we selected the workers only from the largest, most cosmopolitan urban centers in order to heighten the contrast between their geographical setting and that of the moshav members.

The results of this special match in no way showed the moshav members at a disadvantage. On the contrary, in this new match they actually came out *ahead* of the industrial workers by a slight margin.[19]

We see then that the results from Israel confirmed the conclusion reached on the basis of the Comilla experiment in East Pakistan. Cooperative farming evidently has the potential for making men modern at a rate at least equal to that produced by industrial employment. There is nothing inherent about working in the open producing food, rather than under cover producing manufactured material, which prevents a man from learning to be modern through his work experience. If the organizational setting is arranged so as to provide the right stimulus, a man may evidently become as modernized in cooperative agriculture as he would have been by working in industry.

14

Urban Nonindustrial Employment

Although cultivators and industrial workers were to constitute our main sample groups, each field director was expected to interview 100 men who were defined as "urban nonindustrial workers" or UNIs. By this term we designated men who resided in the city and were employed in nonagricultural pursuits, but whose work was done outside the factory. We sought men who worked either alone or in small groups, who used mainly human or animal power, and who were not part of a complex, bureaucratized organization. The type of occupation we had in mind included: in the services, bakers and plumbers; in commerce, street vendors or shop clerks; in transportation, drivers of motorcars or pedicabs; in small-scale manufacturing, artisans or craftsmen; and in general labor, porters, draymen, and the like.

The Problem

In designing our samples we had recognized that most of our factory workers would be living in cities, since most factories are located there. Consequently, for the average industrial employee, each year in the factory also added an additional year in town. This meant that even if men with more factory experience proved more modern it would be difficult to tell whether factory work or urban living had made them so. Our initial interest in the UNIs, therefore, lay in the hope that by studying them we could disentangle the generally intertwined influence of factory and urban experience. As it turned out, we found other ways, discussed in Chapter 11, to establish that the factory could modernize quite independently of any contribution which city living might make to that process. But we were still interested in the UNIs as a group through which we could test how far urban occupational experience outside of a factory, or any other formal organizational setting, might be able to modernize men.

To serve our purpose it was essential that the UNI's come from basically the same background as the cultivators and the industrial workers to whom they were to be compared, in other words, that the only difference between them would be in occupational experience. It was also rather important that the sampling well reflect our objective of representing a wide range of employment situations quite distinct from work in factories. Unfortunately, both these conditions were met only very imperfectly in the samples of UNIs we collected. The main difficulty stemmed from the fact that, by the very nature of their occupations, urban nonindustrial employees are much more dispersed than are cultivators and industrial workers. It therefore required a much greater investment of time to locate the necessary number of individuals who met our sampling requirements as to origin, age, religion, ethnicity, and the like. A further difficulty arose from the fact that urban nonindustrial workers' jobs often were, if not monopolies, at least specialties for particular ethnic, religious, or regional groups quite different from those predominating in industry or agriculture as a whole.

In the face of the high cost of locating UNIs who exactly fitted our sampling requirements, a number of the field directors felt obliged to relax the stringent standard set by their instructions. In Argentina the difficulties of finding eligible men were severe enough that only 56 of the 100 required cases were located, and in Israel we fell 8 short of the goal. Everywhere else the quota was filled, but sometimes in ways which gave undue weight to some group selected only because it was easily accessible in the given country, as may be seen in Table 14–1. Thus, the sampling instructions urged the field director to include up to ten different types of UNI employment, preferably with about ten men to represent each type. Yet in East Pakistan some 80 percent of the UNIs were laborers, porters, stevedores, cart pushers, and rickshaw pullers, men who did extremely hard work for absolutely minimum wages. By contrast, in Chile more than 70 percent of the UNIs were either artisans and craftsmen or street merchants and kiosk venders, in effect men running their own one-man businesses. In Israel we ended up with an exceptional concentration, some 33 percent of the total UNI sample, who were taxi drivers and transport workers, again a group with rather special occupational characteristics. Finally, in Nigeria, we discovered that almost half of the UNIs were doing jobs which the field director classified as "industrially related" even though they were done outside the context of the factory. These jobs included spray painting, vulcanizing, blacksmithing, steel construction, and the like.

Two consequences followed from this sampling outcome. First, it meant

Table 14–1.   Percent of urban non-industrial workers (UNIs) in each country, holding different types of jobs.[a]

Workers	Argentina	Chile	East Pakistan	India[b]	Israel	Nigeria
Craftsmen, artisans, barbers, shoemakers, plumbers, electricians	18	37	0	5	14	54
Bus and taxi drivers, chauffeurs, transport workers	4	6	0	7	33	0
Workers in small retail shops	21	0	4	10	3	24
Hawkers, peddlers, street merchants, vendors	38	34	18	18	0	0
Busboys, waiters, delivery boys, doormen	18	0	0	2	13	0
Domestic personal servants (general unskilled help)	0	13	0	13	0	22
Day laborers, porters, stevedores, coolies	2	9	38	14	36	0
Cart pushers and rickshaw pullers	0	0	40	32	0	0
N [c]	(56)	(106)	(112)	(148)	(92)	(101)

a Columns do not always add up to 100 percent because of rounding errors.
b "Institutional UNIs" are not included here; see the last paragraph of this chapter.
c Figures given are the number of UNIs sampled in each country.

that in some countries we would be comparing industrial workers from a *variety* of industries doing a variety of jobs with UNIs who represented predominantly *one* type of nonindustrial job. Second, it meant that the nature of the comparison of UNIs with any other group would change greatly from country to country. Because we were so dissatisfied with the way we had collected our UNI samples, we seriously considered simply leaving them out of the analysis entirely. Yet to do so was to invite the suspicion that we might be suppressing information which did not support our hypotheses. Since the UNI group had played an important role in our original conception and in the sample design, we concluded that we had an obligation to present the results.

The Findings

We assessed the effect of urban nonindustrial employment by making several match comparisons, the results of which are contained in Table 14–2. First, we placed the UNIs of rural origin in competition with the cultivators. This could be done, using Match 2, in four countries.[1] In all

Table 14–2. Modernity (OM-500) of urban non-industrial workers (UNIs) in competition with other occupational groups: correlations of OM score and occupational variable.[a]

Correlation	Argentina	Chile	East Pakistan	India	Israel	Nigeria
			All experienced factory workers and UNIs[b]			
Simple (zero-order)	.01	−.02	−.26***	−.57***	−.19***	−.37***
Partial, controlling for Set A (early and late socialization)	−.01	.01	−.18***	−.35***	−.15***	−.25***
N	608	621	649	648	515	513
			Matched samples of occupational groups and UNIs[c]			
Rural-origin cultivator vs. UNI (Match 2)	d	.58*** (24)	.16* (69)	.13 (73)	d	.34** (41)
New factory workers vs UNI (Match 50A)	.08 (11)	−.08 (28)	−.08 (22)	−.19 (26)	−.03 (31)	−.14 (40)
Experienced factory workers vs. UNI (Match 1)	.07 (33)	.09 (82)	−.10 (42)	−.39** (29)	−.21** (89)	−.29* (36)

[a] Asterisks denote significance as follows: *, at .05 level; **, at .01 level; ***, at .001 level or better. All correlations are in the direction *from* other occupations *to* UNI. Thus, a positive correlation indicates that UNIs have higher OM scores than the other workers, and a negative one, that they have lower scores.

[b] "Experienced factory workers" include here all factory workers with more than 1 year of experience in the factory.

[c] Figures in parentheses are the numbers of matched pairs in each country.

[d] The Argentine sample contained too few UNIs of rural origin to attempt matches with that group. In Israel there were no men of rural origin.

four the UNIs were more modern than the cultivators, decidedly so in Chile and Nigeria, less strikingly in the other two countries.

However, we could not say whether the UNIs enjoyed a higher standing on OM than their country cousins because of the nature of their jobs or because they were more advantaged by life in the city. Despite our best matching efforts, for example, the UNIs enjoyed statistically significant advantages in both income and newspaper reading in all four countries in which the UNIs scored more modern than the cultivators.[2] Neither could we prove or disprove that the UNIs were more modern because men who were more modern to begin with more often left farming to take up urban nonindustrial work in the city. So this first match result left us in doubt as to how far it was the occupational experience itself which had made the UNIs more modern than the cultivators.

If their occupational experience were making the urban nonindustrials modern, the result should have shown clearly when they were put in competition with *new* workers. The comparison of new industrial workers and UNIs was particularly appropriate because both had previously come from the countryside, thus holding constant any effect which selective migration might have introduced. Yet the UNIs had had long years of experience on the job whereas the new workers as yet had had no work experience apart from having helped out in farming. Therefore, if the experience of urban nonindustrial work had the power to modernize, that power should be clearly reflected in this comparison in the form of significantly higher modernity scores for the UNIs.

For this Match 50A, we chose the new workers by a strict standard, so that even in the extreme case they had less than 6 months of experience in the factory, and none had had UNI experience before entering the plant. By contrast the median length of experience on the job for the UNIs was 6 years. Because the UNIs had been working so much longer they were somewhat older, and, more important, enjoyed higher standing on measures of years in town, income, consumer goods, and mass-media exposure.[3]

Despite these advantages, the urban nonindustrials were less modern than the new workers in five of the six countries, although never at a statistically significant level. Only in Argentina were the urban nonindustrials ahead, but by an inconsequential margin. After quite a few years on the job the urban nonindustrial was, at best, no further ahead in modernity than the man just starting out on his occupational career in a factory. Yet, as we know from the analysis presented in Chapter 11, after a comparable period of time spent in factory employment the experienced worker had forged well ahead of the new worker. All in all these results strongly argued against assuming that employment as an urban nonindustrial worker did anything substantial to make a man more modern.

When we compared the UNIs with the experienced factory workers, differences in urban experience no longer clouded the issue since both sets of men had lived in town a long time, and the factor of selectivity was again very much controlled. The simple (zero-order) correlations, presented in Table 14–2, indicated that we had been correct in assuming that urban nonindustrials would be less modern than factory workers who had had equal time on the job and in the city. An exception had to be made for Argentina and Chile, but in the four other countries use of the occupational variable "experienced worker vs. UNI" yielded correlations unfavorable to the UNIs at high levels of statistical significance. Yet we could not be sure that these correlations were not a consequence of differences in education and other characteristics of the two occupational groups. The matches and partialing permitted us to examine the issue.

Both methods led to the same conclusion. Even under conditions in which numerous other variables were controlled, as in Match 1, four of the six countries showed the factory workers to have a decided edge in modernity over the UNIs.[4] In three of the four countries the difference was statistically significant. Moreover, this advantage held whether the match considered only men of rural origin or urban origin, or combined them in a larger set.[5] The partial correlations for these four countries were all quite significant statistically, and left little room for doubting that factory workers are more modern than urban nonindustrials. In Chile and Argentina, however, the pattern observed elsewhere was, again, absent.

Conclusion

Taking into account all the evidence on the performance of the UNIs, we could make a case either for or against the modernizing effects of urban nonindustrial work. The main evidence making the case for urban nonindustrial employment lies in the fact that the UNIs consistently outperformed the cultivators, who provided our baseline of disadvantage. Moreover, in two countries the UNIs did as well as the factory workers. A reasonable conclusion might then be that at least in some contexts there are aspects of nonindustrial work, certain qualities unanticipated by us, which act to make men more modern.

UNIs did not have the benefit of contact with machinery, nor, usually, of participation in a large-scale bureaucratic organization.[6] But their jobs might have been special in at least one respect, because the work often required interaction with the general public. In our samples, this was most true of the UNIs in Chile and Argentina, the very countries in which the UNIs seemed as modern as the factory workers. To some degree, however, the same kind of special public contact was experienced by at least some of the UNIs in all the countries. Waiters, delivery boys, peddlers, pedicab drivers, barbers, store clerks, repairmen — all have jobs involving interaction with a diverse public. This contact may provide opportunities to acquire new information, may expose one to a variety of points of view, and may require the ability to verbalize, or to reckon, as in making change. Experiences of this sort could perhaps serve as a school in modernization, inculcating an openness to new experience, an awareness of differences of opinion, and a higher level of information, all qualities which contribute to a man's modernity score.[7]

The case against the claim that urban nonindustrial employment normally makes men substantially more modern rests mainly on the fact that there was no instance in which the UNIs proved themselves more modern than new workers to whom they were matched. Indeed, in five of six cases they were less modern. These findings emerged despite the fact that in the new worker–UNI comparison, UNIs had been long on the job, and had had much more urban experience. Given our interest in the factory, however, the critical finding for us was that in four of six countries the experienced factory workers were significantly more modern than the UNIs to whom they were matched, whereas in no case were the UNIs more modern at a statistically significant level. This outcome was observed despite the fact that the UNIs had had as much opportunity to be influenced by the city as had the industrial employees. All this constitutes further evidence that the factory is an effective school for modernizing men, whereas, taken together, the results indicate that work as a UNI has but little ability to modernize a man. Moreover, the factory emerged from this analysis not only as far superior in its role as a school in modernity, but also as largely cleared of the suspicion that its previously noted effects were mere artifacts of the factory's urban setting.

Yet it is important to recognize that occupations other than factory work may be effective schools in modernity for the average man in developing countries. Indeed, we have shown in Chapter 13 that under certain circumstances agricultural work can provide a context in which men become rapidly modernized. There is every reason to believe, therefore, that if UNIs worked in an *organizational* framework comparable to that of the factory they too might also experience more rapid modernization. In fact, we have data which say as much.

In India, and unfortunately in India only, in addition to the usual sample of independent UNIs working alone or in tiny shops, we collected a second set of 100 UNIs who were employed by large-scale organizations such as banks, government offices, and big corporations. We called this second set the "institutional" UNIs. The zero-order correlation of the variable "independent UNI vs. institutional UNI" was .30*** favoring the institutional UNIs. Even with six other variables controlled, the partial correlation remained at the substantial level of .26***. A match confirmed the greater modernity of the institutional UNIs over those not working in organizations. Indeed, a further comparison by matching of the institutional UNIs with comparable industrial workers showed the UNIs who worked in large-scale organizations to be almost as modern as were the factory workers.[8] We hesitate to rest too much on a single case, but we must say that this result strongly indicated to us that just as special features of cooperative organization greatly influenced the cultivators, so evidently can the special features of large-scale bureaucratic organization be a stimulus to the modernization of urban nonindustrial workers.

15

The Quantity and Quality of
Urban Experience

In our earliest thinking about the Project, we did not precisely delineate the components of the modernization experience, but rather thought of them as a syndrome. We initially conceived our task as mainly to achieve an unambiguous demonstration that even in the most traditional national settings one could find dramatic evidence of the transformation of men when they came under the impact of a complex set of modernization influences, of which urban experience was assumed to be but one part. Our first plan, therefore, anticipated our working in only a few very large modern production enterprises set down in the midst of relatively isolated and underdeveloped areas. As appropriate examples of such enterprises we considered studying mainly the large oil refineries built by international capital in desert settings in the Middle East, or the large publicly owned steel mills which the national planning agencies of several countries had located in formerly underdeveloped hinterlands. We reasoned that under such circumstances some of the very principles which characterize the factory as an organization would come to be manifested in the quality of life in the new towns built up around these enterprises. Thus, not only the factory but also the new town would embody the principles of rationality, orderliness, and efficiency which we associate with the modern in social organization. The town would itself become, in some sense, "a school in modernity."

However, some of our methodological consultants strongly urged against limiting our sample to a few dramatic examples of large industries located in isolated settings surrounded by new towns. Part of the argument was practical. Such new towns would be few in number: they might be hard to find and difficult of access. Moreover, effective utilization of such cases called for a before-and-after research design; we would have had to study the area before the new industry was built there, and then come back to study it after it had been in operation some years. Whatever the merits of that research design, it would have required more time, especially time to hold our staff together, than we could count on.

There were also compelling theoretical arguments against our initial plan. If we had tested only a few company towns we would have had difficulty proving that any differences between the "modern" and the "traditional" sectors were really caused by the variables we had in mind, and not by others that were intimately associated with the special character of the few places we had chosen to study. For example, if we had elected to study mainly big oil refineries, we would have had to reckon with the fact that they are usually controlled by foreign capital and employ a large proportion of European technicians. Even if we had found that workers in these establishments had become highly modernized, it would have been unclear whether it was their work in industry which had made them modern, or whether they had become more modern merely because they had had the chance to observe and imitate Western technicians. Also, we would have been left in doubt as to how far the observed effects, if any, were limited to the oil and steel industries and to plants of that particular order of "bigness."

Influenced by such considerations, we increasingly accepted as our goal to establish the effects of industrial experience, if any, as they might be manifested in general. To be able to make statements of a high level of generality, we clearly had to study more than a few exemplary plants; indeed, we had to observe the whole range of industrial establishments.[1] Furthermore, if we were to study many factories rather than a few, we had to go where there were concentrations of industry. Inevitably, this meant going to the large cities. It followed from this imperative, in turn, that most of the industrial workers we studied would live not in new modern towns which were shiny machines for living and models of rational and orderly social arrangements. Rather, the cities we studied would more likely provide their inhabitants the polyglot, raucous, unplanned, often chaotic and even anarchic milieu shaped by the urban explosion so typical of rapidly developing countries. We were not at all certain whether, under such circumstances, the city really would exert a modernizing influence in its own right. It became increasingly clear, therefore, that we should consider the degree and quality of a man's contact with the urban milieu as an important independent variable, one deserving to be measured separately from other modernizing experiences.

In coming to this decision we were, of course, merely bringing our research design into line with what most of the experts would have required of us. After all, urbanization looms large in most theories about societal modernization.[2] Bert Hoselitz summed up the common view quite well when he wrote that "The cities exhibit a spirit different from that of the countryside. They are the main force and the chief locus for the introduction of new ideas and new ways of doing things. One may look, therefore, to the cities as the crucial places in underdeveloped countries in which the adaptation to new ways, new techniques, new consumption and production patterns and new social institutions is achieved."[3]

In Hoselitz's description one may discern elements of our model of the modern man. Indeed, the city would be high on most people's list of the institutions likely to exert a strong influence on individual modernity. That alone made it incumbent on us to study the impact of urban residence on OM scores.

In our case, moreover, we felt it essential to study the independent effects of urban experience, if any, in order to protect the integrity of our main hypothesis, which asserted the special importance of factory experience. Insofar as most of the factories in our sample were going to be located in large cities, it would follow that the men who came from the countryside to work in them would for the first time experience not only a new form of employment, but also a new *urban* context for daily living. If these migrants, tested after the passage of years, then proved more modern than their country "cousins" still on the farm, we would be left in doubt as to whether the observed differences were due to the influence of work in the factory or of life in the city.

To insure, therefore, that when we got to the analysis stage we would be in a position to disentangle the effects of urban residence and industrial employment we took a series of steps to adapt both our sampling procedure and the questionnaire. The measures which the field settings and our sampling framework permitted us to take into account were: the number of years a man had spent in town; the size and relative cosmopolitanism of the city in which he lived as compared to other cities in his country; and the location of his place of work on a continuum from inner city to relatively suburban locations. The first measure permitted us to assess the *quantity* of a man's exposure to urban living, while the second two permitted us to evaluate the importance of the *qualitative* aspect of his urban experience.

The Quantity of Urban Experience

The obvious way to test the effects of urban living as a modernizing influence was to relate the number of years a man had been living in the city to his score on the OM scale. Doing so made the analysis of urban influence strictly comparable to that for schooling and for factory experience, both of which were also measured in terms of "years of exposure."

For the men born and raised in the countryside, and defined by us as of "rural origin," we had recorded exactly how many years they had lived in town after the age of 15. This measure provided the basis for an initial test of whether exposure to urban life exerted a modernizing influence. The measure was available for five countries, Israel being excluded because everyone in that sample was considered to have been of urban origin.

The measure of exposure to urban living showed a strong association with individual modernity scores. Limiting the analysis to the factory workers of rural origin, we found the median correlation of years in town and individual modernity to be .30 significant at the .001 level. Expressing the relation in percentage terms (Table 15–1), we found that as we went up the steps of the urban-experience ladder there was a fairly steady increase in the proportion of men qualifying as high scorers on the modernity scale. For example, in Nigeria, which represented the median case, only 6 percent of those just arrived in the city scored as modern, whereas among those who had spent 14 or more years in town, the proportion scored as modern was 42 percent.

Although some gain in modernity accompanying increased urban experience was, in general, manifested everywhere, we must note that as we moved from one country to the next the pattern was decidedly less regular than that observed earlier for education, and perhaps even for

Table 15-1. Percent of rural-origin men high on OM-500[a] at increasing levels of urban experience.[b,c]

Years of urban experience after age 15	Argentina	Chile	East Pakistan	India	Nigeria
0	—	—	33 (176)	38 (379)	—
1–3	0 (24)	4 (73)	25 (64)	49 (185)	6 (17)
4–5	9 (22)	14 (42)	31 (144)	40 (136)	15 (40)
6–7	14 (44)	7 (43)	36 (113)	42 (106)	21 (52)
8–10	24 (63)	24 (72)	43 (145)	37 (137)	38 (61)
11–13	21 (56)	35 (40)	48 (58)	—	35 (40)
14+	27 (32)	37 (35)	72 (18)	—	42 (24)

a "High on OM-500" means a score in the top one-third of the frequency distribution, in each country.

b Israel is excluded because none of the men in our Israeli sample were considered to be of rural origin.

c Numbers in parentheses are values of N upon which the percentages are based; a dash means that fewer than ten men are at that level of urban experience in our sample.

factory experience. The relative distinctness of the pattern manifested in
each country was also evident when we standard-scored the urban experience and OM measures. These results suggested that the interaction of
urban experience and modernity might be more complex than that between modernity and either education or factory experience. All in all,
however, our initial findings pointed to urban experience as apparently
being a major influence in making men modern, and one whose strength
possibly equaled that of factory experience.

Partialing out the influence of certain of the main variables which
might have been responsible for the apparent effect of urban experience
left its standing relatively unimpaired, as may be seen in Table 15–2.
The control for education, and for the larger set of early socialization
variables, made it clear that, with the exception of India, those with more
years in town were not more modern merely because they came from
relatively more advantaged backgrounds. The control for mass-media

Table 15–2.   Correlations of years of urban experience and individual modernity (OM), for rural-origin factory workers.[a]

Correlation	Argentina	Chile	East Pakistan	India	Nigeria
Simple (zero-order)[b]	.33***	.41***	.23***	.23***	.30***
Partial,					
controlling for—					
Formal education	.36***	.40***	.21***	.07	.24***
Years factory experience	.24***	.29***	.07	.21***	.22***
Mass-media exposure	.27***	.39***	.18***	.29***	.09
Formal education plus years factory experience	.11	.07	.04	.03	.17*
Mass-media exposure plus years factory experience	.09	.08	.02	.08*	.22**
Early socialization experience	.26***	.38***	.22***	.06	.27***
Late socialization experience	.17**	.19**	.03	.14**	.15*
Set A (early and late socialization)	.11	.07	.10**	−.01	.16*
N	239	305	654	700	184

a Asterisks denote significance as follows: *, at .05 level; **, at .01 level; ***, at .001 level or better
b Israel is excluded because none of the men in our Israeli sample were considered to be of rural origin

exposure, one of the most important components of urban experience, yielded partial correlations large and significant enough to indicate that there were yet other elements in the urban experience of these men which in large part accounted for their modernity.

However, when we made allowances for the influence of factory experience, we began to doubt the extent to which the contribution of urban experience was really an independent one. When factory experience was one of a set of variables controlled in the partialing process, as in lines 5–6 and 8–9 of Table 15–2, then half of all the correlations of urbanism and modernity fell below our standard of .10, and usually also failed to register as statistically significant. Only in Nigeria did urban experience consistently make a significant independent contribution after we partialed out the combined influence of factory experience and other late-socialization variables.

These results might well be interpreted as telling us that it was mainly their factory experience which had made these men modern, and that their having lived in cities was merely an incidental accompaniment of their occupation. Before we rushed to this conclusion, however, we had to consider how far these particular results might have involved us in the partialing fallacy.

Given the nature of our samples, the number of years a man of rural origin had spent in urban living was intimately related to how many years he had been working in industry. Indeed, in our samples the correlation of years in town and factory experience was generally about .70 for the rural migrants.[4] Under these circumstances, controlling for factory experience was bound to have a highly depressing effect on the size of the correlation between urban experience and modernity. In other words, it could well be that urban experience *was* actually making an independent contribution to modernity beyond the factory work accompanying it, but that by the method of partialing or by regression analysis one could not satisfactorily establish the facts. Those methods did not permit disentangling the intertwined experiences of urbanization and industrialism.

The matching procedure, however, offered a good alternative, because it did not depend, as did partialing and regression analysis, on an established set of correlation coefficients. Since the men in the match were selected individually, pair by pair, it was quite possible to find men alike in all other characteristics who truly differed in the degree of their exposure to urban influence after the age of 15. In each of the five countries, Israel being excluded as having no rural-origin men, we found a set of men who had, on the average, spent at least 5 years more in town than had the men who were otherwise matched to them on all important characteristics. The matches were of good quality, and the number of cases in each was reasonable.[5]

The results were rather striking. In none of the five countries did the match give evidence of a statistically significant difference favoring those with more years in town. Indeed, only two of the five correlations were above our minimum standard of .10, and in two cases the association was actually slightly negative.[6] These results indicated that it was mainly the occupational experience, that is, the work in factories, which accounted for the apparent influence of urban residence which we had observed earlier. Moreover, in this case, there was much less reason to challenge the results on grounds that we might have committed the partialing fallacy. The 5-year difference in urban residence separating the two sets of men in the match was not a statistical artifact, but a real difference. The match, therefore, raised serious question as to whether urban living contributed very much in its own right to the process of individual modernization. In our data, at least, the effect of urban experience was evidently more apparent than real, in the sense that it had been associated with higher modernity only because urban residence was so highly correlated with factory experience, which was more the real cause.

The matches and the partial correlations offered us our main possibility of disentangling the influence of urban as against industrial experience. We were well aware that in this case, in particular, we would run the greatest risk of committing the partialing fallacy. Nevertheless, we decided to undertake the analysis, prepared to reserve judgment on the outcome. Now that we have seen the results, however, we must commit ourselves to some conclusion.

The combined results of the matches and the partial correlations lead us to the following conclusion: Only in Nigeria did years in town make a substantial and statistically significant independent contribution in modernizing individuals; in the four remaining countries either the match, or the partial correlation, or both, cast serious doubt on the claim that the city, in its own right, makes a significant independent contribution as a school in modernity. The apparent association between urban experience and modernity evidently resulted mainly from the fact that in our samples urban experience was so intimately linked to factory work. The conclusion that factory work was the real cause of the observed correlation seemed the more reasonable because factory experience, subjected to statistical tests strictly analogous to those applied to urban experience, had far more successfully defended its standing as an independent force in shaping individual modernity.[7]

The Quality of Urban Experience

Since the number of years a man spent in town did not in itself significantly influence how modern he became, we wondered whether the nature of the city in which he lived would perhaps make a difference. In other words, we recognized that the critical aspect of urban experience might lie not in quantity but in quality. We could test the quality of city living along two dimensions relevant to our purpose. First, the larger, more cosmopolitan, cities could be compared to the smaller and more provincial towns. This made for a comparison among cities. In addition, we could test the importance of variation within cities, by considering whether our respondents lived in the central or in more peripheral sections of town.

Cosmopolitan vs. Provincial Cities

Whatever it is that makes a city "a city," as we generally think of it, should be more abundant and of better quality in the larger, more metropolitan and cosmopolitan centers. From this it followed, moreover, that if life in the city exerted a modernizing influence, residence in a large cosmopolitan center should exert more influence than life in one of the smaller, more provincial towns. In other words, it seemed reasonable to expect that those living in the more cosmopolitan cities should, on the average, prove to be more modern by our measures.

We were in a good position to test these ideas because in each country we took our cases from at least three cities, and one of these was always the main city of the region or country. Moreover, this main city was usually the capital. In most countries, and especially in the developing nations, the capital cities not only have more people, but they also bring together a greater diversity of activities and individuals of more variable background. The size and political significance of the capital city assure that resources are available there which are not found elsewhere. Lighting is generally better, transportation is more developed, and movies, theaters, newspapers, radio stations, and shops all exist in greater abundance. These larger, more cosmopolitan capital cities might, therefore, be contrasted with the smaller, less complex, more provincial towns to see which type had the greater power to modernize the men in them.[8]

To make this test, we carefully matched the residents of the most cosmopolitan city in each country to those living in the relatively more provincial urban areas. In Argentina, we pitted residents of greater Buenos Aires, a city of world standing, against those living in two provincial cities: Cordoba, center of the automobile industry, and Rosario, a meatpacking and agricultural-processing city.[9] In Chile, men from Santiago, the nation's capital and a decidedly metropolitan city, were matched to men from the seaport city of Valparaiso, from Valdivia, a modest center in a rich agricultural region with a substantial manufacturing sector, and from Concepción, the provincial center of Chile's thinly populated extreme South.[10] For Israel, the obvious claimant to the status of cosmopolitan center was the city of Tel Aviv, and its workers were matched to those from Jerusalem, Haifa, and the more modest industrial towns elsewhere in the country.[11] In Nigeria, the uncontested title of cosmopolitan center went to Lagos, the major port city, modern in architecture, the home of banking and finance, center of industry, and federal capital of Nigeria. To get sufficient cases, Lagos residents were matched to those living in three other places. Two, Abeokuta and Epe, were very modest urban centers having a fair amount of industry. The third was Ibadan, a large city by African standards, capital of the Western Region and home of Ibadan University, but in quality very much a traditional city composed of large family compounds surrounded by mud walls enclosing modest low-lying tin-roofed buildings of a traditional sort.[12]

East Pakistan presented a problem since in the mid-1960's modern Dacca, the capital, was quite a new city, still in process of construction. At that time, its broad avenues and great circles were lined with signs indicating what great complex of government buildings would eventually be located on this or that site, but very few of those buildings had yet been built. The city then gave more the impression of a town about to become a city, but not yet having a truly metropolitan character. Nevertheless, by all standards, it was the most advanced and cosmopolitan place in East Pakistan, and so we matched its residents to those living in the port city of Chittagong and the modest manufacturing center of Khulna.[13]

India also presented us with a difficult coding problem. Ranchi is the capital of Ranchi District. It is also the center of a newly developing steel industry and heavy-machinery complex which will someday make it the Essen of what is often called India's Ruhr. But in the mid-1960s it still had more the aspect of a boom town than of a great city. Giant construction was everywhere visible on the outskirts of town, where huge industrial and housing complexes were being built. In town the streets swarmed with pedestrians, bicycles, pedicabs, and industrial vans intermixed in a chaotic pattern along the main streets lined with low-lying buildings housing numerous small shops and stalls. Yet it was a capital, even if only of a district, the home of a vigorous young university and several other schools, the seat of a very large and modern mental hospital, a focus of industry, and substantial in population. If our Indian cities were placed in competition, we felt convinced that Ranchi had to be rated the most cosmopolitan.

Ranchi's chief competitor was the city of Jamshedpur. Like Ranchi, Jamshedpur is a center of iron and steel making, and of machine manufacturing as well, since Mercedes trucks are assembled there. The home of the famous Tata steel mills, the area is dominated by one company and a large proportion of the residents, representing nearly one-third of the population, live in company housing. There is, however, a considerable independent town in which live other company employees, as well as independent craftsmen, traders, and professionals. Jamshedpur is markedly different in character from Ranchi. It is quieter and more sedate. No important government functions are performed in the city. It has the aspect of a throughly uneventful place, a typical company town, long settled, and not very exciting. For that reason, we classified it with the less cosmopolitan towns even though, technically, it might have claimed precedence over Ranchi on grounds of being the larger of the two cities.[14]

Joining Jamshedpur on the less cosmopolitan side were two towns of rather special character. Muri and Khalari are both small and relatively isolated towns, each built around a single industrial plant. Here, too, a large proportion of the employees live in company housing in the company town. These company towns had not fostered the development of more or less independent sister settlements nearby, as had Jamshedpur, but rather were surrounded by small rural villages in which those men who were not able to get company housing resided. They are decidedly provincial places as compared to the complex, bustling city of Ranchi.

In making the comparison of men from the cosmopolitan versus the provincial cities, we restricted our sample to factory workers. Each worker from the main city was matched to a man from one of the peripheral cities in work experience, education, and some ten other variables. We were able to get an adequate number of cases in each match, and the matches were of generally good quality.[15] The results were striking. In no case was there a statistically significant advantage shown by the larger, more cosmopolitan city. The only near exception was in Argentina, where Buenos Aires did reasonably well in competition with the provincial cities. Elsewhere, the correlations were consistently negative, indicating that, if anything, men became somewhat more modern in the less cosmopolitan cities.[16] It should be recalled, of course, that the matching selected for comparison men from the smaller cities having the same education, skill, income, and other characteristics as the men from the larger cities. When matching thus insured that the individuals compared were alike in most other respects, the presumed cosmopolitanism of the city in which they lived proved to have absolutely no significant effect on individual modernity.

Results based on the match contrasting the larger and more cosmopolitan cities with smaller and more provincial ones were checked by a special regression analysis. In this analysis, a set of variables similar to those used in the matches were also controlled, and again the method was always to pit the single most important city against all the others combined. As in the matches, Argentina alone met the expectation that the more cosmopolitan city should have more modern men, with Buenos Aires having a slight but statistically significant edge over Cordoba and Rosario. Nigeria showed the greatest contrast, but, contrary to expectation, did so by favoring the more provincial cities as against more cosmopolitan Lagos.

Of the remaining three countries, two others also favored the more provincial towns, the third, the cosmopolitan, but in all three cases the figures were at statistically insignificant levels.[17] The special regression analysis thus largely confirmed the results obtained in matching. All in all, we had failed to make a case that the quality of a city as more or less cosmopolitan played any consistent or substantial role in making men more modern.[18]

Location in the Inner vs. the Outer Part of the City

As a challenge to our finding about the poor performance of the more cosmopolitan cities, it might be argued that for the men whom we were studying the criterion we had used was irrelevant. No matter how elegant and sophisticated the chief city might be in comparison with the provinces, that could mean very little to a poor man living in a shanty town on the distant outskirts. Such a man might well never get into the heart of town to share in all that splendor. It could be, therefore, that the modernizing effect of the city on a man would depend mainly on whether his location within his city was central or peripheral. Using his place of work as the key, we therefore classified each worker's factory location as falling in one of three categories: in the central urban district, in an intermediate zone, or outside the main urban area at a suburban or even semirural site.[19]

If it were the case that the more urban the environment the greater men's modernity, then a man's location on this continuum should have been substantially correlated with individual modernity. The data gave but modest support to the argument for urban influence. In three of five countries this "urbanism-of-location" variable failed to show a significant zero-order correlation with individual modernity, and in two of those the expected order was reversed. The results for India and Nigeria indicated there might be some substance to the hypothesis since in those two cases the correlations were statistically significant. However, only one correlation survived the control for the early-socialization variables, the other that for the late variables, and neither coefficient was left significant, or above our usual minimum size of .10, when the full array of variables in Set A was brought under control.[20]

Conclusions

We ran several different tests of the assumption that urban experience has inherent qualities which should make men more modern. On each of these tests the city failed to make a good case. We could not find statistically significant evidence consistent across any major set of our six countries which might prove that the amount or quality of urban experience, in its own right, played any substantial part in accounting for the individual modernity of the men in our samples. This seems to be a most important finding, if for no other reason than that it so far contradicts not only popular expectations but also the established wisdom of so many theorists for whom the city epitomizes modernizing influences. In addition, however, proving that cities are not significant, let alone indispensable, schools for individual modernity could have substantial impact on planning for economic development. Under the circumstances, we felt we should be especially cautious in drawing the conclusion toward which our findings so strongly inclined us.

In this spirit, we were quite ready to view with reserve the finding that the number of years a man spent in town did not generally seem to make him more modern. As already noted, in our samples the association between years in town and factory experience was so high as to render questionable any attempt to disentangle their influence by statistical manipulation alone. One might argue, therefore, that really to test the contribution of urban experience in its own right, we should have had samples in which there were significant numbers of men who had obtained substantial urban experience while not simultaneously gaining industrial experience as well. The men that we have called "urban nonindustrial workers" fit that description, and as we have seen in Chapter 14, they usually lagged far behind the industrial workers in individual modernity, suggesting that the city alone was not very effective in making men modern.

Although doubts based on methodological considerations cautioned us against drawing too firm a conclusion from the data on years in town, the same obstacle did not exist in the case of our comparison of men from the more as against the less cosmopolitan cities, and from the inner city as against the periphery. In those cases, the data seemed to argue rather unambiguously that no special contribution to modernization was made by some essence of the city beyond the fact that urban centers are where we usually find the greatest concentration of modernizing institutions such as the school, the factory, and the mass media.

In thinking about this conclusion, it is helpful to distinguish between direct and indirect influences on modernization. What we seem to have demonstrated is that, with the other major influences controlled, the amount of urban experience per se and the relative cosmopolitan quality of a city per se do not consistently make a significant contribution to modernity scores. In other words, urban experience in itself has little direct effect on OM scores. However, we have reason to believe that urban experience has powerful indirect effects on modernity scores. By indirect effect we mean effects mediated through connections with other variables such as the mass media, formal education, factory experience, and the like.

Census materials and other survey data from developing countries make it clear that urban areas are generally distinguished by greater concentrations of mass media, factories, schools, and higher living standards than are rural areas. We think of these forces as acting directly on the person, to make him more modern. It follows that the opportunity for a number of crucial, direct modernizing experiences is clearly greater in urban areas in most developing countries. Along with these greater opportunities generally goes a greater average exposure to modernizing influences among city people than among rural people. Consequently, city people tend to be more modern than country people.

In the frame of reference of our research, the amount of urban experience, when measured in a global way, as by zero-order correlation, did emerge as having a strong and significant association with higher OM scores when no statistical controls were introduced. Yet the relation proved to be a seemingly spurious one, in the sense that urban experience per se was not the crucial variable. Once we took account of mass-media exposure, factory experience, formal education, socioeconomic status, and other characteristics distinguishing city people, there was little or no impact left that the intrinsic quality of the city had on OM scores, in so far as we mean by such intrinsic qualities the stimuli associated with the size, density, and heterogeneity of the urban population.

This distinction between the city as the place in which certain institutions such as schools, factories, and media of mass communication are concentrated, and the city as the embodiment of some force or "essence" above and beyond that concentration of institutions, seems to us critical. In a classic essay written in 1938 under the title "Urbanism as a Way of Life,"[21] Louis Wirth identified the essence of the city as lying in the facts of size, density, and heterogeneity. Wirth argued that these characteristics of the city gave life there certain special qualities, stimulating its inhabitants to impersonality and inculcating a sense of anomie. Sociologists working in this tradition extended Wirth's ideas to assign the city a special role in the process of modernization. Thus, in his essay on "The City and Modernization," Norton Ginsberg said: "All definitions of modernization refer in some measure not only to change, but, more important, to conceptions of efficiency, increased human and spatial interaction, and extraordinary complexity of human relationships ... Invariably these ideas have come to be associated with the city."[22]

What is notable here, as in so many other discussions of the city, is that Ginsburg assigned basically the same sort of special quality to city life as did Wirth, rather than focusing on the much simpler fact that the city is distinguished by the concentration there of schools, factories, means of mass transportation, and media of communication. Take those away and there will be little power to teach modernity left in such presumably quintessential features of the city as Wirth's size, density, and heterogeneity, or Ginsburg's "extraordinary complexity of human relationships."

The fact that it is not the culture of the city as such which makes people more modern could be of vital importance in deciding on public policy for development. Evidently, to modernize peasants and others in the countryside, we are not required to build more cities and move people to them. Rather, our results suggest that modernizing the noncity dwellers can be accomplished by extending to them benefits of education, mass media, and new occupational experience, while at the same time raising living standards, as was done in Comilla and in the moshavim. More cities and greater urbanization may, in the long run, bring such influences into being, but they are not the only way of creating them. We can accomplish the same purpose without dense urban concentrations if we provide the same opportunities for personal development outside the city which we now normally make available only to city dwellers.

Another important insight the present results give us concerns the city people themselves. Our results permit us to understand more fully the variations in relative modernity within the urban population. If the city in itself were the inherent source of modernizing influence, all the citizens of a given city should be more or less equally modern. In fact, the variation within each city is quite marked. We now see that this variation arises from the fact that it is not urban experience per se which makes men more modern but rather their differential contact with the schools, mass media, and factories which the town contains.

16

Rural Versus Urban Origin

With the exception of education, all the influences shaping modernity which we have so far examined impinged on a man mainly after he had reached adulthood. They are, in the terms of our study, *late socialization experiences*. Yet a man does not come on the urban industrial scene as a *tabula rasa*. At the end of adolescence his character reflects the quality of the family in which he was raised, and the social and cultural attributes of the territory in which he grew up.

Many of those who reviewed our research plans when they were first formulated were quite convinced that each man's *early socialization experience* would very likely be the most important determinant of his modernity. Moreover, they conceived of these childhood influences as likely to produce persistent effects which could not easily be changed by adult experiences. Freudian theory is, of course, in accord with popular psychology in stressing the primacy of early years in shaping character, and the stubbornness of early established traits in resisting efforts to change them. For our part, we were well aware that a man whose character had been cast in the traditional mold would, upon entering the urban industrial milieu, be required to unlearn many of the things he had learned previously. And we knew we had to face the challenge that almost all of experimental psychology argued that "it is much easier to learn something new than to stamp out one set of learned behaviors and replace them by a new set . . . all [the evidence] tends to confirm the tremendous power of early learning and its resistance to later alterations and extinction."[1]

In response to the challenge of the ideas just discussed, we designed this section of our analysis to answer two basic questions. First, how far is a man's modernity determined by the character of his primary group memberships in the early and adolescent years of his life? Second, how resistant to change will these early-established personal characteristics be in the face of later experiences of a kind quite different from those the individual underwent as a youth?

On the first question we had no strong views. It seemed to us quite probable that growing up in a city rather than in a rural village, experiencing the stimulation of a more modern family and school environment, and learning the culture of a less rigidly traditional ethnic group might well make a substantial contribution to shaping a man's modernity. On the second issue, however, we felt quite strongly. We considered it central to our investigation. Our entire study rested on the assumption that men can *learn* to be modern. And we maintained that this prospect exists not just for those who are well prepared for the new experience from the start, but also for those who enter the race with a substantial handicap. We were, in short, convinced that no one is obliged to carry traditional attitudes and values with him all his life, because later experience can bring about a fundamental change from whatever has been true of the individual's formative years.

To test these ideas we selected for particular study here two of the early influences: urban vs. rural residence in the first 15 years of life, and training in a modern vs. a traditional home and school environment.[2]

Criteria for Judging Origins

When Marx derided the "idiocy of village life," he not only spoke for the political left, but also expressed the judgment of a wide spectrum of urban intellectuals for whom the traditional agricultural settlement is the epitome of technological stagnation, cultural backwardness, and mental torpor. Vast arrays of statistics for almost every country in the world provide lugubrious testimony about the numerous disadvantages the typical village farmer suffers in seeking access to education, mass communication, health care, housing, sanitation, transportation, and the like.

Two consequences are generally assumed to follow from these conditions. First, the young man of rural background is expected to come to maturity being much less modern than his "cousin" raised in the city. Second, his backwardness is assumed to persist, so that even if he later has extensive contact with modernizing institutions, the man of rural origin will still lag behind a comparable man who has been raised in an urban setting.

Testing these assumptions required including men of both urban and rural origins in our samples of new and experienced workers. We were able to achieve that objective in only three countries — Argentina, Chile, and Nigeria — but they certainly provide sufficient basis for exploring the issues.

We took special pains to select and classify our respondents on the dimension of origin. Men were accepted into the sample as representatives of the group of rural origin only if their fathers had been employed more or less exclusively as cultivators of the land, and they themselves had lived and gone to school in farming villages. If their village had supported any substantial commercial activity or any government offices of more than purely local significance they could not qualify. These characteristics were supposed to have been constant for the first 15 years of a man's life. If some incidental event took him to the city to live for a total of more than a year during that span, we normally disqualified him as a person of pure rural origin. The city-bred man had to meet comparable requirements to qualify as being of urban origin: to have had a father who did not farm; to have grown up and attended school in a place of sufficient population that, by the standards of his country, it would be classified as an "urban" setting; and, to have spent not more than 1 year out of the first 15 living in an essentially rural area.[3]

The Empirical Outcome

When we placed these two groups in competition there was no doubt that in our samples the average man of urban origin was much more modern than the average man with a rural background. In Argentina 51 percent of urban-origin workers were modern, as against 18 percent of those of rural origin. In Chile the figures were identical, and in Nigeria 46 and 33 percent, respectively. Expressed as a simple correlation, the relation of the origin dichotomy to OM scores was very strong in Argentina at .44*** and in Chile at .41***, and although weaker in Nigeria at .14** it was still statistically quite significant.

These relatively clear-cut results did not occasion great surprise because we knew that on the average urban-origin men had better-educated parents, had themselves had more education, and had had greater mass-media contact and other advantages. From the material presented so far, therefore, we could not tell how serious a handicap rural origin might be in its own right, nor how far men of that background might be able to close the gap separating them from the more advantaged urban-origin men. To settle these issues, we needed different sorts of information.

First, we should emphasize that being rural in origin was no barrier to rapid learning in such schools of modernity as the factory. Men of rural origin gained regularly for each year they spent in the factory, so that in the typical case the proportion of modern men among the more experienced workers was at least twice that among the men newly arrived at the factory. Indeed, rural-origin men got more out of each year in the factory, on the average, than did comparable men of urban origin, and over the years they continued to learn at a rate certainly as regular as that established by their urban "cousins."[4]

Of course, rural-origin men might have learned quite a lot during each year spent in the factory and still have lagged far behind urban-origin men, thus indicating a persistent disability. To test that possibility it was necessary to compare men who were alike in education, factory experience, and other advantages, but were still different in origin.

We were able to make such a comparison using two different methods. When we constructed a match to compare experienced factory workers of urban and rural origin, the results indicated that there were no statistically significant differences separating the matched origin groups. With other variables controlled in the match, the correlations of origin and modernity, while favoring the urban men, were consistently quite low and statistically insignificant.[5]

We also tried partial correlations, applying our standard set of controls. When we did that the strength of the association between individual modernity and origin was sharply decreased. This indicated that the strong simple correlation observed earlier resulted in good part from the advantages urban-origin men had enjoyed through their parents' education, their own schooling, greater mass-media contact, and other institutional benefits more readily accessible to a man raised in the city. When partial correlation adjusted for those differences, the gap between the urban- and rural-origin men was largely closed. Indeed, in Nigeria the partial correlation of .09 was below our standard, only barely statistically significant at the .05 level. In Argentina and Chile, the partial correlations, at .13** and .18***, respectively, while small, were safely in the category of the statistically significant.

While the results of the match and the partialing were not in perfect accord, they certainly did not contradict each other. The difference was one of emphasis rather than of direction. To avoid argument over ambiguous statistics we inclined to the conclusion that those of urban origin were still *somewhat* more modern even when the men of rural origin to whom they were compared had managed to acquire education, factory experience, and other advantages which made the life chances of the two groups reasonably equal.

Nevertheless, we were impressed to discover that the rural-origin men were able to come so near to closing the gap in modernity which *initially* had separated them from those of urban origin. This gap closed most when the men of rural origin obtained as much education as men of urban origin. It was further closed when the groups were rendered equal in factory experience. As their experience was progressively equalized, the advantage of the urban- over the rural-origin men was markedly reduced. In Argentina the gap in OM scores separating the two groups shrank from 9 points to 2; in Chile it fell from 10 points to 1; and in Nigeria it was reduced from 3 points to 2.[6] In political participation, efficacy, independence from relatives, and family planning, the man of rural origin, under the tutelage of his factory and related experiences, had pretty well pulled abreast of the men raised in the city. The experience of the industrial milieu thus proved itself a great equalizer. Men starting out with the handicap of traditional, more rigid, conventional attitudes showed themselves capable of being transformed into more modern men, more open to new experience, more efficacious, more involved in politics, and more self-directing.

Conclusion

In this chapter we explored one of the most critical issues dealt with by our study, and put our theory of modernization to a severe test. Everyone accepts the idea that village people in underdeveloped countries, engaged in agricultural pursuits and living in relatively isolated places, develop more traditional attitudes. Such contrasts as are commonly observed could, of course, be due not to occupational differences and the whole ambience of village life, but rather to differences in opportunity, and in particular to the lesser availability of schooling in rural areas. Indeed, our data show that cultivators can do quite well on our tests of modernity if they have obtained an above-average education. But even holding education constant, the traditionalism of men in the village is, as we have seen, far greater than that manifested by former villagers engaged in urban industrial pursuits.[7]

This difference between farmers and workers cannot be accounted for on the basis of presumed selective recruitment of more modern men from the villages for migration to the factories and the city.[8] The greater part of the difference seems due to the influence of later life in the urban industrial setting. The factory is clearly a school in modernity for the men who work in it. What is most notable, in this context, is the fact that the factory's imprint is not being applied to a *tabula rasa*. Since the extinction of old ideas and habits and their replacement by new ones is one of the most difficult of all learning tasks, it is all the more impressive that the factory seems able not only to teach new technical practices, but also to change already established values, response patterns, and habits in the men of rural origin. This process is carried on sufficiently vigorously that these men gradually overcome their initial handicap. By the time they have been in the factory 8 years or more they have reached almost the same level of individual modernity as have the men born and raised in the city, at least those with whom they share a comparable education.[9]

We take all this as evidence that major transformations are possible in fully matured adults. Even though the progress may be slow and gradual, we consider the evidence to warrant an optimistic conclusion. No man need be permanently left in the condition in which he finds himself on reaching maturity. There is a genuine prospect that he may acquire new, and perhaps expanding and liberating, attitudes, values, and psychological dispositions, so long as he is given the correct setting in which to learn. Furthermore, adult socialization is not limited to learning new techniques and skills. It can affect psychological properties of the most basic character, such as the sense of efficacy, or the way of handling time, and do so by transforming old ways of feeling and relating into newer and more modern orientations.

17

Home and School Background

Our project emphasized that men can become modern through a process of socialization experienced late in life. But many psychologists assert that the important properties of the personality are laid down in childhood and adolescence. They would assume, therefore, that most of the variation in modernity scores could be explained in terms of the early experiences of individuals. In this view, even such later learning of modern attitudes and values as might occur would be largely determined by the individual properties the men brought to the learning situation. According to this reasoning, men who entered the urban industrial complex *predisposed* to be modern would more rapidly and fully learn the lessons it had to teach.

Such individual variation in the propensity to change need not be attributed to "accident" or be considered merely "random." Some of the variation may stem from individual differences in genetic makeup, and from the inborn physiological and temperamental differences which distinguish one person from another. It was beyond the capacity of our project to deal with that kind of variation. Another source of individual differences in personality and in readiness to modernize may lie in the families in which individuals are raised. Although we have very little precise knowledge of why and how such diverse patterns arise, we are all well aware that families do constitute very different social milieus, and that each seems to turn out its own more or less distinctive product.

Just as homes may vary in the atmosphere for learning they create and the values they inculcate, so may schools. We did not assume that a year in one school would necessarily be the equal of a year in any other school, at least so far as its impact on the modernization of the individual was concerned. On the contrary, we considered it likely that schools would vary greatly in the stimulus they provided for learning the attitudes, values, and personal dispositions we associate with individual modernity. Just as we felt that factories could meaningfully be rated on a continuum from modern to traditional, so we assumed that schools could be similarly classified. However, we had no way of getting back to the homes in which our respondents had been raised and the schools in which they had been educated, and even if we had been able to find them, there would have been no ready method for measuring directly what those environments had been like *earlier*. We were obliged, therefore, to rely on more indirect indicators.

A Subjective Measure of Home and School Modernity

To measure the psychosocial properties of the home and school in which our respondents had undergone their early socialization experiences, we relied on a very simple "home and school modernity scale," based on the individual's memory of how his parents and teachers had acted.

The scale was based on eight questions, five to assess relations in the home, and three in the school. Under pressure of limited time, we could touch on only a few of the themes emphasized in our analytic model of adult modernity. Those we selected were: calculability and planning, efficacy, dignity, and time. Thus, we asked: "When you were a boy, did your parents urge you to be exactly on time?" and "Did your teachers keep the promises they made: All the time, Most of the time, Only a few times, Almost never?" Home modernity and school modernity were scored separately and then the scores for each subscale were combined to yield an overall "home-school modernity score" for each individual.[1] The component items of the scale intercorrelated well, and the scale scores were everywhere well distributed over the entire appropriate range.

The simple correlations with OM yielded a mixed picture. In general, the results supported the common-sense assumption that men who came from a home and school background which we classified as more modern would also be more modern as adults. However, it was disappointing to discover (Table 17–1) that this relation met firm standards of statistical significance in only three of the six countries, being immaterial and totally without statistical significance in the other three.

Moreover, even in the countries in which the relation met our expectation, we had to be cautious about assuming the basic issue to have been settled. There was a strong possibility that men who reported their home and school milieus to have been more modern were mainly those who were themselves better educated. Since we knew the individual's own education to be a powerful influence on his OM score, it seemed essential to

Table 17–1.   Correlations of home-school modernity and individual modernity (OM).[a]

Correlation	Argentina	Chile	East Pakistan	India	Israel	Nigeria
1. **Simple** (zero-order)	.11***	.22***	.01	.26***	−.01	.02
2. **Match correlation**[b] (Match 24)	−.03	.02	−.05	.07	−.06	−.01
N's for row 1	817	929	943	1198	739	721
N's for row 2[c]	182	190	90	72	159	102

[a] Asterisks denote significance as follows: *, at .05 level; **, at .01 level; ***, at .001 level or better.
[b] In this match men whose home-school environment was rated traditional were given a score of 1; men whose home-school environment was rated modern were given a score of 2.
[c] Figures given in this row are the numbers of matched pairs in each country.

take such facts into account. We therefore arranged a standard match so that those reporting a modern home-school experience could be compared with others from a more traditional background. The match brought under control differences in education, occupation, and other characteristics which might be related to the modern home and school environment, and thus permitted us to make a less ambiguous assessment of the role played by the "quality" of the individual's early experience in shaping his standing as a more modern or traditional man.[2] The results are summarized in Table 17–1.

Once the influence of other variables was brought under control, even the three countries which had shown significant simple correlations came to join the ranks of the others in showing no statistically relevant association between individual modernity and the quality of home-school background. Men who remembered their parents and teachers as having adopted a more modern approach to childrearing seemed to enjoy no lasting benefits in the form of a higher level of individual modernity, at least when they were matched to men equal in education, occupation, and similar characteristics.

The nature of our method was such that it did not permit us to say whether, at the time of leaving home, those who later recalled having been treated in the way we defined as modern had started out with the advantage of an initially higher modernity score. Our procedure *did* permit us to say, however, that *even* if some men had started out with an initial qualitative advantage, it was not great enough to survive the equalizing effect which later education and occupational experience had for those whose early background was more traditional. Or, to put it another way, it appears that those whose home-school background we defined as modern did not derive from that experience an aptitude for learning to be modern powerful enough to insure them a lasting lead over others who had initially been less privileged, at least when all alike were exposed to later training in modernization under the tutelage of the factory and the mass media.

Explaining the Results

We hesitated, however, to treat these results as definitive evidence for the relative unimportance of the quality of early experience. The reservations were both theoretical and methodological. First, we admit that there was some arbitrariness in our selecting the particular questions we did as defining a modern approach to childrearing. Parents and teachers who strictly train children to be on time and to plan ahead, and who themselves always keep their promises and take care not to humiliate the child, are not necessarily acting in the way most likely to bring their charges up to be outstandingly modern men. There are other themes in our analytic model which will surely seem to many to have been more appropriate issues to investigate — indeed, seem so to us now. For example, it might have been more relevant to inquire whether parents and teachers had encouraged experimentation, taught independence, rewarded initiative, and approved, or at least had been tolerant, of new and unconventional ideas. Some might argue that the qualities we actually tested were, by contrast, as much indicators of traditional as of modern upbringing.

Second, we acknowledge the questionable reliability of a man's memory of the psychosocial atmosphere of his home and school as he recalled it some 20 years or more after the event. In raising this point we are only echoing the caution urged by a whole generation of students of the problem, who learned from bitter experience that childrearing practices can be assessed accurately only by direct observation, which we, unfortunately, could not undertake.

What then is the meaning of the responses we obtained, and the wide distribution of scale scores which emerged? Some light was thrown on this question when we examined the relation of the home-school scale to the scale measuring our interviewees' perception of the treatment they had received as industrial workers. The questions used in that scale dealt with issues, and were couched in language, very similar to the home-school measure, even though the focus of attention had shifted to the job. For example, we asked whether, on the job, a man's superiors had shown respect for his feelings, and we asked: "In your experience when the foreman said he would do something for you . . . did he do it?"

The home-school scale proved consistently to have a statistically significant and fairly substantial relation to the scale measuring the perceived modernity of a man's job experience.[3] Yet there was no particular reason why the relation between the two measures should have been other than random. We concluded that the home-school experience scale tapped a general propensity to see the institutions one had been in, and the authority figures in them, as kind and supportive. Whether both scales merely tapped a common personality disposition whose origin is unknown, or whether childhood experience really shaped the later propensity to see the work environment as benign, poses a question beyond our ability to answer. Nevertheless, our data do permit us to say that the propensity to see oneself as well treated by parents and teachers seems not to have been an important factor in determining how far or how fast men become modern.

Father's Education

The critical weakness of our measure of perceived home-school experience was its subjective character. Fortunately, we had a more objective measure of family background in the number of years of education attained by the father of each of our respondents. Even this figure was, of course, open to error due to ignorance or faulty recall. More serious, however, was the fact that what this measure gained in objectivity it lost in self-evident psychological relevance. Our justification for using it rested on the inference, from general experience, that a household headed by an illiterate father would provide the child a psychosocial milieu quite different from that offered to the child from a home in which the father had even as little as 5 to 6 years of schooling, particularly in a poor country where primary education is not readily available. Since education was itself so good an indicator of individual modernity, it seemed sensible to treat the father's education as an objective index of a potentially more modern home atmosphere. This procedure could be followed in five of the six countries.[4]

The reasonableness of this assumption seemed to be confirmed by the simple correlations between father's education and our overall measure of individual modernity presented in Table 17–2. The correlations for the five countries for which we had data were all highly significant statistically, with the median at .33***. But we knew that the education of fathers and that of the sons in our sample were highly correlated in turn.[5] It could well have been, therefore, that the observed correlation between father's education and son's modernity was only an artifact of the higher education attained by the sons of well-educated fathers.

Through matching we could compare men whose fathers had had either little or much education while controlling for the level of the son's own education. These matches met strict standards, and were based on an ample number of cases.[6] There was, therefore, no reason to fault the statistics presented in Table 17–2. In Argentina and Chile the correlation between father's education and son's modernity was just at our minimal

Table 17–2. Correlations of father's education and individual modernity (OM).[a]

Correlation	Argentina	Chile	East Pakistan	India	Nigeria
I. **Simple** (zero-order)	.33***	.33***	.21***	.44***	.18***
II. **Partial,** controlling for—					
Formal education	.16***	.21***	.07	.18***	.06
Years factory experience	.28***	.25***	.19***	.39***	.11**
Mass-media exposure	.20***	.26***	.15***	.19***	.16***
Early socialization experiences	.15***	.21***	.08*	.14***	.06
Late socialization experiences	.16***	.23***	.08*	.21***	.09*
Set A (early and late socialization)	.09**	.16***	.01	.08**	.03
III. **Match correlation**[b]	.10	.10	−.04	.05	.02
N's for Parts I and II	817	929	943	1198	721
N's for Part III[c]	68	121	130	218	95

a Asterisks denote significance as follows: *, at .05 level; **, at .01 level; ***, at .001 level or better.
b Match 58 pitted men whose fathers had "little" education (punched "1") against men whose fathers had above average education (punched "2").
c Figures given in this row are the numbers of matched pairs in each country.

level, but even there, and decidedly so in the other countries, the result was not statistically significant. So far as the matches were concerned, then, we were obliged to conclude that having had a relatively better-educated father *in itself* gave a man no particular advantage in attaining a high modernity score as an adult.

This rather surprising conclusion could be tempered somewhat on the basis of the partial correlations, also presented in Table 17–2. In two countries the partials confirmed the conclusion that his father's education was in itself no assurance that a man would earn a higher OM score. Argentina, India, and Chile, however, showed consistent statistically significant differences favoring the men whose fathers were better educated. Of those three cases, however, only one correlation also met our standard of being at least .10 or above in magnitude when all the early- and late-socialization variables were controlled. Therefore, taking into account evidence from both sources, we conclude that once other factors, and especially later life experiences, are controlled for, the advantage of having grown up in a home with a presumably "superior" ambience loses most of its importance as a consistent element in the shaping of modern men.

The Limits Of Our Findings

So many of our readers will immediately challenge this conclusion, that we hasten to make explicit the limits within which our statement is meant to apply. First, we are not asserting that the education of the father will under all circumstances fail to confer a lasting advantage in the form of greater individual modernity. Our conclusion is limited to the type of sample we collected. It should not be forgotten that we were working within a narrow spectrum of the full educational range. Even the better educated of the fathers in our matches were men of quite limited education, averaging as little as 4 years of schooling in East Pakistan and at best only about 8 years in the other countries. It could well be, therefore, that if we had gotten into the higher ranges of the distribution on fathers' education, we would have found more evidence that the presumably enriched home atmosphere created by more educated fathers did indeed confer on the sons a lasting advantage in the form of higher adult modernity scores.

A second source of potential misunderstanding arises from the controls we applied in constructing our matches. The crucial advantage the well-educated father bestows on his son may consist in his encouraging that son to get more education than the next man.[7] By matching so that we compared only men who were alike in their own education, we might have suppressed the very indicator which would otherwise have distinguished the men who had come from the more modern homes. However, when we checked this possibility against the facts, we found that our having controlled for a man's own education had not substantially distorted our impression of the relative unimportance of the father's education. As a predictor of a man's modernity score, his father's education played a very modest role compared to the major role played by the man's *own* education.[8]

We are, then, being seriously misunderstood if it is assumed that we read our results as proving that in our samples "there are no significant differences in the characteristics of men whose fathers were better educated as compared to those whose fathers had little education." We are saying no such thing. Men whose fathers had more education were on the average decidedly better educated and more modern than men whose fathers were less educated. This was clearly shown by the simple correlations we presented at the outset of this discussion.

What we *are* saying is that men who came from less-advantaged homes, but who managed to get as much education and factory experience as those whose fathers were better educated, were thereby put on an equal footing with those who had started out with an apparent advantage in their home milieu. In other words, beyond the superior education they secured for their children, the better-educated fathers did not seem also to give their sons much of an *additional* psychic bonus which would later be reflected in still higher modernity scores. Using the language of path analysis, we are saying that a father's education had a substantial *indirect* effect on his son's modernity via the path of the son's own education, but a father's education did not consistently have much of a *direct* impact on that son's modernity score.

We are certainly aware that it is not every man who can manage to overcome early disadvantages. Indeed, the majority do not. The practical outcome, therefore, is that men whose fathers have more education are going to be more modern, on the average. But it remains an important empirical finding that the disadvantage a man experienced by virtue of having a less-educated father *could* be compensated for in the case of those who themselves managed to get more education when young or more factory experience and mass-media exposure when adults, or both.

This finding, in turn, has important implications for public policy in developing countries. All is not settled at birth. The disadvantage of having a poorly educated father is not necessarily borne permanently. If the society will offer a man a chance to get as much schooling as the son of a better-educated man, the boy from the disadvantaged home can close the gap. Even if he misses out in youth, later occupational experience and its concomitants may give him a further opportunity to advance in personal modernization.

The Quality of Education: Rural Versus Urban Schools

Just as father's education served as a less subjective way of estimating the quality of each man's *home* environment, so could urban location serve as a more objective estimate of the quality of his school.

Almost everyone we spoke to expected that rural schools would be much less effective modernizers than would be most schools in the urban centers. The expectation rested on the assumption that the rural schools would be inferior in at least three respects: first, that they would suffer from lack of space, a scarcity of good books, and the almost complete absence of the latest mechanical aids to supplement the efforts of the teacher; second, that the pupils' difficulties in reaching the school over large distances, their lack of proper clothing or sufficient food, and the pressures to help their parents with the farming all would conspire to make attendance more difficult and hence more irregular; third, and most important, that the rural teacher would be likely to be much less well trained than the urban teacher, and would, in his or her own social development, be so close to the common man as to be able to bring little new to the classroom in the way of knowledge, ideas, sophistication, or liberal ways of dealing with people. Insofar as such differences prevailed, we might indeed expect the person whose school had been in a rural village, especially in an underdeveloped country, to be less modernized by the experience than would someone who had had the benefit of being schooled in a more modern urban setting.

To test this idea against the facts we should, ideally, have applied the modernity scale to rural and urban children as they moved through the various grade levels of their respective schools. Unfortunately, our sample design did not permit doing that. The alternative our study did permit was to compare adults whose childhood schooling had been in either rural or urban settings. For this purpose, however, we felt it inappropriate to rely mainly on a comparison of farmers and city workers. Making that comparison it would not be possible to say whether the advantage of the urban-origin men, which we anticipated finding, came from the quality of the school they had attended, or, instead, stemmed from the numerous other differences in life experience which separated an urban-origin industrial worker from a cultivator still living in the countryside. However, in three countries we had available men all of whom were *currently* urban-resident industrial workers, *yet* who differed in whether their childhood schooling had been obtained in the countryside or in the city. Since the later-life conditions of these two sets of men were so much alike, it seemed reasonable to use them as the main basis for judging the effectiveness of the schooling they had received in early life.

Before moving to this comparison, however, we must enter one additional caveat. We felt that to judge the effectiveness of rural versus urban schools, the appropriate test would not lie in comparing the *absolute* score of men from these two backgrounds, but rather in comparing the *gain* in modernity per additional year of schooling which resulted from attendance in either a rural or an urban setting. We insisted on this point because the absolute modernity score could well reflect many influences which had had their effect at any point in life. By contrast, the gain per year of additional schooling could be properly attributed to the effect of the school as such, especially in an analysis in which the effect of other important variables such as occupation was controlled.

In all three countries the urban-origin factory workers were noticeably more modern than the rural-origin men with the same amount of schooling.[9] As we cautioned earlier, however, this absolute difference in OM scores could not properly be interpreted as proving that urban *schools* were more effective. For one thing, men of urban origin might already have been more modern at the time when they first entered school. For another, the two sets of men had likely been exposed to different life experiences by virtue of their origin and those differences could account for the contrast in their raw modernity scores. The point is effectively emphasized by the fact that the gap in OM separating cultivators and rural-origin factory workers was much greater than that separating the two sets of workers, even though the cultivators and the rural-origin factory workers both had gone to the same rural schools.[10]

To test the effectiveness of the school per se under urban versus rural conditions, the appropriate statistic is that which shows the average gain per additional year of schooling. When that statistic was calculated for a set of men all within the same educational range in any given country, we found we could not affirm the superiority of the urban school. In Chile, urban schools did seem to have been the more effective modernizers, yielding a gain of 2.4 OM points per additional year of schooling, as against a gain of only 1.5 points for each additional year in a rural school. But in Argentina and Nigeria the two types of school produced virtually identical results. In Argentina, factory workers had gained 2.6 OM points for each year spent in a rural school, and 2.5 points for each year spent in an urban school. In Nigeria the figures were 3.2 and 3.1, respectively.[11]

Explaining The Findings

We can explain these findings in several different ways. One possibility is that in developing countries urban schools do not actually have the advantages we so often attribute to them on the basis of our social memory of an earlier American experience. If, in our developing countries, crowding, shortage of books, and inadequate preparation of teachers were as common in urban schools as in the rural, there would be no reason to expect superior performance from the former. We do not have the facts for a strict test of this possibility, but we had the impression that whatever the defects of the urban schools in the countries we studied they were actually much more marked in the rural schools.

A second possibility is that a school's quality is marginal in importance compared to the significance of certain basic organizational features common to *all* schools. Whether a school is rural or urban, the important fact about it, from the perspective of modernization, may lie in its embodiment of certain fundamental lessons expressed in its organizational and operational principles. If the modernizing effect of the school came mainly from such organizational features, as we described them in Chapter 9, and if these basic features were present in all schools, whether simple or sophisticated, then rural schools could be expected to do about as well as urban schools. We incline rather strongly to this explanation.

There is, however, a third possibility. Objectively speaking, the urban schools may in fact be richer in those qualities which we assume can produce individual modernity. But subjectively the rural schools might be having a much greater impact than could be predicted solely on the basis of their objective quality. Urban children, when they first arrive at the school, are more likely to have previously experienced in other settings many of the special qualities built into the school as an organization. For rural children, however, their contact with the school will usually be their first, and for some time may be their *only,* contact with certain organizational principles common to the school, the office, and the factory, but not found in the family, on the small farm, or in the rural village. Consequently, for its particular pupils the rural school may be a much more salient experience, since the school contrasts much more markedly with its surrounding milieu than does the urban school with its milieu. Consequently, the rural school, while more weakly embodying the principles of modern organization, could yet have as much impact as the urban school.

This explanation also seems highly plausible to us. We are, unfortunately, not able to test these competing interpretations with the data collected by this project.[12] Our contribution has been limited to showing that, contrary to popular expectation, the quality of a school, as measured by whether it is rural or urban, does not seem to play any consistently clear-cut role in determining how rapidly its pupils become modernized as they pass through its successive grades.

We might be more skeptical of this finding were it not for two facts. On a comparative basis, we note that the massive study of American education known as the Coleman report also failed to find evidence that the quality of public schools made much difference in the academic performance of pupils in the United States. And within our own study, we failed to find evidence that the quality of factories and cities played much of a role in determining their effectiveness as modernizers. These results, therefore, strengthened our conviction that so long as the fundamental principles of organization implicit in the concept of factory, office, and school are met, the basic condition for modernization *through exposure over time* is also met.

There is still another way of looking at these results, which is to argue that how much you benefit from each additional year of schooling depends on what happens *later* in your life. The point may be illustrated by the common phenomenon of loss of literacy. By continuing in school 2 years beyond the second grade, at which stage a man may have been able to read only a few words, he might reach the point where he could read quite well. If, after leaving school, he were somehow stimulated to continue reading regularly, whether it were the Bible or the daily newspaper, then, as an adult, he would almost certainly test out as a good reader. On later testing his literacy, then, we would be led to conclude that the man had gotten a good deal out of his extra 2 years of schooling. If, however, this same man never read anything at all after leaving school, the chances are that his reading skill would have atrophied, and we would have concluded, on testing him, that he had not gotten much out of his additional years of schooling beyond the second grade. In other words, our impression of the impact of additional schooling would be much influenced by what the man had done to keep his skills operational after leaving school.

We believe this illustration applies to the case of the cultivators as a group, who showed much less gain for each additional year in school than did those who left the countryside and went to work in industry. The gain per year of schooling for cultivators versus rural-origin workers, respectively, was: Argentina .4/2.5, Chile 1.2/1.5, Nigeria .9/3.2. Both sets of men had gone to basically the same kind of rural school, and all the comparisons kept constant the grade level at which the men had left school. Yet the men who went on to work in industry seemed to derive much more benefit from each year of their schooling than did the men who went into farming.

It could be, of course, that those who later went to the city had initially been smarter, and therefore had gotten more out of every year in school. But we know, from the evidence in Appendix D, that the men who left the countryside were generally not those more fit, but rather those who were most disadvantaged economically. In any event, whatever role selection may have played, later experience clearly also exerted a substantial influence in determining how much a man got out of a given amount of schooling. Those whose later life experiences were fuller got more out of each year in school than did those whose socialization in later life did little to reinforce the lessons originally learned in school. There was, in brief, an *interaction effect* from the combination of schooling and later-life experience which gave much greater return for a fixed amount of village schooling to those who later combined that schooling with urban industrial experiences.

These results serve to underline a point we have been making throughout this section of our book. An impoverished early environment clearly has important negative effects. But that fact does not necessarily impose a permanent disability. Effective stimulation in adulthood can do a great deal to compensate for a slow or late start on the path to individual modernity. The same limited amount of village schooling can have very different personal consequences when it is linked to adult engagement in the urban industrial milieu rather than being followed by work in traditional village agriculture.

IV

Summary and Conclusion

18

The Behavioral Manifestations
of Individual Modernity[1]

Samuel Stouffer, himself a leading exponent and practitioner of opinion research, once declared that "all research on attitudes and values is haunted by the possibility that verbal expressions by respondents may bear no relation to the subsequent behavior of these people."[2] When we made public our first results we regularly met individuals who, on this basis, seriously questioned the importance of our having found that the OM scales were so sensitive to the influence of educational and occupational experience. Such experience, these critics argued, merely taught men how to give the "right" answers to the sorts of questions we asked. To these critics mere attitude change was ephemeral and unimportant. They considered behavioral change the only kind having substantial social consequences, and indicated they would be impressed only if we could show that men more modern in attitude also behaved in more modern ways.

In our view, responding to a questionnaire is a form of behavior, and we believe that we have found out quite a lot about a man when we discover his ability to work through a long series of complex questions, unerringly discerning and voting for the modern answers. And we certainly do not agree that the sort of change which moves people from the traditional to the more modern end of an attitude and value continuum can properly be described as lacking in social significance. Nevertheless, we acknowledge the importance of knowing how far modern attitudes are translated into modern actions. Moreover, we anticipated these concerns, and took them into account in planning our research. Indeed, the OM scales used throughout this book included many questions which measured not only attitudes and values, but individual behavior as well. Since the issue is of such special interest, however, we decided to give separate and explicit treatment to the link between modern attitudes and modern behavior.

The task of measuring behavior is complex and costly. It requires that one pursue a special methodology suited to the task. We felt our first responsibility was to do the best possible job of measuring and explaining modern attitudes and values, leaving for a later study a full-scale field test of the power of our modernization measures to predict various sorts of behavior. Common sense about the limits of our responsibility, and realism about our resources, therefore dictated that we confine ourselves to one or two main areas of behavior which could be inexpensively assessed. We also strove to find behavior measures which could be objectively verified without reference to some third party. Since these requirements were bound to restrict us to quite a narrow range of behavior, however, we decided also to cast a wider net by getting some behavioral reports from the respondent himself, despite the obvious reservations one might entertain about such reports.[3]

The Relation of Attitudes to Behavior

Our first step was to test how far the discrete claims men made were validated by their having taken relevant concrete action. We put this first because in our opinion it is the most unambiguous, indeed perhaps the only legitimate, test of how far men who talk modern in fact also act modern. Quite a few psychological researchers who studied the relation between attitude and behavior reported that they found very little connection between the two.[4] On closer examination of these studies, however, one often finds that the attitudes and values measured were rather vague and general, whereas the behavior these attitudes were meant to predict was extremely specific, and that the logical connection between the two was far from obvious.[5]

It seemed basic common sense and simple justice to insist that, before we asserted that a man did not act as he said he would, we should be certain that both what he asserted he would do and what he objectively had done were appropriately and unambiguously defined and understood by all concerned. An example of such an unambiguous relation is that between the question: "Can you read?" and later performance on a literacy test. In our project we did not consider a man modern or traditional merely because he asserted that he could read, but if we had, then the literacy test would certainly have been an appropriate behavioral check on the verbal claim to modernity made by answering "yes" to our question. We are pleased to report, incidentally, that of those of our respondents who claimed they could read, between 94 and 100 percent later proved they could indeed do so by passing our literacy test.[6]

Another error commonly found in psychological literature is the conceptualizing of attitudinal statements and performance claims as absolute rather than as relative indicators of behavior. Thus, a study in Jamaica reported that of those who favored family planning "only" 27 percent were actually using birth-control methods. In that light, attitudes seemed a poor predictor of behavior. But this was so only if one insisted on absolutes. Looking further into the matter one discovers that, of those *not* favorable to birth control, only some 8 percent practice it.[7] In a *relative* way, therefore, the attitude is here a good predictor, because people who speak out in favor of birth control are more than three times as likely actually to practice it as are those against the behavior. Moreover, there is the distinction that the people interviewed did not claim to be using birth control, only to favor it. Many a consideration of cost, availability, scheduling, and cooperation with spouse might intervene to prevent someone who wanted a small family from moving over into the category of someone who uses birth-control techniques.

In the light of these considerations we decided to set rather strict limits on the material we might use to test the agreement between verbal claims, on the one hand, and behavior, on the other. We took into account only those instances in which almost anyone would agree that there was an unambiguous link between the claim made and the act itself. Thus, when a man asserted that he took an interest in world news he in effect made a claim — from our viewpoint — that he would be able to identify at least some world figures such as Kennedy, Nehru, and de Gaulle. We therefore defined these two questions as unambiguously linked. In other cases, however, the connection between questions which might be considered linked appeared very tenuous to us. That a man claimed an interest in local news, for example, did not oblige him to be able correctly to identify world figures.

Verbal Claims and Objective Tests of Behavior

To assess whether the link between any two questions was relatively unambiguous, three judges rated every pair of questions which, on first examination, seemed to involve a connection between a claim and some behavior which might test that claim. Only those pairs of claims and validating behaviors between which the judges saw a clear-cut connection were included in our analysis.

We established a further distinction between those behaviors we could test by objective methods and those based on a report by the subject to the effect that he had done one thing or another. An objective test was presented by the question: "Can you please tell me the names of some newspapers?" The interviewee either knew the names or did not; and we could count whether he knew one, two, three, or more newspapers. An example of a self-reported behavior was the reply to the question: "How often do you listen to the radio?" We had no way of establishing directly whether a man did or did not listen.

Table 18–1 presents all those pairs of questions about which our judges felt that there was an unambiguous connection between a verbal claim to modernity and an objective test of that claim. All of the objective tests involved communications behavior, such as the naming of three or more newspapers. Thus we see in the first line of Table 18–1 that those who said they got news from the newspapers every day clearly validated that claim, with as many as 98 percent naming at least three newspapers. Even in the East Pakistan sample, in which many of the men were illiterate, some 60 percent of those who claimed to get news from the papers every day — often by hearing them read aloud in a group — could name not one but three newspapers.

We took these findings as striking validation that those who claimed to get news from newspapers did indeed have contact with the press. The results indicated to us that the people who claimed to read newspapers often really did go down to the newsstand, look over the papers, ask for their favorite paper by name, and so on. Of course, there are other ways of knowing the names of papers than by reading them. That made it particularly important to consider the men who did not claim to read the press. The contrast between the two sets of men was marked indeed. Men who claimed to read the paper regularly could name three or more newspapers as much as nine times more often (in India) as could men who did not make that claim.

Some may wish to discount this finding by stating that people know they can be checked on, and so would not lightly exaggerate their use of the newspaper. But the same argument cannot be made with equal force concerning a man's assertion that he has a strong interest in world affairs. It costs him nothing to say that, even if it is not true, and he would be a suspicious man indeed if it occurred to him that an hour later in his interview he might be asked to identify Kennedy, de Gaulle, or Nehru. Yet the results, using that question, were basically similar to those obtained with the question concerning newspaper reading. Regularly, two and even three times as many men who claimed an interest in world news validated that claim by being able to name more world leaders. Thus, in Argentina, 74 percent of those claiming a strong interest in world affairs could correctly identify three leading world figures, whereas among those who reported they were not very interested in world affairs only half as many, some 37 percent, could identify Kennedy, de Gaulle, and Nehru.

Table 18–1 presents numerous other instances of the same phenomenon. Again and again the men who, in effect, made a verbal claim to the status of modern men by virtue of their approach to the news and to the mass media validated that claim by turning in a far superior performance

Table 10.1. Objective tests of verbal claims to modernity: percent engaging in specific behaviors.[a, b]

Behavior and claim	Extreme response	Argentina	Chile	East Pakistan	India	Israel	Nigeria
Naming 3 or more newspapers among those who claim to get news from papers—	Never	—	53	12	9	52	48
	Daily		98***	60***	83***	89***	91***
Correctly identifying world figures among those expressing interest in world news—	Not at all	37	11	6	27	52	15
	Very much	74	33***	8	52***	69**	24*
Naming 3 or more country problems among those who claim their mass-media exposure is—	Low	0	0	4	0	0	0
	High	45*	25*	8	1**	67*	35*
Ability to read among those who claim to get news from newspapers—	Never	65	73	23	42	67	100
	Daily	99	97***	74***	97***	98***	99
Answering all information items correctly among those who claim their mass-media exposure is—	Low	0	0	0	2	0	0
	High	66***	16***	21***	57***	54***	50***
Naming 3 or more newspapers among those who trust most for local news[c]—	Friend	—	83	34	44	68	77
	Newspaper		88*	34	54*	88***	84*
Ability to identify a radio among those who say they listen to a radio—	Never		—	41	52	—	88
	Daily			69**	94***		95*
Correctly identifying a camera among those expressing desire to own one—	Not at all	21	11	32	51	80	72
	Very much	43***	17*	25	80***	94***	74
Correctly identifying consumer items among those who want to own—	Few items	9	5	21	46	43	60
	Many items	16	7*	33*	73*	52	80*

a This table is based upon more detailed cross-tabulations in which there were between two and five steps for each behavior and claim variable. In order to simplify our presentation we have shown only the percentages of subjects behaving in one way (for example, naming 3 or more newspapers) whose responses on the claim variable put them in an extreme cell (never reads newspaper or reads newspaper daily). We used the two extreme cells only if ten or more men were in those cells to provide a base for percentaging; failing that we added another cell to the set defined as "extreme."

b Asterisks indicate sizes of gamma coefficients generated from the original uncollapsed table mentioned in note a, as follows: no sign, less than .10; *, .11 to .29; **, .30 to .39; ***, .4 or larger.

c In Israel, national news was used instead of local news.

on a behavioral test of their factual knowledge. They could much more often identifying international leaders, distant capitals which figure in the news, local politicians, books, magazines, radios and the like. Moreover, the relation between claim and behavior held up when checked in groups of men selected to have basically the same level of education.[8] We therefore take the results in Table 18–1 to be resounding evidence for the validity both of the claims men make, and of our classification of them as more modern on that basis. Men who were rated more modern on the basis of their expressed claims acted unmistakably more modern as evidenced by their behavior in the realm of information and mass communications.

Verbal Claims and Self-Reported Behavior

Table 18–1 was restricted almost exclusively to behavioral tests of information related to mass communication. We did, in fact, extend the measurement of behavior to other realms, but to enter these realms we had to forego the sort of objective verification of behavior which was possible when we were mainly testing a man's factual knowledge. This relaxation of our standard took two forms.

First, we had to accept what a man said he did, rather than testing his behavior ourselves. This seemed to us not too serious a compromise, however, since the results of the check we made above already indicated that individuals were impressively accurate in reporting their own behavior. Nevertheless, we have to acknowledge that we had no way of proving that a man who claimed to be in some organization, say a trade union, was actually a member.[9] Second, we had to allow a more tenuous connection between the attitude or value claim to modernity on the one hand, and the type of behavior to which we linked the claim, on the other. For example, we felt that a man who urged taking public action to defeat those government proposals of which one disapproves might reasonably be expected to act on his conviction by joining civic or political organizations. But we had to acknowledge that our expectation was somewhat arbitrary, as well as sanguine. After all, one can protest a government decision in other ways than by joining civic organizations. Many judges would, therefore, feel that the connection between favoring active citizenship and the act of joining organizations was problematic rather than compelling.

Even with these more relaxed standards, our questionnaire yielded only about a dozen new opportunities to check the relation of attitudinal claims to behavior.[10] The results were consistent with those obtained earlier in the realm of communications and information. The verbal stances we classified as modern quite regularly eventuated in modern actions, as those actions were reported by the respondent himself. For example, men who claimed to be interested in politics were much more likely to report that they had contacted politicians and public officials. Thus, of the Israeli men who claimed a strong interest in politics, 25 percent had written to a government official, whereas none of the men who expressed little interest in politics had taken that action. Of Nigerian men "strongly interested" in politics, 91 percent had joined a political organization, whereas of those with "little interest," only 43 percent had joined such organizations. The men who claimed that they had frequently become concerned about public issues — as compared to those who were only rarely concerned — were between four and ten times as likely, depending on the country, to report they had taken the trouble to write or talk to an official about some public issue.[11]

A Summary Behavior Scale and Its Relation to Attitudinal Modernity

To be able to test the validity of *specific* claims to modernity we had to treat each instance of modern behavior separately. But having satisfied ourselves as to the validity of the claims men make, the next step was to develop a summary measure, or general index, of modernity based exclusively on behavior. By constructing such a scale we might finally meet an expectation we fostered in the very first chapter of this book. Moreover, we recognized that if we could build a general measure of modernity based exclusively on behavior, we could much more concisely express the relation between modern attitudes and modern behavior.

To construct the behavioral modernity scale we searched our questionnaire for all measures which could be considered tests of behavior. Some we classified as *objective* measures because they were based on tests directly administered by us. Table 18–1 has already familiarized the reader with those items which assessed the individual's knowledge of political figures, consumer goods, newspapers, books, and problems facing the local and national community. Such questions were supplemented by tests of arithmetic, vocabulary, and comprehension. Taken together, this set of items tested mainly how well informed a man was. The subset of *self-reported* behavior measures dealt with the individual's claim to read the newspaper and to listen to the radio often, to have joined organizations, to have voted and contacted government officials, and to have discussed work and politics with his wife. That subset of items tested mainly the extent to which a man was taking an active role as a citizen.

Each set — the objectively tested and the self-reported behavior items — was made up into a separate subscale.[12] In addition, all the items were combined in a single overall scale of behavioral modernity. Evaluated for reliability, the scale based on the objective tests yielded quite satisfactory Kuder-Richardson coefficients, as did the summary scale. The reliability of the scale based on self-reported behavior was of only marginal quality, but we decided it was good enough to support the types of analysis we planned for this chapter.[13] The content and quality of the scales based on objective tests and on self-reported behavior were sufficiently different that we felt it incumbent on us, at some points, to report their interaction with other measures separately, as well as in their combined form in the summary "Behavioral OM." We give prime emphasis, however, to the summary scale, which assigned more or less equal weight to the objective tests and to self-reported behavior, and, clearly, covered the wider range of content.

OM-1 was the obvious candidate to represent attitudinal modernity when we came to study its relation to the behavior measures. Since OM-1 was a measure of modernity based solely on attitudes and values, none of its items overlapped with those in the behavioral scales. This claim could not be made for OM-3, 500, or 519.

When we tested the relation of OM-1 to the behavior scale we found unmistakable evidence that attitudinal modernity is strongly related to modern behavior. The men who held modern attitudes and values were decidedly more modern in their behavior, as exemplified in keeping up with world and local news, joining organizations, and taking the trouble to contact public officials about important issues. The correlations between attitudinal modernity as measured by OM-1 and the overall behavioral scale were quite strong. The median correlation was .48***, and the range was from .41*** in Nigeria to a robust .69*** in India.

The firmness of the connection between attitudinal modernity and modern behavior is more readily grasped if we express the relation in terms of the percentage of the men high in attitudinal modernity who also scored high in modern behavior. The results, presented in Table 18–2, were striking. In each country the proportion of men who scored high in behav-

Table 18–2. Percent of men high on behavioral modernity[a] who are low, medium, or high on attitudinal modernity.[b]

Standing on attitudinal modernity	Argentina	Chile	East Pakistan	India	Israel	Nigeria[c]
Low	13	14	15	5	16	18
Medium	35	32	34	27	35	29
High	52	54	51	68	49	54
N high on behavioral modernity	271	308	373	448	261	286

a "High on behavioral modernity" means a score in the top one-third of the frequency distribution on the summary (objective plus self-reported) behavior scale.
b Attitudinal modernity is measured by scores on OM-1, trichotomized as to the frequency distribution in each country.
c Percentages do not total 100 because of rounding.

ioral modernity rose steadily as we went from those low to those high in attitudinal modernity. Taking Argentina as an example, of some 271 men who scored high on the behavior scale, only 13 percent were on the low side in attitudinal modernity, as against 52 percent who scored on the high side on the attitude measure. Strictly comparable relations were evident in all the other countries. Unmistakably, modern behavior is strongly associated with modern attitudes. Men who express modern attitudes and values do not leave it at that. They also *act* in ways which are more modern.

Personal Correlates of Behavioral Modernity

It was very gratifying to us to find that men modern in attitude were also modern in behavior. This finding was critical in meeting the challenge of those skeptics who argued that it does not mean very much that a man learns to sound modern unless he also acts modern. To fully satisfy the demands of our research design, however, we had to go further and test how far the institutions our project identified as "modernizing" induced individuals to act in more modern ways.

The results, presented in Table 18–3, showed clearly that the same forces which we earlier identified as determinants of men's performance on the general measure of modernity, also worked to determine their scores on the specific behavioral measure. The zero-order correlations expressing the association between the independent variables and the summary behavior scale were of approximately the same magnitudes and stood in approximately the same rank order as did those which we earlier saw linking the independent variables to the more general OM scores. Total years of education and mass-media exposure turned in the best performance, with median correlations of .55*** and .42*** (adjusted for autocorrelation) respectively; years of factory experience clearly played a significant role, with a median of .25***; and consumer goods possessed, taken as a measure of economic well-being, made a very good showing. The independent variables such as age, factory modernity, and home-school modernity, which were weak in their power to explain the general measure of modernity, were also evidently weak in their ability to explain specifically behavioral modernity.

Two additional facts uncovered by correlating the several forms of the behavior scales with the independent variables merit our attention. First, we found that factory experience had about as much influence on the scale based mainly on objective tests of information and vocabulary as it did on the self-report scale measuring mainly political action.[14] This strongly suggests that the factory not only changes men's styles of political participation, but also increases their knowledge of subjects ordinarily assumed to be the distinctive focus of classroom instruction. In other words,

Table 18–3.   Correlations of selected independent variables and scores on summary scale of behavioral modernity.[a]

Independent variables	Argentina	Chile	East Pakistan	India	Israel	Nigeria
1. Education	.55***	.54***	.56***	.74***	.43***	.48***
2. Mass-media exposure[b]	.35***	.47***	.42***	.61***	.40***	.42***
3. Occupational type	.37***	.32***	.20***	.23***	.16***	.39***
4. Years urban since 15	.37***	.36***	.23***	.09***		.22***
5. Years factory experience	.23***	.36***	.26***	.24***	.26***	.22***
6. Rated skill	.26***	.24***	.23***	.36***	.23***	.21***
7. Factory modernity	.07	−.06	.07		−.12**	.09*
8. Consumer goods possessed	.41***	.31***	.40***	.46***	.19***	.35***
9. Home-school modernity	.07*	.19***	.09*	.24***	.02	.01
10. Age	.06	.16***	.04	.06*	.08*	.16***
N for rows 1, 2, 3, 8, 9, 10 (all subjects)	817	929	943	1198	739	721
N for rows 5, 6, 7 (all factory workers)	663	715	654	700	544	520
N for row 4 (rural-origin factory workers)	239	305	654	700		184

a Asterisks denote significance as follows: *, at .05 level; **, at .01 level; ***, at .001 level or better
b These figures have been adjusted for autocorrelation; see note 12.

for men who got less schooling than they should have, the factory may be an effective means of supplementing their education in those very subjects the school is most specialized to teach.

Of course, the factory could not be expected to be as effective as the school in teaching geographical information and vocabulary. After all, the school specializes in those branches of instruction. The school's advantage was, therefore, not surprisingly reflected in the fact that the correlation coefficient relating the objective test to education was generally two or three times that relating the same test to factory experience. Yet it is particularly important to note another fact. When the self-report scale, rather than the information test, was the focus of attention, the correlations with education were not markedly greater than those yielded by factory experience. We should recall that the self-report scale was concerned with civic action — joining an organization, voting, or talking to an official. We consider being an active participant citizen one of the truly distinguishing characteristics of the modern man.[15] These results therefore suggest that we should alter the impression so often derived from the analysis in this book, to the effect that education is consistently much more important than factory experience as an explanation of individual modernity. When it comes to civic actions, the factory seems as important as the classroom in serving as a training ground for modernity.

The Fate of Personal Adjustment in the Modernization Process

In addition to searching for those forms of modern behavior which may be taken as evidence of positive personal development, we felt it our obligation to test how far becoming modern might produce less desirable behavioral consequences. To test the facts we needed a measure of personal adjustment. The instrument on which we placed main reliance was the Psychosomatic Symptoms Test, which had proved remarkably useful in culturally diverse situations as a quick and simple diagnostic assessment of individual psychic adjustment.[16] The test is particularly appropriate in the context of this chapter because it deals with self-reported behavior. In the test, the respondent is asked such questions as: "Do your limbs tremble enough to bother you?" and "Are you bothered by sweating palms even when you are not exercising?" For details see Appendix A, part IV.

In our experience, no belief is more widespread among critics of industrialization than that it disrupts basic social ties, breaks down social controls, and therefore produces a train of personal disorientation, confusion, and uncertainty, which ultimately leads to misery and even mental breakdown among those who are uprooted from the farm and herded into great industrial cities.[17]

Our experience, however, had led us to a rather different conclusion. We noted that the shift in industrial work often seemed to guarantee more income and greater security. Opportunities for self-expression and advancement and increments of status and prestige frequently accompanied the move to the cities. We felt these experiences could actually conduce to better mental health among industrial workers, even in the sometimes chaotic setting of developing countries.

To see which of these interpretations might be correct, we administered a version of the Psychosomatic Symptoms Test to each of the men we interviewed. We obtained good distributions, ranging from those who reported none at all to those who indicated they had all ten of the symptoms on the basic list. We considered men to be suffering from multiple symptoms if they claimed to suffer from half or more of all the symptoms listed on the test in their country. Generally this included about 20 percent of the men, whom one might, on this basis, consider as relatively distressed. We then used these test results to obtain correlations and cross-tabulation percentages to see whether men who were in more frequent contact with modernizing institutions such as the school, the factory, and the mass media showed more symptoms or were more often in distress. The detailed statistics developed in this analysis have already been presented elsewhere, and we will not repeat them here.[18] The conclusions we reached are, however, so germane to the concerns of this chapter that we feel obliged at least briefly to summarize what we found out.

Of the modernizing experiences frequently identified as likely to induce individual disorganization by disrupting personality, creating strain, introducing disturbed stimuli, and the like, none consistently and significantly produced increased maladjustment as measured by the Psychosomatic Symptoms Test. In contrast to our experience in studying the impact of these same independent variables on other psychological scales, such as our measures of modern attitudes, the patterns observed in relation to adjustment were not only weak but decidedly lacking in consistency across the six countries.

Increased education, long ago identified by Durkheim as inimical to social integration and as more likely to lead to suicide, actually had a fairly consistent, and sometimes significant, *positive* effect on adjustment. That is, people with more education had fewer symptoms. Exposure to the mass media operated in the same way, but more weakly. In any event, one cannot say that men exposed to the presumably confusing and jangling flood of music, of desire-arousing advertisements, of distressing world news, and of whatever else is carried by these media were led by this to lose sleep in bad dreams or to break out in cold sweats. Similarly, exposure to the impersonality of urban life, to its plethora of stimuli, to its frenzied pace, and to its crowded conditions did not unmistakably induce psychosomatic symptoms. Men born in the urban centers were not significantly less well adapted than those born in the countryside; men who have lived long in town did not have significantly more symptoms than those with fewer years of exposure; those living in the larger and more cosmopolitan cities such as Lagos, Santiago, Buenos Aires, and Ranchi were not psychically worse off than those living in the smaller and often more traditional cities of Ibadan, Valdivia, Cordoba, and Khalari.

Neither can we say that employment as a factory worker is conducive to psychosomatic complaints. Men who had worked longer in industry did not thereby consistently acquire significantly more psychosomatic symptoms along with their seniority. Indeed, for the more successful men who had high skill, and especially for those who had been able to buy more goods, there was a consistent and often significant tendency toward better adjustment. The size of the factory, often cited as one of the best indicators of the impersonal, bureaucratic, and even inhuman qualities of industrial life, failed effectively to predict psychosomatic symptoms; if anything, work in large factories was less conducive to multiple symptoms. Much the same lack of differentiation was evident when the factories were classified as more modern in technology and personnel policy as against those more traditional.

Whatever may cause psychosomatic symptoms in younger men in developing countries, *it is apparently something other than exposure to the modernizing institutions such as the school, factory, the city, and the mass media.* Moreover, we found no evidence that migration, itself, brings about psychic distress as measured by the development of a large number of psychosomatic symptoms. Men who moved had no more symptoms than those who remained in their home villages, nor did they seem significantly less adjusted than their fellow workers who were raised in the town and hence came to work in industry without the necessity to migrate.

By studying these influences one at a time we might have obscured the fact that their impact was in an important degree cumulative, producing a significant effect only when one slightly negative experience was piled on another. To test that idea we grouped the respondents in each country on a scale from those who had had no contact with modernizing experiences to those with maximum exposure to modernizing experiences.[19] If the effects of modernizing experiences were indeed cumulative, there should have been a steady increase in the proportion showing multiple symptoms as we moved up the scale from minimum to maximum exposure.

Nothing of the kind occurred. In five of the six countries there was no visible pattern of any kind, certainly none giving a basis for asserting that when they acted cumulatively the modernizing institutions produced a substantial or otherwise statistically significant negative effect on adjustment. India was the only country which showed a statistically significant pattern, but it was contrary to the hypothesis being tested. In India each step up the scale of increased exposure to modernizing influences brought with it a *decrease* in the number of psychosomatic symptoms. The one clear-cut result, therefore, argued that if exposure to modernizing influences had had any effect, it was to *improve* personal adjustment.

It was, of course, possible that some combinations of experience would be more distressing than others. To test this possibility we examined the effect of contact with modernizing experience using different sets of experiences, such as migration plus mass-media exposure, or migration plus high exposure to factory work *and* urban living. None of the combinations consistently showed a distinctly greater effect on adjustment than any other.

Finally, as a last resort, one might shift the basis of the argument to assert that even if contact with modern *institutions* did not conduce to more psychosomatic symptoms, *personal* individual modernization would. In other words, it might be argued that what is important about the individual's modernization is not what made him modern, but rather just how modern he has become. Several of the more popular relevant theories certainly assert quite firmly that the more modern a man is, that is, the further he has come from his traditional cultural roots, the more under stress he should be.

This proposition could easily be tested by correlating each individual's score on the OM scale with his rating as to psychosomatic adjustment. The correlations we obtained were as follows: Argentina, .07*; Chile, .03; East Pakistan, .09**; India, .15***; Israel, -.00; Nigeria, .15***.[20] Although the correlations were quite small, five were positive and four statistically significant, indicating that greater individual modernity went with fewer symptoms. Quite contrary to popular expectation, therefore, one is forced to conclude that, if anything holds in this realm, it is that the more modern the individual, the better his psychic adjustment as measured by the Psychosomatic Symptoms Test.

19

An Overview: The Relative and Total Impact of the Explanatory Variables

Most of our analysis up to this point involved testing serially a large number of variables to assess whether they made a statistically significant contribution to individual modernity. Although quite a few life experiences passed the test, some proved much more important than others. We should now turn to an examination of the relative contribution of these more important variables, not only when they stand alone, but also as they enter into more complex interaction and competition with each other. In programming this competition we decided to limit ourselves to small sets of variables, not only to simplify matters, but also to reduce the risk of committing the partialing fallacy. In testing the strength of the individual variables, we elected to enter only three in the competition: education, mass-media contact, and occupational experience. For a still more fundamental contest, we used only two composite measures, putting the combined set of variables representing early socialization experience into competition with the set of variables reflecting late socialization experience.

Education, Mass-Media Exposure, and Occupation in Competition

Education, mass-media exposure, and occupational experience together accounted for about 90 percent of the variance in OM-500 explained by the larger "standard" set of eight independent variables.[1] To place these three alone in competition, therefore, would certainly not give an unrepresentative impression of the total set of forces making men modern. Moreover, education, the mass media, and occupational experience had each been advanced, on theoretical grounds, as a major factor in explaining modernity and, as we saw above, did in fact establish their status as important independent contributors in accounting for OM scores. Each measure quite well represented a larger realm of experience, so that by using it alone we reduced the chances of committing the partialing fallacy.[2] Yet, relative to one another the three variables were minimally redundant.

Since the outcome of this three-way competition would lead to some of the most fundamental conclusions of our entire study, we felt we should check the facts in as many ways as we feasibly could. There were four main procedures available for making the comparison: simple correlation, regression analysis, the calculation of point gains, and analysis of covariance.

Simple Correlation

The zero-order correlations presented in Table 19–1 showed all three variables to be strongly associated with individual modernity, and all within the same range. Looking first at the results for the total sample, we find the median correlation for education to be .52, for mass media, .45, and for occupation, .41. The hierarchy which these median correlations revealed was fairly well preserved in the separate countries, with

Table 19–1.   Correlations of education, mass-media exposure, and occupational experience with individual modernity (OM).[a]

Variable	Argentina	Chile	East Pakistan	India	Israel	Nigeria	Median
			All subjects				
Education	.59	.51	.41	.71	.44	.52	.52
Mass-media exposure	.57	.46	.38	.56	.38	.43	.45
Occupation	.47	.48	.35	.34	.11	.50	.41
N	817	929	943	1198	739	721	
			Rural-origin factory workers				
Education	.36	.22	.42	.68	b	.39	.39
Mass-media exposure	.45	.27	.35	.56	b	.39	.39
Factory experience	.36	.48	.26	.11	b	.29	.29
N	239	305	654	700		184	
			Urban-origin factory workers				
Education	.47	.49	c	c	.48	.43	.48
Mass-media exposure	.28	.33	c	c	.40	.40	.37
Factory experience	.20	.23	c	c	.26	.27	.25
N	423	410			544	336	

a All correlations are significant at the .01 level.
b There were no rural-origin factory workers in the Israeli sample.
c There were no urban-origin factory workers in the East Pakistani and Indian samples.

education always first in rank order, although occupation twice showed itself more important than mass-media contact. The basic hierarchy was also preserved in the figures for the subsamples of urban-origin factory workers. Among workers of rural origin, however, education was challenged for preeminence by mass-media contact in two of five countries, and by factory experience in one. We interpreted the data as indicating that the rural-origin workers arriving at the factory and the town with less than average education, and consequently with lower OM scores, found their new setting especially stimulating, while, at the same time, they were not limited by any "ceiling effect" in how far they could grow in modernity. The result was to strengthen the apparent impact of mass-media exposure and occupational experience, in competition with education, as determinants of OM.

Regression Analysis

A simple correlation may be objected to on grounds that it does not take into account the extent to which any one variable may borrow its apparent strength from another with which it is intimately linked. Mass-media contact, for example, might seem important only because those with more media contact are usually better educated. Regression analysis, like partial correlation, takes into account the simultaneous effects of the other variables, thus giving us a better opportunity to judge the "pure" or "true" contribution of each variable without confounding it with the effect of the others. The regression analysis gave basically the same pattern of results as did partialing. However, since the beta weights, that is, the standardized regression coefficients, have certain advantages as a statistic, we report those. Readers more at home with partial correlation may interpret these beta weights much as they would a partial correlation. The details are given in Table 19-2.

Although the regression analysis did not fundamentally alter the conclusions we reached on the basis of the zero-order correlations, it suggested some modifications. Education again emerged preeminent, almost invariably number one in rank order in the total sample and in each of the worker subsamples. The median beta weight for education was generally at least one-third greater than that for its closest competitor, and in many of the subsamples it was more than double the size of its weakest competitor.

Mass media and occupation, however, shifted their relative standing in the regressions. In the total sample, for example, the median beta weight for occupation at .25 was higher than that for mass media at .23 and each of these two variables was as often in rank order 2 as it was in rank 3. This outcome left no doubt that both mass-media contact and occupational experience made substantial and truly independent contri-

Table 19–2.   Beta weights for regression of OM-500 on education, mass-media exposure, and occupational experience.

Variable	Argentina	Chile	East Pakistan	India	Israel	Nigeria
All subjects						
Education	.41	.34	.32	.56	.33	.32
Mass-media exposure	.30	.24	.20	.20	.30	.22
Occupation	.22	.31	.27	.17	.08	.30
Rural-origin factory workers						
Education	.32	.19	.33	.56	a	.29
Mass-media exposure	.31	.17	.19	.23	a	.29
Factory experience	.30	.45	.22	.15	a	.16
Urban-origin factory workers						
Education	.42	.43	b	b	.37	.30
Mass-media exposure	.19	.22	b	b	.25	.27
Factory experience	.17	.21	b	b	.15	.15
All factory workers						
Education	.48	.42	.33	.56	.37	.31
Mass-media exposure	.24	.21	.19	.23	.25	.27
Factory experience	.20	.30	.22	.15	.15	.16

a There were no rural-origin factory workers in the Israeli sample.
b There were no urban-origin factory workers in the East Pakistani and Indian samples.

butions to making men modern. It also indicated that once the contribution of education was taken into account, the relative impact of mass-media contact and occupational experience was about equal.[3] It should be kept in mind, of course, that this statement represents a kind of averaging of our experience across six countries. In fact, in three countries the beta weight for occupation was greater than that for mass media by one-third or more, and indeed in those countries — Chile, Nigeria, and East Pakistan — it came close to equaling the beta weight for education.

In the sociological literature on modernization, the theoretical and empirical case for education and mass media has been made extensively, but little attention has been given to the contribution which occupational experience can make to shaping men in the modern mode. The results of our regression analysis should serve to redress the balance. Occupational experience, in particular work in modern, large-scale bureaucratic enterprises such as the factory, clearly played a role at least equal to that of the mass media and in some groups almost as great as that of education in the shaping of individual modernity.

The Point-Gain Story

The size of a correlation coefficient or beta weight may be unduly influenced by the particular distribution of cases on which it is based. To escape that problem we needed a measure expressed in absolute rather than relative form, and in terms of a concrete unit having a readily grasped referent in daily experience. These conditions were met by our measure of the number of points a man's score on the OM scale changed with each additional year of experience he obtained either in school or at work in the factory. Unfortunately, there was no comparable unit of measurement for exposure to the mass media, since on that variable we had scored men for the amount of current contact rather than for the number of years they had been using the media. Regrettable as was the loss of our third competitor, the advantages of using the point gain per year of exposure were sufficiently great to warrant our going ahead to compare only education and factory experience.

We computed the point gains (Table 19–3) on the basis of the regression analysis in which education, mass media, and factory experience had been entered in the equation.[4] Under these conditions of competition, every year a man spent in school clearly yielded a substantially greater return in OM points than the same amount of time spent in a factory. Among the urban-origin men the median gain per year of schooling, at 1.9 OM points, was almost five times that for each year in the factory, at 0.4 points. Among the rural-origin men, for whom the factory was a more important influence, the respective median gains of 1.6 points and 0.6 points still put the school ahead by a ratio of about 2.5:1.

This outcome permits of two very different interpretations. The first and

Table 19–3. Point gains on OM-500 per year of schooling and of factory experience.

Variable	Argentina	Chile	East Pakistan	India	Israel	Nigeria	Median
			Country				
			Rural-origin factory workers				
Education	2.2	1.2	1.3	1.6	a	2.3	1.6
Factory experience	0.7	0.9	0.6	0.5	a	0.6	0.6
			Urban-origin factory workers				
Education	1.9	2.1	b	b	1.8	1.7	1.9
Factory experience	0.3	0.4	b	b	0.4	0.4	0.4

a There were no rural-origin factory workers in the Israeli sample.

b There were no urban-origin factory workers in the East Pakistani and Indian samples.

most obvious, is that the school is by far the most effective setting for making men modern. In terms of the yield per hour of exposure, the school is clearly more effective than the factory in inculcating modern attitudes, values, and behavioral dispositions. Effectiveness, however, is not the same as efficiency. To judge the efficiency of the school in comparison with the factory we have to take into account factors other than the sheer amount of exposure over time.

First, the school has the child during his most formative and impressionable years. The factory, by contrast, must work with a mature man whose personality at that age is presumably fully formed and more resistant to change. Second, we should keep in mind that the school is totally devoted to formal instruction. It works full time at trying to get its charges to learn new material. The factory, on the other hand, is geared mainly to production, and devotes little of its energies directly to formal instruction or indoctrination, at least beyond the period of a man's apprenticeship. Third, the cost of any gains in individual modernity attained in school cannot be easily written off as incidental to some other purpose, since the only "product" we get for our investment in the cost of schooling is learning by the children. The factory, however, is mainly engaged in making goods or producing economic services, through which it gives society a direct return on the material and human capital expended. Any increased modernization of the work force in the factory is, therefore, a gain achieved by society with virtually no marginal cost.

Taking these facts into consideration, we are led to a quite different interpretation of the results of the point-gain analysis. Rather than emphasize the greater absolute yield of schooling, we may stress either the school's relative inefficiency or, alternatively, the exceptional efficiency of the factory in achieving as much as it does in individual modernization at so modest a cost to society. We interpret our findings not as showing the school to be inadequate, but rather as indicating the comparative efficiency of the factory as a training ground in individual modernity. The factory brings about a smaller change per year but, considering the cost per unit of change, it accomplishes more for much less than the school, and does so under the handicap of having less malleable material with which to work.[5]

Results of an Analysis of Covariance[6]

While the method which yields an estimate of points gained per year of experience has many virtues, it has one particular disadvantage. It expresses results as an average across a wide range of experience, and may thereby obscure differences in the effectiveness of education or factory experience at different levels in their respective ranges. Thus, it could be that education affects individual modernity, as it does literacy, mainly after the fourth grade. In that case, a country like East Pakistan, with most of its sample having less than 4 years of schooling, would show a much lower average point gain for education than would a country like India, in which over half the sample had more than 7 years of schooling.

Analysis of covariance permits us to determine the OM scores of groups having had different combinations of education and factory experience, while simultaneously adjusting the scores to take account of other variables of the sort previously controlled by the matching process. Table 19–4 presents the results for all six countries. The figures in the cells give the mean OM score of the men at each level of education and factory experience, adjusted to hold constant the effect of four other characteristics: father's education and ethnic origin, selected as appropriate background variables, and mass-media exposure and urbanity of the factory location, representative of current experience.[7]

Examining Table 19–4 we note the following:

Table 19–4. Mean modernity scores of educational and factory-experience groups computed by analysis of covariance.[a]

Education (years)	Factory experience (months)				Education (years)	Factory experience (months)			
	Argentina					**Chile**			
	1–12	13–72	73–108	109–228		0–7	24–60	72–108	120–228
1–4	46	48	52	53	1–3	48	49	52	54
5–6	51	51	52	55	4–5	48	54	54	54
7	53	55	55	56	6	53	55	57	58
8–15	61[b]	60	60	58	7–10	57[b]	58	60	61
	East Pakistan					**India**			
	0–6	35–60	61–96	98–156		1–6	36–52	53–96	97–192
0	46	50	51	51	0	41	45	53	53
1–4	51	52	54	58	1–7	48	54	56	57
5–8	52	56	57	58	8–10	58	58	59	62
					11	61	61	60	64
	Israel					**Nigeria**			
	0–12	13–66	67–102	103–216		0–6	18–40	41–72	73–159
1–5	51	53	57	57	4–6	52	55	55	56
6–7	56	56	58	57	7	56	55	56	54
8	57	58	60	58	8	57	56	57	58
9–14	63[b]	62	63	61					

a OM-3 was used as the measure of individual modernity. Four covariates were controlled: father's education, ethnic origin, mass-media exposure, and urbanism of factory location. Each mean score is based on at least ten cases except where otherwise indicated.

b Score based on fewer than ten cases.

1. Education again emerges fairly consistently as a more powerful influence than factory experience in producing individual modernity, at times winning by a ratio of as much as 2:1.

In India, for example, men in the low-experience category gained 20 points as they went from 0 to 11 years of education; but there was a change of only 12 points for the men of zero education as they rose from no factory experience to 8 years and more. Or, to take another example, in Chile the third step on the experience ladder showed an 8-point change as men moved from the lowest to the highest education level, whereas the comparable third step on the education ladder showed only a 5-point change as men shifted from the least to the most experienced worker categories. East Pakistan and Nigeria, it is true, showed more nearly equal gains for men moving up the education and experience ladders, but it should be recognized that in those two countries the range in education was small, whereas the range in length of factory experience was more or less as it was elsewhere.

The differential effect of education and factory experience became strikingly evident when we examined the modernity scores of men with contrasting profiles of education and factory experience in combination. Even though they were raw recruits just entering the factory, men with the highest education started on their factory experience already having higher modernity scores than those of men who had had the benefit of as many as 10 years of factory work but who had earlier in life suffered the disadvantage of getting very little education. Thus, in Argentina, a man who was just starting out in the factory but came in with 7 years of schooling already had as high an OM score (at 53 points) as a man who had already spent some 13 years in the factory but had suffered the disadvantage of coming to the plant with only 2 years of schooling behind him.

2. Another way of looking at the same facts, however, is to recognize factory work as a great equalizer. The longer men are in a factory, the smaller becomes the gap in their modernity scores, because the men with little education come, through their factory experience, to catch up with those of higher education. The gap separating those with highest and lowest education was generally only half as large among experienced workers as it was among those just starting out in industry. In Israel, for example, the best-educated new workers were 12 OM points ahead of the least educated, whereas, among the more experienced workers, the same educational advantage gave the best-educated men a lead of only 6 points. This "interaction effect" was clearly manifested in four of the six countries, was weakly present in the fifth, Chile, and was absent only in East Pakistan.

Clearly, men who start out with little or no education also start with a psychosocial handicap in the form of low modernity scores. Yet if these same men succeed in getting into factories, then they evidently can, in time, raise their modernity scores to the level of men with far more years of education who have as yet not had the additional benefit of factory experience.

The most dramatic exemplification of this tendency was encountered in India, in which men having no education whatsoever, but enjoying the maximum of factory experience, performed on the OM scale at a level equal to that of men with 6 years of education who had as yet not acquired any substantial amount of factory experience. The record in the other countries, moreover, was not too different. In Argentina the maximum factory experience raised the least-educated men from second-grade level to the equivalent of seventh-grade level; in Chile from second to sixth; in Israel from third to eighth; and in East Pakistan from zero to the equivalent of completing third grade. Most of these figures involve some interpolation, and should therefore be recognized as only rough approximations. Nevertheless, the general thrust of the data is clear and unambiguous. In five of six countries, the average number of modernity points which workers with minimum education had gained by virtue of spending some 8 to 10 years in the factory was the equivalent of approximately four additional grades of formal schooling.

We consider this outcome quite extraordinary, and of exceptional theoretical and practical interest. It confirms in a simple and unambiguous way the main thesis of our project, which is that the factory is a school for modernity. We now see that the factory can step in to serve an important remedial function. Men who have had the misfortune of securing little or no formal education may, in substantial degree, compensate for that deprivation as far as individual modernity is concerned through and in the course of their industrial experience.

3. The ability of factory experience to make men modern is manifested much more powerfully among the men with relatively low education. As they increased their factory experience, those in the lowest education ranges generally gained two or three times as many points in their modernity scores as did the men with relatively more education. This pattern, which can be discerned in Table 19–4, is clear evidence of an interaction effect in the data.[8]

In Argentina, for example, men whose education was in the range from 1 to 4 years, gained 7 points as they went from 0 to 10 years of factory experience, but those with 7 years of education gained only 3 points as a result of the same amount of factory work. Indeed, really substantial benefits from factory work were apparently enjoyed only by men with less than 7 years of schooling. Although some benefits from factory work still accrued to men with more education, the gains they made were very modest. In Nigeria, Israel, and Argentina those in the highest educational brackets actually showed some slight loss of modernity on the average, as they moved from the less experienced to the more highly experienced categories.

4. Some distinctive patterns observed earlier in the samples from particular countries could be understood better once the data from Table 19–4 were available. For example, the data permitted us to explain why the regression analysis done earlier indicated that in Israel, India, and Nigeria factory experience offered substantially less competition to education than it did elsewhere. The variation in the effectiveness of factory experience shown in the regressions evidently resulted from differences in the educational composition of the sample in the several countries. Those country samples which did not include a large proportion of workers with little or no education consequently contained fewer men of the sort who typically experienced the greatest impact from their contact with the factory. This was particularly true of the samples for Israel and Nigeria. On the average, therefore, those countries showed a weak factory effect compared to that for education.[9]

Once we adjusted for the differences in the composition of the several national samples, the performance of factory experience in competition with education became more nearly comparable from one country to another. Take, for example, the group of men who had about 1 to 4 years of schooling, that being the range found most consistently in all the countries, as represented in Table 19–4. As those men moved up the factory-experience ladder, starting as new workers and ending up as veterans with some 8 or 10 years of experience, they gained the following number of OM points: Argentina, 7; Chile, 6; East Pakistan, 7; Israel, 6. By extrapolation we may estimate that for Nigeria the gain would also have been about 6, and in India about 10 points. Clearly, the Indian case is the only one out of line even if in the "right" direction. Otherwise, the effect of factory experience at this educational level was remarkably regular.

5. The reasons why men with more education were less influenced by their factory experience are not obvious. One assumption we can reasonably make, however, is that well-educated men were little modernized by the factory because they entered it so far advanced that the factory had very little to teach them. It would have required a work experience much more sophisticated than that provided by the ordinary factory in developing countries to carry these men still further along on the modernization scale. In other words, the better-educated men may have run up against some kind of ceiling effect.

Unfortunately, our research design did not permit us to test this assumption systematically. To test it we would have had to run some sort of experiment in the field in which we operated superfactories or exceptionally modern work laboratories to see if those presumably more stimulating environments could raise even the well-educated worker to still higher levels of individual modernity. Nevertheless, we know that most men in developing countries around the world are in fact getting only modest education, usually less than 6 or 7 years, and, as we have seen, for them the factory does serve as a powerful supplement, raising the level of their modernity to equal that of men who have had much more formal schooling.

Early Versus Late Socialization

The evidence that occupational experience and mass-media contact performed so well as modernizing forces invites our attention to an issue we earlier designated as fundamental, but which we have not yet dealt with systematically. Our research was motivated, in part, by the belief that significant change in rather basic aspects of the personality — such as the sense of efficacy, the orientation to time, and others tested by the OM scale — could be effected in adult life well after the early formative years had presumably given a man's character its basic set. In the terms of our research design, this implied that the late socialization experiences of a man might play as great a role in determining his OM scores as would socialization forces which impinged on him in the earlier and presumably more impressionable years.

To test this idea we needed to group the variables into two sets. In the early-socialization set we put father's education, own education, own ethnicity-religion, and, in the three countries where it was applicable, urban or rural origin. The late-socialization variables were occupational type, mass-media contact, living standard, and life-cycle stage. In the subsample of factory workers only, "years of factory experience" replaced "occupational type" and a measure of factory quality was added.[10]

We then placed these sets of variables in competition.[11] The results, presented in Table 19–5, seem to us relatively consistent and quite notable. In Part A of the table we see that the late-socialization variables generally came very close to equaling, and in four of twelve cases actually exceeded, the early-socialization variables in their ability to explain OM scores. In the total sample, the median variance explained by the early-socialization variables was 31 percent, and by the late-socialization variables, 37 percent. In the factory-worker sample, the figures were 30 and 29 percent, respectively. Indeed, the pattern did not change materially in any subsample. The evidence seems unambiguous that the experiences a man has mainly as an adult, particularly his job and his contact with the mass media, are at least as important as are his early life experiences in determining what level of individual modernity he will attain.

Table 19–5. Early versus late socialization experiences as determinants of individual modernity (OM-500).[a]

Variable set	Argentina	Chile	East Pakistan	India	Israel	Nigeria
A. Regression of OM-500 on—						
			All subjects			
Early socialization: R	.68	.57	.48	.74	.50	.53
R^2	.46	.33	.23	.55	.25	.28
Late socialization: R	.65	.60	.51	.67	.46	.62
R^2	.42	.36	.26	.45	.21	.38
			Factory workers only			
Early socialization: R	.65	.55	.47	.73	.54	.49
R^2	.42	.31	.22	.53	.29	.24
Late socialization: R	.53	.54	.45	.61	.50	.54
R^2	.28	.29	.21	.38	.25	.29
B. Partial correlation with OM-500 of—						
			All subjects			
Early controlling for late socialization	.53	.47	.30	.56	.37	.33
Late controlling for early socialization	.47	.50	.36	.39	.30	.49
			Factory workers only			
Early controlling for late socialization	.57	.52	.32	.58	.40	.33
Late controlling for early socialization	.40	.50	.30	.36	.33	.41

[a] All correlations are statistically significant at the .001 level.

This conclusion was, however, subject to the challenge that the effectiveness of the late-socialization measures, as we treated them, could have been mainly an artifact of earlier experiences statistically associated with them. It is obvious, for example, that newspaper reading depends on literacy, which comes mainly from the earlier experience of formal schooling. A definitive test of the independent ability of the late-socialization variables to make men modern required that we assess their effect under conditions in which the influence of the early-socialization variables was controlled. To that end we entered both the early and the late socialization sets simultaneously in a regression equation in order to obtain, for each set, its partial correlation with OM-500 while controlling for the effect of the variables in the other competing set.

The resultant partial correlations, presented in Part B of Table 19–5, did not change the impression we had already developed. Placed in competition with each other in a regression analysis, the two sets had a very similar impact on modernity. The early socialization variables seemed much more important in India, but this was offset by the fact that the late-socialization variables emerged as much more important in Nigeria. Across the set of six countries the late-socialization set, with a median partial correlation of .43, was at least as important a predictor of OM as was the set of early-socialization experiences, with a median partial correlation of .42. A separate analysis for the factory-worker subsample required no substantial alteration of the conclusion drawn from the total sample.

We read the evidence as showing conclusively that an individual's personality, at least on the dimensions measured by the OM scale, can be substantially changed after adolescence if he comes into sufficient contact with those institutions which inculcate modernity in mature men. No man need be permanently limited to the attitudes, values, and modes of acting he develops in his early life. No matter how traditional his initial upbringing leaves him, his later-life experiences may compensate for the earlier deprivation. Later experiences may inculcate in him a greater sense of personal efficacy, make him more open to new experience, increase his interest in personal planning, and change his ways of relating to women and children. In brief, his later experiences may transform him from a highly traditional into a relatively modern man.

20

The Process of Individual Modernization

Putting the variables in competition, as we did in Chapter 19, served an important scientific purpose, and also told us things we would need to know in order to make intelligent choices among programs for effecting social change. Nevertheless, by treating the different life experiences as separate forces individually competing for primacy, we unfortunately distort the actual process of becoming modern. In reality the variables we have been concerned with do not work in competition, but rather cooperatively, or at least cumulatively, so that each new modernizing experience adds its impetus to those which came before or to others which are simultaneously exerting their influence. More accurately to represent the actual process of individual modernization, therefore, we should examine the impact of our explanatory variables working together. We need to measure the collective impact of all of our explanatory variables on individual OM scores, and to establish the sequence in which the experiences measured by those variables actually exerted their influence.

The Collective Impact of the Explanatory Variables

To simplify testing the collective impact of the modernizing influences, we reduced the independent variables to a basic set which we felt to be theoretically important, empirically reliable, and minimally redundant.[1] For the total sample this set included eight measures: father's education, own education, occupational type, mass-media contact, living standard, urbanness of adult residence, ethnicity-religion, and a variant on the measure of age we called "life-cycle stage." For the worker subsample the measure of occupational type was replaced by two others, one basically an index of the extent of factory experience and the other an indication of the modern quality of the factory. In addition, in three countries factory workers could be divided into men of rural and those of urban origin. Thus the maximum number of measures in the basic set for workers was ten. With some minor exceptions these variables are already quite familiar from our earlier analysis, but those concerned with the details of definition and measurement will find the relevant information in Appendix C. We should note, however, that once any substantial proportion of the larger set of variables was taken into account, adding or dropping any variable, or changing the approach to its definition and measurement, made very little difference in the general picture which emerged.

For the total sample, including cultivators, UNIs, and factory workers, our basic set of variables yielded very substantial multiple correlations with OM scores, ranging from .56 in Israel to .79 in India, with the median at .69.[2] That this outcome, detailed in Table 20–1, was not the result of contrasting the obvious extremes of isolated cultivators and urban industrial workers became clear when we examined the results for the subsamples limited to factory workers, which yielded a median multiple correlation of .65. Clearly, the variables we had identified as important in accounting for individual modernity produced their basic effect just as well within essentially homogeneous occupational groups as they did when we contrasted people whose life conditions were rather obviously different.

A correlation of .65 is highly significant statistically. With samples as large as ours the probability of our getting this figure by chance alone is extremely remote.[3] But a model of chance is not too satisfactory for judging how well we have done in explaining individual modernity.

Table 20–1. Multiple correlations (R) and percent of variance explained (R^2) in OM-500 using basic independent-variable sets.[a]

	Argentina	Chile	East Pakistan	India	Israel	Nigeria
			All subjects			
R	.76	.71	.58	.79	.56	.67
R^2	.58	.50	.33	.62	.32	.45
			Factory workers only			
R	.71	.69	.54	.77	.61	.61
R^2	.51	.48	.29	.59	.37	.37

[a] The basic independent variables are those in Set A, including eight variables for the total-sample regression and up to ten for the factory-worker group. See Appendix C for description of the variables.

More appropriate, perhaps, are two other standards, one absolute, the other relative.

The absolute standard is provided by the goal of explaining 100 percent of the variance, that is, to attain the perfect correlation of 1.00. This goal is almost never achieved, usually not even remotely, in social-science research. One of the reasons is purely technical. It requires that one have perfectly reliable measures, something virtually impossible to achieve in the social sciences. In our own case OM-500, the main dependent variable, attained a median reliability of only .82. As for the independent variables, we have no way of knowing precisely how accurately our respondents reported their education, length of factory experience, and the like. There is, however, little reason to assume that the reliability of those descriptive measures was any higher. Given these conditions, even if we had measured all possible and relevant causes of individual modernity, the imperfection of our measures would have limited us to attaining a multiple correlation of .82, which would mean explaining 67 percent of the variance in OM scores.

In fact, with our basic set of eight predictor variables alone we accounted, in the median case, for only 47 percent of the variance in OM scores. So, using the standard of absolute perfection, we were generally less than half perfect. However, when we adjust the standard to take account of the ceiling set by the unreliability of our measures, we can see that the variables we did take into account were actually very effective in explaining individual modernity. In the median case for all six countries our small set of basic variables explained just over 70 percent of what would have been the practical limit even if we had measured *all* relevant variables. In the case of India, where the data yielded the best performance, the variables we measured accounted for about 62 percent of the theoretical maximum and about 92 percent of the practical maximum resulting from the unreliability of our measures.

How good a performance is that? Again, it depends on one's standard. Since a perfect performance would consist in explaining 100 percent of the variance in OM scores, we are clearly a long way from perfection. But to use perfection as the standard is rather unrealistic. We consider it far more reasonable to compare our performance in explaining 47 percent of the variance in OM scores with the ability of the leading social scientists in the United States to explain the variance in important measures reflecting individual experience in the American setting.[4]

Viewed in that light, our efforts must be recognized as quite successful. Even in explaining "objective" and seemingly highly determined social facts such as individual educational and occupational attainment, the leading American study could account for only 26 percent and 43 percent of the variance, respectively.[5] Moreover, attempts to explain attitudes in the

American setting have generally been even less successful. For example, at one of our leading centers of social research the investigators used eight predictor variables, very similar to our set, in an effort to explain the variance in thirteen different measures of political attitudes and behavior in the American population. Across the set of thirteen measures the median variance explained was only 13 percent. The measure which could be best predicted by the independent variables they used, namely, that of "liberalism-conservatism," had only 48 percent of its variance explained. This was equal to our median, but well below our best performance of 62 percent of variance explained.[6]

It seems clear, therefore, that we have been able to explain the causes of individual modernity in six developing countries at least as well as social scientists in the United States have been able to explain the determinants of individual social mobility, and rather better than they have been able to explain the factors underlying most political attitudes and values. We did this, moreover, using samples covering only a modest part of the total range of occupational and educational experience. It seems very likely, therefore, that the underlying relation which we identified are, in reality, even stronger than they appear to be in our more limited samples.

A Developmental Model

We have seen that by simultaneously taking into account some eight to ten basic facts about a man, such as his education, his occupation, and his social origins, we can predict a good deal about his attitudinal and behavioral modernity. But the set of variables which we analyzed concurrently to explain individual modernity did not have their impact concurrently. Rather, the impact was built up serially over time. As a final task, therefore, we must give an account of the sequence or the stages of development men follow in moving from traditionalism to modernity.

Since we did not follow individuals through their life cycle, the sequential models we present below are, strictly speaking, only a hypothetical construction from the data at hand. Nevertheless, we feel we can identify the main paths followed by the men in our samples. In elaborating this developmental model we took into account three types of information. First, we drew on the theory and findings of general research into the process of adult socialization. Second, we obviously relied heavily on our detailed analysis of the role of the several separate explanatory variables as presented in the preceding chapters. Our third source of guidance was, however, a new element in this book: a statistical procedure known as path analysis.

Path analysis is a special form of multiple regression which requires that one set forth a detailed hypothetical causal model before any statistical procedures may be undertaken. In this type of analysis the interrelations of the independent variables to each other are taken into account as well as the relation of those variables to the dependent variable. The particular value of path analysis is that it permits one to break down the apparent effect of a predictor variable into direct and indirect components.

The *indirect effects* of a predictor on the dependent variable express the ways in which the predictor affects the dependent variable through the mediation of other variables in the model. This is the effect which appears to vanish when the other variables are brought under control.[7] By contrast, the *direct effect* expresses that element of the predictor variable's total impact which does not depend on the mediation of other variables. For example, schooling itself makes young people more modern in attitude and value, and that fact may shape their behavior all the rest of their lives. It may, for instance, influence their choice of an occupation or their political preferences. Such influences would then be *direct* effects of education. In addition, however, schooling, by conferring literacy and the habit of reading, and perhaps by inculcating more civic consciousness, may encourage men to use the mass media more. Such exposure to mass communication may, in turn, make men more modern. In such a case we would say that some of the impact of schooling had been mediated through contact with the radio and newspaper. Taken together, all such mediated influences represent the sum total of the *indirect* effects of education on modernity.

The method of path analysis used to determine which effects are direct and which indirect involves statistical assumptions and procedures too technical and complex for us to discuss them here. We plan, instead, to report the details in a separate publication. Nevertheless, in elaborating the developmental model of the modernization process which we present below, we drew heavily on a path analysis which we performed. Consequently some of the results will be described as either direct and indirect effects in the technical sense of those terms as defined above. The main facts are summarized in Table 20–2.

The Early Stages of Development

A good deal was foreshadowed by whether a man was born in the countryside or in the city. Knowing no more about a worker than that, one could predict his OM score almost as well as one could by knowing how long he had worked in a factory.

To some extent the rural setting, from the start, inculcates traditional attitudes. But the consequences of being born and raised in the countryside are largely long term, with effects mainly mediated through other life experiences. Men born in the countryside were more likely to have fathers with less education. In part for that reason, and in part for others

Table 20–2.   Total, direct, and indirect effects of main independent variables on OM-500: median for six countries.

Independent variables	All subjects			Factory workers only		
	Total[a]	Direct[b]	Indirect[c]	Total[a]	Direct[b]	Indirect[c]
Rural-urban origin[d]	—	—	—	.28	.10	.18
Ethnicity-religion	.19	.09	.10	.23	.09	.14
Father's education	.27	.05	.22	.22	.03	.19
Education-literacy	.52	.37	.15	.55	.37	.18
Occupational experience[e]	.41	.16	.25	.30	.12	.18
Mass-media exposure	.45	.18	.27	.40	.16	.24
Living standard	.39	.10	.29	.33	.08	.25
Urbanism[f]	.19	.04	.15	.02	.04	−.02
Life-cycle stage[f]	.03	.04	−.01	.06	.01	.05
Nature of present factory	—	—	—	.10	.06	.04

[a] Total effects are the zero-order Pearsonian correlation coefficients.
[b] Direct effects are the beta weights (path coefficients).
[c] Indirect effects are the differences between total effect and direct effect.
[d] Measured only in Argentina, Chile, and Nigeria.
[e] In the total sample this variable measures occupational type; in the worker sample it is a complex measure of factory experience. See Appendix C.
[f] See definitions in Appendix C.

equally obvious, the rural-origin men were much less likely to get very far in school. Since schooling is the main force in shaping modernity, the rural-origin men thus started out with a substantial handicap.

The man born in the countryside was, of course, most likely to enter farming as an occupation, and that type of job gave him little opportunity to develop his modernity. But even if he moved to the city, his lack of schooling reduced the chances of his later getting a job at high skill, of earning extra money, and, most important, of being more exposed to the influence of the mass media. Since all of these contribute to adult modernity, the rural-origin man, precisely because in his case all other things were *not* equal, started out with poor prospects of ever getting very high on the modernity scale.

These were, however, only prospects. They express the odds against a man, but they in no sense represent fixed, unalterable circumstances. On the contrary, as we have seen, and will see again, a rural-origin man who got more than average education, who served a long tenure as a factory worker, and who came into extensive contact with the mass media, ended up almost as modern as one who was born and raised in the city.

The ethnic and religious group into which a man was born operated in much the same way as did his origin in a rural or urban setting. That is, in itself, this characteristic of a man did not have a substantial direct effect on his modernity. A man's ethnicity and religion did, however, influence the accessibility of other important opportunities, education being outstanding among them. Once these indirect effects were discounted, however, the contribution of ethnicity as an explanation of modernity was modest.[8]

Father's education played a similar role. Indeed, its importance dwindled almost to the vanishing point when other variables were taken into account. The explanation lies mainly in the fact that the father's education was a key determinant of his son's education. Fathers with more education were more often urban than rural, and in either case tended to give their sons more education. But the effect of father's education was overwhelmingly an indirect one. Men who had received equal educations tended to be equal in modernity regardless of the differences in the education their fathers had received. Aside from its influence on the son's education, which was no mean consideration, the father's education did not seem to create any special quality in the family's home life which, in its own right, played a substantial role in determining the son's modernity.

Everything so far points in the same direction. Of the early experiences in life, only education was a highly important key to individual modernity. Indeed, standing alone it was by far the single most important determinant of a man's modernity. If we think of points on the OM scale as dispensed from tellers' windows, each representing a different aspect of the life cycle, then the window identified by the sign for "education" alone gave out almost half of all the OM points distributed by all the tellers combined.

Not only was the relative weight of education as a predictor of OM scores very large, but it was also outstanding in the degree to which its effects were direct, rather than being mediated through other variables which it influenced. For most variables their indirect effect equaled or substantially exceeded the direct effect. By contrast, the direct effect of education was in the ratio of at least 2:1 to its indirect effect. This indicates that the greater modernity conferred by education was mainly a result of what had gone on in the classroom and in the schoolyard, rather than following as a consequence of later-life advantages to which education had led.

Later Stages of Development

Taking our sample of men as a whole we can say that at the point at which they left school half the story of their eventual modernity score had been told. But this was true only on the average. Actually, for many men the story really ended at that point. The score they had attained at the time they left school was basically the same one they were going to record when our project staff eventually came by to test them. Others would add a few points over the years. Still others, however, were to have later-life experiences which would raise by many points the OM scores they had had at the time they left school. This increase was frequently as much as 50 percent, and in some cases was almost 100 percent, of the score these men had had on leaving the village. This outcome depended largely on the interaction between the stage at which the men left school and the nature and extent of their later contact with modernizing institutions. Of these later experiences, the two which were critical were the occupations they entered and the extent of their contact with the media of mass communication.

Men of rural origin who stayed in the countryside to farm as their fathers had done were most likely to be frozen at the level of modernity which characterized them when they left school. Few things in the nature of their work stimulated them to new ways of looking at things, to a heightened sense of personal efficacy, or to any of the other changes which would have made them more modern.

Yet it does not follow automatically that a man must have limited horizons merely because he is engaged in agricultural pursuits. We believe our rural men lagged behind not because they were farmers, but rather because the organizational framework in which they worked, and the communities in which they lived, were so traditional. This was made dramatically evident in the case of those few men who had the good fortune to be enrolled in, or otherwise come under the influence of, a vigorous new form of social and economic organization such as the Comilla cooperative movement in East Pakistan. In just a few years those men experienced a quite dramatic improvement in their standing on the scale of individual modernity.[9]

The average farmer, however, could not count on being enrolled in an organization so innovative as the Comilla cooperatives nor, indeed, in anything remotely like it. His chief opportunity for becoming more modern, therefore, lay in maximizing his contact with the media of mass communication. That is, of course, not so easy to do if one lives in an isolated village settlement. Moreover, the mass media were more often available to the better-educated and more prosperous cultivator. Still, they did provide one channel for breaking out of the fixed position in which the farmer otherwise found himself.

As for the men of urban origin, spending their formative years in town presumably exposed them to a whole series of more modern organizations before they actually entered on their occupational careers. In addition, the young men raised in urban areas were likely to have more years of schooling. Both of these factors, as well as other background advantages, contributed to the probability that the urban-origin men would have a fairly high level of modernity at the time they entered the factory. This created a kind of ceiling effect for them, that is, it kept to a modest level the gain in modernity they might attain during each year of factory employment. Nevertheless, urban-origin men also showed an appreciable increase in modernity, year by year, as a result of their work in industry. Their stay in the factory, moreover, had an indirect effect on modernity because it contributed to their readiness to expose themselves to the influence of the mass media. Indeed, across all the given levels of education and factory experience, each step up the ladder of mass-media exposure could raise the OM score of an urban-origin man about 2 points.

The greatest change in individual modernity was experienced by the men who left the countryside and associated agricultural pursuits to take up work in industry. Although the evidence is not unambiguous, it seems that the people who decided to migrate were not necessarily those who were more modern to begin with. However, there is reason to believe that the mere fact of moving a great distance was, in itself, a substantial psychological stimulant. Moreover, the organizational principles on which city living and industrial work were run were almost totally new to the migrants. Generally, their formal education was least extensive, so there was no ceiling holding down the amount they could learn in the new setting. Among these migrants, therefore, the lessons which the industrial establishment had to teach worked with their full force.

Even within the group which migrated from the farm to industry, the men varied in their readiness to absorb what the factory could teach them. Some were quick to grasp the message and changed their thinking, and acting, in ways which made them much more modern men. Others were slow to change. Being a mere sojourner in the factory had some effect, but those men who were sufficiently engaged to raise their skill level seemed to get much more out of their factory experience.[10] More important, those who were stimulated by their new residence and new occupation to expose themselves more fully to the media of mass communication thereby increased their OM scores by as many points as they had increased those scores by working in industry.

As a result of this set of experiences, rural-origin men of modest education, say with 3 years of schooling or less, often moved almost completely to the opposite end of the continuum of individual modernity from that occupied by their former neighbors who continued agricultural pursuits in their natal villages. Indeed, such migrants often benefited enough from the combined stimulus of factory work and mass-media contact to attain a modernity score the equal of that of men who had had twice as much education as the migrants, but had remained in their traditional villages to work as farmers.

Looking to the Future

The basic model of the development of individual modernity just presented accounts, in the median case, for just under half of the variation in OM scores. What then accounts for the rest?

One obvious path to fuller explanation of individual modernity scores would be to improve the reliability of our measures. If both our attitude scale and our measures of individual backgrounds were closer to perfect reliability we would, in the median case, be explaining not half but rather three-fourths of the variations in the OM scores. Yet about one-quarter of the variance in OM scores would remain unexplained. Still further to increase our understanding of what makes men modern, we would have to deal systematically with elements of the personality to which we gave little attention in our research design. In addition, we would have to improve our measures of certain factors which we did study, but without great success.

Probably the greatest gain toward fuller explanation would be made if we could better assess the *quality*, as against the *quantity*, of contact with modernizing social forces. Admittedly, our measures of the quality of the factory, and of the home-school environment, were not very helpful in explaining individual modernity. Yet we continue to believe, with some empirical support, that the quality of such institutions does play a substantial role. In the case of the factory, at least, we have been able to locate certain establishments which seem to have been unusually effective in modernizing men.[11] The difficulty is that we have not yet identified what it is in the more successful factories which gave them their special character as schools in modernity. Identifying and measuring those qualities remains a task for future research.

Just as factories vary in their ability to make men modern, so might other institutions be either more or less effective schools for modernity. For example, we saw that being exposed to the Comilla cooperative had a substantial positive effect on individual modernity. By extrapolation, we might argue that individual exposure to various kinds of voluntary or nonprofit organizations could have a modernizing impact.[12]

When we consider factors which probably influence a man's modernity but which we did not study at all, we must acknowledge that we did little to measure the possible contribution of personality. Certain qualities of personality seem to us to be most promising foci for further research. We should particularly know more about the role of intelligence and of personal adaptability in influencing how rapidly and how completely an individual becomes modern.

In some ways the OM scale is like a measure of intelligence, although it deals with a kind of *social* intelligence, rather than with the kind measured by conventional intelligence tests. Nevertheless, the two kinds of intelligence are likely to be related.[13] Indeed, insofar as individual modernity is something one learns — and we believe it essentially answers that description — it follows that high general intelligence would help people to learn to be modern. The school, the factory, and the mass media may all have special lessons in modernity to teach people, but, no less than in the case of reading, writing, and arithmetic, the learning of lessons in modernity depends not only on the skill of the teacher but also on the mental capacity and the psychological readiness of the learner.[14]

Of course, many individuals whom we believe or know to be very intelligent nevertheless resist learning, for various reasons. Clearly, certain qualities of personality could be critical in determining whether individuals who have the necessary intellectual potential to learn actually use that potential to learn things. For example, those who are rigid might well respond to the new experience of the factory not by opening themselves up to its influence, but rather by defensively resisting its message.

It is, of course, an open question whether we would actually much increase our power to explain the variation in OM scores merely by measuring other kinds of institutional experience, by more perceptively evaluating the quality of institutions, and by more thorough measurement of personal qualities. It may well be argued that to assess the true quality of home and school experience, and meaningfully to gauge the contribution of personal qualities such as intelligence and flexibility, we really should do longitudinal studies. Only then could we measure the quality of the home and the school as they were actually lived in, and not merely as they are recalled. And only then could we examine the role of intelligence or personal rigidity as they truly intervened at the moment a man entered the factory, rather than long after that fact. But these are tasks for the future, to be undertaken in research yet to be launched. So far as concerns the research we have already completed, and reported in this book, it is time to sum up and state our conclusions.

21

Summary and Conclusions on the Social Significance of Individual Modernization

The main purpose of economic development is to permit the achievement of a decent level of living for all people, everywhere. But almost no one will argue that the progress of a nation and a people should be measured solely in terms of gross national product and per capita income. Development assumes, as well, a high degree of political maturation, as expressed in stable and orderly processes of government resting on the expressed will of the people. And it also includes the attainment of popular education, the burgeoning of the arts, the efflorescence of architecture, the growth of the means of communication, and the enrichment of leisure. Indeed, in the end, development requires a transformation in the very nature of man, a transformation that is both a means to yet greater growth and at the same time one of the great ends of the development process.

We have described this transformation as the shift from traditionalism to individual modernity. The object of our research was to delineate the elements of such personal change, to measure its degree, to explain its causes, and to throw some light on its observed and probable future consequences. It is time for us to sum up the progress we made in that task, taking the opportunity, in so doing, to deal briefly with some of the issues we earlier may have left unresolved.

Defining and Measuring Individual Modernity

One who sets out to define and to measure individual modernity is like the animal trainer whose new act requires he learn to ride on the back of his tiger. He may emerge alive, but the chances are very great he will have been knocked about quite a bit in the process. Nevertheless, we accepted as a critical element in the structure of our whole intellectual and scientific enterprise the construction of a reliable, cross-national measure of individual modernity.

We do not claim to have invented the idea of the modern man. The concept was already there when we began our work, even though its content was vague. Inventing types of men has, after all, always been a fundamental preoccupation of sociologists: Marx described the consciousness of the bourgeoisie and the proletariat; Redfield defined the contrasting attributes of the folk and urban types; Stonequist gave us the marginal man; Riesman the inner-, outer-, and other-directed man. These "ideal types" people the pages of almost every well-known sociologist's work. Yet it has been the rare instance, indeed, in which any systematic attempt has been undertaken to measure whether there are real people in the world who, in their own persons, actually incorporate the qualities identified by these ideal types.[1] We were determined to break with this sociological tradition, and firmly committed ourselves to testing how far the set of qualities by which we defined the modern man actually cohered as a psychosocial syndrome in real men.

Our results provide definitive evidence that living individuals do indeed conform to our model of the modern man, that they do so in substantial numbers, and that essentially the same basic qualities which define a man as modern in one country and culture also delineate the modern man in other places. The modern man is not just a construct in the mind of sociological theorists. He exists and can be identified with fair reliability within any population where our test can be applied.

The modern man's character, as it emerges from our study, may be summed up under four major headings. He is an informed participant citizen; he has a marked sense of personal efficacy; he is highly independent and autonomous in his relations to traditional sources of influence. especially when he is making basic decisions about how to conduct his personal affairs; and he is ready for new experiences and ideas, that is, he is relatively open-minded and cognitively flexible.

As an informed participant citizen, the modern man identifies with the newer, larger entities of region and state, takes an interest in public affairs, national and international as well as local, joins organizations, keeps himself informed about major events in the news, and votes or otherwise takes some part in the political process. The modern man's sense of efficacy is reflected in his belief that, either alone or in concert with others, he may take actions which can affect the course of his life and that of his community; in his active efforts to improve his own condition and that of his family; and in his rejection of passivity, resignation, and fatalism toward the course of life's events. His independence of traditional sources of authority is manifested in public issues by his following the advice of public officials or trade-union leaders rather than priests and village elders, and in personal matters by his choosing the job and the bride he prefers even if his parents prefer some other position or some other person. The modern man's openness to new experience is reflected in his interest in technical innovation, his support of scientific exploration of hitherto sacred or taboo subjects, his readiness to meet strangers, and his willingness to allow women to take advantage of opportunities outside the confines of the household.

These *main* elements of individual modernity seem to have in common a thrust toward more instrumental kinds of attitudes and behavior. The more expressive and interpersonal aspects of the OM syndrome tended to be less important, by and large, although still significantly involved in the syndrome. This fits well with the relative emphasis on new and more effective ways of doing things as central to the modernization process, with changes in ways of relating to other people coming largely as side effects. The Japanese case is a good example of how the instrumental aspects of OM can be present with, we would judge, many fewer of the expressive elements.

Although these are the principal components, they by no means exhaust the list of qualities which cohere as part of the modernity syndrome. The modern man is also different in his approach to time, to personal and social planning, to the rights of persons dependent on or subordinate to him, and to the use of formal rules as a basis for running things. In other words, psychological modernity emerges as a quite complex, multifaceted, and multidimensional syndrome.

Different specialists in scale construction often prescribe different standards for judging whether or not a set of questions or subscales cohere well enough to be acknowledged as constituting a general syndrome. Our OM-500 achieved a comfortable median reliability of .80 or above in all six countries, as judged by the Kuder-Richardson formula. In one group of people after another, differentiated by occupation, religion, ethnicity, educational level, and country of origin, the same set of qualities went together. We therefore felt quite confident in affirming the empirical reality of the psychosocial syndrome our theory had originally identified.

While the existence of this particular psychosocial syndrome seems established beyond serious doubt, nevertheless, the reasonableness of claiming that the syndrome defines individual modernity is open to challenge. We can identify objections to that designation on purely theoretical grounds, on the basis of values, and on empirical grounds. Although we cannot hope to allay every last doubt, there are convincing arguments which meet each of these challenges.

Challenges on Theoretical Grounds
We encountered much less concern over the issue of how we measured

individual modernity than over the question of how we conceived it and how we labeled it. Each of the challenges to our approach reflected a different, and sometimes sharply contrasting, theoretical orientation. Since we cannot respond to all of them here, we have selected three of the most commonly introduced and, we feel, most fundamental. These involve disagreement with our choice of the term "modern," caveats as to whether individual modernity should really be thought of as all of one piece, and charges that we may have conceived of modernity too narrowly.

The first of the theoretical challenges we most commonly encountered centered on our use of the term "modern" to describe the syndrome we were studying. Unfortunately, those who found this designation unacceptable were not unanimous in their choice of an alternative. Prominent among the substitutes they proposed were "industrial," "Western," "contemporary," "organizational," and "bureaucratic."

Few things are more fruitless than quibbling over labels. If that were all there was to the issue, therefore, we would readily accept some other designation, secure in the judgment that what is critical is the content of the OM scale and not the label placed on it. But our choice was not arbitrary and, in explaining our preference for it, we can perhaps further illuminate the ideas which guided our research.

Strictly speaking, "modern" merely means that which is new, the most current or latest in styles of dress, art, or thinking. It should be fairly clear that we are not using the term in that sense. The type of man we identify by the OM scale has qualities which have often been manifested in the past and which we believe will be of continuing importance in the future. In one sense, the qualities by which we identify the modern man are timeless.

Yet, in another sense, the issue of time is central. A complex of institutional patterns is being widely diffused throughout the contemporary world. These include large-scale industry, intensive urbanization, rapid transport, media of mass communication, presumptively rational large-scale bureaucratic organizations, mass education, and mass culture. Societies having these characteristics are termed modern, and in this case unambiguously so because this package of institutions is the latest development in national styles. It was our conviction that societies with such characteristics encourage the development of a particular type of man and, indeed, also require that type if they are to function effectively. Since the term "modern" was an already commonly accepted term used to describe the type of society we were interested in, there seemed every reason to use the same term to designate the type of man we assumed to be so intimately associated with that kind of social order.

The term "modern man" also had the advantage that we have become accustomed to juxtaposing it to the term "traditional man," as the other pole of a continuum. Neither the "industrial man" nor the "organizational man" readily suggest such a polar type. Moreover, the term "industrial man" seemed inappropriate because the qualities we were concerned with were relevant to, and could as well be manifested by, men working outside of industry in agriculture, in trade, and in politics. The "bureaucratic man" seemed pejorative, and also inaccurate, in that the term is increasingly used to describe rigidity in the application of rules, whereas we thought of the modern man as flexible and innovative. In addition, of course, we expected to find the modern man quite prevalent outside of bureaucratic settings. Similar objections could be raised to the term "organization man," a designation which, in any event, had already been given rather special meaning by William Whyte's book, *The Organization Man*. Since all the other candidates had serious liabilities as well, and "modern man" had special virtues in our eyes, we settled on that term, hoping that everyone would realize that the critical matter is not the label but the content measured by the scale.

The second challenge to our theoretical position questioned our assumption that it was productive to think of individual modernity as all of one piece. Considering the range of topics covered by our questionnaire, our approach might actually be characterized as quite eclectic. Yet we were guided by the conviction that whatever the nominal social content of the area under consideration, a modern man would respond in a fundamentally consistent way. In other words, we believed there might well be a small number of *general* orientations or dispositions which expressed themselves in different realms of concrete social action. And we further assumed that this small set of general orientations might relate to each other with sufficient consistency to identify a *syndrome* of characteristics which could appropriately be identified as those of the modern man.

Those critical of our approach seriously doubted that the pattern of personal change could be at all consistent across the whole range of dimensions we had in mind when we spoke of modernization. They urged that the model which specified a *general* modernity syndrome be replaced by one that emphasized each dimension of change as a *discrete* entity, or by one based on individual profiles or typologies of change, each represented by different sets of men.

Those who inclined to this position argued that we could not be at all sure that in every one of the many realms we studied, ranging all the way from the sense of efficacy to the readiness to allow one's daughter to work outside the home, there would be evidence of consistent change as men came more and more under the influence of modern institutions. And even if most of these personal orientations changed in some men in some places, it seemed unlikely that they would change more or less equally in all places among all men.

Following the proposed alternative strategy one might look for men who were personally very efficacious, and also favored science, education, and technological innovation, but who were at the same time opposed to giving the common man a voice in village councils and insisted on keeping women in the home. Such a combination of views might well be found in some populations. Indeed it *was* found by us among certain Indian farmers.[2] Men presenting such a profile could get a fairly high score on the modernity scale, yet in many respects we should have classified them as traditional. The summary OM score obscured these facts, and caused us to consider these men equally modern with others manifesting quite a different profile of modern characteristics.

This experience certainly gave weight to the argument that it was unrealistic to consider modernity all of a piece, expressible in a single summary OM score. But it did not require this experience to convince us that our critics had a weighty argument here. We had so considered it from the very beginning of our research. Indeed, our initial assumption was that it was quite problematic as to whether there was such a thing as a really general modernity syndrome, and we were quite prepared to conduct our analysis either measure by measure or on the basis of fairly distinctive profiles each of which might characterize only a small set of men within our larger sample. Nevertheless, the delineation of a general syndrome of modernity had such obvious theoretical and practical interest, and its availability promised so greatly to simplify the task of analyzing our complex set of data, that we found it essential to start with the assumption that modernity might indeed prove to be all of a piece.

One's theoretical assumptions open up issues and lead to predictions, but they cannot settle matters of fact. We felt we had a compelling obligation to ascertain whether, in fact, a general syndrome of modernity really existed. As we now know, it turned out that there *was* an underlying dimension of individual modernity which cut across, and in substantial degree united, the diverse opinions, attitudes, and values expressed over the wide range of situations probed by our questionnaire. These elements are loosely rather than tightly tied to one another, but they definitely hold together well enough to satisfy the most commonly used standards for judging the integration of the elements of an attitude and value scale. In this respect, our experience was similar to that of the psychologists who have tried to develop a measure of "general intelligence" which would simultaneously reflect the many different capacities to which the concept of intelligence can refer.

In sum, our results permit us to say that, despite expectations to the contrary, the different aspects of the personality affected by contact with modernizing institutions do not change in a random way relative to one another. The changes in one realm tend to be significantly related to changes in other realms in such a way as to make it very reasonable to declare that there is a general modernity syndrome, the elements of which respond to external influences in basically the same way.

To affirm the existence of this general syndrome of individual modernity, and the similarity in the way its components respond to modernizing influences, is not to assert that, in a technical sense, individual modernity is unidimensional. Nor do we deny that there may be distinctive profiles of modernity as, for example, in the case of men who are well informed and efficacious, yet have simultaneously closed their minds to any new ideas about birth control or women's rights. Our experience in working with the data indicates, in fact, that the modernity score earned by most men comes from giving about the same proportion of modern answers in all, or at least most, realms. Nevertheless, there are some men with fairly distinctive profiles.

It may also be that some dimensions of modernity are more affected by certain types of experience than by others. Information levels, for example, might be expected to increase more through exposure to the mass media, whereas the sense of efficacy may be more affected by factory experience than by schooling. Our preliminary efforts to uncover such differential patterns of influence have not been very productive, but we still feel that these issues should be studied more intensively and we hope to do so ourselves in the future. Yet the probable existence of such profiles, even their possibly widespread distribution, cannot negate the existence of the general syndrome of modernity which we uncovered. While the study of individual profiles — if they emerge in any significant number — may prove a useful supplement to the analysis we have done, one cannot, in the light of the available facts, properly challenge the legitimacy of our approach.

The third theoretical objection to our conception of the modern man was that we were too selective, having focused almost exclusively on those elements of the syndrome which showed the positive side of the modernization experience. It is widely assumed that becoming modern quite regularly makes men cold and impersonal, rigid and bureaucratic, likely to default on personal obligations, alienated, and psychically maladjusted. Those who hold to this view objected that our conceptualization of the modernizing syndrome simply did not give these more negative attributes a chance to demonstrate their true role in a full characterization of the modern man.

Just for the record, we must declare that it was not our conscious intention to show the modern man in either a good or a bad light. Ours was a much more academic concern, namely, to find that set of coherent personal characteristics most relevant to understanding the impact of the modernization process on the individual. In any event, it is not accurate to assert that our conception of modernity tended to cover up the dark side of the process. We did in fact measure many of the attitudes, values, and conditions which some theorists assume to be almost invariable negative accompaniments of individual modernization.

The simple fact is that generally those negative characteristics did not relate systematically either to the modernity syndrome or to exposure to the institutions we defined as modernizing. The men who were classified by us as more modern were less rather than more prone to believe that possessions insure personal happiness; they were about as likely as the more traditional to urge that old people be treated with respect and consideration; they were as much inclined as anyone else to give support to a relative in need; they had not become so bureaucratic as to propose that an official favor the man whose case rested on legal rights over the man whose case rested on great need. Indeed, we had in our questionnaire many questions of this type, and they generally failed to distinguish effectively between modern and traditional men.

Although they are not reported in this book, we have elsewhere published a description of scales of alienation, anomie, and intergroup hostility which we developed on the basis of our questionnaire.[3] These also failed to show any consistent pattern of association with our measures of individual modernity, but insofar as there was any significant association, it was most often negative, that is, the more modern men were less alienated, anomic, and hostile to other groups in their society. Finally, we have extensive evidence that neither individual modernity nor greater contact with modernizing institutions leads to greater maladjustment as measured by the Psychosomatic Symptoms Test.[4]

In brief, we claim that our approach to the measurement of modernity was not narrow. What failed was not our approach to measurement, but rather the prediction of those who asserted that in becoming modern the men of traditional countries would lose whatever qualities had made them more friendly, humane, personal, warm, open, secure, or otherwise attractive and adjusted in their traditional mode. Modern men may be different, but they are not deculturated, nor are they "bad guys" or "sick."

Challenges Based on Values

It is not so easy to draw hard and fast lines between a challenge to the OM scale based on theoretical assumptions and one based on value premises. Nevertheless, we interpret what is probably the most common challenge to our measurement of modernity as an objection on grounds of value. Is it not the case, we are asked, that the OM scale embodies personal qualities which are distinctly valued only in Western society? To define modernity in those terms would clearly impose an alien standard for judging the progress of development in most non-European countries. Indeed, if we could not meet this challenge some of our critics would be prepared to argue that use of the OM scale borders on being a social-science form of cultural colonialism.

We seriously question the accuracy of the assertion that the qualities measured by the OM scale are distinctively European or even, more broadly, Western. Indeed, the statement seems to us to be itself parochial. Groups as widely separated in space and time as the Plains Indians of North America in the nineteenth century and the Ibo of twentieth-century Africa seemed to manifest and value many of the qualities which make for a high OM score. Indeed, being an active participant in the larger community, being personally efficacious, and being open-minded and flexible are qualities which have been, and are, very highly valued in many cultures, new and old. Such qualities are useful and desired not only in the United States but in Japan, and not only in Communist Russia but in Mao's China and Castro's Cuba.

Moreover, there is no factual basis for asserting that these qualities are, in fact, more characteristic of the peoples of Europe or even of the United States. Every large nation undoubtedly includes a variety of types of men, some like our modern man and others quite different. And each of the countries of Europe is itself home to a distinctive national character, not only setting it off in some respects from other nations in Europe, but also bringing it closer in other respects to nations in non-European parts of the world.

Even if the qualities of the modern man were actually more widespread in Europe and the United States, that would not establish those qualities as necessarily a distinctive element of Western culture. We have presented much evidence to indicate that individual modernity rises with increasing education, with employment in the modern sector of the economy, and with mass-media exposure. Since such experiences, which make for greater individual modernity, are so much more widespread in the conditions of European and North American society, it follows that on those continents there may well be more men who qualify as modern. But those men are modern because of their contact with modernizing institutions, and not because of their national culture. It is of critical importance, in this context, to know that Joseph Kahl, using a measure of individual modernity having broad affinity with the OM scale, has shown that when national groups are matched on education and urban location there are no substantial differences in the modernity scores of people from Brazil, Mexico, and the United States.[5]

Even if the qualities built into the OM scale prove to be more distinctive of some national groups than others, we reject the charge that we are in any way imposing an alien standard of judgment on anyone. The OM scale is not a judgment. It is a description of a type of man. We assumed that this type of man was more likely to develop under certain circumstances than under others. Whether it is good or bad to have more rather than fewer men who fully manifest the qualities we have called modern *is* a question for value judgment, and it clearly is an issue on which men of goodwill certainly may differ profoundly. But it should be clear that we have in no way insisted on the moral superiority of modern over traditional men.

While we have proposed no moral imperative concerning individual modernity, we would be less than frank if we did not acknowledge our belief that there is an empirical imperative suggested by our findings. *We feel our results make it clear that as developing nations acquire more modern institutions, more widely diffused, to that degree their populations will come to include more and more men marked by the characteristics we have termed modern.*

Finally, we should like to emphasize that we in no way mean to deny the appropriateness of attempting alternative ways of defining individual modernity which might seem less influenced by Western models. Indeed, we urged our field directors to test alternative models of individual modernity wherever possible. The Indian field director, Amar K. Singh, aided by a board of local consultants at Ranchi, did actually devise a distinctive Indian measure based on the standards used in that community to judge who is "modern." The scale included questions such as whether food tastes better when, in cooking, one uses charcoal rather than dried cowdung cakes as fuel, whether women should wear ornaments, whether wives should give their husbands better food than they give themselves, and whether a holy man gets candy out of an empty bag by trickery or because he has supernatural powers.

This distinctively Indian scale of modernity proved to be very highly correlated with the standard OM score for India, indicating that our project's standardized conception had nevertheless led us to identify as modern the very men who were classified as modern by purely local criteria. Moreover, scores on the local modernity scale were influenced by the same social forces — schooling, factory work, and mass-media exposure — which we had found to lead to higher scores on the standard OM scale in India.[6] This finding, along with the fact that the same ingredients combined to define the modernity syndrome in the six quite different countries we studied, convinces us that OM is not a syndrome bearing the distinctive cultural stamp of Europe. Rather, we believe it to be of a higher order, indicating a more general human characteristic which is pancultural in meaning and transnational in relevance. No country or culture can claim the modernity syndrome as its distinctive property. Modern men can be found in all societies, and they can come to be the majority in any society, whatever its historic cultural tradition.

Political Perspectives

Analogous to charges that the OM scale gives too much weight to qualities typical of Western culture is the claim that it reflects a political bias,
giving greater weight to qualities one would expect in a capitalist society
while ignoring those which would be valued in a communist or socialist
society. Sometimes this complaint takes the form of asserting that our
model of the modern man gives credit toward modernity for individuals
who support the status quo, but not for those who seek to bring about
basic, much less radical, social change. On both counts we feel that the
respective characterizations of our approach are inaccurate, and rest either
on incomplete information or on a misreading of our questionnaire and its
utilization.

Socialism and modern man. Let us consider, first, the suspicion that the
OM scale may well describe men in capitalist countries, but would not fit
"socialist man." This issue can ultimately be settled only by administering
the scale in socialist countries. We had hoped to include one such country
in the original set but at the time we launched our study our East European
colleagues were not yet ready to undertake the type of research we outlined to them. Subsequently the OM scale was used in at least one country
in the East European bloc, but the results were not available at the time
we went to press.[7] When the results become available they may reveal
some themes to be distinctively important for those countries, but we are
quite certain that the data will also demonstrate that, overall, the modernity scale works as well in the European socialist countries as it did in the
six developing nations we studied.

Our confidence about the results we expect to obtain in the socialist
countries is not merely an expression of blind faith in the universal applicability of our scale. The senior author of this volume spent some 25 years
studying the social structure of the Soviet Union, with special emphasis
on the personal qualities which the Soviet system sought to inculcate in its
ideal citizen.[8] Many of the themes included in the OM scale were selected
with explicit reference to that ideal, so that the OM scale would equally
well describe the modern man in either socialist or capitalist countries.
In the Soviet Union the regime calls for active public participation by
all citizens in "the building of communism"; it urges persistence — or, as
they say, "strength of will" — in the pursuit of personal and communal
goals, calling on the people to eschew passive fatalism in the face of obstacles; and it demands that people shift their allegiance away from traditional authority to the newer political entities of Communist Party and
Soviet State. As Raymond Bauer succinctly summed it up, the Soviet "new
model of man" calls for him to be "conscious, rational, and purposive,"
terms highly congruent with our description of the modern man.[9]

The major point at which the socialist model and our model of the modern man may seem most definitely to diverge is in the former's emphasis on "collectivism" versus the latter's stress on "individualism." Even here, however, the disparity between the communist model and our conception of the modern man is more apparent than real. We acknowledge that we did not introduce many questions which explicitly tapped the existence of a communal orientation, and it therefore remains moot how far this orientation might or might not be part of the modernity syndrome in our samples, let alone in socialist countries. Obviously, much would depend on the specific content of the questions designed to measure communalism. Many forms of communalism, such as the prime identification with one's family, village, tribe, or religion, rather than with the national state, would not be considered modern in the Soviet Union or China any more than they were by us in our work in developing countries.

In addition, we feel it is a mistake to see the element of "individualism" built into our OM scale as in any way the antithesis of "communalism" or "cooperation" as those terms are normally used in the socialist countries. An examination of the questions we actually used makes it immediately apparent that they deal mainly with individual decision-making in regard to very personal matters such as the choice of a job and of a spouse. Moreover, the independence expressed by selecting the modern answers to those questions involves independence of the power of parent, priest, and village elder. In the socialist countries men are also definitely expected to be relatively autonomous in dealing with the incumbents of those social roles. There is, therefore, no reason to argue that the measure of individualism incorporated in the OM scale represents a kind of "anti-communalism" which would be unacceptable in socialist countries. Indeed, other questions used in the OM scale make it quite clear that favoring government planning and community effort are very much part of the modernity syndrome.[10]

All in all, therefore, we feel it is not correct to state that the qualities embodied in the modern man peculiarly suit him for life under capitalism, but would disqualify him as a valued citizen in a socialist country. Of course, we do not argue that "socialist man" and "capitalist man," if there are such creatures, would be alike in all respects. Obviously, many explicit differences in value and attitude would separate the two. Nevertheless, both the capitalist and the socialist systems value and need most, indeed we dare say virtually all, of the qualities measured by the OM scale. And in both systems, formal education, work in factories and cooperatives, and exposure to the mass media are likely to make men more modern than are people less exposed to such influences.

Modernity and the status quo. As for the issue of favoring the status quo, we feel that charge cannot properly be laid against the modern man as we have identified him. If by the status quo one means the social order characteristic of most traditional countries, then it is obvious that one of the essential components of our modernity syndrome is *opposition* to the status quo. What other meaning can one assign to favoring the rights of women to move and work outside the home; the rights of men to choose for themselves, rather than have the elders choose, their jobs and their wives; and the rights of the little man to have an equal voice in village councils and an equal chance to get his children as much education as they are capable of? The essence of the modern man as we defined him, and as he emerged from our empirical studies, lies in his openness to new experience and his readiness for basic change, including change in almost every kind of social organization.

If, in the design of the OM scale, we did not make the readiness for specifically *political* change more explicit, it was not because of any desire on our part to avoid the issue. On the contrary, the initial questionnaire which the project developed incorporated many items designed to measure the conservative-radical dimension, including questions on party preference. However, our local advisors generally considered such questions too sensitive to be asked, especially in a survey sponsored by a foreign university. Only in Chile and Argentina, therefore, were we able to develop a "radicalism" scale, based on questions as to whether the national economic system required a total (and immediate) overhaul. In both countries this measure of radicalism was positively and significantly correlated with overall modernity.[11]

We cannot be sure the outcome would have been the same in the other four countries, because the relation of political orientation and individual modernity is a very complicated subject which requires detailed analysis in its own right.[12] Nevertheless, we believe the outcome would have been consistent with the findings for Chile and Argentina, because favoring change in the basic political and economic system is so clearly consistent with wanting the other changes which were measured in such detail by the OM scale. In any event, it should be clear that the OM scale was not subtly designed to give the impression that the more modern men are particularly prone to support the status quo. We approached the question as an open issue. The evidence we found indicates that modern men are likely to favor fundamental change in political and economic institutions, much as they favor basic changes in interpersonal relations and in social customs.

The Empirical Challenge

What we have termed the empirical challenge to our use of the term modern to characterize the attitude and value syndrome we identified may be simply stated as follows: Granting that we have discovered a syndrome of attitudes, values, and dispositions to act, do we really have the right to say this syndrome identifies individual modernity unless we can show that it is more characteristic of men about whose modernity we have other, and *independent,* evidence.

This argument, of course, plunges us into the necessity of deciding who can, on really independent grounds, be said to be indisputably modern. As we have seen, if we take as our standard the citizens of Western Europe, we will be charged, and properly so, with ethnocentrism. A much more appropriate alternative would be, therefore, to accept as "modern" by definition those individuals, within any given country, who are better educated, more urbanized, more engaged in industry and related non-traditional occupations, and more exposed to the newer media of mass communication. These are "objective" characteristics which can be more or less unambiguously measured. It would probably be generally agreed that such people represent, for their countries at least, what is commonly meant by modern.

Psychologists will recognize this approach as an example of the "criterion method" for judging the appropriateness of one or another designation of a scale's content. Relevant evidence has already been given abundantly in our text.[13] The syndrome measured by the OM scale is many times more common among individuals whose objective characteristics place them in the modern sector of society. As we saw (in Chapter 8), the range in the proportion of men who were classified as traditional went from 97 percent among those who had had least contact with the institutions defined as modern down to a mere 1 percent among those with the most extensive involvement in the modern institutional sector. Using the criterion method for validating scale content, therefore, we seem to be on very good ground in claiming that the psychosocial syndrome measured by the OM scale designates a modern man.

Explaining How Men Become Modern

Having developed a reliable and valid means for measuring individual modernity cross-culturally, we were in a position to attempt our major objective, which was to explain what makes men modern. Just as we had adopted a rather catholic position in considering a wide range of potential elements which might delineate the modern man, so we considered a large number of forces as possible determinants of individual modernity. Many of these were, however, only alternative ways of measuring the same thing, and we were able to reduce the explanatory variables to a basic set of eight to ten major dimensions.

Taken together, this limited set of independent variables produced multiple correlations ranging from .56 to .79. This meant that we were explaining between 32 and 62 percent of the variance in OM scores, with the median at 47 percent. This performance compares quite favorably with results obtained in the more developed countries in studies using comparable measures of complex personal attributes. Of course, it also leaves a good deal of the variation in individual OM scores unexplained. Part of this unexplained variance is undoubtedly due to measurement error, since both the OM scales and the independent or explanatory measures were far from being perfectly reliable. But there must also be factors which we did not measure which very likely played a substantial role, native intelligence and basic personality being two obvious examples.

Nevertheless, our battery of measures taken together explained enough of the variation in OM scores to make it very meaningful to attempt to sort out the *relative* contribution of different sorts of influence on individual modernity. For us, the critical competition was that between influences which exerted their effect early in life and those which came into play mainly in adulthood. We see individual modernity, measured by the OM scale, as being quite a basic personality characteristic. Yet, in the theories of personality most dominant in our time, it is generally assumed that the basic attributes of personality are laid down in the early period of development. If this assumption were correct, there would be little hope of changing people from traditional into modern men, psychologically speaking, once they had reached adulthood. Instead, efforts to increase the proportion of modern men would have to be focused mainly on the family and early schooling.

We assumed, however, that men could be changed in quite fundamental ways *after* they reached adulthood, and that no man need therefore remain traditional in outlook and personality merely because he had been raised in a traditional setting. Putting these ideas to an empirical test, we measured how much variance in OM scores was accounted for by the set of early-socialization variables — notably father's education, own education, ethnicity, and urban or rural origin — as compared to the explanatory power of a set of later socialization influences, including occupation, standard of living, urban experience, and mass-media exposure. We consider it highly notable that in three of our six countries the late socialization experiences played an even more important role in determining a man's modernity score than did the earlier formative influences. Indeed, when each set was used standing alone, the early-socialization variables typically accounted for about 31 percent of the variance while the late-socialization variables accounted for about 37 percent of the variance in OM scores.

Our results indicate that under the right circumstances any man may become modern after he has passed his adolescence. And, since the forces which can make men modern after the formative years seem to be embedded in the institutions which developing countries are most eager to adopt, the prospect is substantial that over time more and more of the men in those countries will develop the attitudes, values, and behavior patterns we have identified as defining the modern man.

In addition to observing the effect of the explanatory variables grouped as early and late socialization influences, we naturally wanted to know how the main variables performed independently, in their own right. In all six countries, education emerged as unmistakably the most powerful force in shaping a man's modernity score. Indeed, judged by the number of points on the OM scale a man gained for each additional year of schooling, education was generally two or even three times as powerful as any other single input. In this, our conclusions are not new but rather confirm findings in several other studies of modernity. Occupational experience and mass-media exposure shared the second rank more or less equally. By showing exposure to the media of mass communication to be a major force in making men modern our results confirmed one of the pioneering studies in the field, that by Daniel Lerner, whose *Passing of Traditional Society* stressed the central role of the mass media as a modernizing institution.

The distinctive emphasis of our project, however, lay in its concern for the potential impact on individual modernity of occupational experience, and particularly of work in modern large-scale productive enterprises such as the factory. The variable of factory experience generally was second in importance after education, although each year in a factory yielded only one-third to one-half the increase in modernity which an additional year in school could bring. One important surprise, however, was our discovery that the men in certain nonindustrial occupations, such as cabdrivers, newspaper vendors, barbers, and street hawkers, showed rather more modernity than we had assumed.

By contrast, some of the institutions most commonly associated with the process of modernization failed to substantiate their claim to standing as important schools for making men modern. Most notable of these was the city, whose failure to qualify as an important independent modernizing influence was not corrected by taking into account either the size or the relative cosmopolitanism of different urban centers. Ethnic origin and religion also proved to be relatively unimportant variables in explaining individual modernity, at least once the educational and occupational differences usually characterizing such groups were brought under control.[14] We were struck, and rather surprised, to find that the quality of the school a man attended and the relative modernity of the factory he worked in, at least so far as we were able to measure them, also played a very small role in determining a man's modernity when compared to the sheer quantity of his exposure to the school and the factory.

These conclusions are of necessity stated here in very general terms, and do not reflect the many variations we observed when the forces at work in making men modern were studied in greater depth. For example, father's education emerged from the matching process and the multiple-regression analysis as having little direct effect on individual modernity. But the path analysis put this finding in perspective by showing that father's education was nevertheless important for its indirect effect on individual modernity. The father's education played a major role in determining the level of the son's education, and that, in turn, had a very powerful direct effect on individual modernity scores.

When seen operating in combination and under varying circumstances, the individual explanatory variables also sometimes changed their standing relative to one another. Thus, we discovered that factory experience had a much greater impact on men of rural background and little education than it did on men of urban origin who had had more education. Indeed, in explaining the OM scores of the less-educated rural-origin men we found that their occupational experience could be of equal, or even greater, importance than was the amount of schooling they had received.[15] This was partly because such men entered the factory with lower scores to begin with, so that they were not yet near the ceiling and hence had more room to develop as modern men under the tutelage of the factory. We also assume the factory effect was greater for men of rural origin because for them the factory was their first extensive contact with modern organizational principles and the large-scale inanimate use of power. In other words, with those men the factory produced a more powerful demonstration effect.

While we were persuaded by our data that the factory was certainly a school in modernity, other results indicated that the factory is probably not the only form of occupational experience which makes men more modern. As already noted, some types of urban nonindustrial employment also seemed to be at least a modest stimulant to modernity, a fact which we attributed to the contact with a diversified public and to relative autonomy in arranging one's own work. In addition, men pursuing traditional occupations, such as those of porter, but doing so in the context of large-scale bureaucratic organizations, also become more modern.

We were most struck, however, by the dramatic changes in the level of individual modernity which were manifested in the East Pakistani farmers who came under the influence of the Comilla cooperative movement. Since the cooperatives did not rely very heavily on new machinery to increase the productivity of the farmers, the exceptional impact of agricultural cooperation in Comilla must be accounted for by reference to other influences. We assume the success of the Comilla co-ops came, in part, from the insistence on self-help, in part from the models of alternative ways of doing things which the cooperative instructors provided, and in part from the new principles of social organization and interpersonal relations which the cooperatives introduced.

Adapting and Extending Our Theory

At this point it becomes obvious that one may justifiably raise the question whether, in the light of the facts now available, the original theory guiding this research should be abandoned for another. Our response is that we see no reason to abandon the theory. On the contrary, we believe it has been shown to be generally correct. But there does seem good reason to adapt and extend it.

First, we wish to emphasize that the critical premise of our research was that later life experiences, coming beyond those of childhood and adolescence, could bring about important changes in basic features of individual personality. The evidence that types of occupational engagement other than industrial employment may also influence men to become more modern in no way challenges our basic assumption that adult men can undergo significant personality change as a result of the influence of their work. On the contrary, these additional findings further confirm the soundness of our general theory, and hint that it may have even broader application than we had anticipated.

Nevertheless, the clear-cut findings in the case of Comilla cooperatives, and the suggestive ones concerning the urban nonindustrial workers, oblige us to broaden our explanation of changes in individual modernity so as to take account of occupational experience other than factory work. The conditions of employment in a factory are evidently a sufficient cause for individual modernization, but they are not a necessary one. What we need is either a set of more explicit propositions indicating all the different conditions which can independently bring about individual modernity, or a more general theory which uncovers what may be common to settings as diverse as work at a factory bench, farming in a Comilla cooperative, or running a newsstand at a busy intersection.

This challenge to theoretical development is not limited to the changes we observed to follow from occupational experience. It applies as well to the clear evidence that contact with the mass media makes men more modern. Moreover, we still have far to go in explaining just what it is about the process of schooling which makes education the single most powerful variable in explaining individual modernity. In the relevant chapters of this book we have given our views on how these several modernizing forces exert their influence, placing particular emphasis on the concepts of modeling, exemplification, and generalization. But we recognize that the theory remains fragmentary and eclectic. Whether a truly general theory applicable in all circumstances can be devised is an open question. In any event, the development of such a theory is still a task for the future. Our ideas, we believe, certainly incorporate a good part of the truth, but exactly how much of the truth we have captured remains to be seen.

It seems appropriate, at this point, to note that we adopted the approach we took in the face of a persistent challenge, which predicted an outcome totally at variance with the assumption guiding our research. We assumed that individuals would incorporate into their own personal value system the principles predominant in guiding the operation of the institutions in which they were employed. Those who challenged this assumption argued that, on the contrary, traditional men would more likely respond defensively, clinging to their past orientations, or might even react by changing in ways *opposed* to the dominant emphases of the modern institutional system with which they now were coming into contact.

This argument always seemed to us one of the most fundamental of the possible challenges to our theoretical assumptions. Those who were skeptical about our expectations were correct in characterizing us as assuming that most men coming into contact with modernizing institutions for the first time would see them not as threatening or hostile, but rather as either neutral or benign. In any event, we were convinced that the chief mode of response would be an adaptive rather than a rejecting one. We expected men to incorporate into their own values the principles which are explicit or implicit in modern industrial organizations, and to accept as their own the ways of approaching and solving problems which typify rational organizations.

Many of our critics assumed quite the contrary. They predicted that men coming from the traditional sector would experience the modern setting as something deeply alien, and would respond negatively. Examples of such negative reactions would be to cling defensively to one's original values and modes of response, or to react by developing a kind of counter-culture. According to this theory the traditional man, entering the factory and finding it preoccupied with strict schedules and planning ahead, was expected to respond by taking contrary positions in his personal life, as, for example, by favoring loose scheduling and a more spontaneous and unplanned approach to daily living.

Now that our research is completed, we need no longer leave the issue unresolved. We can choose, from the two competing perspectives, the one view which is most in accord with the facts. We interpret the results we obtained as unambiguously establishing the correctness of one assumption over the other. *Insofar as men change under the influence of modernizing institutions they do so by incorporating the norms implicit in such organizations into their own personality, and by expressing those norms through their own attitudes, values, and behavior. In the great majority of cases, they do not respond by moving away from, or reacting against, those norms. The defensive-resistance model does not, at least in our samples, answer to the facts.*

It may be true that only a few men change a great deal. Nevertheless, most men change at least somewhat as a result of their contact with modernizing institutions, and in a direction congruent with the dominant emphases of their new environment. Our men developed values, attitudes, and behavior patterns analogous to the norms reflected in the organization and functioning of the modern institutions. The model which predicts a negative reaction, which expects the new labor force in industrial countries to respond to industrialism by developing a counterculture, is simply wrong. That theory may accurately describe some aspects of the youth culture in the more advanced countries, but it is not supported by the evidence from our samples of workers and farmers in six less-developed nations.[16]

Additional Methodological Issues

There remain a few issues related to measuring the process of individual modernization which we have not dealt with systematically in our presentation. They may be put in the form of simple questions, to which we will essay brief answers.

1. Is the process of modernization continuous and lifelong, or is there a definite plateau that people reach, after which they no longer continue becoming even more modern?

As we noted, most contemporary theories of psychology view the personality as something more or less complete by adulthood, and unlikely to change significantly thereafter. Some variation is recognized, of course, in accord with the particular characteristic under study, but by and large it is widely assumed that there is a biologically given plateau which, for most characteristics, is reached by the age of 20.[17]

Our experience with the OM scale suggests that the process of individual modernization can continue, if not indefinitely at least for a very long time, without any obvious limit being reached. This was most clear in the case of education where, at least up to the twelfth year of school, each year of contact produced pretty much the same increment in OM scores as the year before. The growth curve for modernity rose on the chart in virtually a straight line in every country, without any visible dip in the later years. Indeed, preliminary assessment of the results from our samples of advanced high school and university students indicated that the growth in individual modernity continues through at least the first years in college.

Examination of the curve of growth in modernity for men at different stages of industrial seniority indicates that there, too, the process of modernization is relatively continuous over time. During a span of at least 12 years in the factory, which was generally the maximum seniority of men in our samples, workers continued to become more modern, year by year, the longer they continued in industrial employment. The slope of the curve was, of course, much flatter than for education, because in the factory men learned less, year by year, than in school. There were also more irregularities, and in one or two countries some hint that the process might begin to reverse itself after 12 years. All in all, however, the chart line went uninterruptedly upward. We cannot be sure that becoming increasingly modern is a lifelong process, because our samples cut off at age 35. Up to that age, however, a man in the right institutional setting can experience a continuous process of movement up the modernity scale.

2. Granted that change toward modernity is continuous so long as men remain under the influence of modernizing institutions, what happens to those who lose that contact? Is modernity irreversible, or will such men return to the more traditional mold?

This is, unfortunately, a question we cannot answer on the basis of any substantial empirical evidence.[18] We can only say, therefore, that we believe that becoming modern represents a fairly basic change in personality, and that such changes generally tend to be relatively enduring. How long they endure will, of course, depend on various circumstances, including how persistent the given individual is in preserving his character, how deeply rooted were the modern attitudes and values he had adopted, how much his subsequent experience reinforces his newly acquired traits, and how strong are the countervailing environmental forces working to move him in different directions.

For example, we assume men who leave industry to start their own small shops will probably be among the most modern and, furthermore, that their subsequent experience in entrepreneurial activity will itself further conduce to increasing individual modernization. By contrast, a man who leaves the urban industrial setting to resume both peasant agriculture and the whole set of his traditional role obligations would likely become less modern under the influence of such life conditions. Even this reduction would be relative, however, and would probably still leave the returned migrant much more modern than those of his companions who had never had the benefit of contact with modern institutions outside the village. Thus, a recent study in Ecuador strongly indicated that the men who came back after trying out urban-industrial life were more modern than their compatriots who had never left the village, and anecdotal evidence abounds that such returnees become a force for increased modernization within their home communities.[19]

3. Considering that the modernization process seems to work so consistently in so many different cultural settings, is there then no choice?

Must everyone become modern, and to the same degree?

This issue seems to generate the greatest misunderstanding, and satisfying people with regard to it is most difficult. Dispassionate discussion becomes overshadowed by lurid images of modern science turning out a race of automatons, machine-produced golems who are as uniform and unfeeling as are the products of Detroit's massive assembly lines.

Our image of man's nature is not that of a sponge which must soak up everything with which it comes in contact. In our view individual change toward modernization is a process of interaction between the individual and his social setting. Quite contrary to the conception of men as putty passively taking on whatever shape their environment imposes on them, we see the process of individual modernization as one requiring a basic personal engagement between the individual and his milieu. In this engagement the individual must first selectively perceive the lessons the environment has to teach, and then must willingly undertake to learn them, before any personal change can come about.

If the qualities of industrial organization are truly alien to a man, he will not incorporate them. Moreover, even if he finds an organization to be unthreatening or, better, congenial, a man will not necessarily learn new ways unless he personally has the readiness and the capacity to learn. And even if the environment is benign and the individuals are ready to learn, the process will not work if the environment itself is confusing and the messages it conveys are unclear or even contradictory.

In brief, if the process of modernization were at all like the situation described in Huxley's *Brave New World,* the outcome of our study should have yielded a perfect correlation rather than the much more modest figure it attained. Moreover, *all* the men in our samples should have changed, and all should have become completely modern in short order. Instead, as we know, many did not change at all and most changed only to some degree, so that after years of exposure to the modernizing influences only a modest proportion qualified as truly modern. And these, like all others, became modern with some degree of selectivity, changing fully in some respects but holding to divergent and even traditional views in others, as was the case with Nuril, the modern worker from East Pakistan whose views we described in Chapter 5.

All in all, then, we see little reason to fear that the modernization process threatens to impose on us a deadly, passive, totalitarian uniformity, especially if one keeps in mind that among the most outstanding characteristics of the modern man are his openness to new experience and his readiness for change. Indeed, our data indicate that, at least in the kind of developing country we studied, the more modern men were also the more radical, in the sense that they much more frequently asserted the need for immediate and total transformation of the existing socioeconomic system.[20]

4. Since a whole set of institutions, including the school, the factory, and the mass media, all operated to make our men modern, the question arises: Must a nation be able to bring *all* these forces to bear, and do so simultaneously, in order to stimulate the development of individual modernity?

The issue is a sore one, since the key problem of many underdeveloped countries lies precisely in their lack of schools, factories, and media of mass communication. Our experience suggests that it is not necessary that all, or even most, of the more effective agencies be available and working simultaneously in order to bring about individual modernity. On the contrary, any one modernizing institution seems to be able to operate independently of the others. Moreover, contact with any one modernizing institution evidently can be more or less readily substituted for contact with any other, making allowance for the fact that some institutions are more effective than others. Indeed, the evidence from the Comilla cooperative experiment indicates that, even in quite isolated villages, new forms of social organization can be highly effective in making men modern without the aid of machinery or electronic communication. The means for bringing about greater individual modernization are, therefore, potentially within the reach of even the least-advantaged nations and communities.

5. Does the concept of individual modernity and the measurement of it through the OM scale apply to men, or are the concept and the measure relevant to understanding the characteristics and the situation of women as well?

Our project studied only men solely because of practical considerations arising from the limits on our budget and the concentration of men in the industrial jobs in which we were especially interested. We are firmly convinced that the overwhelming majority of the psychosocial indicators we used to identify the modern man would also discriminate effectively among women. And we are quite certain that the same forces which make men modern — such as education, work in complex organizations, and mass-media exposure — also serve to make women more modern. Of course, some adjustments in the content and scoring of the OM scale might be necessary to make it maximally effective in distinguishing modern from more traditional women, and some influences might play a different role in shaping the modernity of women rather than men. Nevertheless, we believe the pattern which will eventually emerge for women will be broadly similar to that we observed in the case of men. We are given confidence in this assumption by some preliminary evidence already available.[21]

6. Are the individual modernization processes we studied in several developing countries likely to take place also in more advanced industrial and postindustrial societies?

Our answer is "yes." Societal modernization is always a matter of degree. Even the most highly developed nations have more and less modern portions of their populations, according to differences in exposure to modernizing experiences. In the United States, we would expect the forces which make men modern to have their most dramatic impact on immigrants from less-developed countries, on rural subsistence farmers who leave their farms, and dropouts who leave school, in order to enter industry, and on members of disadvantaged minority groups. In general, however, we believe that the same qualities which are summed up in the OM scale would distinguish the more from the less modern individuals in the industrialized countries, and that the same forces which made individuals modern in our samples would emerge as important causes of modernity in the economically advanced countries.[22]

The Social Significance of Individual Modernization

To a social psychologist, it is gratifying, indeed it is an activity sufficient unto itself, to be able to measure individual modernity, and to show how far and in what ways schooling and jobs bring about increased modernity scores. But the more pragmatic among our readers, and not only those from the developing countries, are likely to ask: "Is this purely an academic exercise? In particular, does it have any practical contribution to make to national development? Are not attitude and value changes rather ephemeral and peripheral? Can you give us any evidence that all this has much to do with the real problem of underdevelopment?"

In response, we affirm that our research has produced ample evidence that the attitude and value changes defining individual modernity are accompanied by changes in behavior precisely of the sort which we believe give meaning to, and support, those changes in political and economic institutions which lead to the modernization of nations.

We were able to document most extensively those behavioral changes accompanying attitudinal modernization in the realm of political and civic action. The modern man more often took an interest in political affairs, he kept informed and could identify important political events and personalities, he often contacted governmental and political agencies, more often joined organizations, more often voted — and all these by large margins. He was in every way a more active participant citizen of his society.[23]

It seems obvious to us that these are precisely the qualities one needs in the citizen of a modern polity. The introduction of modern political institutions imported from outside, or imposed from above by elites, tends to be an empty gesture unless there are active, interested, informed citizens who can make the institutions really work. And, as we have seen, such citizens are the more modern men shaped by the modernizing institutions we have identified, namely, the school, the newspaper, and the factory.

Beyond politics, the modern man showed himself to perform differently from the more traditional man in many realms of action having practical bearing on the process of societal modernization. The more modern man is quicker to adopt technical innovation, and more ready to implement birth-control measures; he urges his son to go as far as he can in school, and, if it pays better, encourages him to accept industrial work rather than to follow the more traditional penchant for office jobs; he informs himself about the goods produced in the more modern sector of the economy, and makes an effort to acquire them; and he permits his wife and daughter to leave the home for more active participation in economic life. In these and a host of other ways, only some of which we have documented, the man who is more modern in attitude and value acts to support modern institutions and to facilitate the general modernization of society.

While it was important to show that men who were more modern in attitude and value also acted in more modern ways, we feel it even more important to challenge the assumption that a "mere" change in attitudes and values cannot in itself be a truly important factor in the process of national development.

In saying this we are not espousing some form of naïve psychological determinism. We are not unaware that a modern psychology cannot alone make a nation modern. We fully understand that to be modern a nation must have modern institutions, effective government, efficient production, and adequate social services. And we recognize full well that there may be structural obstacles to such development stemming not only from nature, but from social, political, and economic causes as well. Narrow class interests, colonial oppression, rapacious great powers, international cartels, domestic monopolies, archaic and corrupted governments, tribal antagonisms, and religious and ethnic prejudices, to name but a few, are among the many objective forces which we know may act to impede modernization.

Nevertheless, we believe a change in attitudes and values to be one of the most essential preconditions for substantial and effective functioning of those modern institutions which most of the more "practical" programs of development hope to establish. Our experience leads us to agree with many of the intellectual leaders of the third world who argue that, in good part, underdevelopment is a state of mind.[24] It is admittedly difficult with presently available techniques and information to establish the case scientifically, but we are convinced that mental barriers and psychic factors are key obstacles to more effective economic and social development in many countries.

The technology which is, perhaps, the most distinctive ingredient of

modernity can be borrowed by and established in developing countries
with relative ease. Machinery is influenced by temperature and humidity,
but it is otherwise immune to culture shock. Although they travel less well,
political, economic, and cultural institutions can also be relatively easily
imitated in their totality. Systems of taxation and of voter registration,
and even political party systems, are regularly copied from the more advanced countries by those in the earlier stages of development. Patterns
of factory management, forms of administration for business and government, new faculties, research institutions, indeed whole universities are
being created every day in the developing countries as copies of institutions
and procedures originating in the more developed countries.

How many of these transplanted institutions actually take root and
bear fruit in their new setting is not precisely known. But the experience
of almost everyone who has worked extensively on problems of development is replete with examples of the failure of such transplantation. The
disappointment of high hopes and aspirations is endemic among those who
have attempted such transplanting, and the hollow shells of the institutions,
sometimes transformed into grotesque caricatures of their original design,
sometimes barely functioning, often standing altogether abandoned, can be
found strewn about in almost any developing country in which one chooses
to travel.

In the explanations which are offered for this situation, one hears again
and again the echo of one basic refrain: "The people were not ready for
it yet." When one probes this generalization, it quickly becomes apparent
that the material resources, the manuals for repair and maintenance, the
charts and tables for organization, the guidelines for administration which
accompanied the transplanted institutions were meaningless without the
support of an underlying and widespread pattern of culture and personality which could breathe life into the otherwise sterile forms and give
human meaning and continuity to their activity.

In the last analysis, the successful functioning of these institutions was
critically dependent on the availability of individuals who could bring to
the job certain special personal qualities. These new institutions required
people who could accept and discharge responsibility without constant
close supervision, could manifest mutual trust and confidence in co-
workers which extended beyond the situations in which one could keep
them under direct surveillance, could subordinate the special interests of
one's clique or parochial group to the goals of the larger organization,
could be flexible and imaginative in the interpretation of rules, could
show sympathetic consideration for the feelings of subordinates and openness to their ideas and other potential contributions. These, and a host
of other personal qualities requisite to running a complex modern institution effectively, are not in excess supply in any society. In many of the

developing countries, moreover, people possessed of the requisite qualities are actually scarce. And in some cases, the small set of individuals
who possess the qualities necessary for effectively running the new institutions are either not called upon, or may even be socially ineligible,
for service in those roles in which they could be most useful.

Such conditions in the institutions of national standing have their precise analogue in the more commonplace situation of individuals engaged
in very modest pursuits, within purely local and parochial settings. In
such settings we find most widely diffused the qualities our research has
identified as characteristic of the traditional man: passive acceptance of
fate and a general lack of efficacy; fear of innovation and distrust of the
new; isolation from the outside world and lack of interest in what goes on
in it; dependence on traditional authority and the received wisdom of
elders and religious and customary leaders; preoccupation with personal
and especially family affairs to the exclusion of community concerns; exclusive identification with purely local and parochial primary groups,
coupled to feelings of isolation from and fear of larger regional and
national entities; the shaping and damping of ambition to fit narrow goals,
and the cultivation of humble sentiments of gratitude for what little one
has; rigid, hierarchical relations with subordinates and others of low
social status; and undervaluing of education, learning, research, and other
concerns not obviously related to the practical business of earning one's
daily bread.

Of course, not all these qualities are prevalent in all traditional settings,
and they are unequally distributed among the men in them. Yet they are
extremely common in individuals, and exceptionally pervasive across
cultures and settings, in the countries of the less-developed world.

We must acknowledge that some of these qualities of the traditional
man facilitate his adaptation to life. Such qualities help men to make a
successful adjustment to the real conditions which exist in, and indeed
pervade, their life space. But those qualities also tend to freeze people
into the situations and positions in which they are now find themselves,
and this, in turn, serves to preserve the outmoded, indeed archaic, and
often oppressive institutions which hold the people in their grip. To break
out of that iron grip requires, among other things, that people become
modern in spirit, that they adopt and incorporate into their personalities
the attitudes, values, and modes of acting which we have identified
with the modern man. Without this ingredient neither foreign aid nor
domestic revolution can hope successfully to bring an underdeveloped
nation into the ranks of those capable of self-sustained growth.

Economists define modernity in terms of gross national product per
capita, and political scientists in terms of effective institutions for governance. We are of the opinion that neither rapid economic growth nor

effective government can develop, or, if introduced, will be long sustained, without the widespread diffusion in the rank and file of the population of those qualities we have identified as those of the modern man. In the conditions of the contemporary world, the qualities of individual modernity are not a luxury, they are a necessity. They are not a marginal gain, derived from the process of institutional modernization, but are rather a precondition for the long-term success of those institutions. Diffusion through the population of the qualities of the modern man is not incidental to the process of social development, it is the essence of national development itself.

Appendices
Bibliography
Notes
Index

Appendix A
The Questionnaire

PART I. Item Content of OM-1, OM-2, and OM-3

The following set of questions represent the items which comprise the scale called OM-3. These items were selected from the main project questionnaire according to the criteria mentioned in Chapter 6. Inevitably the number and content of items varied slightly from country to country. In some countries the questions could not be used exactly as given here, in which case the field director adapted them to local conditions. Words in parentheses represent alternative expressions which were found to be more appropriate for some settings. Words and phrases in brackets indicate the *type* of expression called for in the question, requiring the field director's discretion in providing the appropriate expression according to the cultural context. For example, the alternative to question AS-3 which here reads, "To read [a holy book, e.g., Koran or Bible] and learn other religious activities," in Chile was simply rendered, "To read the Bible and learn other religious activities."

Although the questions listed here are slight condensations of the questions as they appeared on the project questionnaire, they remain essentially unchanged. Instructions to the interviewer appear in small capitals. For scaling purposes some of the questions were given multiple codings, that is, they yielded more than one item or unit in calculating the OM score. This was the case, for example, when a question was used to measure both verbal fluency (a behavioral item) and attitudes toward change (a basic attitudinal item). In cases where multiple codings were used, the bases for these codings were given following the expression coded for.

The coefficient in parentheses which accompanies each item represents the median correlation of the item to OM-3 across the six countries, adjusted for autocorrelation. In some cases two and even three questions were collapsed into one item, so that there is only one coefficient shared by the bracketed questions. In cases of multiple coding for single questions, coefficients corresponding to each coding are given.

The x's in the three columns on the left indicate in which of the OM scales the various items were included. As indicated in Chapter 6, all items in OM-1 (the core attitude scale) were also included in OM-2 (an expanded attitude scale). The x's in the second column, therefore, identify only those questions added to OM-1 to form OM-2. To these attitudinal items were added some 50 or so behavioral and informational items, here called BI. All items together comprise the "maximum scale," OM-3.

In order to facilitate interpretation, the following key to themal codes is included:

AC	Active public participation	KO	Kinship obligations
AS	Aspirations (educational and	MM	Mass media
	occupational)	NE	New experience
AG	Aging and the aged	OP	Optimism
CA	Calculability	PA	Particularism
CH	Change orientation	PL	Planning
CI	Citizenship	RE	Religion
CO	Consumption attitudes	SC	Social-class stratification
DI	Dignity	TI	Time valuation
EF	Efficacy	TS	Technical-skill valuation
FS	Family size	UN	Understanding
GO	Growth of opinion	WC	Work commitment
ID	Identification with nation	WR	Women's rights
IN	Information		

OM-1	OM-2	BI	Code and Number	Question
		x	AC-1 (.27)	Do you belong to any organizations (associations, clubs), such as, for example, social clubs, unions, church organizations, political groups, or other groups? Yes / No
		x	AC-2 (.22)	If "Yes" to AC-1; what are the names of all the organizations you belong to? *Coded for number of organizations*
		x	AC-3 (.16)	If "Yes" to AC-1; which of these organizations takes a stand on political or public issues such as [a current issue supplied by interviewer]? *Coded for number of organizations*
		x	AC-4 (.18)	Have you ever talked to or written to some government official or political leader to tell him your opinion on some public issue, such as what the government should do about [a current issue supplied by interviewer]?
		x	AC-5 (.14)	How many times have you voted during the past [ ] years? _____
	x		AC-6 (.30)	Have you ever (thought over so much) gotten so highly concerned (involved) regarding some pub-

OM-1	OM-2	BI	Code and Number	Question
				lic issue, such as [a current issue supplied by interviewer]? Frequently / Few times / Never
x	x		AG-2 (.11)	Some people say that a boy learns the deepest and most profound truth from old people. Others say that a boy learns the most profound truth from books and in school. What is your opinion? Most truth from old people / About equal truth from both / Most truth from books and school
	x		AG-3 (.09)	Some people look forward to old age with pleasure, while others dread the coming of old age. How do you personally feel about the coming of old age? Look forward with pleasure / Indifferent or neutral / Dread old age
x	x		AS-1 (.26)	If schooling is freely available (if there were no kinds of obstacles) how much schooling (reading and writing) do you think children (the son) of people like yourself should have? *Coded for number of years*
		x	AS-2 (.15)	What good is an education for an ordinary man? _____ AFTER R ANSWERS SPONTANEOUSLY, USE SINGLE PROBE: What else is it good for? _____ _____
x	A		AS-3 (.12)	Suppose a man has a young son about to begin school. The man is too poor to keep his son in school for more than a few years. Here are some subjects the boy might study in school. Which subject do you think is *most* important for the boy to learn? 1. To learn to read and write [local language, e.g., Bengali] very well 2. To read [a holy book, e.g., Koran or Bible] and learn other religious activities 3. To learn some useful trade, like how to repair modern machines
x	x		AS-4	And which is second in importance for the boy to learn? _____
			AS-5	What in your opinion is the best occupation a person of your experience and ability can hope for? OBTAIN SPECIFIC JOB TITLE. *Coded for:*
		x	(.25)	1. Absolute status level
x	x		(.18)	2. Level relative to respondent
			AS-6	Why is that? _____ *Coded for:*
		x	(.13)	1. Number of themes

OM-1	OM-2	BI	Code and Number	Question
		x	(.13)	2. Number of subthemes
		x	(.12)	3. Number of words
			AS-7	Suppose a man is economically well off and has a son. What is the best line of work he may encourage his son to follow? _____ *Coded for:*
		x	(.20)	1. Job classification
x	x		(.17)	2. Level of occupational aspiration
x	x		AS-8 (.13)	Some people say that the more schooling a person gets the better off he is. Others say that if a man has a good head, he does not need much schooling. What is your opinion?
x	x		AS-9 (.10)	A poor cultivator has only one son, aged 10 years, and greatly needs this son's full-time help in cultivation so the family will be able to raise enough food to eat (well). But the son wishes to continue to attend school rather than working fulltime. What should the father decide on this question? IF R SAYS "BOTH," ASK: Which should the son give his main attention to? Work for father / Continue in school
x	x		AS-10 (.08)	Some people say that a son should try to find a better type of work than his father does. Others say that a son should usually be proud to follow the same work as his father. What is your opinion?
x	x		CA-3 (.12)	There are many things a man wants in those he works with. Which of the following things would you say is most important in fellow workers? That they be friendly and good companions / Reliable, fulfilling their share of the work / Men of good character, respected in the community
x	x		CA-6 (.05)	When you meet someone for the first time, what should you do? Trust him until he proves to be not worthy of that trust / Be cautious about trusting him until you know him better / Not trust him because he may take advantage of you
	x		CA-7 (.08)	Some people say if your relatives know all about your private affairs they may take advantage of you. What is your opinion? There is a good chance they will take advantage of you / Little chance / No chance
	x		CA-8 (.08)	On the whole, when you buy from merchants do you feel you get honest weight and goods which have not been adulterated? Always / Most of the time / Only at times / Never

OM-1	OM-2	BI	Code and Number	Question
x	x		CA-11 (.10)	Some say it is a great burden for a mere boy to be responsible and reliable all the time. Others say he must be taught always to be responsible and reliable even if it is a great burden (very difficult). In your opinion, how often should one excuse a boy who is sometimes irresponsible? Always (excuse him) / Most times / Few times / Never (excuse him)
x			CH-1 (.13)	In your line of work, do you find that things remain the same from year to year, or is there much change in how things are done, with the bringing in of new machines, tools (seeds, fertilizers), and ways of working? Would you say in your work from year to year things: Stay exactly the same / Mostly stay the same / Change much / Change very much
			CH-2	You said that in your work things _____ READ R'S CHOICE FROM CH-1. 1. Now some people consider that an advantage 2. Some think it is a disadvantage 3. Some say it does not matter 4. Some say they never thought about it What do you say?
x	x		CH-3 (.20)	Two 12-year-old boys took time out from their work in the corn (rice) fields. They were trying to figure out a way to grow the same amount of corn (rice) with fewer hours of work. 1. The father of one boy said: "That is a good thing to think about. Tell me your thoughts about how we should change our ways of growing corn (rice)." 2. The father of the other boy said: "The way to grow corn (rice) is the way we have always done it. Talk about change will waste time but not help." Which father said the wiser words?
	x		CH-4 (.01)	These days one often hears people say the old ways are slipping away and many things are changing. Others say that things are holding fast as they used to be. We would like to have your opinion on this question: Do you think the amount of respect young people show to old people is changing: Not at all / Only a little / Quite a lot / Very rapidly
			CH-5	How do you feel about that? Is it (the change): Too fast / Too slow / Just right

OM-1	OM-2	BI	Code and Number	Question
	x		CH-6 (.12)	How about the freedom of women to do things like [working outside the home]? Is that: Changing rapidly / Changing slowly / Not changing at all
			CH-7	How do you feel about that? Is the change: Too fast / Too slow / Just right
	x		CH-8 (.05)	How about the opportunities for a poor man to improve his economic condition? Are these opportunities: Increasing greatly / Increasing somewhat / Decreasing somewhat / Decreasing greatly / Remaining the same
	x		CH-9 (.08)	Some say that the opportunities a boy has to get educated are increasing. Others say they do not see much change in this. What is your opinion? Are a young man's opportunities to get educated: Increasing greatly (rapidly) / Increasing somewhat / Remaining the same / Decreasing
	x		CH-10 (.04)	Would you say that religion is holding its own or that its influence on people is getting weaker? Is the hold of religion: Increasing somewhat / Holding steady / Decreasing somewhat / Decreasing much
			CH-11	How do you feel about that? Approve / Disapprove / Feel neutral
	x		CH-12 (.07)	Would you say that how much attention the government pays to the views of the ordinary man is: Increasing rapidly / Increasing somewhat / Decreasing somewhat / Decreasing greatly / Remaining the same
			CH-13	How do you feel about that? Is it: A good thing / A bad thing / Neither good nor bad
x	x		CH-14 (.06)	Some people say that a boy should be taught to prefer the old, traditional ways of doing things. Others say a boy should be taught to prefer the new and modern ways of doing things. What should a boy be taught to prefer? Only new ways and things / Mainly the new ways and things / Mainly the traditional ways and things / Only the traditional ways and things
			CI-2	If a law that you considered unjust or harmful was under discussion by your (national parliament, or city or village council), what do you think you could do about it?

OM-1	OM-2	BI	Code and Number	Question
				Coded for:
		x	(.21)	1. Number of words
x	x		(.29)	2. Action, Inaction
	x		CI-7	Suppose there was a difference in advice given by two important sides as to what you should think on an important public issue.
			(.22)	Whose advice would you give most weight to if: 1. The religious leaders gave one advice, and 2. The government gave another
	x		CI-8 (.12)	1. And if your political party gave one advice, and 2. Your tribal council (or boss) gave another
	x		CI-9 (.19)	1. Your trade (workers) union gave one advice, and 2. Your extended family council (leader) gave another
x	x		CI-13 (.19)	What should most qualify a man to hold high office? Coming from (right, distinguished, or high) family background / Devotion to the old and (revered) time-honored ways / Being the most popular among the people / High education and special knowledge
	x		CI-14 (.16)	Three men each come with a petition (request) to a government official, but unfortunately only one petition can be granted. 1. One man has the most right according to the law 2. One man is a friend of an influential leader 3. One man is very poor and has the most need Which one petition ought the official to grant?
		x	CO-1 (.39)	Now I would like to ask you about some of the goods (things) people have or may want in the future. PRESENT PICTURE OF (TRANSISTOR) RADIO Here is a picture. Can you tell me what is in this picture? Correctly names "radio" / Don't know / Other (specify)
		x	CO-2 (.32)	What is in this picture? PRESENT PICTURE OF (MOVIE) CAMERA Correctly names "camera" / Don't know / Other (specify)
x	x		CO-4 (.10)	PRESENT PICTURE OF RADIO AGAIN TO THOSE WHO DO NOT OWN ONE Is this something you would like to own: Very much / Somewhat / Not at all

OM-1	OM-2	BI	Code and Number	Question
x	x		CO-5 (.17)	PRESENT PICTURE OF (MOVIE) CAMERA AGAIN Is this something you would like to own: Very much / Somewhat / Not at all
x	x		CO-6 (.12)	SHOW AGAIN PICTURES PREVIOUSLY USED Do you think most of your countrymen will own things like this in 30 years? Yes / No
			CO-7	What other things besides those in the pictures would you very much like to own? DO NOT PROBE OR ENCOURAGE RESPONSES, BUT SIMPLY RECORD EACH ITEM MENTIONED SPONTANEOUSLY — *Coded for:*
		x	(.23)	1. Number of consumption or production items
		x	(.08)	2. Number of production items
		x	(.22)	3. Number of consumption and production items
		x	(.18)	4. Number of consumption items
		x	(.11)	5. Number of high-cost items
		x	(.21)	6. Number of additional items
	x		CO-8 (.13)	Suppose an ordinary man has a good house and can feed and clothe his family well enough. 1. Some people would say that this is enough—that no good can come from always chasing after more and more things to buy 2. Other people would say that a man should always strive to make more money, so that he can buy more, better, and different things Which of these opinions do you agree with?
	x		CO-9 (−.14)	1. Some people say that the more things a man possesses—like new clothes, furniture, and conveniences—the happier he is 2. Others say that a man's happiness depends upon other things beyond these What is your opinion?
	x		DI-5 (−.06)	Suppose your job was changed to that of supervising a group of men in the factory. You are supposed to keep production up at a high level. If one of the men you were supervising made a mistake causing a big loss, how would you talk to him about his mistake? Bawl him out good and loud / Criticize him sharply but quietly / Criticize him mildly
x	x		DI-6 (.06)	If a housewife spends more than the family income allows her to, and this is not the first time it has happened nor the first time he has called it to her attention, what should the husband do?

OM-1	OM-2	BI	Code and Number	Question
				Beat her / Bawl her out severely / Give her a good talking to / Just call it to her attention again
x	x		DI-7 (.03)	There are different opinions about how much one needs to respect the dignity of a boy between about 10 and 12 years of age as against that of an adult man. Which of the following is more correct, in your opinion, regarding a boy's dignity: It is less important than a man's / As important as a man's / More important than a man's
x	x		DI-8 (.18)	Suppose your country was attacked by another country. Your country wins the war. How should you treat the defeated people? *Coded for severity of treatment*
x	x		DI-9 (.08)	A husband finds that his wife has spent some of their very limited savings on an expensive ornament. He is very angry because he had been saving the money for seed, and upbraids (scolds) his wife, saying how wasteful and foolish she is. If the neighbors hear this scolding of the wife, how do you think they will react? They probably will applaud the husband for teaching his wife a lesson / They probably will not like seeing the husband make his wife so unhappy
	x		DI-10 (.11)	Suppose a factory worker makes a grave mistake which causes a big loss. His supervisor finds out about the mistake and loudly berates the worker in front of the other workers. How do you think the other workers would react to this? They would not pay any attention since it is not their problem / They would feel sorry for the mistaken worker and angry at the supervisor
x	x		DI-11 (.17)	Some people say a boy should be taught always to take into consideration the feelings of others. Others say a boy should be taught to protect his own feelings since others can look out for themselves. Should one teach a boy to protect first: ASK FIRST "OWN" VS. "OTHERS"; THEN ASK FOR DEGREE BEFORE RECORDING HIS OWN FEELINGS: All the time / Most of the time OTHERS' FEELINGS: All the time / Most of the time

OM-1	OM-2	BI	Code and Number	Question
x	x		EF-1 (.14)	Some say that a man born into a poor family will not better his condition even if he is ambitious and hard working. Do you think such a man: Will surely fail to get ahead / Will probably fail / Will probably succeed / Will surely succeed
x	x		EF-2 (.21)	Some say that accidents are due mainly to bad luck. Others say accidents can be prevented by sufficient care. Do you think prevention of accidents depends: Entirely on luck / Mainly on luck / Mainly on carefulness / Entirely on carefulness
x	x		EF-3 (.27)	Some say that getting ahead in life depends on destiny. Others say that it depends on the person's own efforts. Do you think the position a man reaches in life depends more on fate or more on one's own efforts? ON FATE: Entirely / Only partly ON OWN EFFORTS: Entirely / Only partly
x	x		EF-4 (.17)	A boy was fated *not* to succeed. But he was very intelligent, capable, hard working, and eager to succeed. Despite what may be fated, do you think he could succeed? Completely / Only partly / Not at all
	x		EF-5 (−.04)	Some people say that we [the local population, e.g., Chileans] are great dreamers (big talkers) but we do not accomplish (do) very much. Do you think this statement: Is absolutely true / Has much truth in it / Is not correct at all
x	x		EF-7 (.13)	In your opinion could a detailed plan be worked out whereby [local social groups, e.g., different tribes of Nigeria] could get along together peacefully? No / Yes / Perhaps
x	x		EF-8 (.25)	Some people like work in which there are many times when a man must face hard decisions. Others prefer work in which it is not necessary to make many hard decisions. What kind of job would you prefer? One requiring: Many decisions / Only a few decisions / No decisions at all
x	x		EF-9 (.09)	To improve the condition of life in this community some say the people must get together to help themselves. Others say that it will require the help of the government. What do you think?

OM-1	OM-2	BI	Code and Number	Question
				To improve this community should the people rely: On themselves alone / Mainly on themselves / Mainly on the government / On the government alone
x	x		EF-11 (.36)	Which is most important for the future of [the country of R]? WRITE #1 NEXT TO R'S CHOICE The hard work of the people / Good planning on the part of the government / God's help / Good luck
			EF-12	Which is the second most important? WRITE #2 NEXT TO R'S CHOICE _____
x	x		EF-13 (.24)	Which of the following statements do you agree with more? 1. Some people say that man will some day fully understand what causes such things as floods, droughts, and epidemics 2. Others say that such things can never fully be understood by man
x	x		EF-14 (.27)	Learned men (scholars, scientists) in the universities are studying such things as what determines whether a baby is a boy or girl and how it is that a seed turns into a plant Do you think that these investigations (studies) are: All very good (beneficial) / All somewhat good (beneficial) / All somewhat harmful / All very harmful
x	x		EF-15 (.13)	People sometimes disagree about whether human nature can be changed or not. What is your opinion? Human nature can be changed for the better / It can change, but probably for the worse / It will always be (remain) the same
x	x		EF-16 (.14)	Some say that a boy should be "easy going," and accept things as they come along. Others say that a boy should always be striving to overcome obstacles as they arise. In your opinion should one teach a boy: To accept all things as they come / To accept most things as they come / To try to overcome most obstacles / To try to overcome all obstacles
x	x		FS-1 (.14)	What do you think is the best number of children for a man like you to have during your lifetime? *Coded for number of children mentioned*

OM-1	OM-2	BI	Code and Number	Question
	x		FS-2 (.07)	Suppose you could well provide for and educate all the children you might have. How many would you want in that case? The same number / One or two more / Even more than that
x	x		FS-3 (.25)	Some people say that it is necessary for a man and his wife to limit the number of children to be born so they can take better care of those they do have (already have). Others say that it is wrong for a man and wife purposely (voluntarily) to limit the number of children to be born. Which of these opinions do you agree with more?
x	x		FS-4 (.21)	A man and his wife have several children. This is as many as they can afford. They do not want any more. Suppose a doctor could give the wife a new kind of pill which would prevent having more children but would not otherwise change her in any way. Would it be right for her to take such a pill / Would it be wrong
	x		FS-5 (.15)	Suppose the government of (the country) recommended to people to limit the size of their families, and showed them how to do it. Should people then follow this advice? Yes / No
	x		FS-6 (.09)	Suppose a husband and wife agreed that they wanted to act voluntarily to limit the number of children they would have. Should the responsibility to see that they carried through their plan fall: Mainly to the husband / Mainly to the wife / Equally to both
			GO-1	Would you tell me what are the biggest problems you see facing your [community, city, village, i.e., type of community in which R lives]? *Coded for:*
		x	(.22)	1. Number of themes
		x	(.27)	2. Number of subthemes and themes
		x	(.21)	3. Number of words
			GO-2	Would you tell me what are the biggest problems you see facing [country of R]? *Coded for:*
		x	(.29)	1. Number of themes
		x	(.33)	2. Number of subthemes and themes
		x	(.23)	3. Number of words

OM-1	OM-2	Bl	Code and Number	Question
x	x		GO-3 (.06)	If we had a female interviewer talk with your wife, do you think your wife would have: The same opinions as you do / Some opinions different from yours / Many opinions different from yours
x	x		GO-4 (.08)	Suppose we talked with other men in this community: Would many have opinions different from yours / A few have opinions different from yours / All have much the same opinions as you do
x	x		GO-5 (.12)	On most matters: 1. Do you think we ought to let the husband speak for his whole family, or 2. Should we be sure to get the wife's opinions also?
x	x		GO-6 (.16)	Suppose we talked to the other men in your town, how much attention should we pay to the common man as against the leaders? Most attention to what the ordinary people of the town say / Equal attention to what the people and the leaders say / Most attention to what the leaders of the town say
x	x		GO-7 (.02)	Some people say a boy should not insist on his own opinion if his group disagrees with him. Others say that a boy should hold to his own opinion even if the whole group disagrees with him. In the face of disagreement by his group, should you teach a boy: Always to go along with the group / Most times to go along with the group / Most times to hold to his own opinion / Always to hold to his own opinion
x	x		ID-1 (.25)	Do you consider yourself first and foremost a (an): [name of nationality, e.g., American / regional or tribal name, e.g., Yankee / state identification, e.g., Massachusetts resident / local town or village identification, e.g., Bostonian]
x	x		ID-2 (−.00)	Suppose a national leader and a local leader disagreed about what should be done about some public issue. Which leader would you feel the greater moral obligation to obey? National leader / Local leader
	x		ID-3 (.09)	In your opinion, to which of the following has a man a greater obligation?

OM-1	OM-2	BI	Code and Number	Question
				ASK THE TWO ITALICIZED ALTERNATIVES FIRST: THEN ASK THE CORRESPONDING TWO NUMBERED SUBALTERNATIVES
				His society or nation: 1. In all circumstances 2. In most circumstances *His own family:* 1. In all circumstances 2. In most circumstances
		x	IN-1 (.39)	Now I would like to ask you about some people who have been in the news recently (important people). Would you tell me who is Lyndon Johnson? Country and office correct / Country only / Office only / Neither
		x	IN-2 (.45)	Would you tell me who is Nehru? Country and office correct / Country only / Office only / Don't know
		x	IN-2x (.39)	Would you tell me who is [some leading national figure nearly everyone would know, e.g., president, prime minister]? Country and office correct / Country only / Office only / Don't know
		x	IN-3 (.43)	Would you tell me who is [a well-known current national political figure]? Correct country and position / Correct position but country only approximately right / Correct position only
		x	IN-4 (.37)	Would you tell me who is [a relatively little–known national political figure]? Country and office correct / Country only / Office only / Don't know
		x	IN-4x (.24)	Would you tell me who is [a national figure almost everyone would know, but not same as in IN-2x]? Country and office correct / Country only / Office only / Don't know
		x	IN-5 (.42)	Now I would like to ask you where certain places are. First of all, where is [a distant, moderately well-known city within R's country]? Correct country and region / Correct country only / Don't know
		x	IN-6 (.42)	Where is (in what country is the city of) Washington? U.S. / Don't know
		x	IN-7 (.46)	Where is (in what country is the city of) Moscow? Russia or Soviet Union / Don't know
		x	IN-7x (.24)	Where is [an easy city, e.g., Santiago in Chile]? Correct / Incorrect

OM-1	OM-2	B1	Code and Number	Question
	x		KO-1 (.13)	To whom should a man feel closest? To his wife / To his mother (father, brother)
x	x		KO-2 (.21)	If a man must choose between a job which he likes or a job which his parents prefer for him, which should he choose? The job he prefers / The job his parents prefer
	x		KO-3 (.01)	Suppose a young man works in a factory. He has barely managed to save a very small amount of money. Now his first cousin comes to him and tells him that he needs money badly since he has no work at all. How much obligation do you think the factory worker has to share his savings with his first cousin? A strong obligation / A not so strong obligation / No obligation
	x		KO-4 (−.03)	Now suppose in the story I told you it was not his first cousin but a distant cousin who came to the factory worker and said he had no money. How much obligation do you think the factory worker has to share his savings with his distant cousin? A strong obligation / A not so strong obligation / No obligation
x	x		KO-6 (.05)	Some people say that a boy should be taught to give preference to a friend or relative, even when others have a more rightful claim. Others say a boy should be taught not to break an important rule even for a friend or relative. Do you think a boy should be taught to give preference to a friend or relative: Always / Usually / Sometimes / Rarely (or never)
x	x		MM-6 (.25)	Which two sources of information do you trust most in finding out the news about what goes on in the world? Coded for type of source, i.e., religious leader, friend, radio, newspaper, etc.
x	x		MM-7 (.13)	Which of the following would you trust (rely on) more to give the truth about a local event: Your newspaper (or radio station) / A close friend
			MM-8	Would you tell me the name of some books? _____ Coded for:
		x	(.37)	1. Names of books
		x	(.28)	2. Kinds of books mentioned
x	x		MM-9 (.06)	All things considered, do you think that the (moral) influence of (foreign) movies on the peo-

OM-1	OM-2	BI	Code and Number	Question
				ple (of this country) is good, bad, or neither good nor bad?
				(Foreign) movies are a:
				Good influence / Neither good nor bad influence / Bad influence
			MM-10 (.27)	Which one of these (following) kinds of news interests you most?
				Your home town (or village) / World events (happenings in other countries) / The nation / Sports / Religious (or tribal, cultural) events (ceremonies) or festivals
x	x		MM-11	Which is second in interest for you? _____
			MM-12	Which is next most of interest for you? _____
x	x		NE-1 (.11)	Suppose you could get along well enough (where you are now), earning enough to provide food and other necessities for yourself and your family. Would you be willing to move to another place far from here where the language and other customs are different, if you could live twice as well there?
				Move / Stay
x	x		NE-2 (.21)	Suppose you met a man who was very different from yourself. He was born in a different region (or country), his customs are very strange, he has a different way of talking, and even a different religion, but he seems friendly.
				1. Would you wish to get to know him well, or
				2. Would you just as soon not
x	x		NE-3 (.20)	Do you like to meet (enjoy meeting) new people or would you just as soon (prefer to) spend your time with people you already know?
				Meet new people / Prefer people already known
x	x		NE-4 (.25)	There are some men who are so much like you that you can easily understand their ways of thinking. There may be other men who differ from you so much that it is really hard to understand their ways of thinking.
				Now consider [an adherent to a religion different from that of R, e.g., a Moslem]. Could you easily understand his way of thinking?
				Yes / No
x	x		NE-5 (.29)	If you were to meet a person who lives in another country a long way off (thousands of kilometers/ miles away), could you understand his way of thinking?
				Yes / No
			NE-6	What is the longest trip you have ever made as an adult?

OM-1	OM-2	BI	Code and Number	Question
				From _____ To _____
				Coded for:
		x	(.16)	1. Number of kilometers/miles
		x	(.17)	2. Relative location of destination, e.g., next state, neighboring country, etc.
	x		NE-7	Which of the following is more true of you?
			(.18)	1. I would prefer to live my life in the village (the country) 'with only occasional visits to the big city.
				2. I would prefer to live my life in the big city with only occasional visits to the country or small towns.
			PL-1	I know a man who does not worry (think) about what he will need to do in the days ahead; he just counts on being able to do each task as it comes up. What would you feel about this man?
				Coded for:
	x		(.09)	1. Approval / Disapproval
		x	(.11)	2. Number of words
x	x		PL-3 (.14)	In comparison with a man who just takes things as they come, do you think a man who plans and arranges things in advance will have: Many less difficulties and problems / Somewhat less difficulties and problems / The same number of difficulties and problems
x	x		PL-4 (.18)	People are different in how much they like to plan and arrange their affairs (lives) in advance. Would you say that you yourself prefer: To plan ahead carefully in most matters / To plan ahead only on a few matters / More to let things come without worrying (too much) ahead
	x		PL-5 (.01)	Men do not agree on the importance (weight) to give the different qualities (characteristics) of women in choosing a wife. Would you advise a young man choosing a wife to consider: Beauty more important than running the house well / Both the same / Running the house well a little bit more important than beauty / Running the house well much more important than beauty
x	x		PL-9 (.02)	Some people say a boy should be taught to handle things as they come up without bothering much about thinking ahead. Others say a boy must be taught to plan and arrange things in advance. What do you think a boy should be taught? To handle all things as they come up / To take most things as they come up / To try to plan

OM-1	OM-2	BI	Code and Number	Question
				most things ahead / To try to plan all things ahead
		x	RE-5 (.18)	(Generally) how often during a day do you pray? _____ times a day
		x	RE-6 (.10)	Do you fast during the time of fasting of your faith? Absolutely without fail / Most of the time / Occasionally / Never
		x	RE-7 (.17)	How frequently do you attend church (mosque)? _____
	x		RE-8 (.19)	There are two sons of an old and noble family, both of whom wanted to help their country. One set out to be a holy man (monk). He gave up all his worldly possessions in order to go about the country showing the path to the good and religious life. The other son set out to establish a great textile mill (factory). His factory gave work to hundreds of his countrymen (all of whom he treated fairly) and also produced inexpensive goods that many people needed. Which of these two men do you personally admire more: Holy man / Factory owner / Both, equally / Neither
x	x		RE-9 (.17)	Which in your opinion has done more for his country: Holy man / Factory owner / Both, equally / Neither
	x		RE-10 (.14)	Which man has best lived up to his religion: Holy man / Factory owner / Both, equally / Neither
x	x		RE-11 (.21)	A man's wife is gravely ill. He obtains the best possible medical care, and he also prays fervently (and with a pure heart). She finally recovers. Which do you think was more important in her recovery, prayer or medical care? Prayer / Medical care / Both
x	x		RE-12 (.21)	Do you think a man can be truly good without having any religion at all? Yes / No
x	x		RE-13 (.11)	A man's only son is killed by a car while crossing the road. The father asks himself, "Why should this have happened to *my* son?" How would you account for this event? _____
	x		RE-14 (.24)	1. Should a man give alms to the poor because he fears (or loves) God, or 2. Because he feels it is the compassionate, kind (generous) thing to do

OM-1	OM-2	BI	Code and Number	Question
x	x		SC-2 (.11)	Which of the following in your eyes (view), should carry the most weight in determining the respect (prestige, honor) a man deserves? Coming from a high or distinguished family background / Having much money / Having much schooling
	x		SC-6 (.01)	I have here a drawing of a hill (ladder, steps, etc.) SHOW RESPONDENT DRAWING. Imagine that this hill represents the social positions of all of the people in the country. This means that in the upper part of the hill are placed persons who have the highest social positions. In the middle of the hill are those persons who have a middle social position, and in the lower part of the hill are those persons who have lower social position. Is it easy or hard for a man to (increase his prestige and) change his position upward on the hill? Easy / Hard
x	x		SC-8 (.10)	In your opinion, which of the following is more important in getting ahead in life? Strength of family connections / Own ability and hard work
	x		SC-9 (.06)	All things considered, and compared with most of the people in this country, how has life been to you? More fair / As fair / Less fair
x	x		TI-3 (.05)	Suppose you had hired a man to work for you. Would you rather: 1. Set a fixed daily schedule for him 2. Allow him a little freedom to set his own daily schedule 3. Leave the daily schedule mostly up to him so long as he finished the job
x	x		TI-4 (.15)	Some people think that a factory (USE "farm" IF R IS CULTIVATOR) should be run with a strict time schedule of work. Others think there should be less concern with time in a factory (farm). Do you feel that having a strict time schedule in a factory (farm), in general, is: Good and necessary / A pity, but necessary / Bad and unnecessary
x	x		TI-5 (.13)	Suppose a friend who said he would meet you at noon did not come right on time. How long would it be before you would consider him to be a little (somewhat) late? TRY TO GET A RESPONSE IN TERMS OF MINUTES OR PARTS OF AN HOUR

OM-1	OM-2	BI	Code and Number	Question
x	x		TI-7 (.07)	Some people say that it is all right for a boy to fail to keep some appointments (be on time) since this is only natural in a boy. Others say that a boy should be taught to keep his appointments and to be on time always. If a boy fails to keep some of his appointments, should we consider it excusable: Always / Most times / Few times / Never
x	x		TS-12 (.16)	Suppose there is a man who has a little shop (factory) and he produces nails. Things have gone well, and he has saved some money. Now he wants to expand his business. Which would get greater output: 1. To hire more workers than previously, or 2. To give the present workers extra training
x	x		TS-13 (.09)	Suppose John's cocoa has got black pod and is dying. What should John do? 1. Consult an experienced cocoa farmer who lives nearby, or 2. Consult the agricultural extension worker (adapt to local crops and specialists)
x	x		TS-14 (.01)	Some people say that it is not too important for a boy to be skillful (handy) with machines and interested in mechanical things. Others say that every boy should be skillful with machines and interested in mechanical things. Assuming he has other abilities, how important is it that a boy also (be skillful with machines and) have mechanical interest? Not at all important / Perhaps a little (somewhat) important / Very important / The most important (thing for a boy)
		x	UN-1 (.14)	There are several ways to determine how much should be paid to a worker in a factory. Many factories pay according to the number of children, but most of them pay workers according to their degree of skill and production. Why do most factories pay according to skill and not according to the number of children: 1. Management pays the workers and has the legitimate right to make the rules 2. Skilled workers are hard to find, so they must be offered more to attract them 3. Paying according to children would be unfair to the unmarried workers
		x	UN-2 (.08)	The manager of a factory does not like the foremen to be too (very) friendly with the workers under him. Why is that?

OM-1	OM-2	BI	Code and Number	Question
				1. Management does not want to encourage disrespect for authority
				2. The factory is a place to work, not to socialize
				3. Foremen can more easily maintain discipline if they are not too friendly with the workers
	x		UN-3 (.14)	At a certain foundry the management does not have a man do several different jobs but, instead, asks him to do one simple job over and over again. Why is that?
				1. The iron can be made more efficiently that way
				2. So that the workers can earn more money
				3. Management runs the factory and has the right to arrange the work
			WC-2	Do you prefer to remain a factory worker (farmer), or would you prefer to do some other kind of work? IF "OTHER KIND OF WORK" IS PREFERRED, ASK: What kind of work would you prefer? *Coded for:*
		x	(.22)	1. Job classification
x			(.11)	2. Level of occupational aspirations
x			WR-1 (.03)	Even a woman who dutifully fulfills all her usual obligations to her husband (such as obeying and serving him carefully) may do it in a way which is affectionate or in a way which is not so affectionate. If you had to choose between these qualities in a wife, would you prefer: 1. A wife who is very exacting in the fulfillment of her obligations even if she is a bit lacking in affection 2. A wife who is very affectionate even if she is a little lax in fulfilling her obligations
		x	WR-2 (−.03)	There are some husbands who discuss (certain) things with their wives that other husbands do not discuss with them. In general, do you (would you) discuss religion with your wife: Often / Once in a while / Not at all
		x	WR-3 (.02)	In general, do you (would you) discuss your work with your wife: Often / Once in a while / Not at all
		x	WR-4 (.20)	In general, do you (would you) discuss politics with your wife: Often / Once in a while / Not at all
	x		WR-5 (.05)	If you found out you had (a serious disease such as) cancer (tuberculosis), to whom would you want to tell it first?

OM-1	OM-2	BI	Code and Number	Question
x	x		WR-6 (.16)	Should an unmarried girl of 18 years who wants to work be allowed to take a job outside of her home town? Under no circumstances / Under few circumstances / Under most circumstances
x	x		WR-7 (.14)	Suppose in a factory, or office, both men and women did exactly the same sort of work, what should be the pay they receive? It should be equal / Men should get a little more / Men should get quite a bit (lot) more
x	x		WR-8 (.16)	Would you vote for a suitable woman to be elected to one of the highest offices of the land? Yes / No
	x		WR-9 (.05)	When a family has several children, both sons and daughters (equally), and a new child is coming, is it preferable that the new child be: A boy / A girl / Either one, it does not matter
x	x		WR-11 (.21)	Should a girl's marriage partner be picked by herself or her parents? IF R SAYS "HER PARENTS" ASK: Should she marry her parents' choice even if she does not like him? Yes / No IF R SAYS "HERSELF" ASK: Should she marry him even if her parents do not approve? Yes / No
x	x		WR-12 (−.01)	Some people say that a husband should help his wife by doing things around the house, such as occasionally caring for the kids or doing some heavier cleaning. Others say that these things are solely the wife's obligation and the husband should not be bothered by them. In your opinion, how much do you think a husband should help his wife around the house? Never / Few times (sometimes) / Often / Always
x	x		WR-13 (.08)	Suppose men and women work together in the same work shop (place). How much should one worry about (illicit) sexual contact (relations) between them? Worry a lot / Worry a little / Worry not at all
x	x		WR-14 (.09)	Suppose adolescent boys and girls are taught in the same school building. How much should one worry about this leading to (illicit) sexual contact between them? Worry a lot / Worry a little / Worry not at all

PART II. Supplemental Questions

The questions in Part I, used in the construction of OM-3, were supplemented by others in the construction of OM-500 and 519, as explained in Chapter 6. The following are those questions which were used as supplements in constructing OM-500 and 519 in either Argentina or India, or both. They are reproduced here both to indicate their similarity with the core set in Part I and to facilitate the interpretation of Part III of this Appendix, which lists the items and themal orderings of OM-500 and 519 in these two countries. The procedure was basically the same in the other four countries. Many of the items listed below were used as supplemental in the construction of OM-500 and 519 in these countries also, but in those countries still other additional items were often used. Here we have included only the supplemental items used in either Argentina or India or both, in order to conserve space. The letters in parentheses after the themal code for some questions indicate that they were asked only in particular countries: A = Argentina; C = Chile; I = India; P = Pakistan; S = Israel. Obviously, questions not asked in a given country could not be used in OM there. But being asked was no assurance the question was used in constructing OM-500 or 519 in that country.

Code and Number	Question
AG(C,A)-50	How much obligation or duty does a young man have to obey old people? Much obligation / Some obligation / Little obligation / No obligation
AG(C,A)-51	Do you think that contradicting an old person: Is very incorrect (a bad thing) / Is somewhat incorrect / Does not have much importance / Has no importance at all
AS-11	Which of these two jobs would you prefer a son of yours to take, assuming he was qualified for either? 1. A (skilled) machine-worker's job at $400 per month 2. Or a white-collar (desk) job (the work of a clerk in an office) at $300 per month
AS(I)-51	Suppose a poor farmer has a son who is very bright, industrious, and intelligent. He says to his father: "I want to study — in a school first and then in a college." The father replies: "I, too, wish to educate you the most. But I have no money, therefore, you have to give this idea up." In spite of this the boy says: "I shall try my best." Do you think that the prospect of his studying in a college is: Very great / Very little / Nothing
CA(C,A)-50	In the place where you work there certainly must be workers who at times don't do their share of the work. In general, how have you acted when they have not done their share? I have not been bothered much (I have not cared about it, been concerned about it) / It didn't seem good, but it was the boss's responsibility / It seemed so bad that I was tempted to say something to them / It seemed so bad that I told them (tried to make them see) that their conduct (behavior) was not right.

CH(I)-51   In the present period, new things, such as motor cars, railways, airplanes, electric fans, radios, etc., are being made. Some people say that these things have brought advantages and comfort to our lives. But others say that there have been more disadvantages due to these things.
What is your opinion? _____

CH(I)-56   Now, please tell me which do you like more:
Prevalence of dowry system / End of dowry system

CI-1   Which is the more important right of a citizen?
His right to vote / His right to free education

CI(C,A)-50   Which of the following forms of celebrating [a national holiday, e.g., the 4th of July] seems most appropriate to you?
Participating in some public, patriotic activity (act) / Treating that day like any other patriotic or religious holiday / Treating that day like any other day of rest (day of leisure, day without working)

CI(C,A)-51   There are different ideas about how [the country of R] can improve its economic situation.
In your opinion, does [the country of R] need:
To do things as in previous times (as in the old days) / To maintain the present ways / To make some changes / To make basic changes

CI(C,A)-52   In your opinion, what is it that [the country of R] needs most?
A total and immediate change / A total but slow (gradual) change / A partial, immediate change / A partial, slow change / No changes

CO(C,A)-50   Is having a car like this [brand name of a good car]:
SHOW PHOTO
A great aspiration (something you want very much) / Something you would like but not a great aspiration / A matter of indifference (something you don't care about)

CO(C,A)-52   SHOW THE PHOTOS OF THE HOUSES
Would you point to the housing in which you think you would have to live in order to feel really satisfied and comfortable with your level of living (living standard)?
MARK THE NUMBER OF THE PHOTO CHOSEN
__1. __2. __3. __4. __5. __6. __7. __8. __9. __10.

DI(C,A)-50   In your opinion, is it more important to respect (have consideration for) the feelings of a woman or to respect the feelings of a man?
To respect the feelings of a woman is:
More important / Equally important / Less important

DI(C,A)-51   Why do you think that? _____

FS(S,P,I)-51   1. Some people think it is not good to have many children, as it becomes difficult to feed and clothe so many.
2. Others say that it is not bad to have many children, as all of them will help in household work.
What is your opinion?

GO(C,A)-50   Do you think that it is necessary for a boy to have the same ideas (opinions) as his father?

In all important matters / In the majority of matters / In certain matters / In nothing

GO(C,A)-54   People have various opinions about different religions. What do you think about the truth that each religion has?

All religions have some truth in them / Many religions have a part of the truth / Only a few have the truth / Only one religion has the truth / None has the truth

NE(C,A)-51   If you won a contest in which the prizes were either to spend two (paid) weeks free at a (nearby) beach, or to make a free (paid) trip for the same length of time through some other country, which would you choose?

The beach / The trip

PA(C,A)-54   In your experience, what do the people you know do when they have to see about some urgent matter in a public office?

1. Try to find a friend in the office or an acquaintance who has friends in the office.

2. See about the matter without looking for help.

PA(C,A)-55   Do you think that is:

Good / Bad / Neither good nor bad

PL(C,A)-50   Some people say that those who are successful in life have generally made plans and arranged things in advance so they would turn out well. Others say that those who are successful in life had better luck than others. Do you think that in order to be successful in life it is:

Much more important to have good luck / A little more important to have good luck / A little more important to make plans / Much more important to make plans

RE(I)-52   Suppose a holy man came to you and showed you his bag which seemed empty. But he took out some sweets and gave some to you. Can you say how he did this? Did he do this by:

Cunning and trick / Supernatural powers

SC-4   Next I would like to ask you some questions about different groups of people and their social position in the community.

I have here (this is) a drawing of a hill (ladder, steps, etc.) SHOW RESPONDENT THE DRAWING. Imagine that this hill represents the social positions of all of the people in the country. This means that in the upper part of the hill are placed persons who have the highest social positions. In the middle of the hill are those persons who have a middle social position, and in the lower part of the hill are those persons who have lower social position. Now, I would like you to point to the position on the hill of the people who have the same social standing (social position) as you.

1. Top position (step)

2.

3.

4.

5. Lowest position (step)

SC-5   A. FACTORY WORKERS ONLY

Now, please point to the position (step) on the hill which you think most farmers have, broadly speaking.

B. FARMERS ONLY
Now, please point to the position (step) you think factory workers have, broadly speaking.
1. Top position (step)
2.
3.
4.
5. Lowest position (step)

SC-9 Taking the good with the bad (all things considered) would you say that compared with the majority (most) of the people in this country, life has been:
More fair (better) / As fair (the same) / Less fair (worse) to you as compared to the majority?

SC-10 Why do you say that? _____
PROBE ONCE. What other reasons? _____
ASK RESPONDENT TO PLEASE COMPLETE THE FOLLOWING SENTENCES IN HIS OWN WORDS:

ST-5 When offered more responsible work, the man . . .

ST-6 If his work materials or tools are not available, the man . . .

TI(C,A)-51 Do you think that the men (people) of today should dedicate themselves:
To assure a good life for the people who will live in the future / To improve the life and welfare of those who live today / To conserve the memory and traditional (old, familiar) ways (customs) of our ancestors.

TS(C,A)-50 You know that vaccinations are given to prevent people from getting diseases such as smallpox, infantile paralysis, diphtheria, etc. In your opinion, are these vaccinations useful:
Almost always / At times / Almost never

WC-9 Now I would like to ask some questions about what kind of work you prefer and why.
As between work in a factory and work in cultivation, which do you generally prefer?
Factory / Cultivation

WC-10 Well, what are the advantages of [R's choice in WC-9]? PROBE UNTIL THREE DISTINCT REASONS HAVE BEEN OFFERED, SAYING: Can you think of other kinds of advantages? AND: What else?

WC-11 There must be some disadvantages to work in [R's choice in WC-9]. What are some of those?
ONE PROBE: Are there any other disadvantages?

WC-12 Well, with regard to [opposite of R's choice in WC-9]. What are some of its advantages as a line of work?
ONE PROBE: Any other advantages?

WC(C,A)-55 In speaking of the advantages and disadvantages of the factory and the country (the farm), you have not mentioned (either) opportunities for promotion (possibilities of getting ahead). Where do you think these opportunities are better?

In the country (on the farm) / In the factory / Not relevant

WR(I)-51   People differ in their opinions on certain things of our society. I
want to know your opinion on some such matters.
1. Some think that a wife should prepare (cook) better food for
her husband than what she partakes of herself.
2. But others think that the wife should take exactly the same food
as her husband takes.
What is your opinion?

PART III.   Content of OM-500 and OM-519 for Argentina and India

The following is a list of themes and questions used in the construction of
OM-500 and 519 for Argentina and India. The text of most of these questions
can be found by referring to Part I of this Appendix. However, as indicated
in Part II, several questions used in these scales did not appear in OM-3. The
numbers of such questions are italicized; their text is found in Part II (Supplemental Questions).

A. Questions Comprising OM-500

Argentina		India	
Themal Code	Number	Themal Code	Number
AC	2, 4, 6	AC	2, 4, 5, 6
AG	3, 50, 51	AG	2
AS	1, 2, 6, 8, 10, 11, 51	AS	1, 2, 3, 5, 6, 9, 10, 11
CA	3, 6, 8, 50	CA	11
CH	1–2, 3, 6–7	CH	1–2, 3, 14, 51, 56
CI	1, 7, 8, 13, 14, 50, 51, 52	CI	2, 7, 8, 13, 14
CO	1, 6, 8, 50, 52	CO	1, 7a, 7b, 8
DI	5, 8, 9, 10, 11	DI	6, 8, 10, 11, 51
EF	1, 2, 3, 8, 9, 11, 13, 14, 15, 16	EF	2, 3, 8, 11, 13, 14, 15, 16
FS	1, 3, 6	FS	1, 3, 4, 5, 51
GO	1, 2, 5, 50, 54	GO	1, 2, 4, 5, 6
ID	1	ID	1
IN	2, 3, 6	IN	2, 3, 6
KO	1, 2, 6	KO	2, 6
MM	8, 10–12	MM	6, 8, 9, 10–12
NE	1, 2, 3, 4, 5, 7, 51	NE	1, 2, 3, 5, 6, 7
PA	54 55		
PL	2, 3, 4, 50	PL	3, 4, 9
RE	10, 11, 12, 14	RE	8, 9, 11, 12, 52
SC	2, 4–5, 8	SC	2, 4–5, 8, 10
ST	6	ST	5
TI	5, 51	TI	3, 4, 5, 7
TS	12, 50	TS	12, 13, 14
		UN	3
WC	9, 10–12, 55	WC	9, 10–12a, 10–12b
WR	4, 6, 7, 8, 9, 11, 12, 13	WR	2, 4, 6, 7, 8, 11, 12, 13, 51

B. Questions Comprising OM-519

Subscale	Constituent questions for—	
	Argentina	India
Active citizenship	AC-2, 4, 6; CI-2	CA-2, 4, 5, 6; CI-2
Change valuation	CH-1–2, 3; CI-*51, 52*; TI-*51*	CH-1, 2, 3, 14, *51*; CO-7b
Dignity valuation	DI-5, 8, 9, 10, 11	DI-6, 8, 10, 11, *51*
Economic aspirations	CO-8, *50, 52*; NE-1	AS-11; CO-7a, 8; NE-1, SC-10
Education valuation	AS-1, 8, *51*; CI-13; SC-2	AS-1, 2, 9; CI-13, SC-2
Efficacy	EF-1, 2, 3, 13, 16	EF-2, 3, 11, 13, 16
Family size	FS-1, 3	FS-1, 3, 4, 5, *51*
Information	CO-1, IN-2, 3, 6; MM-8	CO-1; IN-2, 3, 6; MM-8
Minority-opinion valuation	AG-*51*; GO-5, *50, 54*; WR-4	GO-4, 5, 6; WR-4
Modern family	KO-1, 2; WR-9, 11	CH-56; KO-2; WR-2, 11, 12
Modern religion	RE-10, 11, 12, 14	RE-8, 9, 11, 12, *52*
New experience	NE-2, 3, 4, 5, *51*	MM-9; NE-2, 3, 5, 6
Nonparochial allegiance	AG-50; CI-7, 8; ID-1; MM-10, 12	CI-7, 8; ID-1; MM-6, 10–12
Planning valuation	EF-11; PL-3, 4, *50*	PL-3, 4, 9; TI-3, 4
Responsibility valuation	CA-3, *50*; EF-8; ST-6; TI-5	CA-11; EF-9; ST-*5*; TI-5, 7
Technical-skill valuation	EF-15; TS-12	AS-3; EF-14; TS-12, 13, 14
Urban-industrial preference	NE-7; SC-*4, 5*; WC-*55*	AS-5; NE-7; WC-*9, 10–12b*
Verbal fluency	AS-2, 6; GO-1, 2	AS-2, 6; GO-1, 2; WC-*10–12a*
Women's rights	CH-6, 7; WR-6, 7, 8, 13	WR-6, 7, 8, 13, *51*

PART IV. Psychosomatic Symptoms Test

The development and use of this set of questions is treated in the last section of Chapter 18, "The Fate of Personal Adjustment in the Modernization Process." The letters in parentheses after the themal code for some questions indicate that they were used only in particular countries. A = Argentina; C = Chile; N = Nigeria.

Code and number	Question
PT-1[a]	Now I would like to ask you some questions about your health. INTERVIEWER NOTE: DISCOURAGE GENERAL TALK ABOUT SYMPTOMS OR MEDICAL HISTORY. Do you ever have trouble getting to sleep or staying asleep? Yes / No
PT-2	Do your hands (or legs) ever tremble enough to bother you? Yes / No

PT-3a	Are you bothered by nervousness ("nerves")? Yes / No
PT-4	Have you ever been bothered by your heart beating hard when you were not exerting yourself or working hard? Yes / No
PT-5	Do you ever bite your fingernails? Yes / No
PT-6a	Have you ever been bothered by shortness of breath when you were not exercising or working hard? Yes / No
PT-7	Are you ever troubled by the palms of your hands sweating when you are not exercising or working hard? Yes / No
PT-8a	Are you often troubled with headaches? Yes / No
PT-9a	Are you ever bothered by having dreams that frighten or upset you very much? Yes / No
PT(C,A)-50	Has your work been affected by problems of health in the past 6 months? Frequently / From time to time (at times) / Rarely / Never
PT(C,A)-51	In the past 6 months have there ever been times when you couldn't take care of things because you just couldn't get going? Many times / Sometimes / Few times / Almost never
PT(C,A)-52	In the past 6 months have you been bothered by all sorts of pains and ailments in different parts of your body (at the same time)? Frequently / At times / Rarely / Never
PT(C,A)-53	If you have things to do, do you find it difficult to get up (in the morning) in order to (face and) accomplish them? Almost always / Often / At times / Never
PT(N)-51	Have you ever thought you were being affected by witchcraft? Yes / No

aRepresents a core item, present in the scale for all countries. All others are supplementary, used at the discretion of the field director in each country.

Appendix B
OM-12:   The Short Form

Each of the 14 items included in OM-12 correlated with the larger OM scales, in each of the six countries, at a highly significant level. Moreover, each of the questions was strongly correlated with the independent variables of education, urban experience, and occupation. Ten of our 33 attitudinal sub-themes (listed in Table 7-2) were represented by the questions, as were political activity, verbal fluency, information, and mass-media behavior. For the details of the selection process, see Smith and Inkeles, "The OM Scale."

As we point out in the last section of Chapter 6, the items of OM-12 have been extensively incorporated in cross-cultural research. In coding the 14 items of the scale, the researcher faces those problems which we discuss at the end of the first section of Chapter 6. In particular, as to dichotomization, he should use relative cutting points to maximize within-sample discrimination, and absolute cutting points for cross-sample comparisons. The former approach, which involves finding the midpoint of the frequency distribution within each cultural sample, is of course the one we have preferred in our present analysis. To aid potential users of OM-12, we have included our standardized coding instructions.

We urge those who plan to use OM-12 to pay particular attention to the suggested alternative questions mentioned in the coding instructions. The exact texts of those alternative questions are given in Appendix A, and so are now readily available. Since it is more or less inevitable that one or another question from a cross-national set may not serve well in a particular country, we recommend that all the suggested alternate questions actually be asked. This provides a pool of items which are theoretical equivalents, from which the researcher may select those which are best understood and most discriminating when put to his particular study group.

Purely Attitudinal Items[a]

AC-6   Have you ever (thought over so much) gotten so highly concerned (involved) regarding some public issue (such as . . .) that you really wanted to do something about it?
Frequently / Few times / Never

AS-1   If schooling is freely available (if there were no kinds of obstacles) how much schooling (reading and writing) do you think children (the son) of people like yourself should have?

CH-3   Two 12-year-old boys took time out from their work in the corn (rice) fields. They were trying to figure out a way to grow the same amount of corn (rice) with fewer hours of work.
The father of one boy said: "That is a good thing to think about. Tell me your thoughts about how we should change our ways of growing corn (rice)."
The father of the other boy said: "The way to grow corn (rice) is the way we have always done it. Talk about change will waste time but not help."
Which father said the wiser words?

CI-13   What should most qualify a man to hold high office?
Coming from (right, distinguished, or high) family background
Devotion to the old and (revered) time-honored ways
Being the most popular among the people
High education and special knowledge

EF-11, 12   Which is most important for the future of (this country)?
The hard work of the people
Good planning on the part of the government
God's help
Good luck

EF-14   Learned men (scholars, scientists) in the universities are studying such things as what determines whether a baby is a boy or girl and how it is that a seed turns into a plant. Do you think that these investigations (studies) are:
All very good (beneficial) / All somewhat good (beneficial)
All somewhat harmful / All very harmful

FS-3   Some people say that it is necessary for a man and his wife to limit the number of children to be born so they can take better care of those they do have (already have).
Others say that it is wrong for a man and wife purposely (voluntarily) to limit the number of children to be born.
Which of these opinions do you agree with more?

MM-10-12   Which one of these (following) kinds of news interests you most?
World events (happenings in other countries)
The nation
Your home town (or village)
Sports
Religious (or tribal, cultural) events (ceremonies) or festivals

NE-5   If you were to meet a person who lives in another country a long way off (thousands of kilometers / miles away), could you understand his way of thinking?
Yes / No

RE-12   Do you think a man can be truly good without having any religion at all?
          Yes / No

Behavior-Information Items

AC-1, 2   Do you belong to any organization (associations, clubs), such as, for example, social clubs, unions, church organizations, political groups, or other groups? If "Yes," what are the names of all the organizations you belong to? (Scored for number of organizations.)

GO-2   Would you tell me what are the biggest problems you see facing (your country)? (Scored for number of problems or words in answer.)

IN-6 or 7 Where is (in what country is the city of) Washington / Moscow? (Scored correct or incorrect.)

MM-5   How often do you (usually) get news and information from newspapers?
          Everyday / Few times a week
          Occasionally (rarely) / Never

ªWords in parentheses are alternative phrasing for aid in translation. In every case the items should be adapted to make sense in the particular culture.

Coding Instructions and Notes

Note: Full texts of Alternative items are given in Appendix A.

AC-6. Closed coding. The modern answer is "frequently." In adapting this question to a particular country, it is sometimes advantageous to give examples of public issues, especially if the term "public issue" is not familiar. An alternative item is CI-2, which asks about a proposed law which the respondent considered unjust or harmful. This is coded for action versus inaction, action being the modern response (especially collective action).

AS-1. This is now an open question, but the interviewer is instructed to probe until the respondent mentions a specific number of years or a level of schooling easily converted into years. This makes direct field coding very simple. The more years of education desired, the more modern the answer. An alternative item is AS-5, which asks for the best occupation the respondent thinks a man like himself could obtain. This is coded for status level, with high-status aspiration coded as modern.

CH-3. Closed coding. The modern answer is to think about new techniques. In the more developed of our countries (Chile, Argentina, Israel) we used the following version of CH-3: "While some people say that it is useful to exchange (discuss) ideas about new and different ways of doing things, others think that it is not worthwhile since the traditional and familiar ways are best. Do you feel that thinking about new and different ways (forms) of doing things is: always useful / / usually useful / only useful at times / rarely useful?

CI-13. Closed coding. The modern answer is "high education." An alternative item would be SC-2, which asks whether the basis of social prestige and respect should be education / money / family background, with "education" considered the modern answer.

EF-11, 12. Closed coding. The two responses scored modern are "hard work" and "government planning" given as either the first or the second choice. An alternative is EF-8, which asks whether the respondent prefers work with many / few / or no problems or decisions, with the first response being most modern.

EF-14. Closed coding. Answering that "scientific study is beneficial" is considered modern. In the more developed countries the example, "Why are there earthquakes?" may be used instead of, "How is it that a seed turns into a plant?"

FS-3. Closed coding. Modern answer: "favors birth control." A more extended response scale should be used when the sample of respondents is known to be quite modern, ranging from viewing birth control as "almost always a good idea" down to "never a proper thing to do."

MM-10—12. Closed coding. The more modern answers are considered to be "news about world" and "national events." An alternative is MM-6, which asks what two sources of information about world affairs the respondent trusts most, with the modern response being "mass-media sources" as contrasted to personal, non-mass-media sources.

NE-5. Closed coding. "Yes" is coded as the modern answer. The actual name of a distant, very different foreign country may be used (for example, Japan). Also the response scale may well be extended to include the middle category, "perhaps." An alternative item would be NE-3, which asks whether the respondent enjoys meeting new people or prefers to spend his time with people he already knows. The modern response involves meeting new people.

RE-12. Closed coding. "Yes" is coded as the modern answer. The response scale might be extended to include the middle category, "perhaps." An alternative item would be RE-14, which asks whether a man should give charity to the poor because of generosity or fear (love) of God, with "generosity" treated as the modern answer.

AC-1, 2. To code this item simply count the number of organizations. The modern coding for this item is a higher number. Compulsory unions should, if possible, be omitted from the count. For instance, in Israel membership in the Histadrut was omitted. An alternative would be AC-4, which asks if the respondent had ever written or spoken to a government official about a public issue, the modern response being "yes" or "frequently."

GO-2. The actual name of the respondent's country may be used instead of the words "your country." The most useful coding for this open item involves a count of the number of "problems" enumerated by the respondent. If this proves too difficult in field practice, a simple count of the number of words in the response will serve nearly as well. An alternative item is GO-1, which is identical in all respects except that it asks about the problems facing one's town or village. In both items the modern answer involves more words or themes (problems) than the more traditional answer.

IN-6 or 7. Either IN-6 or IN-7 may be used here, with preference given to IN-7 (Moscow). Semiclosed coding recorded by interviewer. Those who give the correct identification are scored modern. Alternative items are IN-1 and 2, which ask who is Lyndon Johnson (or current U. S. president) and who was Nehru or any other comparable leader of world renown. For more developed countries more difficult international figures or national capitols might be substituted — IN-1, 2, 6, 7.

MM-5. Closed coding. The modern answer is "every day." (For more developed countries one might ask the number of newspapers read each day or per week.) An alternative item is MM-1, frequency of exposure to the radio, with higher exposure being more modern.

Appendix C
The Set A Variables

Our final, full set of independent (or predictor) variables was designated "Set A." The rationale underlying this basic set is suggested at the beginning of Chapter 20, and the division into variables of early socialization and late socialization is dealt with in the last section of Chapter 19. What distinguishes these variables from most of those dealt with in Part III, "Contexts and Causes of Modernization," of this book is that we make heavy use, in Set A, of variable indices. In each case in which an index was created, it was as a combination of standard-scored components. Where dummy variables, as described below, were necessary, they were designed to maximize their correlation with OM. Through performance of factor analyses, we were able to ensure that our various composite variables did indeed measure coherent dimensions. With each of the Set A variables, we did our best to maximize the apparent role of that variable in relation to modernity. That way we would be able truly to program a competition among the variables as predictors of OM.

(*a*) *Education-literacy*. In our study, a man's literacy score was directly related to an actual performance witnessed by the interviewer. Combination of that score with the man's reported formal schooling gave what we considered his true level of education-related functioning and experience. For the six countries, with Israel designated by the letter S, the measures were intercorrelated as follows: A, .58; C, .40; EP, .85; I, .85; S, .42; N, .32

(*b*) *Economic level*. Self-reported consumer-goods possession was used as the index of economic level in analyses of the full sample. For the factory workers, self-reported income was included also, correlating with consumer-goods possession as follows: A, .18; C, .33; EP, .22; I, .33; S, .18; N, .39.

(*c*) *Mass-media exposure*. The index of mass-media exposure combined newspaper reading with radio listening, although television viewing was substituted for the latter in Argentina. Details are given in Chapter 10.

(d) *Life-cycle stage.* The measure of life-cycle stage included age, marital status, and number of children.

(e) *Ethnicity-religion.* The version of ethnicity-religion used in the multiple-regression analyses depended on which ordering of the ethnic or religious groups showed the strongest association with OM-3 scores. In this manner we attempted to give the ethnicity-religion distinctions within our samples from each country the maximum opportunity to influence modernity scores.

(f) *Quality of urban experience.* For the full sample, the composite index of the quality of present urban experience rank-ordered respondents in terms of the centrality of their residence to large urban areas and in terms of cosmopolitanism of the city of residence itself. We used whichever rank-order gave the highest zero-order correlation with OM-3. For the factory-worker subsample, we considered location of work, as well as of residence. Details are given in Chapter 15.

(g) *Father's education.* As a measure of the status of a man's parents, we used the number of years of formal education reportedly obtained by the respondent's father. In Israel, father's occupational status level was substituted. See Chapter 17 for details.

(h) *Occupation type (full sample only).* The occupational index rank-ordered our respondents in terms both of urban and of factory experience, as follows: cultivators, new factory workers, urban nonindustrial workers, middle-experience workers, and high-experience workers.

(i) *Individual factory experience (factory workers only).* This index contained our measures of a respondent's total months of factory experience, his coder-rated skill level, and the number of factories worked in by the man. The average intercorrelations of these three variables for the countries studied were: A, .34; C, .34; EP, .27; I, .24; S, .23; N, .32.

(j) *Nature of present factory (factory workers only).* This index combined rated modernity of the factory, size of the factory, and perceived number of benefits, as detailed in Chapter 12.

(k) *Rural vs. urban origin (factory workers only).* The dichotomous rural-versus urban-origin variable has been described in detail in Chapter 16. It was made use of only in Argentina, Chile, and Nigeria.

(l) *Years urban since age 15 (factory workers only).* This index was made use of only for men of rural origin, as described in Chapter 15.

Appendix D
Migration and Individual Modernity

The role of migration in predicting individual modernity was, though secondary to our research design, still an intriguing one. It is, of course, easy to exaggerate the extent to which men flood in from the countryside to the city. Nevertheless, we must acknowledge that the worker of migrant background is at least substantially present in the labor force of any developing country, and in some cities, such as Dacca and Lagos, he may well represent the majority. For example, in 1950 64 percent of the population of Lagos consisted of immigrants, the majority of those being Yoruba. A significant proportion of these migrants might, of course, have come from other urban centers, such as Ibadan, and the proportion of migrants in the industrial labor force could be different from their weight in the general population. However, we had the impression that close to half of the industrial laborers in Lagos were migrants from the country side. (See A. L. Mabogunje, 1968). In Dacca the industrial labor force seemed to us overwhelmingly of rural origin.

If our men had left the village because they were more ambitious, more adventurous, and more eager to test themselves in a larger arena than that provided by the typical village square, we might well expect some reflection of those motives in the reasons men gave for having left home. In East Pakistan and India, but unfortunately in only those two countries, the field directors asked: "Why did you leave your village and take up factory?" The question was put to all workers, not only those newly arrived from the village. Nevertheless, the answers of all should be relevant since in those two countries all had been cultivators.

In both countries, the overwhelming majorities reported they had left their native villages because of economic necessity — because there was insufficient land in relation to the mouths to feed and no other work to be had there. Fifty-nine percent of the East Pakistani migrants gave such economic reasons. By contrast, when we combined all those who mentioned factors such as the opportunity to use one's education, the chance to acquire skill or knowledge, the prestige of industrial work, or the attractions of life in town, they totaled fewer than 5 percent of the sample. In India it was less easy to divide the answers into simple sets, since one of the main coding categories, accounting for 22 percent of the replies, placed in the same group those mentioning either "need to get a job" or the "opportunity for advancement." Nevertheless, it is notable that fewer than 1 percent mentioned the search for new experience and the desire to see new places; only 3 percent cited benefit to society and nation; and under 6 percent alluded to the intrinsic value or interest of factory work as a reason for migration. By contrast, 45 percent mentioned the need to get money to live, to pay debts, and to help families in need.

All in all these responses provide very little basis for assuming that people — at least in India and East Pakistan — migrated because they had unusual personality attributes or special psychological needs. On the contrary, the overwhelming problems seemed to be the all too ordinary lack of land and work, and the resultant scarcity of money with which to live. But it may be argued that financial problems are endemic in countries like East Pakistan and India, and it is therefore not decisive that the overwhelming majority of the migrants there gave economic needs as the reason for moving. According to this view, those who remained in the village presumably would also have told us that they had great financial need; nevertheless, *they* had not left the villages in search of industrial work. Those who left, the argument runs, might have had more modern attitudes and a distinctive personality and yet still have cited their financial problems as reasons for leaving home. In other words, financial necessity might indeed be the cause of migration, yet not be an explanation of why some leave while most remain. To really test the role of psychological factors in migration, the "psychological-push" theorists argued, we should directly compare the personalities of those who left and those who remained. This we could do by our match procedure, the measure of personality being, of course, the OM scale.

Unfortunately, many of the men we had classified as new workers of rural origin could not claim to represent "inexperienced migrants newly arrived from the countryside," because they had lived in the city for several years before taking a job in industry. Therefore, to compare them with their cousins still in the villages clearly could not serve as a strict test of the role of self-selection in migration. Any differences which emerged from such a comparison could as much result from later exposure to city and industrial life as from earlier self-selection.

To deal with this situation we insisted that when we matched cultivators and new workers the latter had to have less than 3 months in industry and not more than 1 year of residence in town after age 15. Even this requirement was, of course, a compromise forced on us by necessity. Yet when this standard was applied, only East Pakistan, India, and Chile came through with adequate numbers for a proper match. Argentina and Nigeria could not provide enough cases for a suitable match, and Israel had been ruled out from the beginning as not fitting the model requiring men who had migrated from village to town.

The match pitting pairs of cultivators and new workers somewhat favored the new worker, but his advantage was so modest as to lack statistical significance in all three countries. Thus, the correlation of the occupational variable cultivator/new worker run against OM was, by country: for Chile, $-.01$; for East Pakistan, $+ .08$; and for India, $+ .09$. (These results were obtained with Match 3/4 Y, the respective N's being 35, 93, and 88; the match quality was generally good.)

We conclude, then, that while there was some tendency for new workers to be more modern than men who remained in the village this difference could not in itself explain the decision of those workers to migrate. Indeed, we suspect that the migration experience in itself may be behind the small difference in OM scores observed in India and East Pakistan. At any rate, as is clear from Chapter 11 on the effects of factory work, change in individual modernity *after* migration is by far the more dramatic phenomenon.

Appendix E
The Match Control Table

The technique of matching, used extensively throughout our analysis, is described in detail in the last section of Chapter 8. The procedure involves basically the selection of pairs of men who, though differing on one crucial match variable, are statistically indistinguishable on a number of other match controls. Occasionally, statistically significant bias does creep past our control procedure, and wherever this has happened we have reported it in the text. In this appendix, we present merely the pro forma part of the story. For each of the 23 matches cited in the text, we indicate, among our master pool of 14 potential match variables: (1) the crucial match variable itself (*); (2) the attempted match controls (×); (3) other variables not controlled and differing (O); and (4) other variables not controlled but invariate (−).

Table E–1. The match control table.

Chapter number	Match number	Match description	Consumer goods	Factory size	Factory modernity	Gross income	Objective skill	Age	Mass-media exposure	Ethnicity-religion	Urbanism of residence	Years urban since 15	Origin rural-urban	Factory experience	Occupation	Education
9	36Mb	Education: low/high	X	X	X	O	X	X	X	X	X	X	X	X	—	*
10	25	Mass-media exposure: low/high	X	X	X	X	X	X	*	X	X	X	X	X	—	X
10	25A	Mass-media (cultivators)	O	—	—	—	—	X	*	X	—	—	—	—	—	X
11	4	Cultivators vs. rural-origin factory workers	O	O	O	O	O	X	O	X	O	O	—	O	*	X
11	3B	India: Ranchi cultivators vs. factory workers	O	O	O	O	O	X	O	O	O	O	—	O	*	X
11	3C	India: Muri & Khalari cultivators vs. factory workers	X	O	O	O	O	X	X	X	O	O	—	O	*	X
11	13	East Pakistan: original village vs. city	O	X	X	X	X	X	O	X	O	*	—	X	—	X
11	12A	India: village vs. company housing	O	X	—	O	O	X	X	X	*	O	—	X	—	X
12	15	Traditional vs. modern factory	O	X	*	X	X	X	O	X	O	X	X	X	—	X
12	28	Benefits in present factory: low/high	O	X	X	O	X	X	O	X	X	X	X	X	—	X
12	22	Small vs. large factory	O	*	X	O	X	X	O	X	X	X	X	X	—	X
12	59	Quality of factory: low/high	X	O	O	X	X	X	O	X	X	X	X	X	*	X
13	2	Cultivators vs. rural-origin UNIs	O	—	—	O	—	X	O	O	O	O	—	—	*	X
14	1/2C	Cultivators vs. rural-origin UNIs	X	—	—	O	—	X	O	X	O	O	—	—	*	X
14	50A	New factory workers vs. UNIs	O	O	O	X	O	X	X	O	X	O	X	O	*	X
14	1	Experienced factory workers vs. UNIs	O	O	O	X	O	X	O	X	O	X	X	O	*	X
14	1B	India: independent vs. institutional UNIs	O	—	—	O	—	X	O	X	O	O	—	—	—	X
14	1A	India: factory workers vs. institutional UNIs	O	O	O	O	O	X	O	X	X	O	—	O	*	X
15	12M	Years urban experience: low/high	X	X	X	O	X	X	O	X	X	*	—	X	—	X
15	13M	Cosmopolitanism of city: low/high	X	X	X	O	X	X	O	X	*	X	X	X	*	X
17	89N	Origin and factory experience: low/high	O	X	X	O	X	O	X	X	X	O	*	*	—	X
18	24	Home-school modernity: low/high	X	X	X	O	O	X	O	X	X	X	X	X	*	X
18	58	Father's education: low/high	X	X	X	O	X	X	O	X	X	X	X	X	—	X

Bibliography

Adorno, Theodor W., *et al. The Authoritarian Personality*. New York, Harper, 1950.

Allport, Gordon W., Philip E. Vernon, and Gardner Lindzey. *Study of Values: A Scale for Measuring the Dominant Interests in Personality*. 3rd ed. Boston, Houghton Mifflin, 1959.

Almond, Gabriel A., and Sidney Verba. *The Civic Culture: Political Attitudes and Democracy in Five Nations*. Princeton, N. J., Princeton University Press, 1963.

Althauser, Robert P., and Donald Rubin. "The Computerized Construction of a Matched Sample," *American Journal of Sociology* 76 (no. 2, 1970) 325–346.

Bauer, Raymond A. *The New Man in Soviet Psychology*. Cambridge, Mass., Harvard University Press, 1959.

——, Alex Inkeles, and Clyde Kluckhohn. *How the Soviet System Works*. Cambridge, Mass., Harvard University Press, 1964.

Bellah, Robert N. "Meaning and Modernisation," *Religious Studies* 4 (1968), 37–45.

Bergthold, Gary D., and David C. McClelland. *The Impact of Peace Corps Teachers on Students in Ethiopia*. Human Development Foundation, December, 1968.

Blau, Peter M., and Otis D. Duncan. *The American Occupational Structure*. New York, Wiley, 1967.

Blauner, Robert. *Alienation and Freedom; The Factory Worker and His Industry*. Chicago, University of Chicago Press, 1967.

Bloom, Benjamin S. *Stability and Change in Human Characteristics*. New York, Wiley, 1964.

Blumer, Herbert. "Attitudes and the Social Act," *Social Problems* 3 (1955), 59–64.

Bray, D. W. "The Prediction of Behavior from Two Attitude Scales," *Journal of Abnormal Social Psychology* 45 (1950), 64–84.

Breer, Paul E., and Edwin Locke. *Task Experience as a Source of Attitudes.* Homewood, Ill., Dorsey Press, 1965.

Cahalan, Don. "Correlates of Respondent Accuracy in the Denver Validity Survey," *Public Opinion Quarterly* 32 (Winter 1968–69), 607–621.

Campbell, Angus, *et al. The American Voter.* New York, Wiley, 1965.

Cantril, Hadley. *The Pattern of Human Concerns.* New Brunswick, N. J., Rutgers University Press, 1965.

Christie, Richard, and Marie Jahoda. *Studies in the Scope and Method of "The Authoritarian Personality."* Glencoe, Ill., Free Press, 1954.

Coleman, James S., *et al. Equality of Educational Opportunity.* Washington, U. S. Department of Health, Education and Welfare, Office of Education, 1966.

Crozier, Michel. *The Bureaucratic Phenomenon.* Chicago, University of Chicago Press, 1964.

Cunningham, Ineke. *Modernity and Academic Performance: A Study of Students in a Puerto Rican High School.* University of Puerto Rico Press, 1972.

Desmukh, M. B. "Delhi: A Study of Floating Migration," in *Social Implications of Industrialization and Urbanization: Five Studies of Urban Populations of Recent Rural Origin in Cities of Southern Asia.* Calcutta, UNESCO Research Center of Social Implications of Industrialization, 1956, pp. 143–225.

Deutsch, Karl W. *Nationalism and Social Communication: An Inquiry into the Foundations of Nationality.* Cambridge, Mass., and New York, M.I.T. Press–Wiley, 1962.

——— "Social Mobilization and Political Development," *American Political Science Review* 55 (no. 3, September 1961).

Deutscher, Irwin. "Looking Backward: Case Studies on the Progress of Methodology in Social Research," *American Sociologist* 4 (no. 1, 1969), 35–40.

Ehrlich, Harold J. "Attitudes, Behavior and the Intervening Variables," *American Sociologist* 4 (no. 1, 1969), 29–34.

Etzioni, Amitai. *The Active Society; A Theory of Societal and Political Processes.* London, Collier-Macmillan, and New York, Free Press, 1968.

Fennessey, James. "The General Linear Model; A New Perspective on Some Familiar Topics," *American Journal of Sociology* 74 (no. 1, 1968), 1–28.

Fischer, Claude S. "A Research Note on Urbanism and Tolerance," *American Journal of Sociology* 76 (no. 5, March 1971), 847–856.

——— "The Effects of Urbanism: A Review and Analysis of Poll Data." forthcoming.

Fromm, Erich. *Escape From Freedom.* New York, Farrar and Rinehart, 1941.

Ginsburg, Norton. "The City and Modernization," in Myron Weiner, ed., *Modernization.* New York, Basic Books, 1966, pp. 122–137.

Guilford, Joy Paul. *Fundamental Statistics in Psychology and Education.* 3d ed. New York, McGraw-Hill, 1956. (Note: 4th ed., McGraw-Hill, 1965).

Gurin, Gerald, J. Veroff, and Sheila Feld. *Americans View Their Mental Health: A Nationwide Interview Survey.* New York, Basic Books, 1960.

Holsinger, Donald B. "The Elementary School as an Early Socializer of Modern Values." Ph.D. diss., Stanford University, 1972.

Horowitz, Irving Louis. *Three Worlds of Development: The Theory and Practice of International Stratification*. New York, Oxford University Press, 1966.

Hoselitz, Bert F. *Sociological Aspects of Economic Growth*. Glencoe, Ill., Free Press, 1962.

Huntington, Samuel P. "Political Modernization: America vs. Europe," *World Politics* 18 (no. 3, 1966), 378–414.

—— *Political Order in Changing Societies*. New Haven, Conn., Yale University Press, 1969.

Inkeles, Alex, "The Fate of Personal Adjustment in the Process of Modernization," *International Journal of Comparative Sociology*, 11 (no. 2, June 1970), 81–114

—— "Fieldwork Problems in Comparative Research on Modernization," in A. R. Desai, ed., *Essays on Modernization of Underdeveloped Societies*, vol. 2. Bombay, Thacker and New York, Humanities Press, 1971, pp. 20–75.

—— "Participant Citizenship in Six Developing Countries," *American Political Science Review* 63 (no. 4, December 1969), 1120–1141.

—— *Public Opinion in Soviet Russia: A Study in Mass Persuasion*. Cambridge, Mass., Harvard University Press, 1962.

—— *Social Change in Soviet Russia*. Cambridge, Mass., Harvard University Press, 1968.

—— and Raymond A. Bauer. *The Soviet Citizen: Daily Life in a Totalitarian Society*. Cambridge, Mass., Harvard University Press, 1959.

—— and Amar K. Singh. "A Cross-Cultural Measure of Modernity and Some Popular Indian Images," *Journal of General and Applied Psychology*, 1 (1968; Bihar Psychological Association, Ranchi/Patna, India).

Ireland, Rowan Henry. "The Factory as a School in Social Change." Ph.D. diss., Harvard University, 1969.

Kahl, Joseph A. *The Measurement of Modernism: A Study of Values in Brazil and Mexico*. Austin and London, University of Texas Press, 1968.

Kavolis, Vytautas. "Post-Modern Man," *Social Problems* 17 (1970), 435–448.

Klapper, Joseph T., *The Effects of Mass Communication*. Glencoe, Ill., Free Press, 1960.

Kornhauser, Arthur. *Mental Health of the Industrial Worker*. New York, Wiley, 1965.

Leighton, Alexander H., *et al. Psychiatric Disorder Among the Yoruba: A Report from the Cornell-Aro Mental Health Project in the Western Region, Nigeria*. Ithaca, N. Y., Cornell University Press, 1963.

Lerner, Daniel. *The Passing of Traditional Society: Modernizing the Middle East*. Glencoe, Ill., Free Press, 1963.

Mabogunje, A. L. *Urbanization in Nigeria*. London, University of London Press, 1968.

March, James G., and Herbert A. Simon. *Organizations*. New York, Wiley, 1963.

Marshall, Alfred. *Principles of Economics: An Introductory Volume*. 8th ed. London, Macmillan, 1936.

Moore, Wilbert E. *Industrialization and Labor: Social Aspects of Economic Development.* New York, Russell and Russell, 1965.

———— "The Strategy of Fostering Performance and Responsibility," in Egbert de Vries and J. M. Echavarria, eds., *Social Aspects of Economic Development in Latin America,* vol. 1. Paris, UNESCO, 1963.

Nelson, Joan M. *Migrants, Urban Poverty and Instability in Developing Nations,* Occasional Papers in International Affairs, No. 22. Cambridge, Mass., Harvard University Center for International Affairs, 1969.

Pakistan Academy for Rural Development at Comilla. *The Academy at Comilla: An Introduction,* Comilla, no author, no date.

Parrinder, Geoffrey. "Religion in Village and Town," *Annual Conference Report,* Part 1. Ibadan, Nigeria, West Africa Institute of Social and Economic Research, Sociology Section, University College, March 1953, pp. 115–127.

Parry, Hugh J., and H. M. Crossley. "Validity of Responses to Survey Questions," *Public Opinion Quarterly* 14 (no. 1, 1950), 61–80.

Pool, Ithiel de Sola. "The Functions of Mass Media in International Exchange," in *UNESCO Handbook of International Exchanges.* Paris, UNESCO, 1965, pp. 63–75.

———— "The Role of Communication in the Process of Modernization and Technological Change," in Bert F. Hoselitz and W. E. Moore, eds., *Industrialization and Society.* Paris, UNESCO, 1963.

Qakir, S. A. "Land Holdings and Land Use in an East Pakistan Village: Dhanishwar," *Journal of the Pakistan Academy for Rural Development* (Comilla), 1 (no. 2, 1960).

Reddy, Richard D., and David H. Smith. "The Impact of Voluntary Organization Participation Upon the Individual," in David H. Smith, ed., *Voluntary Action Research: 1973.* Lexington, Mass., Heath, 1973.

Robinson, John P., *et al. Measures of Political Attitudes.* Ann Arbor, Mich., Institute for Social Research, University of Michigan, 1968.

Roy, Prodipto, Frederick Brynolf Waisanen, and Everett M. Rogers. *The Impact of Communication on Rural Development: an Investigation in Costa Rica and India.* Hyderabad, UNESCO (Paris) and National Institute of Community Development, 1969.

Russett, Bruce M., *et al. World Handbook of Political and Social Indicators.* New Haven, Conn., Yale University Press, 1964.

Sayles, Leonard R. *The Behavior of Industrial Work Groups: Prediction and Control.* New York, Wiley, 1963.

Schuman, Howard. *Economic Development and Individual Change: A Social-Psychological Study of the Comilla Experiment in Pakistan,* Occasional Papers in International Affairs, No. 15. Cambridge, Mass., Harvard University Center for International Affairs, February 1967.

———— "The Random Probe: A Technique for Evaluating the Validity of Closed Questions," *American Sociological Review* 31 (no. 2, April 1966), 218–223.

Scotch, Norman A., and H. Jack Geiger. "An Index of Symptom and Disease in Zulu Culture," *Human Organization* 22 (no. 4, Winter 1963–64), 304–311.

Sewell, William H., A. O. Haller, and G. W. Ohlendorf. "The Educational and Early Occupational Attainment Process: Replication and Revision," *American Sociological Review* 35 (1970), 1014–1027.

Shaw, Marvin E., and Jack M. Wright. *Scales for the Measurement of Attitudes.* New York, McGraw-Hill, 1967.

Silvert, Kalman H. *The Conflict Society: Reaction and Revolution in Latin America.* New York, American Universities Field Staff, 1966.

Slotkin, James S. *From Field to Factory: New Industrial Employees.* Glencoe, Ill., Free Press, 1960.

Smith, David H., and Alex Inkeles. "The OM Scale: A Comparative Socio-Psychological Measure of Individual Modernity," *Sociometry* 29 (no. 4, December 1966), 353–377.

Srole, Leo, *et al. Mental Health in the Metropolis.* New York, McGraw-Hill, 1962.

Stouffer, Samuel A., *et al. The American Soldier: Adjustment During Army Life.* Studies in Social Psychology in World War II, vol. I. Princeton, N. J., Princeton University Press, 1950.

———— *Social Research to Test Ideas: Selected Writings.* New York, Free Press of Glencoe, 1962.

Stycos, J. Mayone, and Kurt W. Back. *The Control of Human Fertility in Jamaica.* Ithaca, N. Y., Cornell University Press, 1964.

Suzman, Richard M. "The Modernization of Personality." Ph.D. diss., Harvard University, 1973.

Tumin, Melvin M., and Arnold S. Feldman. *Social Class and Social Change in Puerto Rico.* Princeton, N. J., Princeton University Press, 1961.

UNESCO. *Mass Media in the Developing Countries.* Paris, UNESCO, 1961.

Vanneman, Reeve. "The Conditional Effect of Education on the Modernizing Influence of the Factory," from a Memorandum of October 1969, in the files of the Harvard Project on Social and Cultural Aspects of Development, Cambridge, Mass.

Ward, Robert E., and Dankwart A. Rustow. *Political Modernization in Japan and Turkey.* Princeton, N. J., Princeton University Press, 1964.

Weber, Max. *The Protestant Ethic and the Spirit of Capitalism.* New York, Scribner's, 1958.

Weiner, Myron. *Modernization: The Dynamics of Growth.* New York, Basic Books, 1966.

White, Morton, and Lucia White. *The Intellectual Versus the City: From Thomas Jefferson to Frank Lloyd Wright.* Cambridge, Mass., Harvard University Press, 1962.

Wicker, Allan W. "Attitudes Versus Action: The Relationship of Verbal and Overt Behavioral Responses to Attitude Objects," *Journal of Social Issues* 25 (no. 4, 1969), 41–78.

Wirth, Louis. "Urbanism as a Way of Life," *American Journal of Sociology* 44 (1938), 3–24.

Woodward, Julian L., and Elmo Roper. "Political Activity of American Citizens," in Heinz Eulau *et al.*, eds., *Political Behavior.* Glencoe, Ill., Free Press, 1956, pp. 133–137.

Notes

1 Introduction

1. For a discussion of comparable studies and their success in accounting for scale variances see footnotes 4, 5, 6 in Chapter 20.

2. The number of researchers (of whom we have a record) who have used our instrument for measuring modernity has come to nearly 50. Some of the most interesting studies follow. A doctoral dissertation by Ineke Cunningham which has been recently published by the University of Puerto Rico Press as *Modernity and Academic Performance: A Study of Students in a Puerto Rican High School* (1972) used our shortened modernity scale to measure the relation between modernity and academic performance in students, their parents, and their peers. Wayne A. Cornelius, Jr., now Assistant Professor of Political Science at Massachusetts Institute of Technology, used selected questionnaire items in a study of migration in Mexico (1971). Stephen L. Klineberg, now Assistant Professor of Social Psychology at Rice University, used our instrument to study Tunisian adolescents and their parents under the impact of modernization (1971). Dr. Herbert Leiderman of the Stanford University Department of Psychiatry used the instrument in a study of child socialization in Kenya (1969). Donald B. Holsinger, currently a lecturer in Education at Stanford University, used our scale to measure attitudinal modernity among primary-school children in Brazil (1972). In a less strictly academic study, Alfred Bennett, Jr., used the scale to measure attitudinal modernity of corporation managers in the Philippines (1969). Finally, Gary Bergthold and David McClelland used OM in their measurement of the influence of Peace Corps teachers on students in Ethiopia (1968).

3. Since we drew our samples mainly from among cultivators and industrial workers, we were generally testing within a narrower educational and occupation range than that covered by a national sample. In four of our six countries, however, the modernity scale was also applied to university students without

any problems in administration or scoring. This indicates the OM scale could readily be used in studies covering the whole range of social groups normally included in a national sample.

4. For a statement of this viewpoint see Vytautas Kavolis, "Post-Modern Man," *Social Problems* 17 (1970): 435–448.

5. Among the features which may give an institution a strong character are: being governed by strict rules and procedures, being able to dispense powerful reward and punishment, being dominated by very strong sentiments of group solidarity. A naval vessel at sea or a varsity or professional football team would qualify as very strong environments. A large college dormitory would be a much less powerful environment than most Greek-letter fraternities and sororities. For a discussion of the factory as a strong environment, see Chapter 11.

6. For experimental evidence on the ability of highly structured situations to influence the participant's basic attitudes, see Paul E. Breer and Edwin Locke, *Task Experience as a Source of Attitudes* (Homewood, Ill.: Dorsey Press, 1965).

7. James S. Slotkin, *From Field to Factory; New Industrial Employees* (Glencoe, Ill.: Free Press, 1960), p. 31.

8. The Psychosomatic Symptoms Test in our research consisted of a set of questions which had previously been used in the United States and elsewhere to measure the mental health or adjustment of groups. This set of questions is reproduced in Appendix A. A brief discussion of the results of this test appears at the end of Chapter 18. A detailed description of our work in this area is found in Alex Inkeles, "The Fate of Personal Adjustment in the Process of Modernization," *International Journal of Comparative Sociology* 11, no. 2 (June 1970): 81–114.

2   Toward a Definition of the Modern Man

1. Robert E. Ward and Dankwart A. Rustow, *Political Modernization in Japan and Turkey* (Princeton, N. J.: Princeton University Press, 1964), chap. 1.

2. Samuel P. Huntington, "Political Modernization: America vs. Europe," *World Politics* 18, no. 3 (1966): 378–414.

3. Max Weber, *The Protestant Ethic and the Spirit of Capitalism* (New York: Scribner's, 1958), p. 27.

4. Robert N. Bellah, "Meaning and Modernisation," *Religious Studies* 4 (1968): 39.

5. The twenty-four main themes used in constructing our scales of overall modernity are listed in Table 7-1.

6. See Alex Inkeles and Raymond Bauer, *The Soviet Citizen: Daily Life in a Totalitarian Society* (Cambridge, Mass.: Harvard University Press, 1961); Raymond A. Bauer, Alex Inkeles, and Clyde Kluckhohn, *How the Soviet System Works* (Cambridge, Mass.: Harvard University Press, 1964); Alex Inkeles, *Public Opinion in Soviet Russia: A Study in Mass Persuasion* (Cambridge, Mass.: Harvard University Press, 1962); and Alex Inkeles, *Social Change in Soviet Russia* (Cambridge, Mass.: Harvard University Press, 1968).

7. Daniel Lerner, *The Passing of Traditional Society: Modernizing the Middle East* (Glencoe, Ill.: Free Press, 1963).

8. This would have been true for OM-3, OM-500, and OM-519, as described in Chapters 6 and 7.

9. In making this statement we do not mean to suggest that all the themes we were led to by the analytic perspective were original with us. On the contrary, many of those themes had been emphasized by other scholars as well. We have already noted Lerner's interest in the opinion realm, which he expressed in the concept of *empathy*, or the ability to see oneself to encourage fellow's situation. Lerner also asserted that a mobile society "has to encourage rationality" and noted that in it "people come to see the future as manipulable rather than ordained, and their personal prospects in terms of achievement rather than hertiage." We may recognize here much the same emphasis as is contained in our concept of efficacy and our theme of aspirations and technical skill. Further, Lerner speaks of the mobile person as "distinguished by a high capacity for identification with new aspects of his environment; he comes equipped with the mechanisms needed to incorporate new demands upon himself that arise outside of his habitual experience." Again the strong relation this bears to our concepts of "openness to new experience" and "readiness for change" will be readily apparent. (See Lerner, *Passing of Traditional Society*, pp. 48–49.)

Similar parallels may be observed between elements in our conception of modernity and those proposed by several others. Robert Ward, for example, presents a list of elements of what he calls "intellectual modernization," and among them are items very similar to our themes of aspirations for new learning, acceptance of change, dignity, and growth of opinion. (See Ward and Rustow, *Political Modernization*, chap. 1.) Ithiel Pool also defines the modern not in terms of GNP nor the proportion of the labor force in industry, but "rather in terms of values and modes of behavior" shared by a population. Among the values and ways of acting he describes as modern are elements closely akin to our themes of efficacy, aspirations, and openness to new experience. See Ithiel de Sola Pool, "The Role of Communication in the Process of Modernization and Technical Change," in Bert F. Hoselitz and W. E. Moore, eds., *Industrialization and Society* (Paris: UNESCO, 1963), p. 281. Wilbert Moore lists among the more "specific values and principles of conduct appropriate to modernization": rationality in problem solving, punctuality, recognition of individually limited but systematically linked interdependence, and achievement and mobility aspirations, each of which is easily translated into the language of our list of themes. See W. E. Moore, "The Strategy of Fostering Performance and Responsibility," in Egbert de Vries and J. M. Echavarria, eds., *Social Aspects of Economic Development in Latin America* (Paris: UNESCO, 1963), I: 236–237. Indeed, we can find similar themes delineated in work as far afield and as far back as the classical economic writings of the late nineteenth century. Thus, Alfred Marshall asserted that there were qualities that make a great industrial people and are required not in any particular occupation, but in all, such as "to have everything ready when wanted, to act promptly and show resource when anything goes wrong, [and] to accommodate oneself quickly to changes of detail in the work done." See Alfred Marshall, *Principles of Economics: An Introductory Volume* (8th ed., London: Macmillan, 1936), pp. 206–207.

10. Wilbert E. Moore, *Industrialization and Labor: Social Aspects of Economic Development* (New York: Russell and Russell, 1965), p. 74.

11. M. B. Desmukh, "Delhi: A Study of Floating Migration," in *Social Implications of Industrialization and Urbanization: Five Studies of Urban Population of Recent Rural Origin in Cities of Southern Asia* (Calcutta:

UNESCO Research Center on Social Implications of Industrialization, 1956), p. 219.

12. Geoffrey Parrinder, "Religion in Village and Town," *Annual Conference Report,* Part I (Ibadan, Nigeria: West Africa Institute of Social and Economic Research, Sociology Section, University College, March 1953), p. 126.

13. See Irving Louis Horowitz, *Three Worlds of Development: The Theory and Practice of International Stratification* (New York: Oxford University Press, 1966), *passim;* Karl W. Deutsch, "Social Mobilization and Political Development," *American Political Science Review* 55, no. 3 (September 1961): 493–514, Deutsch, *Nationalism and Social Communication: An Inquiry into the Foundations of Nationality* (Cambridge–New York: MIT Press–Wiley, 1962); Alex Inkeles, "Participant Citizenship in Six Developing Countries," *American Political Science Review* 63, no. 4 (December 1969): 1120–1141; Amitai Etzioni, *The Active Society; A Theory of Societal and Political Processes* (Glencoe, Ill.: Free Press, 1968).

14. Lerner, *Passing of Traditional Society,* pp. 46 and 55.

15. See Deutsch, *Nationalism and Social Communication;* Pool, "The Role of Communication in the Process of Modernization;" Lerner, *The Passing of Traditional Society.*

16. It should be noted that the behavioral model cut across both the topical and the analytic models. Its special quality lay not in distinctions of substance, which served to separate the analytic from the topical models, but rather derived from distinctions about the procedures for *measuring* a man's position on any issue. Any one of the themes dealt with in either the analytic or the topical model could be approached either through the measurement of attitudes or through behavioral tests. In effect, therefore, there were logically four components in our approach to modernity: analytic themes and topical themes, each of which could be measured by studying either attitudes or behavior. As stated below, we eventually brought all four components together in our overall measure of modernity, called OM.

3 The Research Design and Sample Structure

1. In selecting factory workers we had to meet various sampling criteria, discussed in the text and summarized in Table 3–1, and we also had to take into account our sampling requirements for the selection of factories, discussed in Chapter 12. Combining these two considerations we decided to seek approximately 10 workers from each of approximately 70 factories in each country. In this way we were able to avoid overemphasizing any one factory.

To draw our sample of men from each factory, the field director was to review the personnel lists to see how many men were eligible in terms of our sampling criteria. If more than 10 men were eligible from a given factory, ten were selected at random from those eligible. However, recognizing that this ideal might be difficult to hold to in given field conditions we authorized the field directors to take more than 10 men, but not more than 20, from a single factory when necessary. Actually, as the results given below indicate, the field directors came reasonably close to the standard of getting approximately 10 men per factory. India is an exception for various reasons discussed in the text. It should be clear from these results that we seldom had to resort to randomization within factories, since in most factories 100 percent of the eligible population was interviewed.

	Argentina	Chile	East Pakistan	India	Israel	Nigeria
Number of factories sampled	85	92	46	11	131	59
Average number of workers interviewed per factory	8	8	14	64	4	9

2. For a full discussion of the role of urban experience, see Chapter 15.

3. The criteria used to distinguish a modern from a traditional factory and the sampling procedures used to select factories are more fully described in Chapter 12.

So far as size is concerned, within each country we devised at least five factory size categories, and we tried to sample so that our set of workers would not come disproportionately from any particular size plant. In Argentina, for example, the numbers of workers interviewed from "small," "medium," and "large" plants (collapsing the five size categories into three) were 215, 211, and 238, respectively. The distribution of cases among small, medium, and large factories in the other countries was also approximately well balanced.

So far as type of product is concerned, factories were sampled with the aim of obtaining a broad diversity, rather than a set of factories representative with respect to the industry of the country as a whole. Thus, although the jute industry dominated East Pakistani industry, jute factories did not dominate our sample there. The field directors were requested to have at least seven types of product more or less equally represented in the set of factories included in the sample. In all countries, a broad range of type of product was represented by the factories sampled. For example, the 85 factories in the Argentine sample broke down by product type as follows: food and beverages, 16; textiles, 12; chemicals, 19; metals, 9; machinery, 8; electrical apparatus, 9; paper and printing, 12.

4. The main participants were Alex Inkeles, Edward Ryan, and Howard Schuman. By that time each had between 3 and 5 months of field experience in pretesting questions and assessing the feasibility of the study in Chile, Nigeria, and East Pakistan, respectively. Amar K. Singh, who was later to become field director for India, sat in on the conference as a consultant. David H. Smith, then a graduate assistant to Professor Inkeles in Chile, served the group as recording secretary. The criteria then agreed on served not only as a guide to the individual field directors, but also as a kind of compact, adherence to which insured the ultimate comparability of the separate country studies.

In Chile and Argentina there were no special criteria of selection on cultural grounds. In Pakistan, however, we included only Bengali Moslems (except for a tiny sample of about 25 Hindus). In Israel we selected only the so-called Oriental Jews, rather than Jews of European origin. In Nigeria we confined ourselves to various subtribes of the Yoruba. In India we included equal members of Bihari Hindus and so-called "tribals" according to a complex special scheme.

The selection of industrial factory workers and of urban nonindustrial workers is further discussed in Chapter 4, note 6, and Chapter 14, respectively. So far as cultivators were concerned, in each country we drew them from at least ten, and generally more, different villages. The villages sampled were selected because they were in the districts, indeed often were the very villages, from which had come the industrial workers we had previously found in the factories. In addition we made certain that these villages were appreciably isolated from the modern world, that they were as far as possible from such influences as good roads, bus services, railroads, and various forms of mass media.

Since the cultivators in our sample were selected after the sampling of factory workers of rural origin, we were able to match the two groups moderately well, not only on specific area of origin, but also on education, religion, and the like. However, the rural-origin factory workers had, in their turn, been selected according to the same criteria as had been used for urban-origin workers, which meant having a higher education than was common for the average farmer. It followed that the cultivators in our sample were often somewhat above the countryside average in educational attainment. However, we definitely selected only the typical "peasant" cultivators, rather than rich owners of large farms, farm supervisors, or farm foremen.

Ideally we expected to draw experienced and inexperienced "new" workers in a ratio of 5 to 2 from each factory, in accord with our overall design. In doing so we were deliberately trying to oversample new workers, relative to their true proportion in the total factory-worker labor force, because of their crucial theoretical importance to the major hypothesis of our study. However, really inexperienced or "new" factory workers meeting our other criteria proved to be especially hard to find. Therefore, special arrangements were allowed to provide for greater numbers of such interviewees to be selected; for instance, (a) new factory workers were sought by themselves from additional plants in which no experienced workers were sampled; (b) new workers were drawn in greater than their proportionate number from large plants where they were more plentiful; and (c) men were interviewed as new workers who had just been accepted by a factory for production-line employment even though they had not yet started to work. For further discussion of the new- vs. experienced-worker classification see Chapter 12.

A rural area was taken to mean an isolated house, or a compound of houses in the countryside or a small community, usually with 2,000 or fewer residents, whose members did mainly agricultural work. An urban area was taken to mean any settlement with a population of 20,000 or more. On these definitions the ambiguous middle range of settlements from 2,000 to 20,000 inhabitants was omitted from the sampling.

Going beyond the size distinction, we tried to select as rural areas villages which were agricultural, rather than small towns which might be mainly commercial and administrative. Thus we eliminated from consideration those settlements with many shops, offices, and government buildings even if they were small and otherwise rural. Thus, an attempt was made to make urban and rural origin clearly differentiable polar types, ignoring men with part urban and part rural experience in their first 15 years. No more than 1 year of experience in the opposite type of setting was allowed among respondents.

In Argentina, Chile, and Nigeria we were able to obtain more or less equal numbers of men of urban and rural origin meeting our other sampling criteria. However, in Israel we were able to find extremely few rural-origin men, even among cultivators, owing to the generally urban residential patterns of the Jews who made up the set of Oriental Jews on whom we based our Israeli sample. In East Pakistan and India, given the preponderantly rural nature of the populations, the field directors decided to simplify their task by including in the samples only men of rural origin.

5. We did, at first, look for urban origin men in East Pakistan, and found 26. But we had to screen so many men to find these that we concluded the cost would be prohibitive to reach the total of 100, the minimum number for our type of statistical analysis. We therefore suspended the search. Our regular sampling brought us 20 additional men who were partly urban in background.

6. The matching technique is more fully described in Chapter 8, especially in note 8, and in Appendix E.

4 The Conduct of the Fieldwork

1. Israel was a partial exception to this statement, since there we relied on the services of the well-established Israel Institute for Applied Social Research for the recruitment and training of interviewers.

2. Alex Inkeles, "Fieldwork Problems in Comparative Research on Modernization," in A. R. Desai, ed., *Essays on Modernization of Underdeveloped Societies* (Bombay: Thacker, 1971), II: 20–75.

3. *Ibid.*

4. We were, from the outset, aware that how far men were modernized by experiences like education and factory experience might depend on the special features of the sociopolitical system in which they lived. For this reason we hoped to have available pairs of nations which were alike in culture and general level of development, but which had contrasting systems of political and economic organization. For example, East Pakistan was Muslim, was ruled (in 1963) by a military dictatorship, and relied almost exclusively on private enterprise. India was Hindu, was ruled by a multiparty democratic parliamentary system, and relied on many socialist enterprises.

5. Since Israel was one of the countries which had been receiving large shipments of surplus food from the United States, and was paying for it in blocked local currency, ample funds in Israeli currency were available to cover the cost of field work. In addition, we could count on the cooperation of the Israel Institute of Applied Social Research, an experienced and highly competent research center which regularly undertook surveys of the Israeli population and had previously conducted several researches in cooperation with American groups. These advantages meant that adding Israel to our sample would place minimum additional strain on our financial and personnel resources.

6. The method for the selection of factories to reflect a range of characteristics by size, product, and modernity is described in Chapters 3 and 12. Of the factories selected for inclusion in the sample according to the selection criteria, we were actually permitted to enter and work in 100 percent of those in India and East Pakistan, in 99 percent in Nigeria, and in 97 percent in Israel. The rejection rate was relatively high only in Argentina, where we were allowed to enter only 75 percent of the factories selected by us. We had no formal count from the field director in Chile, but his experience was evidently closer to that in Argentina than that in the other countries.

7. Each field director was given the right to unrestricted use of the data in the preparation of a separate publication focused on the distinctive needs and interests of the audience in his country. To facilitate preparation of these reports, copies of all computer runs for a given country were made available to the respective field directors free of charge. For our senior staff, we ran

informal seminars on the theory and methods of research, especially as they related to the social psychology of economic development. In addition, each of the local field directors was assured a period of additional training at Harvard University, and use of the computer and other facilities there.

8. Our rules for identifying factories as "modern" or "traditional" are described in Chapter 12.

9. We could not always carefully select our interviewers or maintain appropriately close supervision. For example, in Chile and Argentina we were obliged to subcontract some of the interviews which were to be done in cities rather distant from the capital. In those cases we could not follow our usual verification procedures, but external checks on the performance of our interviewers could be supplemented by checks internal to the questionnaire.

10. Some interviews had to be discarded, either because we were not confident about the conditions under which they had been done or because evidence internal to the questionnaires threw doubt on their veracity. The largest block of such discards was accounted for by two interviewers in Buenos Aires, all 18 of whose interviews we did not use. Dr. Singh also discovered one interviewer who came to his attention because the man seemed to discharge his duties with exceptional speed. A careful check revealed that he had indeed contacted all his interviewees, but had skipped large segments of the questionnaire, checking those items at random. This man was discharged, and all his interviews were withdrawn from the sample.

11. Items were taken directly or adapted from the questionnaires of the following studies: Gabriel A. Almond and Sidney Verba, *The Civic Culture: Political Attitudes and Democracy in Five Nations* (Princeton, N.J.: Princeton University Press, 1963); Melvin M. Tumin and Arnold S. Feldman, *Social Class and Social Change in Puerto Rico* (Princeton, N.J.: Princeton University Press, 1961); Alex Inkeles and Raymond A. Bauer, *The Soviet Citizen* (Cambridge, Mass.: Harvard University Press, 1959); Hadley Cantril, *The Pattern of Human Concerns* (New Brunswick, N.J.: Rutgers University Press, 1965); J. A. Kahl, *The Measurement of Modernism: A Study of Values in Brazil and Mexico* (Austin and London: University of Texas Press, 1968); Julian L. Woodward and Elmo Roper, "Political Activity of American Citizens," in Heinz Eulau, *et al.*, eds. *Political Behavior* (Glencoe, Ill.: Free Press, 1956), pp. 133–137; Daniel Lerner, *The Passing of Traditional Society: Modernizing the Middle East* (New York: Free Press, 1963); and Kalman H. Silvert, *The Conflict Society: Reaction and Revolution in Latin America* (New York: American Universities Field Staff, 1966).

12. We conducted an early pretest in 1962 in Puerto Rico to ascertain the general feasibility of our approach. At that time we tested only a small set of questions, selected to represent the range of topics we then thought to investigate and the several styles of question wording we then considered using. The pretest sample was limited, moreover, to several dozen individuals.

13. Our procedure assumed that all concerned were equipped to make basically the same apperceptions and could converse well in English. For both Professors Perla Regina Gibaja, field director for Argentina, and Juan Cesar Garcia, field director for Chile, this was not the case so far as English was concerned. Their briefing, therefore, was in part conducted in Spanish by Inkeles and Smith.

14. This maximum number of questions was for Argentina. It included the core set of approximately 166 attitudinal and behavioral questions considered

relevant to measuring individual modernity *and used in all six countries,* the background and sampling questions, all the questions in the "optional" category, and a large number of those designated "unique." "Optional" questions dealt with our main interest in individual modernity, and were designed to be cross-nationally comparable, but, as their designation suggests, they could be left out of the questionnaire if the local field director so desired. "Unique" questions were developed on the initiative of each field director without consultation with other field directors, and could be of purely local interest without necessary reference to the theme of individual modernization.

15. One of the most difficult tasks in training interviewers is to teach them not to lead the interviewee. The situation can become very problematic in cultures in which interviewers tend spontaneously to adopt positions of authority, as in Nigeria. During the early stages of interviewer training there, one interviewer was assigned a respondent who was evidently confused by the questions, kept changing his mind, and took a very long time to answer. It was late at night, and getting later, and in a fit of exasperation the interviewer said, in Yoruba of course: "For Christ's sake, answer the question. If you don't, we'll be here until midnight." As Dr. Ryan reports the incident: "Not surprisingly, the interview blew apart. The respondent rushed into the lounge area, greatly agitated, and declared he would not continue." The insult was patched up by Dr. Ryan, who drove the man home. More important, it formed the basis for new training sessions designed to change the behavior of the interviewer at fault and to help the others to be more aware of the problems created by leading interviewees, or by passing audible judgments on their performance.

16. There were some 440 question "units," that is, questions or subquestions, to which the R score applied in Chile and Argentina. These men, therefore, averaged 1.3 repetitions per question unit. Of course, the necessity for so many repetitions could have been a consequence of deafness, rather than inability to comprehend our questions. Moreover, we are not unaware that the apparent individual variation in R scores could have been significantly a function of the interviewer's conscientiousness in noting repetitions.

17. We found no review systematically summarizing the experiences of the pollsters, but a rate of about 5 to 10 percent of DK/NA for the average question seems normal. In all fairness we must acknowledge that this is not necessarily a serious defect in most public-opinion polls. Their purpose is mainly to estimate the distribution of opinion. The loss of cases as DK/NA is, therefore, not of great concern. In our study, however, the type of intensive analysis we planned to undertake made it important not to lose cases in this way. In this connection, it is germane to compare our results with those of research rather more nearly comparable to ours, specifically that on the civic culture. Almond and Verba contracted their field work out to commercial polling agencies, which were to draw representative national samples. Within a subset of 18 of their questions, selected because they were roughly comparable to ours, the highest proportion of DK/NA answers ranged from 11 percent in the U. S. to 38 percent in Italy. The average percentages of DK/NA answers in the U. S. and the U. K. were 3.6 and 4.6, respectively. But in the less-developed countries more comparable to ours, namely, Mexico and Italy, the averages were 8.1 and 17.5, respectively. These rates were four to nine times those in our study, and yet the Almond and Verba studies included all levels of education, whereas our samples included only

those with very little education and hence those more prone to respond "I don't know."

18. The random-probe technique was developed by Dr. Howard Schuman and is more fully described in Schuman, "The Random Probe: A Technique for Evaluating the Validity of Closed Questions," *American Sociological Review* 31, no. 2 (April 1966) : 218–223.

5   Two Case Studies

1. The random-probe technique is described in Chapter 4.

6   Constructing the OM Scale

1. Many of these themes, such as politics, religion, efficacy, and family relations, will be treated separately and in detail in our project's second volume, "Explorations in the Study of Individual Modernization," in preparation.

2. In our article which appeared in the December 1966 issue of *Sociometry,* the number of questions testing self-reported behavior was given as 17. That figure represented the 12 referred to here, plus 5 questions in which the interviewee reported his exposure to mass communication — for example, how often he read a newspaper. Those questions were included in a version of the OM scale, OM-4, not dealt with here. In this book, however, we have treated the individual's report of his communications behavior as an independent variable used to explain modern attitudes and values, rather than as a dependent variable constituting part of the syndrome of individual modernity. See David H. Smith and Alex Inkeles, "The OM Scale: A Comparative Psychological Measure of Individual Modernity," *Sociometry* 29, no. 4 (December 1966): 353–377.

3. The actual number of questions we asked to test information was 23, as reported in Smith and Inkeles, "The OM Scale." The answers to some of these questions were coded on several different dimensions. Each such separate coding we referred to as an "item." A single question could thus generate several items. In CO-7, for example, we asked the respondent to name the things he would like to own. The answer was coded not only for the number of things he mentioned, but also for the number which we defined as "modern" as against "traditional" goods, and for the proportion which were for production rather than merely being useful in consumption. Each of these three aspects of a man's answer was separately scored to give the respondent points toward his OM score. This procedure resulted in the original 23 questions having a possible total weight as 35 "items" in calculating an individual's OM score.

4. Several versions of this planned scale were eventually constructed. The standard form was based on 28 questions: 17 which probed attitudes and values, plus 11 which tested self-reported behavior and objective information about political events. See Alex Inkeles, "Participant Citizenship in Six Developing Countries," *American Political Science Review* 63, no. 4 (December 1969): 1120–1141.

5. The question, "Are you satisfied or dissatisfied with your job?" exemplifies those we did *not* include in the pool of secondary OM items. The intrinsic interest and usefulness of that question (WC-5) is obvious. Furthermore, we acknowledged it as not improbable that modern men might, on the average, be more often found on one side or the other of this question. Yet we could not see any compelling reason for the answer to be considered as *defining* a

modern or traditional man. We therefore excluded the question from the OM set, classifying it as an item in the area of personal adjustment. On the other hand, we left in this secondary pool the question (AG-3) in which we asked our interviewees whether they looked forward to old age or dreaded it, for the reasons given in our discussion of aging and its role in the "topical model" of the modern man described in Chapter 2.

6. The obvious alternative would have been to score each answer as modern or traditional in exactly the same way in all six countries. If this could have been done, it would certainly have facilitated certain types of cross-national comparison. But that approach was poorly suited to our materials and to our scientific purpose.

Our purpose was to ascertain how far individual modernity was influenced by modernizing institutions such as education and factory experience in a variety of different cultures. To clarify that relation it was highly desirable that the individual modernity scores have a distribution as close to normal as possible in each country. If all the answers were to be scored in the same way in all countries, there was the risk that most of the people in the countries with high average education would receive very high OM scores, whereas in other countries almost everyone would receive very low scores. In other words, the test would then have discriminated well *across* countries but poorly *within* countries. For our purposes a test "calibrated" separately in each country to yield a normal distribution within that country was far preferable to one scored the same way in all countries but yielding a highly skewed distribution in each country.

Furthermore, if we had scored all answers precisely the same way in all countries we would have been reduced to working with only that small number of questions which were exactly alike in all respects in all six countries. Unfortunately, at least from this point of view, a substantial number of the alternative answers used in the different countries did *not* exactly agree. This was due to adjustments made by the field directors. For example, Howard Schuman, our field director in East Pakistan, often presented only two or three alternative answers for questions which elsewhere used four alternatives. As a result of comparable adjustments made elsewhere, the number of questions *and answers* worded so exactly alike in all six countries as to permit scoring by an absolute standard was reduced to approximately 33. We felt that this number would yield an OM scale with reliabilities too low for the sort of analysis we planned in this book.

We did, however, create scales on this basis to use in a later phase of our study which, unlike this book, will focus on differences in modernity observed when one compares the men from one country with those of another.

7. This effect is achieved simply by multiplying the score originally given in the range 1.00 to 2.00 by 100 and then subtracting 100.

8. One of the disadvantages of the method of cutting at the median is that it may group people who perhaps should logically be kept apart. Consider, for example, the question: "What should one do with a boy who is always tardy?" for which the alternatives were: "Forgive him (1) every time, (2) almost always, (3) rarely, or (4) never?" Using the method of cutting at the median, one might end up grouping those men who said that you should "never" forgive a tardy boy with those who said he should be forgiven "almost always," merely because about half the sample selected the very last alternative in the continuum, that is, the answer "forgive him every time."

We are satisfied, from experimenting with other methods, that the loss of information following upon adoption of our system of dichotomization was minimal, at least given the number of items used in our major scales, and especially in the OM scales. To test this assumption we reconstructed one of our longer special subscales, the politics scale, using not the OM type of dichotomization, but rather standardized Z scores of the raw responses. Unlike the more arbitrary dichotomization approach, the Z scoring took full account of exactly where each individual fell on the actual continuum of alternative answers available for each question. The reliability resulting when this Z-score method was used in constructing the politics scale was basically the same as that obtained by our dichotomization method. In Chile, for example, with 56 items in the scale, dichotomization yielded a reliability of .74, whereas the Z-score method yielded .77, both reliabilities computed by the Spearman-Brown formula for split-half reliability. In India, with 40 items in the scale, the Z-score method yielded a reliability of .84, against .83 for the dichotomous-cut method. There is evidently little reason here to prefer one method over the other.

A second test of the adequacy of the dichotomized scales was made by reference to an external criterion, by comparing the correlation of our independent variables with scales built by dichotomizing *and* with scales based on Z scoring. When this was done in Chile, the evidence suggested no reason to prefer the Z-scoring method or the dichotomization. For example, the correlation with years of education put the dichotomized-item version of the politics scale slightly ahead of the Z-scored version, the figures being .46 and .45, respectively. On mass-media exposure the correlations were both approximately .49. Such fluctuation in a narrow range was found in other independent-variable correlations with the politics scale. As with the scale reliabilities, these data gave no reason to fault our method of building scales by dichotomizing each item at the median.

Although the evidence just cited indicated that for all practical purposes the dichotomized scales were as good as the Z-scored ones, it was nevertheless only indirect evidence of the equivalence of the two types of scale. Decisive evidence of their true equivalence required that the two scales be correlated with each other. When that was done for Chile and India, the resultant correlation in both countries was .97! Clearly, either method gave a virtually identical scale.

9. See footnote 4 of this chapter.

10. These calculations were made, as were all others in this section, using item-to-scale correlations which had been adjusted to take into account the element of "autocorrelation," that is, the correlation of the item with itself. Autocorrelation is a problem whenever any item is correlated with a scale in which the item itself has been included.

Even in the case of scales which are fairly long, the effect of this autocorrelation, while modest, is certainly not negligible. In our experience, even with a scale containing 100 items, up to one-third of the value of the item-to-scale correlation for each item is accounted for by the fact of autocorrelation. This may readily be observed in Table 6–1 by comparing the averages of item-to-scale correlations which are adjusted for autocorrelation with those which are not. Applying the adjustment obviously substantially reduces the number of items in the typical scale which can qualify as having a significant item-to-scale correlation. For example, the proportion of all items in OM-1 having positive item-to-scale correlations significant at the .05 level or better in Argentina fell from 86 to 70 percent when the correlations were adjusted. In Israel, the decline was from 95 to 76 percent, and the results in other countries were comparable. In the light of this experience it should be evident how unfortunate it is that in most research the item-to-scale correlations are reported without adjusting for the autocorrelation effect.

The adjustments we made in the item-to-scale correlations used information readily available in our computer printouts, and were computed by Guilford's formula for corrected point-biserial r (modified for convenience). As Guilford points out, "the chief contribution to spuriousness . . . is the ratio of the item variance to the total-score variance." In our case the total-score variance so dominates the denominator of Guilford's formula that we get at least two-figure accuracy by just using the handy corrected r = original r - s.d./(total score s.d.). See Joy Paul Guilford, *Fundamental Statistics in Psychology and Education,* 3d ed. (New York: McGraw-Hill, 1956), pp. 349–440.

11. The formulas we used to compute the reliability of scales varied somewhat during the history of the project, depending on the preference of the particular analyst. Those we relied on most consistently were the following:

Spearman-Brown: S-B $= nr^2/[1 + (n\text{-}1) \ r^2]$,

Kuder-Richardson: K-R $= [n/(n\text{-}1)] \ (1\text{-}\Sigma V_i/n^2 V_s)$,

where n is the number of items, r the average item-to-scale correlation, V_i the variance of the ith item, and V_s the variance of a scale which is the average of the items.

12. After reviewing several hundred scales of social attitudes and values, Shaw and Wright concluded that scales yielding reliability coefficients of .75 and up could be described as at least "moderately reliable." They did not, however, place this standard in the context of the "internal-consistency" formulas which we have been using. Moreover, the scales they discussed attained their reliabilities only after a kind of "cleaning" process, that is, after items which did not fit well were discarded and the scales were reapplied using only those items which earlier experience had indicated already held together. By contrast, the reliabilities we presented for OM-1, and will later present for OM-2 and OM-3, are for scales which were not thus cleaned for further field use. In addition, few of the researches cited by Shaw and Wright had subjected their questions to so thorough a "scrambling" as we did ours, as described in the section of Chapter 4 on "Response Bias and Comprehension of Our Questionnaire." Nor, it may be noted, were many of their scales so broad and multifaceted as is the OM scale. Against these considerations, however, one must weigh the fact that the OM scales gained a lot in the "reliability race" because of the large number of items they included. See Marvin E. Shaw and Jack M. Wright, *Scales for the Measurement of Attitudes* (New York: McGraw-Hill, 1967), p. 570.

13. The number 40 is approximate. Field directors occasionally dropped certain questions used everywhere else, added questions, or split a single question into two.

14. Only 47 percent of the gain in reliability over OM-2 can, however, be

attributed to the special virtue of the information and behavior questions. The remainder of the improvement was due to the lengthening of the scale.

15. See note 12 in this chapter.

16. The assertion that a man identified as modern at one time would be so defined by the OM scale at another time rests on the results of the split-half reliability test. Using the test as the basis for such prediction has become a convention in attitude testing. However, the only really accurate way to judge whether the test score obtained at one time will actually agree with the score at a second time is to administer the test a second time to the same individuals. This method yields a measure of "test-retest" reliability. How well such second test scores will agree with the first depends, of course, on the time elapsed between the tests, the range of scores among those selected for retest, and many other factors. Test-retest reliability is reported in the psychological literature only infrequently, at least by comparison with the Spearman-Brown and Kuder-Richardson indices. In general, however, test-retest reliabilities are quite a bit lower than those for the other indices. Shaw and Wright report for a number of scales having some degree of comparability with OM a series of test-retest reliabilities ranging from .68 to .84 after lapses of time up to 7 weeks. Bloom reports on seven studies of retesting after a year's lapse, with test-retest scores ranging from a low of .30 on a scale of attitudes toward war to a high of .74 on a religious-values scale, with the median score at .55. See Shaw and Wright, *Scales for the Measurement of Attitudes;* Benjamin S. Bloom, *Stability and Change in Human Characteristics* (New York: John Wiley, 1964), pp. 171–172.

We reinterviewed 16 East Pakistani men, after a median interval of 40 days, using a modified form of the OM questionnaire. The longest form of the OM scale we could reconstruct for this group had 57 items. Using that form, the test-retest reliability was .64. A shortened list of 60 questions, all dealing with attitudes and values, was submitted twice to a class of 33 students at the University of Southern California, the second test coming 2 months after the first. Using these 60 questions, nine variations of the OM scale were constructed. The test-retest reliability of these versions ranged from .47 to .78, with the median at .65. These results are not brilliant, but they indicate that the OM scale has test-retest reliability broadly comparable to that obtained with attitude and value tests commonly used in the United States and Western Europe.

17. This point should be emphasized, because the reliability of a scale is equal to the maximum amount of variance that the scale can have in common with any other variable. In other words, a scale's reliability sets the effective limit on how good its relation can be to any other variable. Thus the true relation between things may be greatly obscured if either of the key variables is unreliably measured. Let us assume, for example, that education was, in fact, perfectly correlated with individual modernity, and that we had a perfectly reliable measure of education. If the measure of individual modernity also had a perfect reliability, the observed correlation would be perfect, namely, 1.00. As the reliability of the modernity measure fell, however, the maximum observable correlation would also fall drastically. With a reliability index of .90, the maximum observed correlation would be .95; with rel. = .70, the maximum $r = .84$; with rel. = .50, the maximum $r = .71$, *even though the true relation remained $r = 1.00$.* If the second measure is also unreliable, the effects are magnified. Thus, if the reliability of our measure

of education were only .90, which is very likely all it was, then the maximum correlations obtainable with modernity measures at given levels of reliability would be: .95 with OM rel. = 1.00, .79 with OM rel. = .70, and .67 with OM rel. = .50. All of these calculations make an assumption which may not be met in practice. While a scale's reliability does set an effective limit, sampling variation of that limit must be taken into account. For this reason one cannot be certain that the "true" correlation will be larger than that obscured by imperfect reliability. One does occasionally get correlations above the effective limit or even the true correlation. See J. P. Guilford, *Fundamental Statistics*, pp. 401–402.

18. Table 2–1 shows that we used 32 different alphabetic codes to identify our questions. Of these, 2 — SAM and BD — were used only to screen and identify our subjects. Four others — AR, OT, PT, and ST — identified the special psychological tests we administered to all subjects. That left 26 themes treating attitudes, values and behavior. However, since two of those, OP and PA, were investigated only in a few select countries, and therefore were not used in the general analysis, we were left with 24 themes which had been treated everywhere.

19. The expression "carry twice the weight of" is used here in a nontechnical sense, merely to indicate that one theme was represented by twice as many questions as another. In determining a man's score, therefore, such questions did carry twice the weight of a set represented by half as many items. Insofar as the reliability of the scale is concerned, however, the influence of any theme cannot safely be judged by the number of items representing it. If items are redundant, in the sense of being highly intercorrelated with one another, but have near zero correlation to the larger set of scale items taken as a whole, then the sheer number of such redundant items will not necessarily greatly influence the reliability of a large scale to which they have been added. By contrast, a scattering of items, a few here and a few there, may have a substantial impact on the reliability of a scale if the items are weakly intercorrelated with one another but all are strongly related to the underlying or common dimension measured by the scale.

20. This rule was applied to the items and scales for each country separately, that is, it was not required that the items make a significant contribution to the scale score in all six countries.

21. After the questions were regrouped into the standard themes, we eliminated all items which were not making a statistically significant contribution to the measurement of individual modernity, repeating the procedure for each country. To qualify for further competition, a question had to have an (adjusted) item-to-OM-3 correlation which was significant at the .05 level or better. Moreover, the minimum requirement was that at least three items in any one theme had to be making a statistically significant contribution. If that number could not be found, the theme was broken up and its qualifying items were relegated to the miscellaneous category. We had originally had 24 standard themes, as indicated in note 18. Using this new standard we eventually ended up with nineteen themes, plus a miscellaneous twentieth category of qualified items. In the process, the initial set of themes was somewhat changed, but the basic structure of the original model was preserved. Moreover, the 5 themes which could not stand alone were not totally eliminated. Those of their items which qualified were represented in OM-500 in the miscellaneous category, and thus could exert their influence.

We then selected the questions which would represent each theme on the basis of their adjusted item-to-OM-3 scale correlation. Within each theme, separately for each country, the five items having highest item-to-scale correlation were chosen to represent the particular theme in the scale for that country. Use of this procedure meant that the items making up the scale in each country were not identical, a departure from our practice in OM-1, OM-2, and OM-3. We were, in effect, taking the position that any item, once it had in advance been classified as belonging to a given theme area, had relevance equal to that of any other item similarly classified as a potential representative of the theme. This gave us great flexibility, freeing us from being prisoners of the inevitable measurement errors which crop up when one attempts to use a single question to mean the same thing in several very different cultures.

This very flexibility may worry some as having been likely to encourage the development of themes which were too "mushy," since they had been created opportunistically rather than in a theoretically rigorous way. We admit the technique was rough and ready, but feel that it served to give OM-500 and OM-519 a much more balanced character, in terms of equal weighting of themes, than was the case for OM-1, OM-2, and OM-3.

In any event, to resolve any lingering doubts about the possibly opportunistic quality of the OM-519 subscales, we constructed still another OM scale subject to the requirement that each of our original set of alphabetic themes had to be incorporated in the scale, with the further requirement that each theme would be equally weighted by virtue of the fact that it was to be represented by exactly two questionnaire items. The items selected to represent each theme were the two with strongest item to OM-3 correlations. This "themal OM," as we called it, proved to be very highly correlated with OM-519, the median correlation for the six countries being .80. There should, therefore, be no residue of doubt about the degree to which OM-519 truly reflected our original theoretical conception.

22. The procedure used to construct OM-519 meant that it did not have exactly the same items as had been used in OM-500. The overlap was, however, very nearly complete. See Appendix A Parts II and III for further details on the content of the themal OM-500 and OM-519.

23. This was possible because each subscale was scored by the same method as used for OM in general, that is, 2 for a modern answer, 1 for a traditional answer, with the sum then divided by the number of items in the subscale. Since each of the subscales was scored from 1.00 to 2.00, the total score could be expressed in the same terms, that is, the subscale scores were summed and then divided by the number of scales, yielding overall scale scores expressed in the range 1.00 to 2.00, which by our usual procedure could be recorded as going from 0 to 100.

24. The fifth series of OM measures we constructed included more than OM-500 and OM-519. OM-52 was based on the 20 items in each country having the best item-to-OM-3 correlations, as adjusted, for the given country; OM-51 had the best 20 qualifying as strictly the same across all six countries; OM-53 was based on the best 40 items in each country; and OM-56 included the best representative of each alphabet-coded theme area. These were used in various ways to clarify the nature of the overall measure of modernity, but do not figure in the analysis in this book. For the record, however, it is important to report that these additional scales correlated with OM-500 and OM-519 about as highly as the latter did with the other scales, as shown in

Table 6–3. This was especially notable in the case of OM-56, because those results showed that the full range of themes included in the original model of the modern man was well reflected in OM-500 and OM-519. For further evidence on the issue of how well the OM scales represented our initial model of the modern man, see Chapter 7, especially Tables 7–1 and 7–3 and the discussion thereof.

25. The main virtue lost was some degree of strict cross-national comparability of content. OM-1 preserved strict comparability in all countries. That is, the same 79 questions were used everywhere. In OM-3 there was some variation from country to country, but the proportion of items alike in all six countries was about 85 or 90 percent, depending on how strict was the definition of "strictly alike." In OM-500, using a rigid standard. the proportion "strictly alike in all countries" was only 36 percent. However, 54 percent of the questions were strictly alike in at least five countries, and 79 percent were strictly alike in at least four countries. Moreover, we considered the rest of the questions, while not exactly alike, quite equivalent as one moved from country to country. Although the content of OM-519 was not identical with that of OM-500, it shared the same general pool of items. Hence, at the level of items, it had the same degree of cross-national comparability as did OM-500. Moreover, exactly the same 19 theme subscales were created for each of the six countries. To that degree, therefore, OM-519 was more strictly comparable from country to country than was OM-500.

26. The comparison of the reliability of OM-3 and OM-500 is, however, unfair to the latter if one does not take into account the length of the scale. So long as the additional questions even very weakly tap the same general dimension, a much longer version of a scale, such as OM-3, will thereby benefit considerably in its reliability rating. Considering that OM-500 had only 100 items, compared to the 166 in OM-3, we should conclude that it is really decidedly the better scale.

27. OM-12 included measures of exposure to the mass media. Since in this book we treated contact with the mass media as an independent or explanatory variable, OM-12 would have been quite unsuitable as a dependent variable in most of our analysis. Even if this decisive consideration did not exist, we would have preferred to use the longer form of OM. For one thing, the questions in OM-12 touched on only 11 of the 24 themes reflected in OM-3 and OM-500. In addition, OM-12 had median K-R reliabilities of only .62 compared to .83 for the much longer OM-3 and OM-500. For a reproduction of OM-12 and a detailed description of its development see Smith and Inkeles, "The OM Scale." See also Appendix B for the scale and coding instructions.

28. We recognize that under certain special circumstances a group of items can yield a scale with adequate reliability even in the absence of any common underlying theme, and we will address ourselves to that challenge more fully in the next chapter.

29. For a discussion of response set, and how we avoided its impact, see Chapter 4.

7 The Content of OM

1. Since we had predicted the direction of the association, a one-tailed test might have been more appropriate. As it turned out, if we had used a one-tailed test our results would have been even more striking, since so large a proportion of our predictions were in the correct direction, and a correlation

significant at the .01 level by a two-tailed tes would be significant at the .005 level by a one-tailed test. The importance of adjusting item-to-scale correlations to take account of autocorrelation effects is discussed in note 10 to Chapter 6.

2. Just how many times more strict our criterion was depended on the number of items in a theme. The larger the number of items considered, the less likely it became that our criterion could be met by chance from a null hypothesis. Where we had as many as 100 correlations to consider — as in the case of all the information items combined for six countries — the 10-percent rule was very much tougher than, say, a 1-percent rule. With 100 items drawn independently at random, and specifying the null hypothesis that there is *no* correlation to the scale, the probability of getting at least *one* correlation significant at .01 is $P(1 \text{ or more in } 100) \cong 0.634$, whereas the probability of getting 10 or more is approximately $P(10 \text{ or more in } 100) \cong$ .00000008. Clearly, in this case, the 10-percent rule would be very much tougher than the usual 1-percent rule. At the other end, however, we had some themes with only 2 questions, yielding a total of only 12 correlations to consider. In those cases the probability of satisfying the 10-percent rule was not so small, being $P \cong .01$. With three items, hence 18 correlations, the chances of getting two or more items significant at the .01 level is $P \cong .01$. So, for the smaller themes, we can say that the *effective* significance of the 10-percent rule was a shade stricter than the standard 5-percent level, but the rule in effect got markedly more strict as it was progressively applied to larger and larger themes.

3. For details see note 8.

4. The observed result could, however, also have been obtained if some of the themes were actually multidimensional rather than truly "themal." We will deal with that challenge further on in this chapter.

5. If each country contributed strictly proportionately, it would have yielded one-sixth of the significant items, and any two countries combined would have yielded one-third. There was no objective criterion for deciding just how much higher a country should go before being charged with holding a monopoly position. We felt that doubling the proportionate contribution of two countries set a reasonable standard for claiming that they had an excessive impact on the performance of a theme.

6. It may be noted that insofar as the two strongest contributors combined gave only half or less of the total, then, at the maximum, only two of the six countries could have been failing to make any contribution at all. In practice it was very rare for even one country to fail entirely to make any contribution to the total pool of items within any theme which correlated with OM at the .01 level or above.

7. The complete list was first presented in Chart 1, page 354, of Smith and Inkeles, "The OM Scale," and is given again in Table 2–1 of this book. The questions which went into each theme are presented in Appendix A.

8. The first procedure required that each subtheme pass both parts of a two-part test based on the adjusted correlations to OM-3 of the items in the subtheme. One-third had to be at the .01 level of significance or better, and at least one-half at the .05 level or better. With the smallest subtheme, having only 2 questions and therefore 12 correlations over the three countries, the one-third rule would require getting 4 or more correlations significant at the .01 level, which would come about by chance only with $P \cong .000005$.

The value of P in all other cases, that is for all larger themes, would be very much smaller. In other words, we were working here with an effective significance level of $P \leqq .000005$. The second method used as the standard of judgment a measure of the departure of each subtheme from the average performance of all items in OM-3, 62 percent of which had had item-to-scale correlations significant at the .01 level or better. For each subtheme, the proportion of its items significant at .01 or better was calculated as in Table 7–2. Then, a one-tailed t test was used to calculate the significance of the difference between the percentage of items which qualified overall and those which qualified for the subtheme. When the proportion of items qualifying for a subtheme was lower than the overall average, then tests significant even at the .05 level were considered as calling the given subtheme into question as a member of the set defining individual modernity.

9. The subtheme CA(2), which measured trust, was ineligible under both procedures we used to test the relevance of the subthemes to modernity. This subtheme was represented by three questions asking how far one can trust a stranger, a relative, and a merchant (CA-6, 7, 8). Two of these had been ruled by the project staff to be not particularly relevant to judging a man's modernity, as indicated by their exclusion from OM-1, but they had been included in OM-3. The suspicions of the staff were apparently correct. The modern man is not substantially more trusting than the traditional man.

10. At issue here was subtheme KO(1). On the first test it was borderline, meeting the requirement that one-third of its items correlate with OM at the .01 level, but failing to meet the requirement that half the items be at the .05 level. The t test indicated that its proportion of correlations significant at .01 (38 percent) differed from the standard to a degree significant at .05. The subtheme KO(1) contained a mélange of questions on relations to wife and cousin, namely, KO-1, 3, 4, 5 and WR-5. The project staff had indicated it doubted the relevance of four of these five questions by excluding them from OM-1. We interpreted the result to mean that modern men are neither more nor less likely to fulfill their obligations to a relative than are traditional men. We note in passing, however, that another subtheme dealing with kinship obligations, namely, KO(2), which tested whether a man would follow his own preferences over that of his parents in selecting a job or a wife, came through with flying colors. Indeed it had a perfect record. Insuring his own autonomy and freedom is evidently so strong an element in the modern man that he is prepared, on that account, to defy his parents' wishes at least in selecting a spouse or a job.

11. The subtheme on consumer values designated CO(2) was borderline on the first procedure, and its proportion (33 percent) of items significantly correlated with OM-3 was below standard, with t significant at .05. The subtheme included two questions (CO-8, 9): whether a man should continuously strive for more goods, and whether material possessions bring happiness. Both questions were considered poor indicators of modernity by our project staff, as evidenced by their exclusion from OM-1.

12. At issue was the subtheme GO(1), testing awareness of differences of opinion. It included two questions (GO-3, 4), inquiring whether the opinion of one's wife and one's peers would differ much from one's own. The theme just barely passed both tests in our first procedure, but its proportion of significant item-to-OM-3 correlations (at 33 percent) was different enough from the standard to yield a value of t significant at .05. We cannot take any credit

for anticipating this challenge, since both items had been certified by our staff as appropriate measures of modernity.

13. At issue was the subtheme DI, dealing with questions about personal dignity. In this case the theme and the subtheme had identical content. It passed both parts of the test under our first procedure, but was called seriously into question by the second since the proportion of significant correlations (at 38 percent) differed from the standard enough to yield a t test significant at .005. The questions which turned in a particularly poor performance were those mainly inquiring how one should respond to people who fail to do their job well (DI-5, 6, 9). Of the seven items in the theme, only two had been rated by our staff as poor indicators of modernity. The dignity theme was one which had proved particularly hard to measure reliably. However, we were later able to build a suitable subscale to test this dimension in all six countries. It was, therefore, included in the construction of OM-500 and OM-519. To do that, however, we had to accept the use of a somewhat different assortment of dignity related questions in each of the countries. For details see Appendix A, Parts II and III.

14. The Spearman-Brown prophecy calculation was made as follows:

$$.82 = .77K/[1 + .77 (K - 1)], \text{ where } K = 166/119.$$

15. We should perhaps here again briefly review the division of our questions into themes. The questionnaire (Appendix A) makes clear our original classification of the questions by theme through the use of the alphabetic code, so that AC represents active citizenship, and so on. There were 24 such themes we considered "main" or "standard." These were arrived at a priori, according to our theory.

Since some of the themes were represented by many questions, and therefore may have constituted too broad a topic, the larger units were, for one part of our analysis, divided into subthemes, so that the original 24 became 35. In this arrangement, as set out in Table 7-2, there were 33 of the usual alphabetic codes with some of the original set appearing more than once, plus a set for all information items treated as a single theme, plus a set of objective behavioral measures which had no alphabetic code. The grouping of items into subthemes was made on the basis of face content, with Inkeles and Smith acting as judges. In other words, the coherence of the sets of items was not tested statistically, theme by theme.

Since many of these subthemes contained as few as 2 items, however, they seemed likely to be unstable or unreliable measures. In constructing OM-519, therefore, we sought to have 5 items to represent each theme. This forced the reduction of the 35 subthemes, indeed of the original 24 main themes also, to a smaller set of 19. All three sets, however, overlap greatly, basically preserving the original theoretical structure established by the list of 24 alphabetically coded main themes.

16. A factor loading may be interpreted much like a correlation coefficient. The square of any loading will describe how much in common any variable has with the dimension. Thus the information subscale, with a loading of .62 in East Pakistan, may be considered to have a common variance of .38 with the factor defined by the entire set of 19 subscales. In the case of India the loading was .76, and the common variance .58. We can see the relation to the results obtained through correlational analysis by considering the analogous correlation of the information-scale scores with the overall OM-500 score. The

correlation for East Pakistan was .58, indicating common variance of .34 between the measures. For India the figures were .75 and .56, respectively. It will be observed that the relative standing of the countries was preserved in both methods, and that the common variance accounted for by the two methods was in the same general range. We should note, in passing, that this similarity between a factor loading and a correlation coefficient cannot be expected automatically. It will occur only if the data yield a large, central first factor, which is what we expected and got with OM-519. The significance of this outcome is further discussed in note 17.

17. There is, unfortunately, no absolute standard for judging how far the loadings in a factor analysis are discontinuous. Factor loadings can range from +1.00 to −1.00, and one often sees results covering most of the range. By that standard the factor loadings in Table 7–3 were unusually tightly clustered in the same range. On the other hand, if the standard of judgment is the amount of variance which any theme has in common with the dimension defined by the factor, then the fact that the information measures had loadings so much higher than did some of the other themes could be used to argue that the information tests were more central, whereas the measure of urban industrial preference, among others, was more peripheral to the OM syndrome. Further on in this chapter we return to a discussion of the status of the several themes as central and peripheral. For now, we note that each of the themes may well be considered as doing roughly equal work in the factor's construction, even though its ultimate closeness may be discrepant from the average. This is a property which follows from the virtual identity of the factor with OM-519, an outcome discussed more fully in note 27. OM-519 was, of course, constructed giving equal weight to each of the subscales. The situation is very much like that of a regression analysis in which, though the individual items showed some variation in their initial, zero-order, correlation coefficients, their ultimate B-weights were extremely similar. In more specific technical language, the raw-score weights for building the first factor were virtually the same across all 19 subscales in each of our six countries.

18. The experiment was performed with OM-520, identical to OM-519 except that a miscellaneous theme had been added to the standard 19, giving a total of 20 subthemes and hence the code number OM-520. In East Pakistan we reran the factor analysis of OM-520, first leaving out efficacy, thus reducing the set to 19 subscales, and again by omitting information plus verbal fluency, which left 18 subscales. The latent roots did fall from 3.68 when we used all 20 subscales, to 3.45 and 3.23, respectively. Since there were fewer elements considered, however, the percentage of variance explained fell only negligibly, from an initial level of 18.4 percent to 18.1 and 18.0 percent, respectively. The factor structure resulting with only 19 and 18 subscales, respectively, was very similar to that with 20. With 20 subscales, all but two had loadings above .30, whereas with only 18 all but one had loadings above .30. Moreover, the general rank order of the subtheme loadings was extremely well maintained. The loadings in the 18-theme factor analysis correlated with those in the original standard 20-theme scale at .98 (Pearsonian). In Argentina we took the more extreme measure of simultaneously omitting three subscales: information, verbal fluency, *and* efficacy. The result was basically the same as in East Pakistan. With all 20 subscales considered simultaneously, the latent root was 4.55, accounting for 22.7 percent of the total variance. Even with 3 scales removed the latent root of 3.68 accounted for 21.7 percent of the

variance. All 17 of the residual subthemes had loadings of .30 or above, as they had in the set of 20 subthemes. Indeed, when we correlated the 17 theme loadings as they appeared in the first 20-theme factor analysis and then as they figured in a separate factor analysis as a set of 17, we obtained a correlation of .99. Again the agreement was virtually perfect. This indicates that the removal of even 3 scales left the structure of the factor almost exactly as it was before.

19. One way of making more precise what we mean when we say that no one element can stand for the whole is to ask how far we could generate a man's score from knowledge of his standing on some component subordinate to the larger summary scale. Specifically, we ask how far we can generate a man's overall modernity score from knowledge of his score on information alone. For a fair test of how well the information score predicts overall modernity we should use OM-2, which does not itself contain any information questions, thus helping us avoid problems of autocorrelation. The correlations of OM-2 with the total-information scale ranged from .47 in East Pakistan to .68 in India. This means that from knowledge of a man's information score we could predict or generate only between 22 and 46 percent, respectively, of his overall modernity score as measured by OM-2. An alternative way of expressing the relation, by reference to the factor analysis of OM-519, is to say that the information subscale, with its median loading of .73 on the first factor, would thereby account for approximately 50 percent of the variance in the overall syndrome. Either way, these facts mark the information score as a relatively good indicator of individual modernity, but it is also clear that half or more of a man's general modernity score, as measured by OM, is determined by characteristics other than the level of information he possesses.

20. The question whether the items actually used in OM were alike or different did not apply to OM-1, in which we used 79 items very much alike from country to country, nor to OM-12, the short form described at the end of Chapter 6, which used the same 14 questions in all six countries. Even with these shorter scales, however, most of the work being done in giving the scale its reliability could have been done by somewhat different items in each country. The issue becomes more acute in the case of the longer scales, such as OM-3 and especially OM-500, because in them a substantial proportion of the items in the respective country scales were not used everywhere and, with a larger set of items involved, there was an increased chance that quite different subsets of items played the key role in defining the modernity syndrome in each country.

21. The number 154 is smaller than the 166 reported earlier as the number of entries regularly used in constructing OM-3. For purposes of running the competition for the top 50 items, however, we had to exclude from consideration any question not used in all six countries. Doing this brought the number of units down from approximately 166 to approximately 154 in each country.

22. The probability of obtaining these results by chance alone was, as we have seen for OM-2, exceedingly small. It was more minute in the case of OM-3, since the probability of the kind of outcome we obtained gets rapidly more remote as the number of items in the scale gets larger. The probability of finding 38 items on top in all four countries goes from less than 10^{-23} in OM-2 to less than 10^{-45} in OM-3. These probabilities were calculated for us by Dr. Bonnie Erickson. To present the reasoning and the calculations would require more space than we feel we can allow.

23. In any one country the chance of an item being in the top 50 is clearly $50/N$, or say about $1/3$ (a trifle less since for OM-3, $N = 154$ or so). For six countries with $N = 154$, $P = (50/154)^6 \cong .001$.

24. The most obvious reason for using the scale based on the subthemes was that it most accorded with our original theoretical conception of the general modernity syndrome, as indicated in Chapter 1. We originally conceived that syndrome as a complex of themes, and not as a summary score based on discrete questions. Each question derives its standing as relevant to modernity on the grounds that it reflects a theme. We initially built OM on the basis of individual items because we wanted a quick approximation of the overall score, whereas it would have taken us a very long time first to construct the subscales for each theme area and then to combine them in an overall scale-based OM. Only at a later stage in our work were we able to build OM on the basis of distinct scales measuring the different themes. Since we consider the theme scores as the cleaner, more reliable, and more valid measures of the underlying variables, we deemed it most appropriate that the factor analysis used as a test of coherence of the OM scale should be based on it.

Quite apart from these considerations, however, we do not feel that the coherence of a long, complex, and multifaceted scale such as OM-3 or OM-500 can appropriately be judged by means of a factor analysis. It is in the nature of factor analysis that when applied to such a long and complex scale it would tend mainly to identify the very subthemes which we combined to form the larger OM scale. Furthermore, it is a general characteristic of factor analysis that if one starts with a small, neatly factored set of elements and keeps adding other related elements, the first factor emerging from a principal-components factor analysis will very likely account for less and less of the total variance as one adds more and more items from the larger pool of related items. By contrast, the *reliability* of the very same scale will increase as one adds the additional items.

The point is readily illustrated. We constructed OM scales in the fifth series to include, successively, the 20 best items, the 40 best, and the 100 best, "best" being defined as the items with the highest adjusted correlations with OM-3. The reliability of the scales thus produced rose markedly with each increment of items, but the percentage of total *variance* accounted for by the first factor in a principal-components factor analysis went progressively down! In Chile, for example, the Kuder-Richardson reliability rose from .66 in the 20-item scale to .78 in the 40-item scale, and topped out at .82 in the 100-item scale. The percentage of total variance accounted for by the first principal component, however, fell as the number of items in the scale was augmented, dropping from 14 percent in the 20-item scale to 11 percent in the 40-item scale and to 6 percent in the 100-item scale. The same pattern was observed in the other five countries. A really long complex scale such as OM-3 or OM-500 is, therefore, at a great disadvantage if subjected to an item factor analysis for purposes of judging its overall coherence.

We acknowledge that any item taken alone will be a poor measure of OM; in other words, there is a lot of error variance. The themes reduce this error variance; they are cleaner, more reliable measures of the theoretically relevant dimensions. Furthermore, they were selected a priori, and not on the basis of an antecedent factor analysis — which gave some point to later using factor analysis to decide how well they cohered as a set.

25. To test the coherence of OM-519 we set the following three standards:

(1) the first unrotated factor should account for at least 20 percent of the total (not the common) variance;

(2) the first unrotated factor should have a latent root twice that produced by the second unrotated factor, and the rate of falloff from factor one to factor two should be considerably larger than the falloff as we moved from factor two to three, from three to four, and so on; and

(3) two-thirds of the units in the factor analysis, namely the subthemes, should have factor loadings of at least .30 or above.

The reasoning behind the selection of these three criteria was as follows:

(1) Factor analysis, especially by rotation after a principal-components analysis, is ordinarily used to discover the subordinate or distinctive elements which cohere as themes within the framework of some larger and generally relatively inchoate mass of discrete elements. Our use of factor analysis was quite different. We were using it not to show how the elements of OM break into distinctive units, but rather to show that they have much in common. Hence the rule that we should have one rather large factor prior to rotation.

(2) The rule that at least two-thirds of the units considered relevant to OM should have loadings of .30 or above was to insure that the strong first factor would in fact represent the OM syndrome more or less as we conceived it, rather than representing some arbitrarily selected subset of the themes.

(3) Even if this first factor were of reasonable size, if the second was not much smaller that would suggest that our approach to combining all the themes in one main factor was more arbitrary than we believed it to be. We wanted the first general factor to be not just larger, but so much larger as to stand out qualitatively — hence the rule that it be at least twice the second factor.

26. A glance back to Table 7–3 reveals that the three criteria described in the preceding note were generally met by OM-519 in all the countries. Condition (3) was met most decisively. Not merely two-thirds but close to 90 percent of the subthemes in each country had loadings of .30 or above. The departures from this standard were relatively minor, and even then the loadings certainly pointed in the right direction. Moreover, when we looked at the factors other than the first, we failed to find any of the themes having a factor essentially unto itself. We could say, then, that while all the themes tied into the same main factor, none formed an exclusive one.

Criteria (1) and (2) were less resoundingly met, but they were basically satisfied. The percentage of total variance accounted for ranged from 18.6 in East Pakistan, admittedly borderline by our criterion, to 28.9 in India, well above the standard we had set. The first factor was, on the average, not merely twice but almost three times the second in all six countries. Moreover, the falloff from the first to the second factor was considerably larger than the falloff from the second to the third. Indeed the second factor was, on the average, only 1.3 times the fifth. This helps emphasize that the first factor was not only of good size but was relatively distinctive in its quality.

27. On the basis of the factor analysis of the OM-519 subscales we assigned factor scores, and then correlated those with the original OM-519. In every country the correlation between OM-519 and the factor exceeded .98. This finding of virtual identity between the two measures gave us even greater confidence in our earlier method of constructing OM-519, and it underlies much of the discussion in this chapter.

28. As we have noted before, our emphasis on the common element which unites the various subthemes is not meant to deny the extent to which each subtheme also measures something different from what it holds in common with the others. We are also aware that the summary score may lump together men who would show quite different profiles if one took account of their scores on the several subthemes one by one. At a later point in our analysis, but not in this book, we hope to deal more fully with the distinctive profile of subtheme scores characteristically manifested by different individuals and subgroups.

Again the analogy between our work and the measurement of intelligence is relevant. If past history in regard to the measurement of intelligence is any guide, we may expect some scholars to deny the validity and usefulness of the OM concept, citing as evidence the fact that factor analyses show the OM scales not to be unidimensional. But we already know and admit that fact at the outset. Indeed, it is an integral part of our conception of OM and the individual modernity concept. Yet the various disparate elements and aspects of OM do have some substantial statistically significant common threads running through them, rather like a common-factor glue that makes them part of a loose but clearly integrated larger whole. The fact that the loose whole is loose and can be broken down into more tightly related subclusters in no way negates the existence of the larger whole nor reduces its theoretical and practical importance.

29. We hope to include several such themal/topical reports in our second volume under the title "Explorations in the Study of Individual Modernization." A published example of this sort of detailed study of major subthemes is already available in Alex Inkeles, "Participant Citizenship in Six Developing Countries." In addition, some descriptions of the interrelations of the OM-519 themal subscales and the independent-variable measures for education, factory experience, and mass-media exposure are given in note 18 to Chapter 9, note 13 to Chapter 10, and note 16 to Chapter 11, respectively.

8   The Social Correlates of Individual Modernity

1. This was for OM-1 in India, as described in Table 6–1. The more typical spread obtained with the long forms of the OM scale in most countries was approximately 60 points, between a low of about 20 and a high of about 80.

2. The variables used were: years of education, years of urban residence, home-school modernity, mass-media exposure, consumer-goods possessed, months of factory experience, father's education, urbanism of residence, objective skill, and number of factory benefits. In Chile and Nigeria the index was based on only nine of these variables, but there too the summary scores were divided into deciles. In selecting the set of variables we were guided by the following considerations. First, only those which our theory identified as probable causes of individual modernity were to be considered. On that basis we excluded certain measures, such as those for age and ethnicity, to neither of which we assigned any theoretical standing as schools for modernity. Second, only one variable was to be included from any set of alternative measures of basically the same dimension. For example, we included the number of benefits provided by the factory as a measure of factory quality, and therefore did not also use the factory modernity rating; having selected consumer goods as an indicator of a man's standard of living, we did not also use the alternative

measures of income or housing quality. Third, we excluded measures not available in all the countries, such as rural-urban origin, as well as those which could not be meaningfully scored on a scale from 1 to 4. These exclusions from our originally quite large pool of independent variables left us with the ten discrete independent variables cited above.

3. Throughout this book men are defined as "high" on OM, or modern, if their individual scores on the scale placed them in the upper third (33 percent) of the frequency distribution for the total sample from their given country. Although the choice of a particular cutting point is perforce arbitrary, the use of some such distinction obviously facilitates presentation of our results, as we are sure our readers will appreciate. For a discussion of how such distinctions may give a spurious impression of threshold effects, see note 5 to Chapter 9.

4. Throughout the data analysis in this book we have attempted to be consistent in our descriptions of the strength of relations. We established a minimum standard of $r = |.10|$ for all correlations, both zero-order and partial. We use the same standard for beta weights. When a statistic is $|.10|$ or greater, we use the term "appreciable," whether or not it is statistically significant. Statistical significance is much affected both by the size of the sample (for example, in a particular match) and by the type of significance test used. By reporting both the significance and the magnitude of association, a more accurate overall picture of the data can be given.

The direction and magnitude of relations become especially important because our study can be seen as six separate tests of our theory and various specific relations. In this situation, an appreciable but not statistically significant association that is consistent in direction across several or all countries becomes noteworthy. Such a finding indicates a reliable though weak relation between the variables involved.

We have also attempted to use a consistent terminology with regard to the levels of magnitude of correlation above $|.10|$. Associations in the $|.10|$ to $|.19|$ range we have termed "small." Between $|.20|$ and $|.34|$ we have called them "substantial." When they were between $|.35|$ and $|.49|$ we have termed the relations "strong." Correlations at $|.50|$ or above we refer to as "robust." This set of designations takes into account the usual range of correlations in sociology and social psychology. We believe that these standards are quite reasonable, especially when one is dealing with single predictor variables in relation to OM scores. For the interpretation of multiple R's, however, higher standards can be required. In that situation, the ranges we use may be taken as referring to R^2 or variance explained, rather than to an association between one predictor and OM scores.

5. Only in Israel was there any consequential departure from the high standard of performance turned in by OM in the other countries. There, in some degree, we faced the dilemma we earlier feared we might run into. In Israel it is unclear whether the OM scale did not do as good a job in identifying the modern men, or whether what we thought of as presumably modernizing experiences simply failed to produce the same degree of expected effect as elsewhere. To anticipate our later findings, we may note that the fault lay less in the Israeli OM scale than in our summary measure of modern experience as it applied to Israel. The "exposure" scale gave substantial weight to industrial as against agricultural employment. Israel, however, was the one country in which, as we will see later, factory workers were not markedly more modern

than the farmers. We attribute that fact in good part to the influence of the agricultural cooperatives in which the Israeli farmers lived. For details, see the analysis of the moshavim in Chapter 13.

6. For a discussion of some current studies of a nature comparable to ours see notes 4, 5, and 6 of Chapter 20.

7. For one thing, cross-tabulation is generally extremely crude, and may, therefore, be thoroughly misleading. Suppose, for example, as in some instances we found in our study, that the typical peasant of limited education was illiterate whereas the typical worker in that category had about 4 or 5 years of education. It happens that a common way to divide men into groups of those with more and less education is to consider all those with less than 6 (or 8) years of schooling as in the low category. To have done so in our case would have been to treat as equal in education men who in reality were most unequal. Thus, the usual control procedure could lead to the unwarranted assumption that occupational factors accounted for individual modernity when, in fact, poorly controlled educational factors were the real explanation.

A second defect of the conventional method of controlling for extraneous variables by cross-tabulation is that it becomes awkward simultaneously to take into account more than two extraneous variables. As the number of variables controlled goes up, the crudity of the distinctions made must increase, else one quickly runs out of cases to fill the rapidly multiplying number of cells appearing in one's table. Some few studies have sought to meet this challenge by greatly increasing the sample size, up to 10,000 cases and more in a single country. Such numbers were quite beyond our means, especially considering that we had to conduct such a long interview requiring considerable investment in each case. Of necessity, therefore, we had to turn to some other solution.

8. The matching technique has not been extensively used in sociological research. A discussion of its virtues and defects will be found in Robert P. Althauser and Donald Rubin, "The Computerized Construction of a Matched Sample," *American Journal of Sociology* 76, no. 2 (1970): 325–346.

9. The Multigroup Match Program, written in OS 360 Fortran, is designed to examine a sample of cases divided into any number of groups, and to find cases across the groups whose difference on any number of variables is within specified tolerance limits. The program then compares paired t-statistics for all possible combinations of the groups, as well as the mean and the standard deviation of each controlled variable with each group. Compatible correlation matrices are also produced. By adjusting tolerances on subsequent reruns the differences between the groups may be reduced so that each matched set of cases is statistically alike. The controls and statistics available in the program provide great flexibility in manipulating data to conform to research criteria and precise information about the characteristics of the resulting matched groups.

10. Briefly, the partialing fallacy involves believing that applying statistical controls in a multivariate analysis generally removes the spurious effects of one or more confounding influences (variables) without affecting the true underlying relation between an independent variable (IV) and a dependent variable (DV). Instead, what usually happens is that the very process of applying statistical controls not only removes the indirect (or, from some viewpoints, spurious) effects of certain variables on the DV as mediated through a given IV, but also removes some of the true direct effects of that IV on the

DV as revealed by the partial correlation, partial regression coefficient, or other similar statistic. This occurs because of multicollinearity (or lack of independence — the presence of substantial correlations) among some of the predictor variables. Only when all of the predictors are statistically unrelated among themselves (which occurs, in general, only when the predictors are factor scores derived from an orthogonal factor extraction procedure) does statistical partialing work so as to avoid all risk of the partialing fallacy.

The practical result of the partialing fallacy is not an error in a statistic, but an error in the interpretation of a statistic. One is often led to conclude, erroneously, that an IV had no true effect on a DV since the partial coefficient (of whatever type) is insignificant or close to zero in magnitude. In fact, an insignificant or near-zero partial coefficient can result either from the partialing process (application of statistical controls) itself or from a true lack of relation between IV and DV. If there is multicollinearity among the predictors, as is usual, then nearly any true relation (in particular, a weak or moderate relation) between IV and DV can be made to appear insignificant merely by applying a sufficient number of statistical controls for variables correlated both with the IV and DV in question. The greater the degree of multicollinearity among the predictors, the greater the possibility of finding insignificant or near-zero partial coefficients as a statistical artifact and hence the greater the likelihood of committing the partialing fallacy.

11. This example should help to make clear an important but little-noted fact, namely, that partialing, just as much as matching, is in effect altering the data base. With both of these methods one is no longer really dealing with a sample representative of the whole original population, but rather with one heavily influenced by the selectivity of the control procedure.

9   The School as a Context for Modernization

1. Almond and Verba, *The Civic Culture*, p. 379.

2. We caution against the temptation to interpret the variation in the size of the correlation coefficients from country to country as reflecting the relative modernizing effect of a year in school in one country as against another. Correlation coefficients are notoriously sensitive to the sample distribution on the variables measured. In India, for example, the higher correlation reflects, in great part, the fact that the sample size did not decrease at the ends of the continuum. In the Indian sample, 299 people had no education at all and 303 had 11 or more years of schooling, with lesser frequencies for all the years between! The comparative effectiveness of each year of education is, therefore, more reliably indicated by the point-gain measures described in Table 9–4. The evidence given there would not support the assumption that each year of education in India is more effective in making men modern than is a year of education in one of the other countries.

3. Using the full range of education from primary school to university, Kahl's scale "Modernism I" yielded correlations with education of .55 in Mexico and .57 in Brazil. (See Kahl, *Measurement of Modernism*, p. 45.) Lerner's measure of empathy, similar to some components of our definition of individual modernity, yielded a correlation with education in Syria of .47. (This figure was calculated by us from the table given on p. 436 of his book, *The Passing of Traditional Society*, in which the education groups ranged from "illiterate" to "secondary or more.") For a national probability sample of the United States, Angus Campbell's data indicate a correlation of .43 be-

tween education and the sense of political efficacy, another measure akin to an important component of our OM scale. (This figure also was calculated by us, on the basis of a cross-tabulation given in Angus Campbell et al., *The American Voter* (New York: Wiley, 1965), p. 479.) A NORC ADL study based on a nationwide representative sample of the U. S. yielded a correlation of −.54 between education and authoritarianism as measured by a five-item "F-Scale." (Reported in Richard Christie and Marie Jahoda, *Studies in Scope and Method of "the Authoritarian Personality"* (Glencoe, Ill.: Free Press, 1954), p. 170.) These represent the upper reaches attained. The more common experience is to find correlations between most attitude measures and education in the range between .10 and .25.

4. The observed range of years of education in our main sample was: Argentina, 1–15; Chile, 1–14; India, 0–11; Israel, 2–14; Nigeria, 4–13; East Pakistan, 0–8. The median education, in all cases very close to the mean, was, respectively: 7, 6, 7, 8, 8, 2 years. Our separate student samples included those with advanced high school and university standing but they are not dealt with in this book.

5. Table 9–1 may be interpreted by some of our readers as revealing a threshold effect such as has been found in other studies of the impact of education; see Prodipto Roy, Frederick Brynolf Waisanen, and Everett M. Rogers, *The Impact of Communication on Rural Development: An Investigation in Costa Rica and India* (Hyderabad: UNESCO [Paris] and National Institute of Community Development, 1969). The most critical evidence against the threshold assumption lies in the fact that the same pattern was not evident when we used mean scores on OM, instead of the percentage in the upper third of the distribution, as may be seen in Fig. 9–1. In other words, the apparent threshold suggested by Table 9–1 is an artifact, at least in this case, of our method of choosing a cutoff point. Our impression is that there is no threshold, and that modernity increases fairly regularly all along the educational continuum, from the lowest grades up to at least the end of secondary school.

6. The matching and partial correlation methods are described in Chapter 8.

7. We caution the reader not to assume that the results given in the text at this point apply to urban schools only, merely because we use the industrial-worker sample. All the industrial workers in East Pakistan and India, and approximately half of those in Chile, Argentina, and Nigeria had attended rural schools. In Chapter 17, on the modernity of home and school as factors influencing individual modernization, we take up in some detail the relative effectiveness of rural versus urban schools.

8. The fact that partialing out other early-socialization factors leaves the correlation of education and modernity so strong has bearing on the possibility that each grade in school is more modern mainly on account of the effect of a selection process rather than because the children learned to be more modern in the classroom. A selection effect could have produced the observed results if each year the less modern children were screened out, either voluntarily or by the school authorities, leaving only a residue of the more modern, a residue becoming more and more concentrated with each passing year. If we adopt this model, however, we are left with the challenge of explaining why some children were already so much more modern at the time they entered the first grade. Sociological and psychological theory points to factors such as the father's oc-

cupation, his education, his ethnic group, and his residence as the most likely causes of such early differences. These, however, are the very early-socialization variables we have already controlled, without thereby seriously diminishing the correlation of education and modernity. This seems to cast serious doubt on the plausibility of the theory that education and modernity are correlated only because the school acts selectively to retain the more modern and successively screen out the more traditional. However, a definitive demonstration of the effect of education on individual modernity in early life would require that we restudy the same individuals at different grade levels as they moved through the school, just as we restudied adult workers after they had spent 4 or 5 years in a factory, for which see Chapter 11. Our project was able to make such a study in Brazil, with pupils in grades 3 to 5. A set of these pupils were interviewed at both the beginning and the end of the school year. We found clear evidence that the school experience itself rather than maturation or self-selection, accounts for the greater modernity of those in higher grades. See Holsinger, "The Elementary School as Socializer," 1972.

9. The eight variables included in Set A for the total sample were: education-literacy; mass-media exposure; father's education; life-cycle stage (essentially age); ethnicity-religion; living standard; occupation; and urbanism of present residence.

For the worker sample, length of factory experience substituted for occupation, and we added a factory-modernity measure and, where applicable, a measure of origin as rural or urban, making a total of ten variables.

Set A consisted of a subset of our complete list of independent variables selected to represent that larger set. The principle for selecting the smaller set was theoretical relevance, and screening was done within that framework to reduce redundancy and eliminate measures our experience had shown to be unreliable. Thus, mass-media exposure was represented by an index based on both newspaper reading and radio listening, and father's education rather than father's occupation was used to represent parental socioeconomic status. In addition, variables which could not be soundly ordered on a theoretical basis, such as religion or ethnic origin, were arranged in Set A on the basis of their empirically demonstrated most effective ordering. The special adjustment of these variables is described in Appendix C.

10. The average number of years of schooling separating those classified as having "more" and "less" education in Match 36Mb was: Argentina, 3.2; Chile, 3.4; East Pakistan, 4.8; India, 9.0; Israel, 5.0; Nigeria, 2.4. Even the smallest of these educational differences yielded a t-test significant at well beyond the .001 level.

11. The match was of good quality, and there were no significant departures from the standard of strict matching.

At the time the first set of matches was prepared, some of the project staff still favored defining mass-media exposure as a dependent variable, whereas others wanted it defined as an independent variable. We resolved the tension by inaction, and so mass-media exposure was not included as a control variable in many of the matches. It was, however, brought under control in most of the partial correlations we report throughout the book, and in many matches done in the later stages of the project. To keep the partial correlations and the matches as comparable as possible we used the match with mass media controlled wherever it was appropriate and available. The facts may be checked in each case by reviewing the list of controls given for each match used. Generally, with so many other variables already controlled, the addition of one more control, even for so important a variable as mass-media exposure, could not materially change the picture given by the match without that control.

All of the control variables for the above and subsequent matches are listed in the Match Control Table in Appendix E.

12. There is good reason for wanting to separate the direct impact of education on OM scores from its indirect impact as mediated through mass-media exposure. Neither the matching procedure nor the partial correlations permit us easily to make distinctions as to direct or indirect impact, whereas the path-analysis procedure to be taken up in Chapter 20 does. By path analysis we can show that part of the reduction in the apparent strength of education, when mass-media exposure was controlled, was due to the indirect effect of education upon OM scores, as mediated through mass-media exposure.

13. In the case of the matches, the point gain was obtained by dividing the mean difference in OM scores between two matched groups by the mean difference in their schooling. For example, in India an 18-point difference in OM score, divided by a 9-year difference in education, yielded a gain of 2.0 points per year. In reporting the point gain per year of schooling from the regression analysis, we simply utilized the raw score weights (called B-weights) from the regression equation.

14. The regression results given are from the separate analysis for factory workers only, and represent the median gain for six countries using OM-500. Results for the total sample, for urban nonindustrial workers, and for cultivators, were in basically the same range. A separate treatment comparing rural and urban schools is presented in Chapter 17.

15. The few-controls regression was not strictly comparable with the few-controls match. The two approaches were alike in controlling factory experience, but the regression analysis added only mass-media exposure whereas the loose match added only ethnicity-religion and urban-rural origin.

16. Another way to express the contribution of education, as against other factors, in explaining individual modernity would be either a beta weight or a measure of relative weight, drawn from a regression analysis in which education and the other relevant variables were included in the predictor pool. Such estimates are offered in Chapter 19.

17. In a study by Bergthold and McClelland, using measures both of need achievement and OM, it was demonstrated for several thousand Ethiopian high school students that education increased OM scores year by year when students were tested at the school, rather than later in life as our subjects were tested. Results of a study of Puerto Rican school children by Ineke Cunningham, and another by Donald B. Holsinger, of pupils in the third to fifth grades in Brasilia, also provide evidence that the effect of schooling on OM is already evident as children complete each grade. See Gary D. Bergthold and David C. McClelland, *The Impact of Peace Corps Teachers on Students in Ethiopia* (Human Development Foundation, December 1968); Ineke Cunningham, *Modernity and Academic Performance*; Donald B. Holsinger, "The Elementary School as an Early Socializer of Modern Values" (unpublished dissertation, Stanford University, 1972).

18. These claims of specific effects were based on the known content of the OM scale, but were substantiated by reference to the cross-country median zero-order correlations of formal education with each of the separate themal subscales in OM-519, as follows: active citizenship, .24; change valuation,

.20; dignity valuation, .26; economic aspiration, .12; education valuation, .24; efficacy, .25; family size, .19; information, .50; minority-opinion valuation, .20; modern family, .22; modern religion, .20; new-experience valuation, .25; nonparochial allegiance, .24; planning valuation, .20; responsibility valuation, .24; technical-skill valuation, .22; urban-industrial preference, .22; verbal fluency, .19; and women's rights, .16. All these medians apply to the total sample from each country, and each coefficient is significant at well beyond the .001 level. It is noteworthy that over 80 percent of the figures are in the narrow range from .19 to .26, which suggests the overall evenness of the impact of formal education on OM scores. The same point could be demonstrated by reference to the specific questions, as against the scales, tapping the dimensions of change sketched in the text. To present those results, however, would require more space than we can allow.

10 Modernity and the Mass Media

1. Data drawn from Bruce M. Russett *et al., World Handbook of Political and Social Indicators* (New Haven: Yale University Press, 1964), and UN sources; see particularly *Mass Media in the Developing Countries* (Paris: UNESCO, 1961).

2. This statement is based on an unpublished MIT study by Howard Rosenthal and Whitney Thompson, cited by Ithiel Pool in "The Functions of Mass Media in International Exchange" in *UNESCO Handbook of International Exchanges* (Paris: UNESCO, 1965), p. 63.

3. In many sociological studies mass-media contact is treated as a dependent rather than as an independent variable. It will be seen from the analysis in this chapter that we are reversing the emphasis. We had three reasons for treating mass-media contact as an independent rather than as a dependent variable.

First, this treatment seemed most consistent with our theoretical interests and our general mode of analysis. Our objective was not to give the broadest description of the characteristics of a modern man, both social and psychological, but rather to provide the best explanation of the way in which certain social institutions shaped the character of men to make them more modern. The mass media are a distinctive feature of modern society, along with the school, the factory, and the urban center. Since we treated the other institutions as independent variables, it was appropriate to accord the mass media the same status. This was clearly the more conservative stance with regard to our main hypothesis, because it meant that when the impact of education and the factory were studied we could control for the effect of mass media. In other words, we made it a more difficult test for the main hypothesis.

Second, we took cognizance of the fact that whether a man had the opportunity to listen to the radio or read a newspaper, at least in a developing country, would in good part be determined by his objective social situation rather than by his personal disposition. A man's residence as rural or urban, his financial resources, and the cultural standards of his community, all influence the degree to which he can use the mass media. Where there are no radios and no printing presses, no degree of individual psychological modernity will assure much contact with the media. Conversely, where the newspaper and the radio are readily available to all, using them may become a customary reflex which tells little about the motivation of the user.

Third, we felt that even if men more modern in spirit were more likely to use the media, the case for treating mass-media exposure as an independent variable was sound so long as their contact with the media in turn made the users still more modern men.

For further discussion of whether the mass media are more properly seen as independent or dependent variables, see the section of this chapter on "Reservations and Affirmations."

4. Joseph T. Klapper, *The Effects of Mass Communication* (Glencoe, Ill.: Free Press, 1960), p. 8.

5. Kahl, in *The Measurement of Modernism,* used as his main independent variable a composite SES measure based on occupation, education, income, and identification. His dependent variable of "modernism" included a subscale called "mass-media participation." That scale, however, did not measure exposure to the media. Rather, it dealt with interest in the news and knowledge of public figures, in much the same way as did the information questions of the OM scale. Although Kahl reported on the relation of this scale to the other subscales he used to measure modernity, he reported no facts about the correlation of mass media use or exposure to either the general measure of modernism or the subscale based on his information questions.

Almond and Verba collected data about mass-media exposure in their five-nation study on *Civic Culture,* but did not report the effect of such exposure on their measures most relevant to judging individual modernity such as the sense of civic and subjective competence.

Lerner's *Passing of Traditional Society* assigned central theoretical importance to the role of the mass media in the process of individual change in developing countries, yet curiously it failed to document the case systematically. The basic typology which distinguished individuals as "modern," "transitional," and "traditional" was a composite based on measures of literacy, urbanism, media participation, and empathy. In Lerner's study, therefore, there is no way of ascertaining whether mass-media exposure, standing alone, accounted for the various forms of modern attitude and behavior which he showed to be more common among his "moderns." Lerner did, however, note that "among illiterate rurals, those with a significant measure of media exposure scored higher than those without such exposure" (p. 72).

6. With some minor variation from country to country, we had asked: "Do you listen to the radio (or read the newspaper) never, rarely, a few times a week, or every day?" The answers were then assigned 1, 2, 3, or 4 points, respectively, so that with both questions combined a man's score could range from a low of 2 to a high of 8 points, making a seven-step scale. We actually constructed several forms of the scales to measure exposure to the mass media. Each combined our measure of newspaper exposure with that of radio exposure (except in the Argentinean regression analysis, where we looked at combined newspaper and television exposure). In Argentina, Chile, and Israel, the three more-developed countries, the lower end of the scale was generally collapsed; for our correlational analyses, the combination was of two standardized scores. We also assigned weights to each measure according to a multiple regression on OM, in a process which was designed to yield the highest possible multiple R. That the several scale forms are functionally equivalent was ascertained by comparison of their correlations with OM-500 in relation to which they yielded nearly identical coefficients of association.

7. The median correlation for the subsample of factory workers only, was .40, as noted in Table 10–2.

8. For six countries the median correlations of the mass-media score with

other independent variables were: education, .36***; occupational type, .27***; urbanism of present residence, .22***; consumer goods possessed, .29***; years of factory experience, .14***.

9. If one squares the zero-order correlation for any given country, and then subtracts from it the square of the corresponding partial correlation, one obtains an indication of the reduction partialing has produced in the ability of the mass media to explain OM.

10. On the whole, the gap separating those in the match treated as "frequently" exposed, and those defined as "seldom" exposed, to the mass media was about two points on the basic seven-point scale. This gap was statistically significant at the .001 level or better in all six countries.

11. Match 25 included not only industrial workers, but a small proportion of urban nonindustrial workers as well. However, we have evidence that the results were basically the same for the subsample of industrial workers only. Match 25A included cultivators only. With no exceptions, all of the control variables in both matches were successfully matched so that differences in the group means were not significant at the .05 level.

12. The basic problem in the Chilean and Nigerian cultivator samples was that they represented only an extremely narrow range on variables such as education and mass-media exposure. Such narrow ranges tend to have depressing effects on correlation coefficients, a tendency technically called attenuation.

13. In this connection, it is interesting to know the cross-country median zero-order correlations of mass-media exposure with each of the OM 519 thermal subscales, as follows: active citizenship, .26; change valuation, .20; dignity valuation, .20; economic aspiration, .13; education valuation, .16; efficacy, .21; family size, .14; information, .44; minority-opinion valuation, .19; modern family, .14, modern religion, .18; new-experience valuation, .20; nonparochial allegiance, .20; planning valuation, .18; responsibility valuation, .16; technical-skill valuation, .18; urban-industrial preference, .16; verbal fluency, .14; and women's rights, .16. As with formal education, all coefficients are medians applying to the total sample from each country and are statistically significant at the .001 level. Most are in a very narrow range, here from .16 to .20, and this gives emphasis to the overall evenness of the OM score's relation to mass-media exposure, similar to the evenness of effect noted earlier for education.

11 The Factory as a School in Modernity

1. Benjamin S. Bloom, *Stability and Change in Human Characteristics*, p. 218.

2. *Ibid.*, p. 223.

3. A test-retest correlation of about .60 may, of course, reflect forces other than actual personal change over time. It could result mainly from the low reliability of the test. The tests under consideration, however, were of rather high reliability, and so the correlation of .60 may be interpreted as due, at least in good part, to the fact of personal change over time.

4. Bloom, *Stability and Change*, p. 223.

5. *Ibid.*, pp. 229–230.

6. In this example we are here also touching on the GO theme (Growth of Opinion Diversity). Obviously it is not possible to treat the dimensions of factory experience as watertight compartments. Useful as the distinction between analytic and topical perspectives may have been for theoretical clarity and effective exposition, in the reality of factory experience the different dimen-

sions are intertwined and the influence of the factory diffuses itself across all of them.

7. Israel had to be excluded because the workers there were migrants not from villages, but rather from other countries. Moreover, they were almost exclusively of urban origin.

Match 4 was of good quality with only one minor flaw: there was a moderately significant difference in age, factory workers being older than cultivators, for both India and Chile.

8. In the nature of the case, however, certain variables more closely associated with industrial experience could not be controlled in the matching of cultivators with industrial workers. Inevitably the workers had more urban experience, enjoyed greater earnings, and had more contact with the media of mass communication. To weigh the influence of these usual accompaniments of industrial experience requires that we conduct an analysis limited to industrial workers only.

9. The six steps (in total months of factory work experience) are defined for each country as follows:

Step	Argentina	Chile	India	Israel	Nigeria	East Pakistan
1	1–12	0– 7	1– 6	0–12	0– 6	0– 6
2	13–63	24–48	36–51	18–63	18–33	35–57
3	64–87	60–72	52–75	64–93	34–51	58–81
4	88–111	84–96	76–105	94–123	52–75	82–111
5	112–141	108–132	106–192	124–216	76–159	112–156
6	142–228	144–228	—	—	—	—

Except for the first step, which was limited to those defined as new factory workers, the steps were chosen by means of three criteria: (1) that each group have an adequate number of men to produce meaningful statistics; (2) that (since men reporting their experience had often rounded to the nearest year or half year) groups be divided halfway between these points of concentration; and (3) that at least the middle groups not represent extremely different amounts of experience.

10. The low correlation of .11 for India should not be automatically interpreted as indicating that there the impact of factory experience was less regular than in the other countries. In India, the correlation was adversely affected by an inverse correlation of education and factory experience found only in the Indian sample. For details see note 13.

11. The issue could be settled definitively only by doing a study of men who had been in industry and then left. We had meant to do such a study in each country, but were unable to mobilize the necessary resources. Limiting ourselves to the workers in our sample who were still in industry, we found that the longer a man had been an industrial worker, and the higher his modernity score, the greater was his preference for a job running his own small business *outside of agriculture*, or for any job of higher status than the one he had. The preference for a higher status job was more clear-cut when predicted on the basis of modernity scores (for five countries median $r = .16^{**}$) than when predicted from years in the factory (median $r = .07$). This finding is a definite challenge to the idea that the factory retains the modern men. On the contrary, the more modern the man the greater his readiness to leave the factory.

Interestingly enough, the variable job *satisfaction* (as opposed to job *preference*) was not systematically related to modernity; indeed, the association was weakly negative in four of six countries. This suggests, quite reasonably, that modern men more often wanted to leave the factory not so much because they *disliked* that type of work, but rather because they were *ambitious* to get ahead on their own.

12. For evidence that the modernizing effect occurred throughout the range of factory experience, see note 22.

13. In India, the most experienced workers actually had substantially less education, with a mean education of 6.9 years as against 8.6 years for the mid-experienced workers. In the other five countries the median gap in average years of schooling separating the experienced workers from the new workers was only one-half a school year. In no case was the gap as great as one full year, and in only three of those five countries did the difference favor the more experienced men.

14. The median correlation of the variable "number of factories worked in" and OM-500 was .14, and the statistic was significant at the .01 level or better in five of the six countries. We recognized, of course, that men who had worked in more than one factory would probably have also been longer in industry, and therefore ran a control for years of experience. Although the correlations were thus reduced, all in all the results supported our assumption that it is the less rather than the more modern men who are likely to remain in the same factory year after year.

The correlations of number of factories worked in and OM-500, with and without control for years factory experience, were:

	Argentina	Chile	East Pakistan	India	Israel	Nigeria
Without control	.20***	.18***	.15***	.12**	.08	.13**
With control	.10*	.02	.08*	.11**	.00	.01

The asterisks denote the level of statistical significance, as usual, with * = .05, ** = .01, *** = .001.

15. As noted above, India provided the only country sample in which education was at all strongly correlated with factory experience. In our sample, the new workers were increasingly recruited from among men with more education, and the older workers had a disproportionately large number of men with very low education. The effect of this feature of the sample's composition was to depress the zero-order correlation of factory experience and modernity. Partialing for education brought the correlation of factory experience and modernity in India into line with the figures elsewhere.

16. As to whether the factory workers' journey toward modernism was even with respect to all the various subthemes included in the OM scale, the answer is: less so than with formal education and mass-media exposure, but still quite consistently so. Of the nineteen OM themal subscales, four had median zero-order correlations with factory experience significant at the .001 level: information, .26; responsibility valuation, .24; active citizenship, .21; and change valuation, .13. Five of the correlations were significant at the .01

level: dignity valuation, .12; efficacy, .12; modern family, .12; verbal fluency, 12; new-experience valuation, .10; and technical-skill valuation, .10. Three of the remaining median correlations were significant at the .05 level: modern religion, .09; minority-opinion valuation, .08; and planning valuation, .08. That left six themal subscales which failed to yield a median correlation with factory experience that was significant. They were: nonparochial allegiance, .07; family size, .06; women's rights, .06; education valuation, .04; urban-industrial preference, .04; and economic aspiration, .00. At least these last figures point in the right direction, even if they do not attain statistical significance.

17. By the time we got around to doing the reinterviews, we no longer had a collaborating field director residing in Argentina, Chile, or Nigeria, and we could not afford to entrust the work to a commercial agency. Reinterviews were also being done in India, but the results were not available at the time we went to press.

18. Because of the obvious expense and difficulty of relocating men, our instructions to the field directors did not specify that the 100 men to be reinterviewed should represent the original population in the precise way they would have if we had used strictly random selection procedures. We set a more relaxed standard, merely asking the field directors to try to represent a variety of educational and factory experience levels. As it turned out, however, the reinterviewed men had almost exactly the same characteristics as did the entire original factory-worker sample. In years of education, perhaps, the most critical variable, the relation of the original sample to the reinterviewed was, for East Pakistan, 2.6 to 2.4, and for Israel, 7.3 to 7.2. On other important variables, such as mass-media exposure, skill level, and the like, the two groups were equally close.

19. To ease the burden of the reinterview, we limited ourselves to a shortened version of the OM scale, containing approximately 40 questions, supplemented by sufficient background questions positively to identify each respondent as the man who had been interviewed earlier and to judge what changed experience he had undergone since the first interview.

The 40 questions in the reinterview were those which we had used to develop a short form of the OM scale with question wording strictly comparable in all six countries and with items all known to have significant correlations to the longer form of the OM scale. At least 18 of our 24 basic alphabetic themes were represented among the 40-odd questions.

The items were scored, as they had been in the original OMs, by dichotomizing the responses to each question as close as possible to the midpoint. The dichotomization was based on the distribution of responses in the reinterview. Obviously, this meant that for a meaningful comparison we had to recode the 40 reinterview questions for these men from their first interview, in order that their scores at "time 1" and "time 2" could be based on an *identical* instrument scored in the *identical* way. Of course, we did so. The reason for using the reinterview cutting point was to maximize response variance in this particular subsample of men. We are certain, however, that the results were basically those we would have obtained using the original dichotomous cuts. *The critical point is that exactly the same cutting points were used to code the original interview and the reinterview.*

Following the pattern of our work with the long form of the OM scale, we derived for each man several OM scores based on this shorter set of questions. The results given in the text are for the short-form equivalents of the longer OM-1, 2, and 3, the equivalents being used at both "time 1" and "time 2." These equivalent scales had between 30 and 40 items. The Kuder-Richardson reliabilities for Israel ranged from .66 to .70, and for East Pakistan from .67 to .75.

20. The OM gains presented are medians for abbreviated forms of OM-1, 2, and 3. The significance level of .001 applies to each of the forms (in both of the countries), and it results from the use of a paired t-test.

21. Some might argue that part of the observed gain in OM could be attributed to familiarity with the test, a familiarity acquired by having taken the interview earlier. However, it does not seem too likely that, from having answered these questions once 4 or 5 years earlier, men would have learned how to take the test in order to get a higher OM score. That reasoning might apply in evaluating gains on a test of skill but, given the nature of the OM scale, it does not seem likely that gains in OM scores over time can be attributed to learning through test-taking.

22. It was apparent, also, that the impact of factory experience on modernity was manifest throughout the range of factory experience. When we computed the correlations between experience and modernity for men of at least 1 year's tenure in the factory, and then partialed out both education and exposure to the mass media, we obtained the following correlations: Argentina, rural origin, .29***, urban origin, .17***; Chile, rural origin, .24***, urban origin, .17**; India, .18***; Israel, .08; Nigeria, rural origin, .15**, urban origin, .16**; East Pakistan, .18***. Although one of the coefficients had fallen below the .05 significance level, it was nevertheless clear that the factory's ability to modernize generally extended throughout the range of the experienced workers. Selective retention of the new workers, therefore, could not explain the correlation of factory experience with modernity, nor could that correlation be primarily attributed to the special impact on new workers of their initial contact with the factory.

23. In our samples, factory experience was correlated with gross income at a median of .45***, with urban experience at a median of .63***, and with age at a median of .55***. The effect of partialing in such a case is not to sharpen one's understanding, but rather to place a successively larger amount of the variable-to-modernity correlation in limbo. In other words, if we did partial out all other elements of the urban-industrial milieu, we would be left not so much with a true picture of the role of factory experience as with an estimate of some residue representing only that which could not possibly be attributed to anything else. In such cases, partialing comes to have not a positive clarifying role in the analysis, but a negative corroding one.

24. By country the results were: Argentina, .21***; Chile, .30***; India, .22***; Nigeria, .12**; and East Pakistan, .17***.

25. The most relevant case was that described by Match 3B for India, which dealt with men all of whom lived in villages near Ranchi and pitted those working in industry against those still farming. The match was of good quality with no departures from our standards. With 45 men in each group, the match yielded a substantial correlation of .31**, favoring the men who worked in factories. Their mean OM score was 60 compared to 53 for the cultivators. Only 9 percent of the cultivators were scored as modern as against 34 percent of the factory workers.

Match 3C for India combined those living in villages near either Muri or Khalari, two relatively isolated industrial establishments each surrounded mainly by a small company town. Here again there were no deviations from standards of strict matching. The factory workers again came out ahead of the cultivators but, given the small N of 26 pairs, not at a statistically significant level. The match correlation was .17; the mean OM score for the workers was 61 versus 57 for the cultivators.

Unfortunately, in East Pakistan we failed to sample any cultivators from the villages (near Dacca) from which we drew the "rural-resident workers," so there we could not construct a match comparable to the two cited above for India.

26. Match 13 in East Pakistan compared factory workers living in their original home village outside Dacca with workers living in Dacca in so-called "factory-worker colonies." These were large housing compounds provided by the mills and factories, similar to what would be called "company housing" in the United States. The number of pairs in the match was a healthy 77. The match was of good quality, with no departure from our standards for strict matching. On the critical match variable, the village residents had had an average of 1.8 years of urban experience at some point in their lives, the factory-colony residents an average of 4.8, the 3-year gap producing a paired t of 9.9 significant at the .001 level. The match correlation (on OM-3) was a minuscule and insignificant .01, and the mean OM scores of the two groups were exactly the same, at 51 points.

Match 12A in India compared factory workers who continued to reside in their original home villages in the vicinity of Ranchi, Muri, or Khalari with workers who had moved from other villages and now resided in either company housing or other communities near the factories. This match, too, was of good quality. The average industrial experience of the men in the match was about 111 months, so that both residence and factory experience had had ample time to take effect. The N of 20 was unfortunately small, but it seems worth noting that the correlation was an insignificant and minuscule .02, and both sets had a mean OM score of 61.

27. We compared workers around Dacca living in their own village with those living in town, and did the same for Ranchi in India. In the Dacca case, the partial correlation of factory experience and OM, with education and mass media controlled, was .13 for the village residents ($N = 69$), and .16 for the town residents ($N = 313$). Thus, the effect of factory experience was in basically the same range, regardless of residence. In Ranchi the comparable partial was .07 for village residents ($N = 194$) and $-.04$ for the town residents ($N = 74$). These correlations were so low as to make no case for the modernizing influence of factories in Ranchi, but it is worth noting that the village residents did at least as well as the town dwellers. In short, the evidence here does not make a case for the influence of urban living.

28. Clearly, the longer a man is in the factory, the older he must become. There is no escape from that association. Of course he need not automatically secure increased earnings the longer he works, but the usual rules of seniority generally get men more earnings as they extend their stay in the plant. Indeed, it might be argued that a man who fails to earn more after spending a long time on the job is a poor learner. Accordingly, he might well also fail to learn the lessons of modernity. His case, therefore, could not properly be used to prove that the factory is a poor teacher. To make that point, one should restrict oneself to the men who had shown the ability to increase their earnings year by year.

29. For details, see note 23.

30. The respective country figures were: Argentina, .19***; Chile, .23***; India, .17***; Israel, .13**; Nigeria, .05; and East Pakistan, .18***. We may also note the partial correlations for men of rural origin when urban experience was added to age, income, education, and mass media as controls. The country figures were: Argentina, .18**; Chile, .25***; India, .17***; Nigeria, .08; and East Pakistan, .13***.

12 Factory Modernity

1. At one point, desperate for more eligible cases, Ryan experienced a moment of weakness and decided to stretch the size criterion to include this plant. As he later reported: "I was smitten for this transgression. The one 'eligible' respondent we found there turned out to be a sample error, after being interviewed, and the case had to be put aside." Thus, the purity of the factory-size criterion was preserved in Nigeria.

2. After reviewing the local situation, Dr. Ryan concluded that too many establishments might meet the size requirement merely because they indulged in the extensive use of apprentice labor, thus giving a spurious impression of the size of their industrial labor force. In most cases such places did not really unambiguously qualify as factories on other grounds, and so a general rule was established limiting the proportion of apprentices a plant could have and still qualify for the sample in Nigeria. The heavy use of "apprentices," incidentally, was often adopted to keep the wage bill artificially low. In addition, by taking many men on at this artificially low wage a manager could nevertheless build up good will by dispensing some kind of job to larger numbers of friends, relatives, and associates of people worth influencing. In short, it involved a substantial component of what was, on the Nigerian scene, a traditional approach to staffing a work project.

3. To standardize the ratings by experts we provided each with a detailed written description of what the project considered important in judging a factory as modern or traditional on both the technical and the human-relations dimensions. In some countries this description was accompanied by a graphic scale with illustrations.

4. A preliminary analysis based on some of the detailed information we collected about the factories is presented in the unpublished doctoral dissertation of Rowan Ireland, "The Factory as a School in Social Change," submitted to the Department of Sociology, Harvard University, Cambridge, Mass., December 1969.

5. The measures of factory size and reported benefits are described more fully below. The correlation of rated factory modernity with size ranged from $-.02^{NS}$ in East Pakistan to .44*** in Nigeria, with a median of .24***, and perceived-benefits correlations ranged from $-.10**$ in Chile to .40*** in Argentina, with a median of .30***. India was not included. The low correlation of size and modernity in East Pakistan does not mean the association would not prevail in the larger population of factories there, even if it was not evident in our sample. Dr. Schuman was more exigent than the other field directors in sampling factories so that there was a modern and traditional representative matched at each size level.

6. Asterisks denote significance levels as follows: *, at .05 level; **, at .01 level; ***, at .001 level or better.

7. One measurement problem we realized after the fact was that our cod-

ing procedure obliged us to rely on the *number* of benefits offered by each factory. A classification in terms of the *type* of benefit might have been more relevant. Examples of the kind of service we scored as benefits are given below in note 12.

8. The Indian sample differed from the others in that the men were drawn from a few factories, because of the special emphasis in that sample on finding factories in the countryside. Only 11 factories were included in the Indian sample, and by Indian standards all were at the modern end of the distribution.

9. These correlations, and all the rest of the analysis in this chapter, took into account the response of all factory workers, not merely those who had worked exclusively in the factory being evaluated. Some men had worked some part, perhaps in some cases even the greater part, of their industrial career in factories other than the one we found them in. To be certain that this fact had not distorted our results, we later reran the basic correlations using as a sample only those workers who had worked in but a single factory, namely, the one they were in when we interviewed them. There were no substantial differences in the correlations obtained using the sample of all workers and the narrower sample of those who had worked only in the same single factory. For example, the correlation of factory modernity and OM, using the total sample of workers versus the subsample, was, by country: Argentina, .18/.18; Chile, −.01/−03; Israel, −.11/−.11; Nigeria, .11/.14; East Pakistan, .13/.13.

10. This was a probability which proved, on the whole, to assume the character of a concrete reality when we looked more closely at the facts. The factory-modernity rating was correlated with the formal education of the workers at a level significant above .01 in Argentina, Nigeria, and East Pakistan, the median r for the five available countries being .14.

11. In Match 15, the number of benefits reported by the worker to be given by his factory was not controlled, which somewhat reduced the danger that this match involved us in the partialing fallacy. The matching procedure was quite successful, in that the matched pairs did not show statistically significant differences on any of the ten variables which we attempted to control.

12. The benefits included in our standard check list were: bonuses, free medical service, housing, loans, sport and recreation facilities, and social-welfare assistance. "Other" benefits to be specified by the interviewee were also listed. These included a wide variety of services, including paid vacations, external or inhouse training to increase one's skill, insurance schemes, and educational aid to children.

13. We used Match 28 for this comparison. In East Pakistan the residence of those getting more benefits was somewhat more urban and in Chile the "more benefits" group had a moderately higher gross income, which is understandable under the circumstances. All of these match biases would, normally, have increased the chances that the group reporting more benefits would emerge as more modern in the match.

14. It could be said that the partialing fallacy was committed in this match because we controlled for the project director's modernity rating. That rating was an alternative measure of the same basic quality which we intended to measure by the benefits count. Moreover, as noted in the text, the two measures were fairly strongly correlated. Controlling for factory size as well further increased the risk of committing the partialing fallacy in this match. For the results of a match on factory benefits in which there were controls neither for rated modernity nor for size, see note 18.

15. The range of factory sizes varied greatly in the different countries, however. As a result, the number signified by the terms "small" and "large" differed a good deal from one country to another. In East Pakistan the average "small" plant in the match had about 100 workers, whereas in Argentina it had about 300. This meant that if there were some important threshold, the crossing of which made a great difference, that effect might be obscured in a particular country. If the hypothesized modernizing effect were more evenly felt as one went up the size ladder, however, the variation in these cutting points would have little influence so long as in each country there was a set of nominally "small" and "large" factories.

16. In Match 22, the number of benefits was not controlled, thus somewhat reducing the chances that we might be caught in the partialing fallacy. There were no departures from the standards of strict matching in four of six countries. In Chile, the factory workers from larger factories had moderately higher scores on consumer goods. In Israel, factory workers from smaller factories had somewhat higher self-rated skill scores. These seem minor flaws, and unlikely to substantially affect the outcome of the analysis.

17. James S. Coleman *et al. Equality of Educational Opportunity* (Washington: U. S. Government Printing Office, 1966). The measures of physical facilities taken into account were features of the school such as its age, the ratio of pupils to teachers, the presence of special facilities such as gymnasiums and laboratories, and the provision of free school lunches; measures of curriculum dealt with the accreditation of the school and the presence of music and art teachers on the staff.

18. In rerunning the matches, we controlled only for education, ethnicity-religion, origin, and factory experience. We also took advantage of this rerun of the matches to limit ourselves exclusively to men who had worked only in the factory being rated, so that their modernity score could not be the outcome of experience in a factory having different characteristics from the one being rated. The resultant correlation of OM scores and standing as "high" or "low" on the matches in no way contradicts the conclusion from the earlier matches to the effect that neither a factory's rated modernity, nor its size, nor its benefits policy, standing alone, makes a consistent independent contribution to individual modernity.

19. Robert Blauner, *Alienation and Freedom: The Factory Worker and His Industry* (Chicago: University of Chicago Press, 1967); Michel Crozier, *The Bureaucratic Phenomenon* (Chicago: University of Chicago Press, 1964); James G. March and Herbert A. Simon, *Organizations* (New York: Wiley, 1963); Leonard R. Sayles, *The Behavior of Industrial Work Groups: Prediction and Control* (New York: Wiley, 1963).

20. Our approach will not quell the doubts of those who would argue that our failure to find a connection between the quality of a man's factory and his individual modernity came from measuring factory quality at the wrong level. It may be argued that instead of looking at the factory as a whole we should have been more concerned with "microenvironments." Some studies in the field of complex organization have shown, quite sensibly, that within a single factory or firm different departments may produce quite distinctive social atmospheres, to say nothing of variable conditions of work. It was beyond our resources to collect information about the immediate work environment of each man in our sample.

21. The appropriate scales were developed by Rowan Henry Ireland, and are more fully described in Ireland, "The Factory as a School in Social

Change." The scale content varied somewhat from place to place according to both the availability of information and the intercorrelation of the relevant items in each country. Lack of appropriate data obliged Dr. Ireland to omit India and Israel entirely, leaving four countries in which to test the hypotheses.

22. The covariates entered into the analysis of covariance were: education, years of factory experience, years of urban residence after age 15, and rated skill.

23. From some factories as many as 15 or more men entered our sample. We considered this number large enough to support a separate correlation analysis for each subsample of 15 or more to assess the association between length of industrial experience and individual modernity. We recognize that with such a small number of cases one or two erratic scores could have a substantial effect on a correlation. Nevertheless, we could not help but be struck by the great variability in the correlation of OM and years of factory experience we observed as we moved from factory to factory. In East Pakistan, for example, one factory showed individual modernity and years of experience to correlate as high as $+.80***$, whereas in another factory it was as low as $+.04^{NS}$, with the others spread over the whole range in between. Similar results were obtained in other countries, suggesting that our factories really did vary greatly in their ability to act as schools in modernity for the men who worked in them. We take it as a major challenge to later research to explain these marked differences in the evident effectiveness of different factories to serve as schools for individual modernization.

13   The Role of Agricultural Cooperatives

1. In preparing this description of the Academy for Rural Development in Comilla we relied heavily on Howard Schuman, *Economic Development and Individual Change: A Social-Psychological Study of the Comilla Experiment in Pakistan*, Occasional Papers in International Affairs, No. 15 (Cambridge, Mass.: Harvard University Center for International Affairs, 1967). We also drew on two unpublished reports, one by Mohammed M. Zaman, a Fellow of the Center for International Affairs from Pakistan, and another by David Eaglesfield, a research assistant to the Project. Mr. Eaglesfield also aided in the data analysis for this chapter.

2. This was the median size of a plot in a typical village in Comilla District. See S. A. Qakir, "Land Holdings and Land Use in an East Pakistan Village: Dhanishwar," *Journal of the Pakistan Academy for Rural Development* 1, no. 2 (Comilla, 1960).

3. The Academy was also supported by the Ford Foundation, and received technical assistance from Michigan State University.

4. There were 7 experimental thanas in 1967, and a government commission then recommended its extension to all 20 thanas in the Comilla District.

5. From the booklet *The Academy at Comilla: An Introduction*, published by the Pakistan Academy for Rural Development at Comilla, with no stated author.

6. The match used was number 45. All the pairs were perfectly matched in religion, district of origin, and father's social status, yet inevitably in a match involving so many groups there were some departures from our standards. There were, for example, very small but statistically significant age differences between most of the pairs. The factory workers tended, quite understand-

ably, to be somewhat ahead in mass-media exposure and consumer goods, yet, as we will see, this did not serve to put them ahead of the co-op members in modernity. In the critical comparison of co-op members and nonmembers living in the same village, there were no statistically significant differences on any of the eight variables controlled in the match.

7. Since the first cooperatives were started in 1960, and our field work was done in mid-1964, it seems a generous estimate to assume that the average exposure to co-op influence was about 3 years. Match 45e, which compared cultivators from co-op villages who were not co-op members with cultivators from nonco-op villages elsewhere in Comilla, yielded a gap in OM mean scores of 5. Match 45f, pitting cultivators from co-op villages who *were* co-op members against cultivators from nonco-op Comilla villages, yielded a gap in OM score of 14 points. Dividing 5 and 14, in turn, by 3, yields the two estimates, respectively, given in the text for the point gain resulting from living in villages with cooperatives. The figure for point gains for each year of factory work is based on Match 4 as presented in Table 11–1. The estimate of the gain per year of additional schooling is based on Match 36Mb presented in Table 9–4.

8. We ran a separate regression for East Pakistan based exclusively on cultivators, in which the occupational variable was defined as "cultivators of nonco-op villages versus cultivators of co-op villages." The set from co-op villages included members and nonmembers. This regression was run for OM-3 only. Five other main variables — education, mass media, consumer goods, age, and father's education — were in the predictor pool. The beta weight was a resounding .36. Adding this occupational variable to the predictor pool increased the multiple R from .57 to .66, raising the total variance explained by over 9 percent. In all our efforts at regression analysis with five or more variables already in the predictor pool there were very few instances in which adding another variable, even education, produced so large an increment in the variance explained.

9. Match 49 permitted us to compare men from villages in Comilla District (but outside the range of the Academy's influence) with those from other districts. The match, which had a healthy N of 44 pairs, was of good quality, only age showing a significant difference between groups. The match produced a trivial correlation of .01[NS]. In addition, Match 45, the main basis for the analysis in this chapter, permitted a similar comparison. The match correlation again was an inconsequential .05[NS].

10. This fact is evident from Table 13–1, as may be seen by averaging cells 2 and 3, and pitting the total against cell 1. However, we also tested the point directly in Match 47, which compared 24 men from Comilla villages having co-ops with the same number from Comilla villages without co-ops. The groups were perfectly matched with but one exception. Only on mass media was there a moderate difference between the groups, but this favored the nonco-op villagers, who nevertheless proved to be less modern. The match correlation with OM was a strong .41**, favoring the men from cooperative villages.

11. For supporting evidence see Schuman, *Economic Development and Individual Change.*

12. For the factory group we were able to show that, even if they were recruited on psychological grounds, men became more modern year by year after they entered the factory. And we later developed decisive evidence by

reinterviewing some factory workers 4 years after we first had encountered them. For details, see Chapter 11.

13. Table 13–1 establishes that within Comilla District nonmembers living in co-op villages were more modern than those living in villages without co-ops. To make a comparison with men living in other districts we used Match 45b. Again the nonmembers living in co-op villages showed to advantage when compared to men living in nonco-op villages. Those living in co-op villages had a 6-point lead in OM scores, and the match correlation was substantial at .29, although just failing to reach statistical significance at .05.

14. Indeed, the mean education of members, at 1.7 years, was actually lower than that of nonmembers, at 2.2 years. Moreover, on scanning our several dozen independent variables we discovered only two persistent differences. The members of the cooperatives were older than the nonmembers, and they were generally economically better off. This latter fact, so far as we could tell, had come about because the co-ops' provision of loans, seed improvement, fertilizers, and the like led to improvement in the economic condition of the members. But it clearly could not have changed their age. And it is unlikely that being older the members were also more modern. Indeed, our experience with cultivators everywhere was that they did not become more modern as they became older. We concluded that older men more readily joined the co-op because they were more mature and so could more readily see its advantages, or that they felt more pressed to join it because they had the burden of maintaining larger families and therefore needed to raise more food.

15. The original members of the moshav were the fathers of the men we interviewed. Sixty-one percent of those fathers were characterized by their sons as having pursued "wholly urban" occupations, and only 30 percent were described as having been "full-time cultivators." Even among these full-time cultivators there were certainly many who took up that occupation only after coming to Israel.

16. The figures given for all countries, including Israel, are for the standard match of cultivators and factory workers (Match 4), as used throughout this book. For a special Israeli match using distinctive controls see note 19 of this chapter.

17. The respective correlations for Match 2, all favoring the UNIs over the farmers, were: Chile, .58***; India, .13; Nigeria, .34***; East Pakistan, .16*. There were insufficient cases to complete the match in Argentina.

18. The basic facts are set out in Chapter 11, especially in Tables 11–2 and 11–3.

19. The match correlation of .15 favored the moshav members over the workers, but with an N of 22 pairs the figure was not significant. The mean OM score for moshav members was 63, for workers, 60; 50 percent of the moshav members scored as modern as against 41 percent of the matched workers.

14 Urban Nonindustrial Employment

1. In Argentina we did not get enough cases of rural-origin UNIs on which to base a match and in Israel there were no men considered of rural origin. In the other countries with a Match 2, the UNIs, having lived and worked in town for some time, showed considerable advantages, often at significant levels. In Chile they were significantly higher on mass media and consumer goods. In Nigeria they were significantly higher on mass media, although this

may have been offset by their being lower on consumer goods. In India the UNIs were much higher on mass media, but they were somewhat lower on parental SES. Similarly in East Pakistan, the UNIs were much more exposed to the mass media, and had more consumer goods.

2. In Match 1/2C we successfully controlled for consumer goods possessed, but the mass-media control failed. The score of the UNIs on the scale was much higher, the difference significant at .01 level in the four countries used in the match. The additional control somewhat reduced the advantage of the UNIs over the cultivators, but did not eliminate it.

3. In Match 50A new factory workers were matched to UNIs only if they had no record of prior UNI experience, and had worked in industry less than 6 months. In fact, everywhere except in Israel their actual average factory experience was under 3 months. Given the greater work experience allowed the UNIs, certain differences between the matched groups inevitably emerged. The UNI group was significantly older in Israel, Nigeria, and East Pakistan. The UNIs also had a significantly higher income in Chile, Israel, and East Pakistan. And, of course, the UNIs had generally been much longer in town than the new workers. Almost all of these differences should, normally, have given the UNIs a substantial edge in modernity which, in fact, they did not show.

4. There were some departures from standard in Match 1, the most consistent of which was for industrial workers to have higher income or consumer goods; the departures were significant in Israel, East Pakistan, and India. In Chile, however, the UNIs were significantly higher on literacy, the vocabulary test, and consumer goods, and showed a nearly significant advantage in mass-media exposure. These persistent advantages of the Chilean UNIs may have played some role in the UNIs' giving the Chilean worker such stiff competition in the match.

5. The separate analysis by origin was undertaken in two matches not shown in Table 14–2.

6. In the last paragraph of this chapter, however, we note an exception to this rule about the work experience of the UNI, observed in the case of a special sample of Indian UNIs working in large-scale bureaucratic organizations.

7. An alternative explanation for the greater modernity of the urban nonindustrial worker, as against the cultivator, would be that men who are more modern in spirit to begin with are more often attracted into work as urban nonindustrials. After all, these jobs may involve less supervision, allow for more initiative and autonomy, and hold open better prospects for gain and personal advancement, all features likely to appeal to a modern man. We have no evidence for settling this point. It certainly is plausible, but no more plausible than the assumption that industrial workers were recruited on psychological grounds. And we have cast doubt on the latter assumption. See especially Appendix D.

8. The zero-order and partial correlations cited were for OM-3, the figures not being available for OM-500. The variables controlled were: education, age, ethnicity, mass exposure, consumer goods possessed, and father's education. For consistency we also used OM-3 in the matches. In Match 1B, the institutional UNIs were ahead of the noninstitutional by 4 points on the OM scale, and were favored by the correlation of .19[NS]. In Match 1A the institutional UNIs came out essentially equal to the industrial workers, both having a mean OM-3 score of 55.

15   The Quantity and Quality of Urban Experience

1. The procedures used for sampling factories are described in Chapter 12.

2. For a succinct review see Norton Ginsburg, "The City and Moderniza-tion," in Myron Weiner, ed., *Modernization: The Dynamics of Growth* (New York: Basic Books, 1966), pp. 122–137. For a critical perspective, especially as applies to popular politics and modernization, see Joan M. Nelson, *Migrants, Urban Poverty and Instability in Developing Nations,* Occasional Papers in International Affairs, No. 22 (Cambridge: Harvard University Center for In-ternational Affairs, 1969).

3. Bert F. Hoselitz, *Sociological Aspects of Economic Growth* (Glencoe, Ill.: Free Press, 1962), p. 163.

4. In the samples of rural-origin workers, the correlation of years of urban residence since age 15 with years of factory experience was, by country: Argentina, .71***; Chile, .75***; Nigeria, .43***; and East Pakistan, .70***. It will be recalled that in India we selected several factories precisely because they were located in the countryside. All of their experienced workers were coded as "zero years in town." When this group was not excluded from con-sideration, the correlation of factory experience and years in town in India was only .13***; when they were excluded, it was .36***. In Israel there were no men of rural origin, so the measure could not be applied there.

5. Match 12M was limited to men of rural origin. The controls produced nonsignificant differences in all but one case: in Nigeria, the "high years urban" group had a somewhat higher skill level than the "low" group. City of work location was not controlled. More important, neither was mass-media exposure.

The difference in urban experience between the two groups was in all cases at least 5 years and significant at beyond the .001 level. Although length of factory experience was controlled, the "high years urban" group had, not sur-prisingly, more UNI experience prior to entering the factory, except in Nigeria. In our Nigerian sample, those with longer time in the city seemed, generally, to have slightly more years of education, making it necessary to match exactly on the education variable and thereby reducing the number of possible matches in this instance to 19. The number of pairs elsewhere was: Argentina, 37; Chile, 29; East Pakistan, 32; India, 46.

6. The correlations of the match and OM, with a positive coefficient favor-ing greater urban experience, were: Argentina, −.01; Chile, .20; East Pakistan, .06; India, −.02; and Nigeria, .18. Although none of these correlations was statistically significant at .05 or better, it should be noted that two of the five correlations were figures above our minimum standard of .10 in magnitude. Moreover, in the case of Nigeria, the match result accorded well with the partial correlation reported in Table 15–2.

7. The main evidence is given above in Chapter 11. In the extreme test we ran the partial correlations of OM with years urban and with factory experi-ence, controlling for four basic background variables: father's education, own education, ethnicity, and literacy. Then, in addition, we alternately controlled for the analogous fifth variable: years urban in the case of factory experience, factory experience in the case of years urban. The results were as follows:

	Argentina	Chile	East Pakistan	Israel	Nigeria
Years urban	.08	.07	.03	−.05	.20**
Years factory experience	.05	.26***	.15***	.27***	.09

In three of five countries the effect of factory experience was highly significant, whereas only in Nigeria did urban experience continue to show a significant effect.

8. The three indicators cited in the text — size, cosmopolitanism, and status as the capital of the largest appropriate territorial unit (nation or region) — did not in every case point to the same city as the one appropriate to put in competition with all the others. In the cases where the three indicators did not all designate the same city, we resolved the issue by selecting that city which, in the opinion of our local judges, was clearly the most cosmopolitan. Cosmopolitanism was defined as being, independent of size, a quality measured by cultural diversity, concentration of business, industry, banking, and government headquarters, richness of artistic and intellectual resources, and extent of contact with the outside world and sophistication about it.

9. Circa 1960, the population of the city of Buenos Aires was 2,967,000, and the population of the metropolitan area from which we drew our sample was 6,763,000. The population of Cordoba was 589,000, and of Rosario, 672,000.

10. Circa 1960, Santiago had a population of 646,000 people in the central city, with about double that number in the metropolitan area. The populations of the other cities, each the capital of a province bearing the same name, were: Valparaiso, 225,000; Concepción, 170,000; Valdivia, 70,000.

11. The population of Tel Aviv was estimated (circa 1968) to be 388,000, but the metropolitan-area population was probably double that. In the same period, Jerusalem was estimated to have a population of 260,000 and Haifa one of over 185,000.

12. Circa 1963, the population of Lagos was 412,000, but this was exclusive of large compounds which were basically part of the capital city's metropolitan area even though technically located in the Federal Territory just outside the city of Lagos. This fact gave the technical edge in size to Ibadan, at 627,000. Abeokuta had 187,000, and Epe 136,000. Despite its large size, Ibadan depended mainly on the cultivation of cacao for its economic standing, had little industry, and was quite unimportant, compared to Lagos, as a center for business, government, and banking.

13. Circa 1961, Dacca had about 557,000 people, mainly concentrated in old Dacca, which was the very densely populated remnant of what had once been a great city. Chittagong held some 365,000 people, and Khulna 128,000.

14. In 1961 Jamshedpur had 328,000 inhabitants, whereas Ranchi had only 140,000. Although Ranchi was growing at a fantastic rate, its population was still almost certainly below that of Jamshedpur in 1964 when we did our field work there.

15. In Match 13M we matched experienced factory workers from the main city in each country to experienced factory workers in the other, lesser cities. The controls produced nonsignificant differences between the groups except in the case of factory size in Argentina and Chile, where workers in the lesser cities work in slightly smaller factories. In the Indian match, where it was not possible to control this variable without cutting drastically the number of matches, the workers in the lesser-cities group worked in much larger factories. Mass-media exposure was not controlled. However, the group differences on this measure were neither consistent in direction nor significant except in Chile, where Santiago workers showed somewhat higher mass-media exposure. The number of pairs in each country was: Argentina, 34; Chile, 66; East Pakistan, 55; India, 51; Israel, 65; Nigeria, 25.

16. With the men from less cosmopolitan cities scored 1 and from the more cosmopolitan scored 2, Match 13M yielded correlations with OM as follows: Argentina, .17; Chile, −.00; East Pakistan, −.12; India, −.03; Israel −.05; Nigeria, −.08.

17. In this regression we arranged the cities in which our factory workers lived as a dummy variable so that the main, most cosmopolitan city was arrayed against all the others, as described in the text. This dummy variable was then entered into a regression analysis on OM-3, in competition with eight other variables: total factory experience; objective skill; mass-media exposure; consumer goods; education; age; ethnicity-religion; and father's education. A positive beta weight indicated that the city classified as more cosmopolitan had more modern men, and a negative beta indicated the cosmopolitan city had fewer modern men. The beta weights for the cosmopolitanism variables were, by country: Argentina, .10*; Chile, −.05; India, −.03; Nigeria, −.12**; East Pakistan, −.03.

18. We were not alone in reaching this conclusion about the relative unimportance of cosmopolitanism as a determinant of modernity. In his study of capital cities and provincial towns in Brazil and Mexico, Joseph Kahl reported: "Of course we found [the modern man] more often in the metropolis than in the provinces, but somewhat to our surprise, we discovered that he is quite common in the middle strata of society in small provincial towns . . . Taking into account that our samples did not include peasants, and also that we had deliberately excluded men from the very bottom and top of the status hierarchy, we concluded that about a third of the measured variation in modernism was accounted for by socioeconomic status, and slightly less than a tenth by metropolitan versus provincial location." Kahl, *The Measurement of Modernism*, p. 134.

19. We considered the urbanism of the work place an important fact in its own right. Nevertheless, we recognize that the location of a man's place of work is not a certain indicator of the urbanism of his place of residence. We attempted to rate the urbanism of each man's place of residence, but technical difficulties with the measure in several countries prevented our using it. Since in some countries we had both measures, we checked their agreement. Using the measure of urbanism of residence did not lead to a conclusion different from that based on the urbanism of the work place as reported in the text.

20. The correlation of "urbanism of factory location" and OM was, by country: Argentina, −.08; East Pakistan, −.04; India, .03; Israel, .16***; Nigeria, .12**. Controlling for the variables in Set A reduced the correlations for both Israel and Nigeria to .08.

21. Wirth's article appeared in the *American Journal of Sociology* 44 (1938): 3–24. For a critical evaluation and testing of some of his ideas, see Claude S. Fischer, "A Research Note on Urbanism and Tolerance," *American Journal of Sociology* 76, no. 5 (March 1971): 847–856, and "The Effects of Urbanism: A Review and Analysis of Poll Data," forthcoming.

22. Ginsburg, "The City and Modernization," p. 122.

16   Rural Versus Urban Origin

1. Bloom, *Stability and Change,* pp. 215–216.
2. Our research design also acknowledged the potential importance of ethnic

and religious differences as background factors. The fact that representatives of several different religions, and, in addition, of a number of different ethnic groups, could all be found in a single national sample, made the analysis of our data from this point of view quite complex. We decided, therefore, to postpone presentation of those results for a later and separate publication.

3. These rules were subject to some discretion on the part of the local field directors. In Chile, men were still considered to be of rural origin if they had spent any one year of their first 15 living in a city of less than 20,000 inhabitants, or if they had spent 2 to 3 years in such a city when these had been the first years of life. In Argentina similar exceptions were made, accepting as "rural" in origin those who had lived in cities of more than 2,000 inhabitants for periods of less than 2 years total. As for the definition of urban origin, in Chile and Argentina, men qualified with up to 3 years of rural residence if the experience came before the age of 7. In Nigeria, the sample was very pure with regard to early residence and required no special exceptions. In general, considering all three countries, almost all the cases actually collected met the more stringent general requirements.

4. For men of rural origin in Argentina, Chile, and Nigeria the median correlation of years in the factory and modernity was .32, whereas for men of urban origin in those countries it was .23. Details are given in Table 11–3. A point-gain analysis based on matches indicated that rural-origin men made absolute gains in modernity generally double those achieved by the urban-origin men to whom they were matched. It was this greater gain per year of exposure to the factory which enabled the rural-origin men to pull more abreast of the urban-origin men, as noted below.

5. The main match pairing men of rural and urban origin (89N) yielded correlations with modernity of .10 for Argentina, .10 for Chile, and .11 for Nigeria. All favored the urban origin, but the three coefficients barely satisfied our minimum size criterion, and none were significant at the .05 level. The match was of good quality, and the N's, respectively, 17, 32, and 15 pairs.

6. The initial gap was based on the mean OM score for the basic sampling group of new workers divided into urban and rural origin, with no other variables controlled. The terminal gap was computed from the mean OM scores of experienced workers divided by origin with controls for education and other variables as in Match 89N.

7. This point was established by our analysis of Match 4 and of the related partial correlation in Chapter 11, where we showed that industrial workers of rural origin, when matched to men still living in the village as cultivators, scored much higher on the OM scale.

8. See Appendix D on migration.

9. The figure 8 years is, of course, approximate. We use that figure because it reflects the difference in factory time between the new and the experienced workers in our origin match. Actually we cannot say precisely how many years of factory and town experience it takes for the rural-origin man finally to pull abreast of the urban-origin man. We can only say that, among men matched on education, after 8 years of factory experience the rural-origin men appeared to have nearly caught up with the urban-origin men.

17   Home and School Background

1. The eight standard questions were: CA-9, CA-10, DI-3, DI-4, EF-10, PL-8, TI-2, TI-6. Two additional questions were added in Chile and Argentina:

CA-51 and GO-51. The exact wording of the questions may be ascertained by consulting Appendix A.

2. In Match 24 father's education was not controlled, thus somewhat reducing the chances of committing the partialing fallacy. The quality of the match was good with no departure from standards.

3. The zero-order correlation between the measures was: Argentina, .29; Chile, .23; East Pakistan, .20; India, .29; Israel, .13; Nigeria, .31. All but the Israeli coefficient were significant well above the .001 level, the Israeli at .01. In the match comparing those "low" and "high" on the home-school measure, all the countries but Israel showed a significant group difference on the perceived work-experience scale.

4. We had the data for father's education in Israel, but internal evidence suggested that some systematic error had crept into the coding of this variable. We therefore excluded Israel from consideration in the analysis in this section. At other points in the book, however, we substituted a measure of "father's status" for the father's education variable in Israel.

5. The correlation of father's and son's education was: Argentina, .36; Chile, .32; East Pakistan, .37; India, .44; Nigeria, .24; all were significant at .001 or better. Because of our lack of confidence in the Israeli measure of father's education, we did not compute the correlation there.

6. In Match 58 fathers in the "less-educated" group generally had no schooling, and those in the "more-educated" group generally had about 6 years of schooling. The t test of the difference between the less- and more-educated groups was significant at well beyond the .001 level in all six countries. Overall, the match met rigorous standards, with only two differences significant at .05 in some 60 or more controls applied across the five countries.

7. This assumption was definitely borne out by the path analysis we undertook. The indirect effects of father's education, as mediated through the respondent's own education, were relatively much stronger, more consistent, and more important than the direct effects once other variables were controlled in the path analysis. For example, using the total sample, and reporting figures which are the median for six countries, we found the following: the total effect on OM of father's education, equal to the Pearsonian correlation, was .26; the direct effect only .05; but the indirect effect .21. The relative weight of father's education was only .03, indicating it was not a very important variable compared to the son's own education, with a relative weight of .47, or compared to the respondent's occupation, which had a relative weight of .15. In this analysis Israel was included, but a measure of "father's status" was substituted for the measure of father's education. For further details see Table 20–2.

8. When we ran our basic Set A of eight control variables excluding "own education," the partial correlation of father's education with OM predictably rose somewhat. In East Pakistan, for example, the partial rose from .01[NS] to .09**, and in Chile from .16*** to .21***. The real meaning of these changes, however, cannot be assessed unless we consider what happened when the shoe was put on the other foot, and the partial correlation of own education and OM was obtained with and without father's education controlled. When that was done we discovered that the correlation of own education and OM was very little affected by releasing the control on father's education. For the total sample, the partial correlation coefficients of own education and OM, first with father's education included in Set A, and then with father's education not included in Set A, were: Argentina, .37***/.39***; Chile, .34***/.37***;

East Pakistan, .26***/.28***; India, .52***/.54***; Nigeria, .29***/.39***. These figures indicate that the earlier impression we had of the effect of father's education derived mainly from its incidental correlation with our respondents' own education.

Another way of looking at the results is to consider the variance explained when we added to a basic pool of predictor variables either own education or father's education. The predictor pool used was the set of late-socialization variables, measuring occupation, mass-media exposure, life-cycle stage, and urban residence. Adding own education to that set raised the variance explained (in the median case for five countries) by 10 percent; adding father's education to that initial set raised the variance explained in the median case by only 1 percent.

9. In Argentina, in the educational range between 4 and 8 years of schooling, the urban-origin workers, on the average, scored more than 4 OM points higher than the rural-origin workers, at each grade level. In Chile, in the grades from third to seventh, the lead of the urban-origin workers at each grade level was also generally 4 points; in Nigeria it was about 1.5. In these comparisons, variables other than education and origin were not controlled. We restricted ourselves to the narrow range of grades indicated above in order to ensure an ample base of cases in all cells used in the comparisons.

10. This may be seen clearly if, for each country, we give first the OM points separating a cultivator from a rural-origin industrial worker, and then the gap separating those same rural-origin industrial workers, from the urban-origin men. The figures are, respectively: Argentina, 9.0/4.5; Chile, 9.5/4.5; Nigeria, 9.0/1.5. In each case we were comparing men who had left school at the same grade level, in the educational range between 4 and 8 years of schooling. Clearly the cultivators, despite going to the same rural schools for the same length of time as did the rural-origin workers, were more distant from their rural-origin "cousins" than those same rural-origin workers were from the urban-origin workers, even though the latter had gone to urban schools.

11. These results were again based on the scores of men who left school at grades between the fourth and eighth years. To be certain that our use of this more limited school range had not misled us, we ran a regression analysis in each country, utilizing the entire educational range in our samples. In each country two regressions were run, one for urban- and one for rural-origin men. The raw-score regression (B) weights for education obtained by this method were comparable to the results obtained by the simpler technique of comparing the mean gain in OM score that men secured by each step up the educational ladder.

12. If our assumptions were correct, then rural-origin children would already have been less modern than urban-origin children at the time they entered school. To test this assumption one would need measures of the modernity of children at the moment they entered school in rural and urban settings, respectively. We have discovered that a modified version of the OM scale can be used reliably and validly as early as the third grade, but we have not as yet obtained an appropriate rural and urban sample on which to test the point raised above.

18   The Behavioral Manifestations of Individual Modernity

1. In preparing this chapter we benefited from the assistance of Shirley Weitz, who searched the relevant literature, and Metta Spencer, who ran some

of the original analyses of data. Both contributed substantially to the elaboration of the ideas and information presented here.

At a later point Harriet Wasserstrum helped in the creation of the behavior scales, and in all other phases of the final analysis. Her assistance was critical in the development of the materials for this chapter.

2. Samuel A. Stouffer, "Attitudes as Related to Subsequent Behavior," in *Social Research to Test Ideas* (New York: Free Press of Glencoe, 1962), p. 193. For a more recent discussion of this general issue, see Irwin Deutscher, "Looking Backward: Case Studies on the Progress of Methodology in Sociological Research," *American Sociologist* 4, no. 1 (1969): 35–40; Harold J. Ehrlich, "Attitudes, Behavior and the Intervening Variables," *American Sociologist* 4, no. 1 (1969): 29–34; Allen W. Wicker, "Attitudes Versus Action: The Relationship of Verbal and Overt Behavioral Responses to Attitude Objects," *Journal of Social Issues* 25, no. 4 (1969): 41–78.

3. The obvious reason for suspecting self-reports is that individuals may give inaccurate information either to enhance their prestige or to appear more consistent with their expressed attitudes than they actually are. This leads some researchers arbitrarily to distrust most of what their respondents tell them. They insist on some external criterion of behavior, some official record, or the judgment of some third party whose job it is to keep the score. Yet such records can be falsified too, and often are. Even a time clock can be punched for you by a friend, and production records are notoriously subject to manipulation by the work crews which generate them. The judgment of a third party, moreover, is as prone to distortion by motives, attachments, prejudices, and situational perspectives as is the report of the party being judged. One may well wonder whether it really is so much more sensible to trust a foreman's opinion in preference to a man's own report as to whether he is hard-working and conscientious.

4. For a conventional statement of the argument, see Herbert Blumer "Attitudes and the Social Act," *Social Problems* 3 (1955), pp. 60–62. For current reviews of the issues and the evidence see the articles by Deutscher, Ehrlich, and Wicker cited in note 2.

5. See, for example, Bray's experiment, in which he sought to determine the power of two popular tests of prejudice to predict behavior. The attitude tests were conventional: Likert's scale of attitudes toward Negroes and the Levinson-Sanford Scale of attitudes toward Jews. However, the behavioral test Bray used had no relation to either topic dealt with by the attitude tests, nor, indeed, to any other natural situation. Rather, the "behavior" had to do with accepting or rejecting the judgment of Black and Jewish confederates as to how far a light moved in an autokinetic experiment. The two situations were clearly very different in content and significance. The attitude tests did not successfully predict behavior in the experiment. See D. W. Bray, "The Prediction of Behavior from Two Attitude Scales," *Journal of Abnormal Social Psychology* 45 (1950): 68–84.

6. The literacy test contained extracts from local newspapers selected to represent three levels of difficulty. Interviewees were asked to read the text, starting with the extract we considered to be the least difficult. If they read that well they were invited to read the extract we had rated at the next level of difficulty. The respondent's reading ability was then rated on a scale, in most countries having four steps from "not at all" to "good."

7. J. Mayone Stycos and Kurt W. Back, *The Control of Human Fertility in Jamaica* (Ithaca: Cornell University Press, 1964).

8. Table 18–1 presents the results for the total sample, without a control for level of education. The table was rerun with a division into high and low education for each of the six countries. The gamma statistic, which we used as a measure of association, was basically the same for each pair of questions in both the high- and low-education sets; and both agreed very well with the gamma statistic obtained for the total sample. This argues that even among better-educated men — who might because of that fact alone have been more or less equal in knowledge — those who had more modern attitudes and values seem to be led, thereby, to more active and effective communications behavior than was shown by their educational peers who lacked the special interest of the men more modern in spirit.

9. By searching appropriate records, some research has sought to test the accuracy of the personal facts which people are so often asked to report. In a wide but intensive study in Denver, Colorado, it was found that on facts which are current — such as whether one has a telephone at home — people gave a virtually perfect account of themselves, the proportion of correct answers being well above 90 percent. But for events more distant in the past, or less important in the individual's life, the accuracy of the self-report fell considerably. Of those who claimed to have voted in the presidential election a year earlier, 86 percent had their claim validated by the voting records of their town. But only 56 percent of those who claimed to have contributed to the Community Chest Drive a year earlier had that claim validated by the records. Of course, they might have contributed, but in amounts too small to have been recorded anywhere. See Don Cahalan, "Correlates of Respondent Accuracy in the Denver Validity Survey," *Public Opinion Quarterly* 32 (Winter 1968–69): 607–621. For an earlier related study see Hugh J. Parry and H. M. Crossley, "Validity of Responses to Survey Questions," *Public Opinion Quarterly* 14, no. 1 (1950): 61 80.

10. Here again three judges rated every pair of questions linking an attitude or value to a behavioral claim on a 3-point scale. We took only those questions which the judges considered to involve a clear-cut connection between attitude and behavior. By limiting ourselves to this high standard, we excluded about 20 pairs of questions deemed to present an ambiguous connection between attitude and behavior.

11. We computed correlations for the 12 pairs of questions which, as described above, our raters considered to present an unambiguous test of the relation of a claim to a self-reported behavior. There were 66 such correlations across the six countries, six observations being missing. Of the 66 correlations, 41 were positive and significant at the .01 level or better. Only one coefficient was significant at that level and negative.

12. Included in the objective-test subscale, with some variation by country according to availability, were the following: an arithmetic test score, the word-opposites test score, the question-repetition score, and the literacy test score; number of consumer goods identified (CO-1, 2), number of city problems cited (GO-1), number of national problems cited (GO-2), world figures identified (IN-1, 2), national figures identified (IN-3, 4), national city identified (IN-5), world city identified (IN-6, 7), and number of newspapers named (MM-8).

Included in the self-report subscale were a measure of self-rated absences from work, and the man's responses to questions on number of organizations belonged to (AC-2), correspondence with the government (AC-4), radio listening (MM-1), obtaining news from the union (MM-3), obtaining news from a local leader (MM-4), newspaper reading (MM-5), discussing work with wife (WR-3), and discussing politics with wife (WR-4). The inclusion of MM-1 and MM-5 in this subscale, and in the summary behavior scale, made advisable adjustment for autocorrelation when correlating these scales and our independent variable mass-media exposure, as in Table 18–3.

13. Using the Kuder-Richardson formula 20 the behavior scales showed the following reliabilities across the six countries: for the objective test sub-scale, .70 to .85; for the self-report scale, .27 to .55; for the summary (Behavioral OM) scale, .71 to .80. It should be kept in mind that these scales had not been "cleaned" by eliminating items which failed to show strong relations to the overall scale score. All the items we had selected on a priori grounds as either an objective test or a self-report of behavior were included and weighed equally.

14. Country by country, the correlations of years of factory experience with the two behavior subscales, the objective (information) and the self-report (political participation), respectively, were: Argentina, .20/.15; Chile, .28/34; East Pakistan, .31/.05; India, 11/.33; Israel, .18/21; Nigeria, .17/.18. Except for East Pakistan, the results for the two scales were rather similar. By contrast, education had a markedly different impact on the two scales. The correlations, in the same order as above, were: .61/.18; .54/.32; .56/.29; .82/.28; .44/.23; .48/.23.

15. For a fuller discussion of the place of participant citizenship in the modernity syndrome see Inkeles, "Participant Citizenship."

16. The set of questions which comprise the Psychosomatic Symptoms Test is included in Part IV of Appendix A. For related readings, see Samuel A. Stouffer *et al., The American Soldier: Adjustment During Army Life,* Studies in Social Psychology in World War II, vol. I (Princeton, N. J.: Princeton University Press, 1950); Leo Srole *et al., Mental Health in the Metropolis* (New York: McGraw-Hill, 1962); Gerald Gurin, J. Veroff, and Sheila Feld, *Americans View Their Mental Health: A Nationwide Interview Survey* (New York: Basic Books, 1960); Arthur Kornhauser, *Mental Health of the Industrial Worker* (New York: Wiley, 1965); Alexander H. Leighton *et al., Psychiatric Disorder Among the Yoruba: A Report from the Cornell-Aro Mental Health Project in the Western Region, Nigeria* (Ithaca: Cornell University Press, 1963); Norman A. Scotch and H. Jack Geiger, "An Index of Symptom and Disease in Zulu Culture," *Human Organization* 22, no. 4 (Winter, 1963–64): 304–311.

17. For a review of these ideas in Western thought see Morton White and Lucia White, *The Intellectual Versus the City: From Thomas Jefferson to Frank Lloyd Wright* (Cambridge, Mass.: Harvard University Press, 1962).

18. See Alex Inkeles, "The Fate of Personal Adjustment in the Process of Modernization," *The International Journal of Comparative Sociology* 11, no. 2 (June, 1970): 81–114. We are grateful to the editors of the journal and to E. J. Brill, publishers, for their kind permission to reproduce part of the material in this book.

19. The no-contact group consisted exclusively of cultivators who, by definition, had not experienced migration, and were further selected as being in the lower half of the total sample distribution on education, exposure to mass media, years of factory experience, and years of urban residence. Each of these four measures defined an additional potential exposure, up to a maximum of five, for the people of rural origin who had migrated to the

city. In the last cell, which represents highest exposure, we placed those of urban origin who were also in the upper half of the distribution on education, mass media, and years of factory work. This procedure was basically like that used to construct the index of exposure to modernizing experiences described in Chapter 8, but at the time we first analyzed the PT test that index had not yet been constructed.

20. In the version referred to in note 18 we used OM-2 for these correlations, whereas the figures given here are for OM-500. They consequently differ slightly from those given in the journal article.

19 An Overview

1. As may be seen in Table 20–1, Set A, which included eight variables for the total sample, accounted for variance in OM-500 scores, across the six countries, in the range 32 to 62 percent, with the median at 47 percent. The three main variables alone, not shown in the table, accounted for variance in the range 28 to 57 percent. Country by country the proportion of variance accounted for by the three main variables fluctuated between 87 and 93 percent of that accounted for by the larger set of eight variables.

2. There were other variables we had measured which could meet the criteria of theoretical relevance and empirical importance, but they seemed to us to be somewhat redundant and therefore more likely to involve us in the partialing fallacy if they were included in this final competition. Thus, years of urban experience might have been included, but, as we have seen, in our samples this measure seemed largely an artifact of occupational experience. In addition, income or living standard might have qualified, but again in our samples differences in living standards depended substantially on occupational position. To have included them would, therefore, have been merely to put the measure of occupation at a disadvantage relative to education and mass-media contact. To have included a measure of literacy, or the vocabulary (antonyms) test score, would, in similar fashion, have put the educational variable at a disadvantage in competition with mass media and occupation.

3. The statement in the text is based on a regression in which both mass media and occupation were entered, and hence were potentially mutually interacting. Some might consider it a purer test of the relative contribution of mass media and occupation to add each separately to education, measuring the increment in variance explained by the separate additions. Adding mass media to education yielded a median increment in variance explained of 7 percent in the regression for the total sample, and 6 percent in the worker sample. Adding occupation, essentially meaning factory experience, to education yielded a median increment in variance explained of 10 percent for the total sample, and 5 percent for the factory-worker sample. On a proportional basis, adding mass media or occupation to education increased the variance explained by 36 percent and 33 percent, respectively. So we see again that mass-media contact and factory work contributed about equally to explaining individual modernity.

4. Mass media could be entered into the competition in a regression analysis even though, as noted above, we could not, in this case, assign the same specific meaning to the raw-score regression (B) weights as we could to the measures of years of schooling and years of factory work.

5. Moreover, while focusing on the gain per year of factory experience we should not forget that in developing countries the factory is likely to have

men for a much longer time than will the schools. It would have been quite possible, therefore, for the cumulative total impact of factory experience to equal, or even surpass, that of schooling, at least for many men. Our data, however, do not permit us to determine whether men would continue to increase in OM scores indefinitely, since in our samples we included men only up to 33 years of age and none had more than 15 years of factory experience.

6. We are indebted to the creative research assistance of Reeve Vanneman for much of the information presented in this section. A staunch advocate of analysis of covariance as a tool in survey research, he adapted our data to the requirements of the MANOVA computer program, ran the preliminary analysis, and wrote a highly perceptive report on the results.

7. Vanneman also performed the analysis with seven covariates, the three additional ones being consumer goods owned, skill level, and age. In the case of both the four- and the seven-covariate analyses he used OM-3 rather than the OM-500 most commonly used in this book as the dependent variable. As a check, therefore, we later ran a three-way analysis of variance on OM-500, considering only education, mass-media exposure, and factory experience. That analysis yielded results consistent with those reported in this section for OM-3.

8. Despite the apparent evidence of substantial interaction in Table 19–4, the interaction effect was statistically significant only in India ($F=4.6$, significant at .01). In addition, in Argentina the interaction, while not significant, accounted for about 1 percent of the variance; elsewhere it was negligible. In a way, this was encouraging, since most of our procedures of analysis assumed that such interaction did not occur in our data. Yet it obviously is difficult to reconcile the statistics on interaction effects with the conclusions we drew in the text after examining Table 19–4. We have no better answer than that offered by Reeve Vanneman, the member of our staff who first conducted this part of the analysis, and responded to the same challenge by saying: "The problem lies in the distribution of the samples. The factory modernizes lower educated workers more than it does highly educated workers. But, in terms of our samples, this interaction effect becomes statistically a problem only in India, and perhaps in Argentina, because only in India is education evenly distributed among the sample of workers. In the other countries in which interaction is observed, roughly half the workers fall into one education level. The statistic for percentage of the variance explained, is greatly affected by the nature of this distribution."

9. In Chile and East Pakistan the lower reaches of the educational range were proportionately heavily represented. Thus, in East Pakistan 35 percent of the workers had zero education and 38 percent between 1 and 4 years of schooling. In Chile 16 percent had a mere 1 to 3 years of school, and 28 percent between 4 and 5 years.

As we have seen, these low ranges were precisely the educational levels in which the largest factory-experience effect was manifested. By contrast, the Israeli and Nigerian samples included no illiterates and relatively few men in the lower educational range. At the other end of the scale, Nigeria and Israel each had over 50 percent of their samples in the groups with 8 years or more of schooling. Since they had so few men whose educational level made them eligible to show the effect of factory experience, the Israeli and Nigerian samples produced an overall weight for the direct effect of factory experience which was comparatively weak. The Indian sample also had many men of high education, but there the impact of those groups was partially offset by the presence in the sample of large numbers of men with zero, or very few, years of schooling.

10. For a description of how each variable was defined and the measure of it constructed, see Appendix C. It will be seen there that the two sets, early and late, together comprise our standard Set A of control variables.

11. Insofar as the set of variables representing early socialization was smaller, by one variable, than the set defining late socialization, the latter might be thought to have been put at a disadvantage in the competition of the sets. In fact the results were not materially different when we took pains to be certain both the early- and the late-socialization sets included exactly the same number of variables.

20   The Process of Individual Modernization

1. Problems of redundancy and unreliability were the especially important ones in guiding our decisions to eliminate certain variables from the larger set. For example, we had built into our questionnaire three different measures of standard of living, namely, monetary income, housing quality, and consumer goods possessed. Our experience in working with the data indicated that the latter was generally the most reliable index of the respondent's economic condition. In the interests of reducing redundancy while emphasizing reliability, we kept consumer goods possessed in the final set and eliminated the other two. In most cases we combined the alternative measures into a summary scale. A similar procedure was followed for the entire set of almost 50 measures which we built into our questionnaire as independent variables, and described above in Table 3–3.

2. Applying a correction factor for the number of respondents and the number of predictor variables involved in the analysis produced very little shrinkage in the figures given in Table 20–1. The shrinkage was usually 0.5 percent, and never above 1 percent. See Guilford, *Fundamental Statistics*, p. 399, for the correction factor.

3. We could also use an OM scale constructed at random, to test directly what amount of variance might be explained by chance, using our eight final independent variables as predictors in a multiple-regression equation for each of our samples. We had constructed such a random scale, designated OM-13, described below. When regressions were computed using that scale we found from 1.4 to 2.3 percent of the variance in OM-13 could be accounted for by the eight final variables across the six countries. Thus, no more than about 2 percent out of roughly 47 percent of the variance in regular OM-scale scores explained by our eight final independent variables can be explained away as an artifact of our statistical method of computing linear multiple-regression equations to predict OM scale scores.

The Random OM-13 is, in fact, not an OM scale at all in any meaningful sense. It was created by selecting, with a table of random numbers, 34 items from the pool of 119 attitudinal OM items comprising OM-2, and then randomly assigning the answers to the question to either the "modern" or the "traditional" category. The result was a scale in each country with approximately 34 items, about half of which were scored in what was the wrong direction from the point of view of our theory of the nature of psychological modernity, while about half were scored in the right direction. In practice, then, the parts of this scale tended to cancel themselves out, with items pulling in opposite directions, rather than all pulling in the same direction as in the regular OM scales.

4. There is no obvious criterion for selecting studies which might most appropriately be compared to ours. Our standard was that the research should deal with a fundamental aspect of society, that it contain measures broadly comparable with those we used, and that the work have a general reputation as the most successful and outstanding of its kind. On that basis we selected the work of Blau and Duncan, on the attainment of educational and occupational status, as an example of efforts to explain a fairly objective social fact, and the research of the Michigan University Survey Research Center as the outstanding example of efforts to explain popular attitudes and values. See Peter M. Blau and Otis D. Duncan, *The American Occupational Structure* (New York: Wiley, 1967) and John P. Robinson *et al., Measures of Political Attitudes* (Ann Arbor: Institute for Social Research, University of Michigan, 1968).

5. Working with a national sample, and relying on two antecedent explanatory variables, Blau and Duncan were able to explain only 26 percent of the variance in the educational level attained by individuals, and 33 percent of the variance in their first jobs. Taking into account the rather obvious measure of "first job" as well, 43 percent of the variance in current occupational status could be explained.

6. Robinson *et al.* reexamined the results of an election survey based on a U. S. national sample collected in 1964 by the Michigan Survey Research Center. They worked with 8 independent variables: sex, race, education, income, age, community size, party identification, and actual vote (for either Johnson or Goldwater). They included as dependent variables 13 attitudinal and behavior measures, ranging from nostalgia for the past, through trust, efficacy, and participation, to information about Congress. Thus, their measures were very much akin to many of those used in the OM scale. From data given by Robinson (in Tables 1 and 2, pp. 488 and 490) we calculated the multiple correlations of the 8 independent variables with each of the 13 dependent variables in turn. The multiple correlations ranged from .20 to .69, with the median at .37. The political-efficacy scale was most like our OM scale in content. Nevertheless, the 8 descriptive variables accounted for only 23 percent of the variance in that scale. The scale whose variance was most fully accounted for among those in the set of 13 measures studied was that measuring the liberal-conservative dimension. On that scale 48 percent of the variance was explained. But this outcome was largely determined by the rather obvious connection between the liberalism-conservatism scale and the facts about party affiliation and actual party vote, which had been included among the 8 predictor variables.

7. Since path analysis is, to some degree, a rather mechanical statistical procedure, one must exercise discretion in interpreting the paths of influence with which the computer printout confronts one. Indirect effects are often designated "true" if the path analysis points to a sequence we can accept as theoretically meaningful. On the other hand, such effects will be designated "spurious" if the causal sequence suggested by the path analysis seems not to make sense on theoretical grounds. In the simplified model we present here all the indirect effects were, by this test, seemingly true indirect effects.

8. Our conclusion concerning the importance of ethnicity and religion rests, in good part, on a detailed set of comparisons based on our matched groups,

the results of which will be reported in a separate publication. In those matches, ethnic groups were placed in competition with each other one pair at a time. In the path analysis, however, the ethnic groups were arranged in a continuum from least to most modern, on the basis of dummy-variable analysis. This empiricist mode of arranging the groups obviously contributed to maximizing the beta weight attained by the ethnicity-religion variable.

9. For details see Chapter 13.

10. Although we mentioned only skill explicitly, the role of income as a concomitant of increasing seniority in the factory should not be neglected. Our path analysis indicated a substantial indirect effect of living standard on OM scores, especially as mediated by mass-media exposure. We believe this follows from the fact that increased income permits the individual to devote more income to the utilization of the mass media. Since skill, seniority in the plant, and income are all fairly strongly intercorrelated, it is very difficult to measure the effect of any one while controlling for the others. Government programs to give a guaranteed income to citizens who are not gainfully employed will create the equivalent of an experimental design in which we may hope to assess the impact of increased income on modernity under conditions where the increased income does not require that the recipient first gain increased occupational seniority.

11. For details see note 23 of Chapter 12.

12. In the present study we used our measures of voluntary-organization participation as part of the summary OM-scale dependent variable. But like mass-media exposure, voluntary-organization participation can be seen as both a cause and consequence of increasing individual modernity. We know from research in developed nations that voluntary-organization participation *can* have an impact on aspects of the OM scale. For example, see Richard D. Reddy and David H. Smith, "The Impact of Voluntary Organization Participation Upon the Individual," in David H. Smith, ed., *Voluntary Action Research: 1973* (Lexington, Mass.: Heath, 1973).

13. In our samples, at least, a conventional measure of "general intelligence" yielded correlations with OM which ranged from substantial to robust. The general-intelligence measure we used was a test requiring the identification of antonyms, which we designated the "opposites test." The correlations of scores on that test and OM-500 were: Argentina, .55; Chile, .58; East Pakistan, .37; India, .57; Israel, .45; Nigeria, .30. All were significant at better than .001.

14. In a study of Black men and women living in Boston, Richard Suzman has shown that individual modernity is intimately connected with a wide range of personality and cognitive variables, such as ego development, intellectual functioning, and field independence. After a large set of independent variables, similar to ours, has been partialled out, personality and cognitive variables were able to explain an additional 10–20% of the variance in OM. See Suzman, "The Modernization of Personality" (Harvard University Dissertation, 1973).

21   Summary and Conclusions

1. There are, of course, some notable exceptions. The most important early example was the effort by Gordon Allport to test Spranger's belief that men could be classified according to the predominance in their personality of "theoretical," "religious," "social," or "economic-and-political" values. See Gordon Allport, Philip Vernon, and Gardner Lindzey, *Study of Values;*

A Scale for Measuring the Dominant Interests in Personality, 3rd ed. (Boston: Houghton-Mifflin, 1959). Probably the best-known and most widely studied syndrome is that first proposed by Erich Fromm under the rubric "the authoritarian personality" in *Escape From Freedom* (New York: Farrar and Rinehart, 1941) and later built into the famous "F scale." See Theodor W. Adorno *et al., The Authoritarian Personality* (New York: Harper, 1950).

2. The farmers in question were above the average in education, were generally Brahmin by caste, and owned more than average landholdings which they exploited more efficiently than their neighbors. These and related social-status characteristics made those men dominant figures in their villages, where they served an important function in supporting technological and educational innovation, while simultaneously playing a conservative role in resisting changes in the power structure. They also upheld conservative patterns of interpersonal relations, especially as they affected the family and the status of women.

3. The scales themselves, and information on how they relate to individual modernity, are described in Inkeles, "Participant Citizenship."

4. See Chapter 18 and Inkeles, "The Fate of Personal Adjustment."

5. Kahl (*Measurement of Modernism*) administered his Modernism III scale to 503 housewives from medium-sized and large cities in the United States. Going from low to high status, as judged by education, the range of scores for the American women was basically the same as for the Latin American men over the same status range, and at any given educational level the absolute scores obtained were much the same regardless of nationality. Kahl concluded that "comparisons of groups from Brazil, Mexico, and the United States show no nationality differences when education and urban location are controlled" (p. 51). One may, of course, raise serious reservations about the appropriateness of comparing women from one country with men from another, since there may well be systematic sex-linked differences in the scores people obtain on measures of individual modernity. Our project has developed an international modernity (IM) scale. The IM scale is calibrated and scored the same way in all countries, unlike the OM scale, which is somewhat different in each country. This IM scale will permit us to compare the absolute scores of matched samples from our six different countries. The results will be presented in a separate publication.

6. The Indian scale was of relatively low reliability, yet it correlated with OM-2 at .59***. The content of the special Indian modernity scale and its relation to the regular OM scale are described in Alex Inkeles and Amar K. Singh, "A Cross-Cultural Measure of Modernity and Some Popular Indian Images," *Journal of General and Applied Psychology* 1 (1968; Bihar Psychological Association, Ranchi/Patna, India).

7. The negotiations we conducted in Eastern Europe at the outset of the project were with sociologists in Poland. The subsequent use of the OM scale was with students in Rumania, the scale having been administered by Professor Karoly Varga of the Institute of Sociology in the Rumanian Academy of Sciences. The results were not available, at least in the United States, at the time we went to press.

8. See Inkeles and Bauer, *The Soviet Citizen,* and Inkeles, *Social Change in Soviet Russia.*

9. Bauer, *The New Man in Soviet Psychology.*

10. In Question EF-11 we asked: "Which is most important for the future of this country: the hard work of the people; God's help; good planning on the part of the government; good luck?" In four of the six countries the strongest positive correlation between the choice of any one of these alternatives and overall modernity was associated with the preference for good planning on the part of the government. In those four countries the median correlation between OM-3 and selecting government planning as first choice among the alternatives was .23***. In India and East Pakistan, however, the modern men were much more likely to select the alternative calling for hard work by the people, with correlations of .36*** and .29***, respectively. In those countries the correlations between OM-3 and preference for planning were only .03 and .08, respectively. Evidently people in India and East Pakistan do not have too much confidence in government planning. This finding should help to emphasize that the relation between modernity and political orientation is complex, and tends to be patterned differently according to the nature of the political system and political climate prevailing in each country. For additional data and further discussion of this issue see footnote 11, and Inkeles, "Participant Citizenship."

11. The "radicalism" index was based on a special question, CI-52: "In your opinion what is it that Chile (Argentina) most needs: (1) a total and immediate change; (2) a total but gradual change; (3) a partial but immediate change; (4) a partial, slow change." The correlation of position on this scale and overall modernity was for Argentina .39 and for Chile .34, both significant at better than the .001 level.

12. See Inkeles, "Participant Citizenship," for the analysis of the complex pattern of relations between measures of modernity and indices of political orientation.

13. We have presented considerable evidence in this volume regarding the criterion validity of our OM scale. But in so doing we have already made some assumptions and prejudgments, based on theory, regarding which end of the response scale for each *item* is "modern" versus "traditional." In a later publication we shall look at what was an even more strictly empirical test of the relation of each item of the OM scale to individual modernity by measuring the item's ability to distinguish between criterion groups of modern and traditional men so classified on "objective" grounds. In that analysis we made *no* assumptions about the "direction" of each answer in modern or traditional. Only the relation of each answer to the "objectively" defined modern characteristics was measured. When presented, the item analysis results will support the conclusion reached here regarding the criterion validity of OM scales composed of those items.

14. For lack of space the evidence for this assertion has not been presented in this book. It will, however, be reported later in a separate publication.

15. This was most notably the case for Argentina and Chile, as judged by the beta weights of a regression including education, mass media, and years of factory work as predictors. See Table 19–2 for details.

16. We are not convinced the model is accurate even in the case of the more developed countries. One element in the youth culture in the affluent countries certainly does seem to be a negative response to many of the features of modern large-scale bureaucratic organization and advanced technology. We consider it important to note, however, that often the youth generating this culture have not themselves worked in large-scale, bureaucratic, produc-

tive enterprises. Moreover, a very large proportion of them were probably raised in affluent and libertarian home atmospheres and later attended progressive schools. Insofar as that was the case, the personal style adopted by these youths could be taken as further evidence of the correctness of our theory, since our theory holds that men most reflect the dominant qualities of the sociocultural milieus in which they have been mainly living. For an interesting discussion of the issue see V. Kavolis, "Post-Modern Man," *Social Problems* 17 (1970): 435–448.

17. Freudians argue that the conscience is laid down in its basic form by the age of 16. We know that the clarity of the image of one's future occupational role is not great in the young child, and remains highly unstable until the age of 14. Thereafter, the individual's image of "what he wants to be" undergoes rapid development up to age 20. After that it generally changes very little for the next 20 years. Thurstone has shown that our verbal fluency continues to develop slowly, so that even at age 20 we still perform at only 80 percent of our eventual full capacity. But what of attitudes and values of the sort dealt with in the OM scale? For these one cannot specify either a biologically determined growth pattern or a genetically given plateau. Yet personality psychologists have tended to treat such attitudes and values as if they were subject to the same limits which govern physical growth and the development of intelligence. For our part, we are of the opinion that such attitudes and values as are measured on the OM scale are not governed by the kind of biologically determined growth pattern or genetically given plateau which determine individual attributes such as verbal fluency. The qualities measured by the OM scale can, in our view, be changed quite profoundly after the age of 20 and up to and even beyond the age of 40.

18. It will be recalled that we had hoped to interview at least 100 men in each country who had originally migrated from the countryside to work in industry, and then had left to return to other, more traditional, pursuits. Unfortunately, such men proved so hard to find that the field directors soon gave up the search in order to concentrate their energies on more accessible cases.

19. Personal communication from Hayes Keeler, graduate student in Political Science at Stanford University, who conducted the as yet unpublished study in Ecuador.

20. See note 11.

21. A special version of the OM scale was administered by Donald Holsinger of Stanford University to boys and girls in the third to fifth grades of schools in Brasilia. At each grade level, the modernity scores of the girls were equal to those of the boys, and the girls gained as many points on the OM scale as did the boys during each additional year of schooling. (See Holsinger, "The Elementary School.") In a study of Negro women in Boston, Richard Suzman, of Harvard University, administered a modified version of the OM scale. Basically the same items as had been used with our men in underdeveloped countries combined to yield a reliable OM scale for the Boston women. Moreover, the OM scores for women, using the Boston scale, could, in turn, be explained by much the same influences which explained the modernity of men in our samples from underdeveloped countries. (See Suzman, "The Modernization of Personality," dissertation, Harvard University, 1973.) It should also be noted that Kahl's modernity scale, originally developed for use with men in Brazil and Chile, evidently worked quite well when used to study the

responses of women in the United States. (See Kahl, *Measurement,* pp. 49–50.)

22. In order to capture the full range of individual modernity in a developed nation like the U. S., it would be necessary to adjust the response alternatives of most OM items to permit finer gradations at the modern end of the continuum. It would also be necessary to lengthen the OM scale in certain areas where there is "high consensus modernity" in the U. S. One could thereby avoid imposing any artificial ceiling on the OM scores of the most modern people.

Nevertheless, we may expect a somewhat lessened impact of later socialization experiences on OM scores for *most* people in highly developed countries even if the OM scale's upper limits were extended. In the U. S. and in other highly developed countries, many aspects of individual modernity have become institutionalized, and have been absorbed into the general culture. As a result, the modernizing of most individuals is likely to occur during the early years in the home, the school, and the neighborhood, and through contact with the mass media. For most people in an advanced industrial society their experience in the factory, the city, the government agency, and other institutions important for modernizing adults may be very little different from the experience they had had previously in the environments in which they had been raised. Consequently, the "contrast," or "demonstration," effect we observed the adult experiences to produce in developing countries might well be weaker in the more developed nations.

23. The evidence concerning these differences in political behavior is built into the OM scale, and may be observed by checking the list of questions in Appendix A. A full account of the 39 items dealing with political orientations and behavior covered by our questionnaire, the scales those items yielded, and their relation to the independent variables is given in Inkeles, "Participant Citizenship."

24. In his unpublished contribution to the conference on Alternatives in Development sponsored by The Vienna Institute for Development in June 1971, Dr. Salazar Bondy, a leading intellectual of Peru, wrote as follows: "Underdevelopment is not just a collection of statistical indices which enable a socio-economic picture to be drawn. It is also a state of mind, a way of expression, a form of outlook and a collective personality marked by chronic infirmities and forms of maladjustment."

Index

Publications Written under the Auspices of the Center for International Affairs, Harvard University

Turmoil and Transition: Higher Education and Student Politics in India, edited by Philip G. Altbach, 1969. Basic Books.

Protest and Power in Black Africa, edited by Robert I. Rotberg, 1969. Oxford University Press.

The Process of Modernization: An Annotated Bibliography on the Socio-Cultural Aspects of Development, by John Brode, 1969. Harvard University Press.

Agricultural Development in India's Districts: The Intensive Agricultural Districts Programme, by Dorris D. Brown, 1970. Harvard University Press.

Taxation and Development: Lessons from Colombian Experience, by Richard M. Bird, 1970. Harvard University Press.

Lord and Peasant in Peru: A Paradigm of Political and Social Change, by F. LaMond Tullis, 1970. Harvard University Press.

Korean Development: The Interplay of Politics and Economics, by David C. Cole and Princeton N. Lyman, 1971. Harvard University Press.

Higher Education in a Transitional Society, by Philip G. Altbach, 1971. Sindhu Publications (Bombay).

Studies in Development Planning, edited by Hollis B. Chenery, 1971. Harvard University Press.

Political Mobilization of the Venezuelan Peasant, by John D. Powell, 1971. Harvard University Press.

Peasants Against Politics: Rural Organization in Brittany, 1911–1967, by Suzanne Berger, 1972. Harvard University Press.

Latin American University Students: A Six Nation Study, by Arthur Liebman, Kenneth N. Walker, and Myron Glazer, 1972. Harvard University Press.

The Politics of Land Reform in Chile, 1950–1970: Public Policy, Political Institutions, and Social Change, by Robert R. Kaufman, 1972. Harvard University Press.

The Boundary Politics of Independent Africa, by Saadia Touval, 1972. Harvard University Press.

University Students and African Politics, by William John Hanna, 1974. Africana Publishing Company.

Economic Nationalism and the Politics of International Dependence: The Case of Copper in Chile, 1945–1973, by Theodore Moran, 1974. Princeton University Press.

The Andean Group: A Case Study in Economics Integration Among Developing Countries, by David Morawetz, 1974. M.I.T. Press.

Kenya: The Politics of Participation and Control, by Henry Bienen (sponsored jointly with the Center of International Studies, Princeton University), 1974. Princeton University Press.